The Philosophy
of Society

'D'où Venons-Nous? Que Sommes-Nous? Où Allons-Nous?'

Paul Gauguin

(From where do we come? What are we? Where are we going?)

The Philosophy of Society

EDITED BY

Rodger Beehler

AND

Alan R. Drengson

METHUEN: LONDON

1978

First published 1978
by Methuen & Co Ltd
11 New Fetter Lane, London EC4P 4EE
Introductions © 1978
Rodger Beehler and Alan R. Drengson
Chapters 4 and 11 © 1978 John Cook

Typeset by Red Lion Setters, London
and printed in Great Britain by the
University Printing House, Cambridge

ISBN 0 416 83480 9 (hardbound)
ISBN 0 416 83490 6 (paperback)

Contents

Preface   vii
Acknowledgements   ix

Part I   *Forms of social life*

Introduction	Rodger Beehler	3
1 Nature and convention	Peter Winch	12
2 Morality and pessimism	Stuart Hampshire	32
3 Understanding a primitive society	H.O. Mounce	59

Part II   *Social reality and social inquiry*

Introduction	Rodger Beehler	81
4 Behaviouralism in political science	John Cook	91
5 Psychology and ideology	Noam Chomsky	110
6 Interpretation and the sciences of man	Charles Taylor	156

Part III   *Social institutions and social change*

Introduction	Alan R. Drengson	203
7 Aestheticism, perfectionism, Utopianism	Karl Popper	212
8 'Social engineering'	Rush Rhees	235
9 Between obedience and revolution	Clyde Frazier	250

Part IV   Cultural relativism

	Introduction	Alan R. Drengson	271
10	Anthropology and the abnormal	Ruth Benedict	279
11	Cultural relativism as an ethnocentric notion	John Cook	289
12	On seeing things differently	Richard Norman	316

Part V   Community

	Introduction	Alan R. Drengson	347
13	Reason, rules and the 'community'	A.E. Murphy	355
14	Oppression	Simone Weil	381
15	Alienation and anomie	Steven Lukes	400
	Select bibliography	Rodger Beehler	425
	Index		431

Preface

Brought together here are fifteen contributions to our understanding of human society. Two of the papers are published here for the first time. The others are gathered from journals and volumes where they have appeared before. Our intention has been to provide materials for a course of study in social and political philosophy; but it is hoped that the book may find its way into the hands of anyone who desires to understand better human social life, and to appreciate morally certain of its features. The desire for such an understanding is itself the outcome of reflection. But it can only be answered by further reflection and by study.

We have chosen, wherever possible, papers marked by simplicity, clarity, and completeness in their treatment of a subject, as well as by the fundamental importance of the questions discussed. In each paper the need to distinguish between different issues, questions, and arguments is stressed, and close attention is paid through the use of examples to the detail of the practices, institutions or conditions of life being examined. More than one of the essays is a response to an influential contemporary thesis, and in two instances this original writing is printed here as well. The student is thus able to examine both sides of the disagreement, and in doing so seek to increase not only his understanding of social life but also his capacity to assess arguments and evidence, and to reason more carefully himself.

A number of the subjects treated are matters in the discussion of which moral considerations must be taken into account. Among these subjects are freedom, community, alienation, oppression, and revolution. Included as well are investigations of the relation of morality to social life, of the problems confronted in understanding alien societies, and the possibility of controlling, and explaining, social change. Indeed the question of *explanation* runs throughout the volume, and we have thought it important to include three papers which discuss the mode of study and explanation appropriate to human social life.

The book is divided into five parts which roughly correspond to the contents of the papers. But more than one paper interlocks with another paper in a different section. (Thus certain questions about human needs raised in part II by Noam Chomsky in his essay are returned to in part V in the writings by Simone Weil and Steven Lukes.) The reader may wish to overlook the order of these divisions and read where his questions and difficulties take him.

We have prefaced to each of the five parts an introduction, written by one of the editors, in which we seek to outline in an elementary way the subject or subjects common to the papers in that section and to suggest some of the questions which need to be asked. In more than one case we have reacted critically to one or other of the papers in a section, where it was felt that this could be done helpfully, and in a way that would encourage the student's own thinking and inquiry. Our hope is that the introductions will assist students to identify the argument of each essay and appreciate the extent of its achievement. But once more, they are meant to be preparatory and elementary, and may be ignored by the reader who has no need of them.

Appended at the end of the book is a list of selected readings where the subjects treated in the papers may be further pursued, or a question touched on in an introduction followed up. An attempt has been made to include recent and accessible writings in this list.

H.J.N. Horsburgh and Kai Nielsen have in different ways given us help and encouragement. We should like to thank them here. We should also like to thank the authors, editors and publishers who generously gave us permission to reprint; and John Cook, for agreeing to publish his papers here.

Rodger Beehler
Alan R. Drengson
Victoria, Canada

Acknowledgements

The editors and publisher would like to thank the following for permission to reproduce material from the publications listed below:

The Editor of the Aristotelian Society for 'Nature and Convention' by Peter Winch from *Proceedings of the Aristotelian Society*, Vol.LX (1960); Stuart Hampshire and the *New York Review of Books* for 'Morality and Pessimism' from *New York Review of Books*, Vol.XIX, Nos 11 and 12 (25 January 1973), and for his reply to the criticisms in *New York Review of Books*, Vol. XX, No. 4 (20 September 1973); H.O. Mounce and *Philosophy* for 'Understanding a Primitive Society' from *Philosophy*, Vol.48, No. 186 (October 1973); Pantheon Books and William Collins Sons & Co Ltd for 'Psychology and Ideology' from *For Reasons and State* by Noam Chomsky; Charles Taylor and *The Review of Metaphysics* for 'Interpretation and the Sciences of Man' from *The Review of Metaphysics*, Vol.XXV, No. 1 (1971); Sir Karl Popper, Princeton University Press and Routledge & Kegan Paul for 'Social Engineering' from *The Open Society and Its Enemies* (1966); Rush Rhees and *Mind* for 'Social Engineering' from *Mind*, Vol. LVI (1947); Clyde Frazier and Princeton University Press for 'Between Obedience and Revolution' from *Philosophy and Public Affairs*, Vol.1, No. 3 (1972); The Journal Press for 'Anthropology and the Abnormal' by Ruth Benedict from *The Journal of General Psychology*, Vol.10 (1934);

Richard Norman and *Radical Philosophy* for 'On seeing things differently' from *Radical Philosophy*, Vol.1, No. 1 (1972); Open Court Publishers for 'Reason, Rules and the "Community"' from *The Theory of Practical Reason* by A.E. Murphy (1965); Routledge & Kegan Paul for 'Oppression' from *Oppression and Liberty* by Simone Weil (1973); A.D. Peters and Company for 'Alienation and Anomie' by Steven Lukes from *Philosophy, Politics and Society*, Third Series, edited by P. Laslett and W.G. Runciman (1967).

PART I
Forms of social life

Introduction

RODGER BEEHLER

We observe that all nations, barbarous as well as civilized, though separately founded because remote from each other in time and space, keep these three human customs: all have some religion, all contract solemn marriages, all bury their dead. And in no nation, however savage and crude, are any human actions performed with more elaborate ceremonies and more sacred solemnity than the rites of religion, marriage, burial. For by the axiom that 'uniform ideas, born among peoples unknown to each other, must have a common ground of truth', it must have been dictated to all nations that from these institutions humanity began among them all, and therefore they must be most devoutly guarded by them all, so that the world should not again become a bestial wilderness.[1]

Are there institutions or customs which every society, every nation or people, possess? Certain difficulties attend this question from the start. In order to appreciate whether two societies have the same customs we have first to appreciate what their individual customs are. Until we do this we shall not be able to judge whether two separate customs are the same. A problem we immediately encounter is that the customs and institutions of different peoples differ. How then are we to know when we are confronted with *the same* institution?

We are accustomed to allowing that markedly different religious beliefs and practices are still religious beliefs and practices. Quite different accounts may be given of a supernatural realm and its relation to the natural world, and quite different practices may be described as the manifestation of religious faith, and yet the general character of what may be strikingly differing beliefs and practices may incline us nevertheless to identify each of them as religious. But is the situation more difficult in the case, for example, of marriage? May it not sometimes be open to persons to object that the sexual, social, and procreative relationships of an alien society are so different from our own that what some of us are inclined to call 'marriage' in this alien society is not marriage, is not *the same* institution, at all? If disputes of this kind arise they must, at least in principle, be capable of being settled. The project of comparing social customs and institutions to see whether they are the same entails something like criteria in terms of which we correctly or incorrectly apply the expressions 'religion', 'marriage', 'burial of the dead'. What is it about our own practices which entitles us to continue to describe them as 'marriage', 'religion', 'burial of the dead'? And in what respects must the practices of other peoples reproduce our own to be correctly identified by us as religion or marriage or burial? Marriage, compared with burial of the dead, is especially troublesome, precisely because the institution of marriage is a much more complex and many-sided social fact than burial. But in respect of all three customs spoken of by Vico, what we require for the project of comparing our ways of life with others' is first to understand our own institutions, customs and practices. What *is* marriage, religious faith, interment of the dead among our people?

But we must also come to understand what it is that other nations and peoples do. We must appreciate correctly their institutions and customs. And here the difficulties appear to be even greater. For our efforts to find this out may be hampered by a natural inclination to apprehend and interpret their customs in terms of our own. We come to what they do under the impress of our own ways of living in the world. We shall perhaps inevitably try to make sense of their life in terms of our own. The result may sometimes be not understanding but mistake; misinterpretation, not appreciation.

If we go back to the question whether there are social institutions which are to be found in every human society, we can easily be brought to see that this is a question about what each human society has, in fact, come to be like. But the remarks of Vico with which we began point towards a different question: whether there are social institutions or customs which every human society not only does but *must* possess. Are there customs or observances which exist in every society, not by choice or accident, not by coincidence or 'convention', but because they are 'natural' requirements of social life?

Many philosophers hold that there are such 'natural', or necessary, requirements of human social life, but they are not all agreed concerning the way in which these requirements are 'natural' or necessary. Most philosophers see these requirements as necessary and natural in being imposed by the nature of human beings and the character of their natural environment. Because human beings require sustenance, because they are vulnerable to physical injury, because they are sometimes selfish or indifferent to others (and so on), some kind of laws, some kind of morality, some sort of property arrangement and other sorts of regulatory customs, are necessary, or things would fall apart. No human society could survive without these kinds of things.

A rarer view of a 'natural requirement of social life' (which gets nearer to the sense of Vico's remarks) is of something which every human society must possess, not in order to survive or flourish, but in order *to be a human* society ('...from these institutions humanity began among them all...'). The idea is that there is something, or more than one thing, which is the same in each human society, but which exists in each, not because human beings could not survive or flourish without it, but because without it there could not be among them human *society*.

In his paper 'Nature and convention', Peter Winch asks whether any of the *moral* observances of mankind are of this kind. Winch, when he wrote his paper, hoped to show that there is at least one moral observance which must inescapably be present in every human society: telling the truth. Winch undertook to show that truth-telling is a necessary condition of human communication, and so of much that goes to make up human social life.

There attaches to this understanding an intractable difficulty which Peter Winch has himself called attention to in a recent comment on his paper[2]. This difficulty concerns the alleged *moral* status of the practice which is claimed to be necessary. Let us allow for the moment (what Peter Winch seeks to show) that for communication by means of language to be possible, speaking the truth must be the rule rather than the exception. Members of any society must as a rule tell the truth if there is to be *speaking* and *telling* among them at all. Does it follow from *this* fact that truth-telling must be a *moral* observance among every human people?

There are two questions at issue here. One is: by virtue of what is a social practice or observance a moral practice or observance? The other is: is any particular moral practice or observance inescapable wherever there is human social life? The central difficulty in Winch's essay proceeds from his failing to pay enough attention to the first question. To show that a social practice is a necessary requirement of human language is one thing. But is what makes it a necessary requirement *the same thing* as what makes it a moral requirement? If it is not, then half of what was embarked upon remains to be accomplished.

Stuart Hampshire, in his paper 'Morality and pessimism', draws our attention from the notion of social life to particular ways of life. Hampshire's intention is to resist conceptions of morality according to which it is a body of injunctions and prohibitions whose claim to be heeded derives from the beneficial consequences which follow upon observing them. On such utilitarian accounts of morality moral observances are conditionally required of persons just in the sense that if the circumstances of life were to change in such a way that observance of these prohibitions and injunctions no longer contributed to human well-being, then we should cease to be under any *moral* requirement in respect of them. Hampshire considers this reason for repudiating any utilitarian account of morality. He puts forward a rival view which locates the peculiar character of moral requirements in the unconditional assent of persons to ways of life.

On Hampshire's understanding of morals, the moral requirements which a person comes to recognize and observe are partly constitutive of, and are seen to be integral to, a desirable way of life. The necessity which people feel themselves to be under in respect of the demands of morality — 'I *must* help him', 'You *can't* do that' — is explained by their being unconditionally claimed by the way of life of which these specifically moral requirements are a part.

Are there difficulties and obscurities with this account of morals?

If someone is claimed by a way of life then he or she will appreciate that certain things are ruled out by the commitment to live in this way. Now one of the things moral philosophers have felt the need to explain is the special sort of difference which attaches to something's being *morally* ruled out or required. Stuart Hampshire appeals to the notion of assent to a way of life to explain this difference. But won't this notion of 'assent to a way of life' have first to explain the *existence* of morality, before it can explain the *difference* morality makes? And can it explain the existence of moral considerations, moral offences, moral judgments?

Not everything which goes to make up a way of living will be a moral observance or practice. What is it then which explains that certain of the forms of conduct which go to make up a particular way of life are morally required of those whose way of life it is? Also, certain ways of life are in conflict with morality (the way of life of a Nazi street thug, for example, or of some ruthless careerist in some profession). Not every way of life even gives rise to moral prohibitions and injunctions. How then can the notion of 'assent to a way of life' explain the fact that there are such things as the demands of morality? Surely even in the case of all those ways of life in which there is moral sensitivity and appreciation there is still something to be explained which cannot be explained simply by pointing to the fact that here we have assent to a way of life. For the others are ways of life too, and there we do not find moral concern or moral observances at all.

Furthermore, if one holds, as Stuart Hampshire does, that certain observances are inseparable from morality (not murdering persons, for example, or not violating them) then this must seem especially incompatible with any account of morality as generated by 'a way of life'. For whether a way of life incorporates morality will now obviously depend on something other than the fact that it is a way of life. But let us go farther. Suppose a particular way of life does incorporate morality. If the allegiance of individuals is to this way of life, then any moral prohibitions or enjoinments which this way of life involves must appear as conditional after all. For one accepts and heeds these *as required by this way of life*. But have we not been taught that morality may (and must) cast judgment *upon* any way of living? If one's living rightly is to go on within a wider 'way of life' (and could anyone ever live just the life of 'living rightly'?) must we not continually judge that way of life by the standards of right living? But if the necessity we feel ourselves to be under in respect of moral observances is to be explained, as Hampshire says, by our unconditional assent to a way of life, will the situation not be reversed? The necessity moral observances impose is now explained as proceeding from the claim upon us of this way of life. But then how (if Hampshire were right) could one scrutinize with the terrible necessity of moral judgment *that way of life*?

Reference to the scrutiny of ways of life brings us to the subject of Howard Mounce's paper 'Understanding a primitive society'.

There exists among a people of Africa known as the Azande a group of practices which anthropologists of the European civilizations have termed 'witchcraft', or 'magic'. The Azande believe that

there are persons who are witches, who possess the power to bring
events about by other than natural means, or at least by means which
it is outside the power of ordinary persons to command. The Azande
also believe that there is a way of detecting witchcraft, which involves
feeding a certain substance to a fowl and asking a question which the
survival or death of the fowl then answers.

Confronted by practices of this kind many anthropologists have
been inclined to say 'they are irrational'. Asked to justify this
judgment these anthropologists reply that there is nothing in reality
which corresponds to what these practices presuppose. There are no
such things as witches or oracles. Howard Mounce discusses in his
paper a certain philosophical reply to these anthropologists which
takes the form of seeking to show that alien social practices cannot
be judged in this way. This reply is made in a paper by Peter Winch
from which Mounce's own paper takes its title. Mounce's intention is
to reveal what is correct and what is incorrect in Winch's position.
This involves him in an attempt to elucidate what a correct
understanding of the Azande practices would be.

I would like to raise one question about Mounce's paper. But
before I do so I would like to sketch briefly a slightly different way of
approaching the issue of the rationality of alien social practices from
that Mounce develops[3].

The anthropologist who declares the Azande practices irrational
does so because he considers them to have no basis in fact. This is
why they are irrational. The anthropologist's reasoning, I want to
argue, is mistaken. What is rational, or irrational, is always what it
is rational, or irrational, *for some particular person* (or group of
persons) to *do* or *believe*. But what it is rational or irrational for a
particular person to do or believe depends on what that person
knows, or believes, *or could be expected to find out*. Thus, what it is
irrational for some particular man to do, or believe, it may be
entirely rational for a different man (or that same man in different
circumstances) to do or believe. Rationality is a property which
attaches to beliefs and actions by virtue of the reasons persons have
for accepting or performing them. It attaches to beliefs and actions
qua cognitive performances. But persons are always particular
historical persons, and what counts as an acceptable reason is always
in part, therefore, a matter of the present state of knowledge in the
community. To take a simple example: it used to be the case among
European and North American communities that people avoided
draughts in order to avoid colds. It has since been claimed that the
common cold arises from a virus, not from exposure. Suppose this

medical claim eventually comes to be established as true. Does this make it the case that we were all acting irrationally in the past when we avoided draughts?

What it is rational to believe is not what is true if believed but what one is justified in believing. But what one is justified in believing is contextually dependent. It depends upon who it is that believes, what he knows, and could be expected to find out; which depends on where he is historically and culturally, among other things. It follows that judgments as to the rationality of beliefs (which are always the beliefs of *particular historical* persons) are not transitive. They cannot be disengaged from the details upon which they must be erected, and set loose to apply indiscriminately across cultures and societies. Because a practice would be irrational for *us* to follow, because of what we know, it does not follow that it would be irrational for persons of a different time or place or culture to follow it.

Consider the Azande. They do not have the long-developed (but still, by anthropological standards, recent) traditions and achievements of empirical inquiry that we do. There is much that we know about natural phenomena that they do not know. It is possible then, and not only possible but likely, that some of what they believe to be true is in fact false, and known to be false. *But it is not known by them to be false.* And they are not in a position to appreciate that it is false. Isn't it perfectly acceptable, then, to say that while the practices of the Azande which are in question would be irrational practices for us to engage in, they are not irrational for the Azande to engage in? I deliberately ask but do not answer this question, because it requires, to be answered, an investigation into Azande culture. It may be that the Azande do know what should enable them to appreciate that witchcraft and oracles have no basis in truth. It may as easily be that the Azande cannot be expected to appreciate this because they have not developed the forms of understanding and explanation which would enable them to see this or that phenomenon as evidence against witchcraft. Instead, they receive these phenomena within a quite different mode of understanding, a quite different conception, of what is going on. But so long as the Azande, who are unacquainted with our ways of conceiving and explaining things, believe what they believe, are they irrational to proceed according to their beliefs?

' — But this misses the point, which is that it is irrational to *believe* what the Azande believe. It is irrational to suppose that the world is as the Azande conceive it to be.' This charge carries the implication that the Azande can *help* conceiving of the world in the way they do. The suggestion is that they are guilty of some fault of reasoning or logic in believing what they do. They ought to see that they have no reason to believe what they believe.

But can the Azande help conceiving of the world — of reality — as they do? Is reality, which includes not just 'what there is', but 'what is happening', simply *there*, to be directly apprehended? Or is anything which is a conception of what there is or what is happening bound up with some tradition in terms of which the different 'things' which go to make up 'reality' are discriminated, understood, made sense of? Or, to get directly to Peter Winch's position, is 'our idea of what belongs to the realm of reality given for us in the language that we use'[4] (use, notice, in describing, explaining, telling, speculating about, what happens in the world)? Certainly, a man, or a people, may be judged irrational for believing what their society's concepts and traditions of explanation, together with their own experience, deny them reason to believe. (I say 'may'; no blanket assertion can be made here.) But can they be judged irrational *because of* the concepts and traditions of explanation they have, and what these 'determine' reality to be? Is this part at least of what Peter Winch in his paper meant to ask?

Turning from what it is rational to believe to what it is true to believe, it is an indisputable fact that among most peoples of the earth, non-magical conceptions of reality, whether developed natively or introduced from without, have prevailed over practices such as witchcraft. How is this to be explained?

One is perhaps inclined to answer that it has been repeatedly discovered that reality is not as magical practices require it to be. But Peter Winch avers (in an argument Howard Mounce outlines and accepts) that this answer is not in the logical cards. The core of this argument is the claim that 'Reality is not something that underlies language and gives it sense, but rather what is real and unreal shows itself in the sense that language has'. This claim is connected to another claim by Winch already quoted: that our idea of what belongs to the realm of reality is given for us in the language we use.

But is our idea of what belongs to the realm of reality *entirely given* for us in the language, the concepts, we use? Our idea of what belongs to the realm of reality is, I take it, our idea of what there is. But our idea of what there is depends surely not only on language but on experience. We ordinarily distinguish between objects, actions, and experiences. In respect of physical objects, which are a part of the 'realm of reality', are *they* 'given for us' in the language we use? It is true that in learning to speak we learn what to call — how to discriminate between — the furniture of the world. But is our idea of what objects *are real* given to us in this way?

Human actions admittedly cannot be observed in the way objects are. The hospitable action, for example, cannot be simply 'perceived' in the movements of outstretched arm and vessel. Explanations of many non-human phenomena too are more than mere 'perceivings'. They frequently involve appeal to what is not (or is not directly) perceivable, such as forces, fields, particles. In these cases our idea of what belongs to reality *is* inextricably bound up with linguistic concepts. But can we not always ask concerning any idea of how things are, or any account of what is going on, whether that idea or account is correct, or at least in keeping with the evidence? (In other words, in respect of 'what objects there are', do we need to distinguish between the power of language to multiply what there is, by further and further discrimination, and the lack of power of language to establish *as real* that which is further and further discriminated?) Peter Winch is right to remark that reality does not give language sense. Persons give language the sense it has, by using words as they do: And what persons take reality to be *will* show itself in the sense their language has; i.e. in what they say. But in respect of what is real, or unreal, as distinct from what is said to be, is *this* to be found out, to show itself, in the sense which language has? Or is it to show itself, to be found out, in the world?

Notes

---

1 Giambattista Vico, *The New Science*, s.333.
2 See his introduction to the collected volume of his essays *Ethics and Action* (London, 1972). See also the paper by Roy Holland, 'Is Goodness a Mystery?', *The Human World*, 1971.
3 For a position similar to mine see Alasdair MacIntyre, 'Rationality and the Explanation of Action', in *Against the Self-Images of The Age* (London, 1971).
4 Peter Winch, *The Idea of a Social Science* (London, 1958), p. 15.

1

Nature and convention

PETER WINCH

I

There is a celebrated discussion of the distinction between the
natural and the conventional in Aristotle's *Nichomachean Ethics*,
Book V, Chapter VII, from which I shall quote:

> There are two forms of justice, the natural and the conven-
> tional. It is natural when it has the same validity everywhere and
> is unaffected by any view we may take of the justice of it. It is
> conventional when there is no original reason why it should take
> one form rather than another and the rule it imposes is reached
> by agreement, after which it holds good.... Some philosophers
> are of opinion that justice is conventional in all its branches,
> arguing that a law of nature admits no variation and operates in
> exactly the same way everywhere — thus fire *burns* here and in
> Persia — while rules of justice keep changing before our eyes. It
> is not obvious what rules of justice are natural and what are legal
> and conventional, in cases where variation is possible. Yet it
> remains true that there is such a thing as natural, as well as con-
> ventional, justice.

Many philosophers in our time would dispute the last statement of

Reprinted from Proceedings of the Aristotelian Society, *Vol. LX (1960), pp.231-
52, by permission of the Editor.* © 1960 The Aristotelian Society. This article was
also reprinted in Peter Winch, Ethics and Action (*Routledge and Kegan Paul,
1972*).

Aristotle's I have quoted, being of the opinion that justice is conventional in all its branches. Karl Popper is perhaps the leading exponent of this view[1], holding that all norms of human behaviour are logically akin to decisions and that there is such a 'dualism of facts and decisions' that any talk of 'natural' morality or law must involve a confusion between two logically quite distinct modes of utterance: laws of nature of the sort established and used in the sciences; and prescriptive norms which are decided upon and adhered to or enforced in the regulation of human behaviour in society. Fire burns here and in Persia, while rules of justice keep changing before our eyes.

I intend to dispute this view. First, I shall try to show, negatively, that Popper fails to establish his desired dualism; later I shall argue, more positively, that there are certain aspects of morality which make it necessary to say that it is not entirely based on convention but that, on the contrary, it is presupposed by any possible conventions. Such a view need not imply, as Popper thinks it must, the nonsensical idea that norms can be laid down 'in accordance with natural laws' in the scientific sense.

II

Like the Sophistic thinkers to whom Aristotle was referring, Popper lays great stress on the alleged fact that whereas norms of behaviour are variable and alterable, laws of nature are not. But his discussion suffers from his tendency to run together that point with the quite different one that it makes sense to speak of men breaking and contravening the norms current in their society, but no sense at all to speak of scientific laws of nature being contravened by the things the behaviour of which the laws are used to describe or explain. It belongs to the grammar of the word 'norm' that it is intelligible to say that a man may choose not to adhere to any given norm; but this does not entail that it is always intelligible to speak of the possibility of *altering* any given norm. Often of course it is: as with norms governing rates of income tax; but that this must always be true remains to be shown. There is, it is true, an important logical relation between the possibility of saying that a norm of behaviour holds good in a society and the fact that people in that society do in fact adhere to the norm more often than they break it, or at least that they tend to manifest some sort of hostile reaction to breaches of it, by way, for instance, of condemnation or remorse. But in order to use this relation to prove that all norms are necessarily alterable in principle, one would have also to show in addition that in respect of *any* given norm, it must always be possible to imagine people in a society *not* adhering to it more often than they break it, or *not* tending to manifest disapprobatory attitudes to breaches of it. I shall try to show subsequently in this paper that this latter condition is not fulfilled for some fundamental cases; not because people's adherence to such a norm is guaranteed by any scientific law of nature but because the idea of their non-adherence is made unintelligible by certain features of the concept of the social life of human beings.

However, it is certainly true that a great many very important norms of human behaviour *are* variable and changeable as between one society or historical period and another. But do they differ from scientific laws of nature in *this* respect? Science develops, and modern physics, for example, cannot be expressed in a set of propositions that would have been uttered by Aristotle, or even Newton, any more than modern morality can be expressed in a series of propositions that would have been uttered by Abraham. Of course, the logic of scientific development is not the same as that of moral change; but then, I am not arguing that there is no logical difference between science and morality, only that this difference cannot be elucidated in terms of Popper's concept of alterability.

Popper would perhaps say that when different laws of nature come to be accepted in science, this is because those accepted previously have been shown to be false, insufficiently precise, or too narrow in scope; that this has been shown by a more searching investigation of the facts, whereas human norms do not change as a result — at least not as a direct result — of any 'investigation of the facts', but rather as a result of human decisions. But the role ascribed here to 'the unchanging facts and regularities' in science has not been made sufficiently clear. What *is* true is the following. Modern scientific theories could be used to describe and explain natural phenomena occurring in the time of Abraham as well as they can be used for phenomena occurring now; but modern *moral* concepts could not be used to describe and explain the actions of Abraham and his contemporaries. The relation between moral ideas and human behaviour is different from that between scientific ideas and the behaviour of natural phenomena.

Nevertheless, we cannot say without qualification that modern scientific theories are about the same sets of facts as the theories of earlier stages of scientific development were about. I do not mean simply that new and more precise observations have been made, which have had to be taken into account by the new theories; scientific *concepts* have changed too, and with them scientists' views on what is to count as a relevant fact. 'Time' in Relativity Theory does not mean what it did in Classical Mechanics. Of course, the two concepts are related, in a way which could be brought out by describing the historical development of physics between then and now. But we shall obscure the nature of this development if we think of it in terms of the building of new and better theories to explain one and the same set of facts; not because the facts themselves change independently, but because scientists' criteria of relevance change. And this does not mean that earlier scientists had a *wrong* idea of what the facts were; they had the idea appropriate to the investigation *they* were conducting.

If it is true that men's moral standards change as a result of human decisions, this is equally true of men's scientific ideas. The relevant decisions here are to adopt this rather than that line of enquiry, to develop particular techniques of investigation, and so on. Scientific concepts and theories can only be understood in the context of the ways in which scientific investigation is carried on, and, *a fortiori*, changes in the one can only be understood in the context of changes in the other.

> If you think of some of the things which enrich the present time: atonality in music, or the structure of the genetic material which gives to all living things the quality of life, or such a notion as parity, which has been prominent in discoveries in basic physics, these are not things which were quite so simply given and there to be found, simply, by anyone. It required a tradition, a culture, a background, even to come to these things, even to define them, even to know the means by which they can be found. *It depends on where you are, what you are, how you talk.*[2]

The barrier that stands in the way of a layman who wants to understand something in modern physics is a cultural barrier. 'The deep things in physics, and probably in mathematics too, are not things you can tell about unless you are talking to someone who has lived a long time acquiring the tradition'[3]. Something formally analogous to this is also true of our difficulty in understanding the *moral* ideas and practices of a historically or culturally remote society. Consider, for instance, the practice of child sacrifice in pre-Abrahamic Hebrew society. This is a practice which, in terms of our own way of living and the moral ideas that go along with it, is just unintelligible. To try to understand it is to try to understand something of what life and thought must have been like in that society. What I want to emphasize here is that the main problem about this is one of *understanding* what was involved; not just one of taking up an attitude, for without understanding we should not know what we were taking up an attitude *to*. And it would be no more open to anyone to propose that this practice should be adopted in our own society than it is open to anyone to propose the rejection of the Second Law of Thermodynamics in physics. My point is not just that no one would listen to such a proposal but that no one would understand what was being proposed. What made child-sacrifice what it was, was the role it played in the life of the society in which it was practised; there is a *logical* absurdity in supposing that the very same practice could be instituted in our own quite different society.

What this indicates is that *decision* is not the fundamental concept in morality. For a decision can only be made within the context of a meaningful way of life and a moral decision can only be made within the context of a morality. A morality cannot be *based* on decisions. What decisions are and what are not possible will depend on the morality within which the issues arise; and not *any* issue can arise in a given morality.

Popper's account does not really make room for the question whether a decision is intelligible or not. This is important, since it is only when questions of intelligibility can be raised that the concept of a decision can have application.

What makes a decision intelligible is its relation to the facts of the situation in which it is made; and this relation is a logical one. Popper seems to deny this with his Humeian doctrine that 'decisions can never be derived from facts (or statements of facts), although they pertain to facts'[4]. Now it is true that in any situation where I can be said to have made a decision it must be conceivable that I might have decided differently; but this does not mean that a different decision would have been necessarily intelligible. Suppose that two men, *A* and *B*, are arguing about a proposed relaxation of the divorce laws. *A* convinces *B* that the divorce laws as they exist generate much human misery and that the proposed relaxation would not bring with it any deleterious after-effects, such as a weakening in public respect for the institution of marriage. Suppose then that *B*, having accepted all this and without raising any counter-considerations of his own, then says that he has decided to oppose any relaxation in the law. Of course, we can imagine *B* acting like this; but I suggest we should find what he was doing unintelligible. And if he were *always* to act like this, we should say

he was incapable of rational decision. It is true that the relation
between factual premises and decision in this example is very much
unlike the relation between a scientific theory and the experimental
evidence cited in its support by a scientist. But this difference
provides no support for Popper's dualism. There are very many, and
very diverse, kinds of relation between factual premise and factual
conclusion which are quite unlike anything to be found in theoretical science: for instance, the relation between the evidence an
historian appeals to and his interpretation of the events he is
relating. And again there are very many different ways in which
decisions can be supported by facts; consider, for instance, the
differences between the appropriate ways of supporting decisions in
morality, politics, business. Rather than a dualism, we have here a
highly variegated and overlapping pluralism of different kinds of
factual statement and different kinds of decision. The dualistic view
obscures the fact that what counts as a relevant fact in a given mode
of life is logically related to the kind of decision which is appropriate
in that mode of life. One could not make clear what is meant by a
'business fact' without taking into account the kind of decision
which has to be taken in the running of a business.

It is important to emphasize in this connection that making a
statement is just as much a human action as is taking a decision. If a
conclusion follows logically from a set of premises this does not
mean that we can be confident that anyone who accepts the
premises will also accept the conclusion. For men often act
irrationally, *both* in the way they argue *and* in the way they act and
decide. The notion of logic is the notion of what is and what is not
intelligible in human behaviour and it can be applied to anything
men do. If it is abstracted from the ways in which men live it loses its
significance *as* logic even as applied to relations between statements,
for a statement is essentially something which men may make in the
course of their lives.

'Facts are *there*, whereas decisions have to be *made*.' This is the
kind of view suggested by Popper's discussion. And there is a sense in
which this is true: when it is a question of investigating a particular
set of facts, we have to find out what they are; this is not a matter for
decision. But Popper is discussing the general concept of a fact and
its relation to the concept of a decision and the matter cannot be left
there. We may be able to say that particular facts are given; but
that is not to say that the concept of factuality is given; it arises out
of the way men live. We have to consider the conditions which make
it possible for us to have a concept of 'the facts', which involves

taking into account the modes of human life, together with the kinds of decisions involved in them, in which the concept of 'the facts' plays a part and from which it receives its sense.

> Knowledge itself cannot be described independently of volition; the ascription of sensible knowledge and of volition go together … The identification served by colour-names is in fact not primarily that of colours, but of objects by means of colours; and thus too the prime mark of colour-discrimination is doing things with objects — fetching them, placing them — according to their colours. Thus the ascription of sensible discrimination and that of volition are inseparable; one cannot describe a creature as having the power of sensation without also describing it as doing things in accordance with perceived sensible differences.[5]

There are in human life many different kinds of 'doing things with objects', as many ways in which facts may be important to men — in science, morality, business, law, politics, etc. — and as many different kinds of fact and ways in which facts may be related to decisions.

III

However, to abandon the dualism of facts and decisions is not in itself to refute the idea that norms of behaviour are conventional in character. For even if we admit that standards of what is acceptable in social behaviour colour all our thinking, even our conceptions of what are to count as the facts, still, such standards are not fixed and established for all time. Modes of social activity vary and differ greatly from time to time and from place to place, and so do men's associated conceptions of what is permissible and what is not. So it may seem a completely contingent, purely historical or sociological, matter *what* norms of behaviour are adhered to in any particular society.

I shall not deny that there is an irreducible historical contingency in the norms that a society adheres to; neither shall I claim that what is thus contingent is any the less morally important for a member of the society. But I do wish to argue against the idea that there need be no fixed points in all this change and variety, that there are no norms of human behaviour which could not be different from what they are in fact, and that everything in human morality is therefore ultimately conventional in character.

To this end I shall examine a conception which plays a leading role in A.I. Melden's recent book, *Rights and Right Conduct*, the conception of a 'moral community'. Melden argues, with great force, that moral conceptions only have sense within the life of such a community and that a fruitful moral philosophy is only possible if such conceptions are placed in the mode of life which gives them their meaning. Now this philosophical procedure is of course familiar from other branches of philosophical enquiry: in the philosophy of science, for instance, one cannot get far without relating the realm of scientific discourse that one is concerned to elucidate to the context of the investigatory procedures established in the scientific community within which it is spoken. Nevertheless, the notion of a 'moral community' is in some fundamental respects quite unlike that of a 'scientific community'[6]. I shall argue that although there may be and are human societies which are not, and do not contain, scientific communities, there could not be a human society which was not also, in some sense a moral community. In trying to show this, I shall also try to indicate more specifically certain moral conceptions which, in one form or another, must be recognized in any human society.

Notice first that morality cannot be called, in the same sense as can science, a 'form of activity'; it is not something one can choose to engage in or not at will. It would hardly make sense, for instance, for someone to say he had spent six weeks working hard at morality (unless this meant something like moral *philosophy*), though it would be perfectly in order for him to say he had spent the time working hard at science. A connected point is that whereas a man can become involved with scientific problems only by choosing to concern himself with science, he does not become involved in moral problems by choosing to concern himself with morality. (It is also significant that in the previous sentence 'involved *in*' seems more appropriate to the case of moral problems than the 'involved *with*' I used of scientific problems.) Moral issues may force themselves on you whether you want to be concerned with them or not. If you are morally obtuse, or corrupt, you may fail, or refuse, to see the moral issues with which your situation faces you; but that will not mean that your situation does not in fact face you with them. Moreover, you will render yourself liable to a moral judgment in not facing up to them. You cannot put yourself outside the sphere of moral discourse by saying it does not interest you. But a man who refuses to concern himself with scientific issues does not thereby expose himself to *scientific* judgment; if somebody like Sir Charles Snow tells him he ought thus to concern himself, that will be a *moral* judgment.

This suggests that moral conceptions arise out of any common life between men and do not presuppose any *particular* forms of activity in which men may engage together. I shall now examine some features of this notion of a 'common life' which are particularly important here.

It belongs to our notion of a social community that such a community should contain a shared language and that specifically human intelligence should be exercised in the life of its members. This has always been recognized as important by social philosophers, but everything turns on precisely *how* it is thought to be relevant. Hobbes, for example, tries to use this feature of human life to prove precisely the opposite of the position I wish to maintain: to prove, namely, that the natural state of men living together is the *bellum omnium contra omnes*. His conception of the 'state of nature' follows directly from his individualistic conception of human language and intelligence.

> It is true that certain living creatures, as bees, and ants, live sociably one with another, which are therefore by Aristotle numbered amongst political creatures, and yet they have no other direction, than their particular judgments and appetites; nor speech, whereby one of them can signify to another, what he thinks expedient for the common benefit: and therefore some man may perhaps desire to know, why mankind cannot do the same.[7]

The points Hobbes makes in reply to this objection all rest on the fact that man has language and the sort of prudential intelligence that his philosophy envisages as providing the basis for language[8]. 'Competition for honour and dignity', a man's 'joy in comparing himself with other men', his belief that he is better able to administer the common business than another, 'that art of words, by which some men represent to others, that which is good', the ability to 'distinguish between *injury* and *damage*'. 'Lastly, the agreement of these creatures is natural; that of man, is by covenant only, which is artificial: and therefore it is no wonder if there be something else required, besides covenant, to make their agreement constant and lasting.'

The last point is crucial, because it is on Hobbes's conception of the relation between rationality and agreement and the related conception of agreement as covenant that everything turns. Briefly,

Hobbes holds that covenant is the only/form of agreement possible between human beings; it is made /possible by rationality, which in its turn is what rules out the possibility of any other kind of 'natural' agreement. Thus everything comes back to his analysis of rationality and his belief that it can be elucidated in purely individual terms, without presupposing any sort of developed social life and institutions. It is this point which bears the weight of Vico's attack on Hobbes.

I shall not here restate the case for saying that human rationality is essentially social in character which on another occasion I based on Wittgenstein's treatment of the concept of *following a rule*. Instead, I want to carry the argument a stage further by suggesting that the social conditions of language and rationality must also carry with them certain fundamental *moral* conceptions.

To this end I shall offer some reflections on what Wittgenstein says about the kind of *agreement* that must exist between users of a common language. I am thinking here not so much of the agreement in using words in the same way which plays such an important part in his account of linguistic rules, as of the different though related conception of the 'agreement in *judgements*', which he argues is a condition of the possibility of anyone's ever *saying* something.

> 242 If language is to be a means of communication there must be agreement not only in definitions but also (queer as this may seem) in judgements. This seems to abolish logic, but does not do so. — It is one thing to describe methods of measurement, and another to obtain and state results of measurement. But what we call 'measuring' is partly determined by a certain constancy *in results* of measurement.

> 241 'So you are saying that human agreement decides what is true and false?' — It is what human beings *say* that is true and false; and they agree in the language they use. That is not agreement in opinions but in form of life.[9]

The 'agreement' that is referred to here is very complex, as can be seen by noticing the various ways in which it might *not* be achieved. This might, for instance, be due to the erratic behaviour of the things we wanted to use as measuring rods; or to the failure of people to react in the appropriate way to teaching, as the chimpanzee in the Kellogg experiment failed, beyond a certain point, to do.

Might it also be because nobody, or hardly anybody, could ever be relied on to *speak truthfully*? We can hardly put it in this way, since a distinction between 'telling the truth' and 'not telling the truth' presupposes a going system of communication. But one can say that the notion of a society in which there is a language but in which truth-telling is not regarded as the norm is a self-contradictory one. The conception of a distinction between true and false statements (and therefore the conception of statements *simpliciter*) could not *precede* a general adherence to the norm of truth-telling. The relation between these is totally unlike that, say, between a conception of the distinction between the left hand and the right hand side of the road and an adherence to the norm of driving on the left hand side; for here we could first contemplate the two alternatives and *then* decide which one to adopt. But adherence to the norm of truthfulness *goes along with* the distinction between true and false statements; without the one there could not be the other. I am not here speaking of what a given individual may do, but of what must be the case generally in a society. An individual who can talk can of course deliberate on a given occasion whether to tell the truth or not. But he will already have learned what telling the truth *is*; and what I wish to argue is both that learning this is part of the process of learning to speak and also that learning this involves at the same time learning that speaking truthfully is the norm and speaking untruthfully a deviation. What kinds of 'norm' and 'deviation' I shall consider more closely shortly.

Let us suppose, *per absurdum*, that the 'other alternative' were adopted: that what we now call 'true' statements were always uttered in place of what we now call 'false' statements, and *vice versa*. All that would happen would be that statements would come to be taken in the opposite sense from that which they now carry. That is, those utterances which, as things are, express true (false) statements would then express false (true) statements. So the supposition that telling lies could be the norm and telling the truth a deviation from it is self-contradictory. And again, if *per absurdum* the incidence of 'true' and 'false' statements were statistically random, there could be no distinction between truth and falsity at all, therefore no communication. For to communicate it must be possible for people's utterances to be taken in certain specific ways by other people.

It would, then, be nonsense to call the norm of truth-telling a 'social convention', if by that were meant that there might be a human society in which it were not generally adhered to. Of course, the existence of this norm is possible only in a society in which there are also certain (linguistic and other) conventions; but that is quite different from saying that it is itself conventional. Rather, general adherence to such a norm is a feature of any society in which there are conventions, that is, any society *tout court*.

IV

Somebody who assented to much of what has gone before might still hesitate to accept my statement that the existence of a norm of truth-telling is a *moral* condition of language. It might be supposed that before we can say that truthfulness is regarded in a given society as a moral virtue, and not merely that people as a matter of fact make true statements more often than they make false ones, something more has to be added that is only contingently, and not logically, connected with the conditions for the existence of a society with a common language as such: perhaps something like a specifically moral approbation of those who adhere to the norm and disapprobation of those who contravene it. I shall try to meet some forms of this objection shortly[10]. But first I should like to point out that even if the objection be conceded, what I have said so far, if sound, would still be enough to refute the view that there could be a society in which telling the truth were generally regarded as a moral *vice*. For this would surely entail that it was something that people tried to avoid doing as a general rule; which would be absurd.

I shall also point out that what I have said does not commit the obvious mistake of equating cases of truthfulness with cases in which merely true statements are made; I do not exemplify the virtue of truthfulness every time I say something true. What I *have* said is that some concern with the virtue of truthfulness is a necessary background condition in any society in which it is to be possible for anyone to make true statements.

Now it might be said that in attaching moral significance to truth-telling as I have discussed it, I have confused two quite distinct senses of the word 'right': namely as meaning (a) *morally* right and (b) *correctly* used. For someone who uses the language incorrectly is not thereby a moral delinquent; and all that is needed for the existence of language is agreement on its correct use. But while the first half of this last statement is true, the second half is false. To lie is not to use language incorrectly. One has to use language correctly (at least within certain limits of grammatical error) in order to make a statement at all, whether a truthful or a lying one. Again, someone who believes another's said lie, has not failed to understand what the speaker has *said*; for only if he has understood this is he in a position to believe the lie. But there is something about the situation that he has failed to understand; and this we might express by saying he has failed to understand the *speaker*, in the sense that he has failed to understand what the speaker has *done*, or where the speaker stands. And this understanding of the role played by the speaker of an utterance is an essential part of language. Communicating is not *just* understanding and using *words*.

Failure to make this distinction mars the presentation of a case with similar import advocated by Michael Polanyi[11], who rightly lays great emphasis on the notions of 'commitment' and 'trust' as essential to the understanding of what language is. The trouble lies in his talk about 'commitment', 'heuristic passions', 'fiduciary acts' as 'tacit *components*' in acts of assertion, often as if they were a sort of *feelings*. 'Unless an assertion of fact is accompanied by some heuristic or persuasive feeling, it is a mere form of words, saying nothing'[12]. This leads him to 'the paradox of self-set standards; if the criteria of reasonableness, to which I subject my beliefs, are ultimately upheld by my confidence in them, the whole process of justifying these beliefs may appear but a futile authorisation of my own authority'[13]. Polanyi embraces this paradox with the words 'Yet so be it', and never really succeeds in making it look less paradoxical.

Yet the paradox could have been avoided if the vital distinction had been observed between 'what a statement means' and 'what a person means in making the statement'. Polanyi says: 'It is not words that have meaning, but the speaker or listener who means something by them'[14]. To this the proper answer is: words may have a meaning and so, in a different though related sense, may a speaker mean something by the words he uses. But this latter kind of meaning would be impossible if the words used did not already mean something in the first sense — something which the speaker did not himself *make* them mean. Humpty-Dumptyism is an absurdity. Of course words may be defined arbitrarily for a special purpose, but only in terms of other words with an established common meaning or of commonly understood techniques such as ostensive definition. Nobody can make his words mean something simply by willing that they should, still less by having a feeling when he utters them.

Because of his confusion over this Polanyi misconstrues the significance of the lie.

> Every conceivable assertion of fact can be made in good faith or
> as a lie. The statement remains the same in both cases, but its
> tacit components are different. A truthful statement commits
> the speaker to a belief in what he has asserted: he embarks in it
> on an open sea of limitless implications. An untruthful state-
> ment withholds this belief, launching a leaking vessel for others
> to board and sink in it.[15]

I call this a misconstruction, because the liar is no less *committed* to
a belief in what he says than is he who speaks truthfully. One is
committed by one's words and deeds and, given these, one cannot in
addition *will* that one shall or shall not be committed in certain
ways. The point about the liar is that he is letting down those with
whom he *has* committed himself.

The notion of commitment marks the distinction and the connection between the following two concepts: *what words mean* and
what people mean by words. People can only say something and
mean it if they use words that mean something; and it belongs to the
kind of meaning that words have that they can be used by people in
statements that they (the people) mean. But this is only possible in
a society where people are so related that for one person to say
something is for him to commit himself with others; and an
important part of such a relation is that there should be a common
respect for truthfulness.

Consider now another objection[16]. To say that something is
regarded as a moral virtue in a society is to say that people regard
non-compliance with it with a special sort of disapproval. But could
there not be a society in which nobody ever in fact failed to comply
with the 'norms'? Where the possibility of doing this never occurred
to anyone? Here there would be no concept of a breach of the norms
and correspondingly there could be no recognizably moral attitude
either to 'breaches of' or 'adherences to' the norms. In fact there
would be no norms, as we understand them. People would just
naturally be truthful, kind to their friends and neighbours, etc.: a
society like that of Swift's Houyhnhnms.

I shall argue that this apparent description of a possible society is
not in fact as intelligible as it may appear. Consider first the case of
'natural kindness', which was the one particularly urged by
Wisdom. Such a people would have no conception of unkindness;
but in this case to say that they 'act kindly' cannot mean quite the
same as it means when applied to the behaviour of somebody in our
own society. For us this is a description which presupposes the

possibility of acting *un*kindly. Now Wisdom might say: 'Very well. We should not call such behaviour "kind", because this is a *moral* term and moral virtues do require the possibility of choice between alternatives which is lacking in my postulated society. But my point was that there could be a society like that, *i.e.*, a society lacking what we should call "moral values".'

This argument is hard to answer so far as the example of kindness is concerned. But consider now the much more fundamental case of truthfulness[17]. Swift's Houyhnhnm argues thus:

> That the use of speech was to make us understand one another and to receive information of facts; now if anyone said the thing which was not, those ends were defeated, because I cannot properly be said to understand him, and I am so far from receiving information that he leaves me worse than in ignorance, for I am led to believe a thing black when it is white, or short when it is long.

A confusion very like Polanyi's is committed here. It is true in a sense that if someone gets me to believe his lie 'I cannot properly be said to understand *him*', for I understand him to mean what he says when he does not. But it does not follow that I do not understand *what he says*; for unless I do I am in no position to *mis*understand *him* in the way I do. Furthermore, this latter sort of misunderstanding must be possible if anything is to take place that we can call 'communication'; for a speaker must be able to mean what he says and a hearer to understand him as meaning what he says. And this can only be so where the speaker may *not* mean what he says, since meaning something is not an event that can just *happen*; and where it makes sense for the hearer to ask whether the speaker means what he says or not. None of these questions could arise in Wisdom's 'society'; hence one could not speak of any 'communication' between its members; hence it is not really a possible *society*.

It may now be said that even if all this is true, it still does not follow that truthfulness must have any *moral* significance[18]. Certainly, the maintenance of established (linguistic and other) standards involves an agreement in reactions, including an agreement in reactions to deviations from the standards. But does this mean there must be an agreement in *moral* reactions? Consider a gambling game between card-sharpers, mutually recognized as such[19]. There clearly must be rules which the players are expected to adhere to; but in what sense of 'expected to'? Might not Hobbes's description apply here: 'only that to be every man's, that he can get:

and for so long, as he can keep it'? These players might *expect* their opponents to break the rules if they think they can get away with it, and not think any the worse of them for that, but simply try to ensure that they cannot by the threat of their guns on the table.

Clearly such a situation is possible; but it does not follow that it is a possible microcosm of a whole society. That would mean that a man's expectation that others will, in general, tell the truth would have to be of a similar kind, as would his own attitude to the alternatives of speaking truthfully and lying. Speaking could only be regarded as a means of attaining some advantage by manipulating the reactions of other people in a desired way: the view of language as rhetoric put to Socrates by his Sophistic opponents in Plato's *Gorgias*. Of course an individual can, at least sometimes, regard his utterances in that way, but not all, or even most, uses of language in a society could be generally so regarded. For one can only use words to manipulate the reactions of other men in so far as those others at least think they *understand* what one is saying. So the concept of understanding is presupposed by the possibility of such manipulation of reactions and cannot be elucidated in terms of it.

Richard Rovere writes of that arch-manipulator of reactions, Senator Joe McCarthy:

> He never really took himself seriously. He was the leader of a fanatical movement, and he gave his name to a fanatical doctrine, but\ he was no kind of fanatic himself.... The most successful and menacing of all our apostles of hatred was himself incapable of true rancour, spite, and animosity as a eunuch is incapable of marriage.... Basically, of course, he was a great sophisticate in human relationships, as every demagogue must be. He knew a great deal about people's fears and anxieties, and he was a superb juggler of them. But he was himself numb to the sensations he produced in others. He could not comprehend true outrage, true indignation, true anything.[20]

McCarthy's operations presupposed the existence of men who *were* true fanatics, who *could* experience true outrage and indignation, and so on. Similarly McCarthy's use of the 'paraphernalia of rationality' — stuffed brief-case, footnotes, etc. — in order to impress people presupposed the existence of the real thing: something that could not be accounted for in terms of its usefulness in getting people to do and believe certain desired things, but which implies that certain values are respected for their own sakes.

Wittgenstein writes:

> A rule *qua* rule is detached, it stands as it were alone in its glory; although what gives it importance is the facts of daily experience. What I have to do is as it were to describe the office of a king; in doing which I must never fall into the error of explaining the kingly dignity by the king's usefulness, but I must leave neither his usefulness nor his dignity out of account.[21]

Because there is rational discourse and understanding men can often induce others to act as they want. But the nature of rational discourse and understanding cannot be accounted for in terms of this fact.

V

I have said that there could not be a human society in which truthfulness were not in general regarded as a virtue. This does not mean that no one can ever be justified in lying. But it does imply that a lie always needs special justification if it is not to be condemned. What is regarded as such a justification will depend on the particular institutions of the society in question.

I am not committed to saying that truthfulness must have precisely the *same* moral significance in any human society. Its peculiar role in *our* lives, for instance, has to do with the importance for us of commerce, with its necessity for reliance on contractual fulfilment and accurate specification of goods; and again with the importance for us of scientific research with its concomitant need for trustworthiness in the reports of experiments and integrity in argument. To say that the virtue of truthfulness must play some part in the life of any society is not to describe the peculiar part it plays in the life of a particular society.

There is a more general concept for which my argument could be adapted: that of *integrity*, which is to human institutions generally what truthfulness is to the institution of language. There are important formal analogies between language and other social institutions; for to act in the context of a social institution is always to commit oneself in some way for the future: a notion for which the notion of being committed by what one *says* provides an important parallel. But the concept of integrity is inseparable from that of commitment. To lack integrity is to act with the appearance of fulfilling a certain role but without the intention of shouldering the responsibilities to which that role commits one. If that, *per absurdum*, were to become the rule, the whole concept of a social role would thereby collapse.

Of course, the particular form integrity will take, what will count as 'integrity' and 'lack of integrity', will depend on the particular institutions within the context of which the question arises. And it is not necessary that the concept of integrity should always be singled out and made a matter of special explicit emphasis, as it is for instance in the climate of culture we call 'Romanticism'[22]. But a people can show a regard for particular manifestations of integrity without necessarily building a whole ethos round the concept.

What I am saying about the relation between the general idea of these virtues and their particular social manifestations is expressed in the following remark of Vico's, with whose conception of the 'natural law of the peoples' my thesis has certain similarities:

> There must in the nature of human things be a mental language common to all nations, which uniformly grasps the substance of things feasible in human social life, and expresses it with as many diverse modifications as these same things may have diverse aspects. A proof of this is afforded by proverbs and maxims of vulgar wisdom, in which substantially the same meanings find as many diverse expressions as there are nations ancient and modern.[23]

Vico could say this while being more alive than most to the extraordinary variety in the qualities of life and thought to be found at different periods of human history.

In some respects integrity is to human institutions generally what fair play is to games. What constitutes fair play in a particular instance must be specified in relation to the particular rules of the game in question. It is a foul to handle the ball in Association Football but not in Rugby; and of course handling the ball does not enter at all into what is meant by cheating at patience. We might, it is true, teach someone the meaning of 'fair play' by introducing him to a number of different examples like this. But his grasp of the concept would not be shown by his ability to remember and recognize just these examples, but by his ability to use the concept in connection with *other* games which did not enter into his training in the concept. The sense of the notion of fair play has to do with its importance for the general idea of a game rather than with its particular manifestations in the rules of any particular game. Similarly, the sense of the concept of integrity has to do with its importance for the general idea of a social institution.

I have not of course contended that one is under an obligation to admire particular manifestations of integrity; that would be to mistake my logico-philosophical thesis for a quite absurd moral doctrine. The concentration camp commandant towards the end of Irwin Shaw's *The Young Lions* exhibited integrity of a peculiarly revolting sort from the point of view of Western liberal morality. He was morally revolting because of the unspeakable role he was playing; to say that he was playing it with integrity is, for most of us, an additional count against him, not a point in his favour. But the propensity of people to act like that was none the less an essential factor in the continued existence of such institutions. There could not be a convention to the effect that such attitudes should not, *in general*, be adopted.

I think that there are other virtues for which a similar case could be made, that of *justice*, for example. But I do not at present see how to go about making such a case; and fortunately there is no more space to start investigating that here.

Notes

---

1 See *The Open Society and Its Enemies*, 3rd edn (London, 1962), vol. I, chapter 5.
2 Robert Oppenheimer, 'Tradition and Discovery', *American Council of Learned Societies Newsletter*, vol.X, no. 8 (October 1959), p.5. The italics are mine.
3 Ibid., p.13.
4 Op.cit., p.62.
5 G.E.M. Anscombe, *Intention* (Oxford, 1969), p.67.
6 I am not suggesting that Melden denies these differences. They are not important for the kind of issue he is discussing in his book.
7 *Leviathan*, part II, chapter 17.
8 Ibid., part I, chapter 4.
9 *Philosophical Investigations*, p.88. I have transposed the order of these two sections in order to make the train of thought, out of context, more intelligible.
10 In what followed I am particularly indebted to criticisms made of an earlier draft of this paper at meetings of the Cambridge Moral Sciences Club and the University College of Swansea Philosophical Society.
11 In his *Personal Knowledge*, especially sections II and III (London, 1962).
12 Ibid., p.254.

13 p.256.

14 p.252.

14 p.253.

16 Made in discussion by Professor John Wisdom.

17 Of course these cases are connected, as Aristotle makes clear in Book VIII of the *Nichomachean Ethics*, where he speaks of 'friendship' as one of the most fundamental of social virtues. But he strains this notion, especially when he speaks of 'the friendship because of advantage' which is 'the connecting link of shopkeepers', and 'legal friendship', where 'the friendly element is the delay in requiring the discharge' of a contractual obligation. But he is certainly talking of something important which is overlooked by writers like Hobbes.

18 The following line of argument was suggested in discussion by Rush Rhees, though I do not think he regards it as capable of being pressed to its apparent conclusion.

19 Rhees's example.

20 *Senator Joe McCarthy*, by Richard Rovere. My quotation is from an excerpt in *The Observer* of 10 January 1960.

21 *Remarks on the Foundations of Mathematics*, V-3, p.160.

22 This was pointed out to me by Sir Isaiah Berlin.

23 *The New Science*, paragraph 161.

2

Morality and pessimism

STUART HAMPSHIRE

I

There are currents of moral ideas which are partly philosophical
and partly something less precise, changes in public consciousness.
The honourable, even glorious, school of British utilitarianism, as
represented by Bentham, J.S. Mill, and Sidgwick, was a school of
moral thought, and a school also of general philosophy, that set out
to do good in the world, even though it was only a philosophy; and it
may even be judged to have succeeded in large part over many years
in this aim.

It is certainly not easy, and perhaps it is not possible to calculate
the real effect upon men's lives of any new system of moral ideas and
of any new philosophy. But the utilitarian philosophy brought new
interests into the study of political economy; into the theory and
practice of public administration; into the rhetoric, and into the
programmes, of movements of political and social reform in
Britain. Indeed the utilitarian philosophy became part of the
ordinary furniture of the minds of those enlightened persons who
would criticize institutions, not from the standpoint of one of the
Christian churches, but from a secular point of view. In the minds

Reprinted from New York Review of Books, *Vol. XIX, Nos 11 and 12 (25 January
1973), by permission of the author and the* New York Review of Books. © NYRB,
Inc. 1973. *A slightly shorter version was published by Cambridge University Press
(1972).*

of liberal and radical social reformers everywhere, the utilitarian philosophy was until quite recently a constant support for progressive social policies. Even the rare and strange adaptation of utilitarianism that appeared in the last chapter of G.E. Moore's *Principia Ethica* pointed toward liberal and improving policies: at least it did in the minds of Keynes, of Leonard Woolf, and of others whose lives were seriously influenced by Moore.

Moore himself wrote of his own moral conclusions as prescribing the aims of social policy, and, like Mill, he was marking the target of social improvements. The utilitarian philosophy, before the First World War and for many years after it — perhaps even until 1939 — was still a bold, innovative, even a subversive doctrine, with a record of successful social criticism behind it. I believe that it is losing this role, and that it is now an obstruction.

Utilitarianism has always been a comparatively clear moral theory, with a simple core and central notion, easily grasped and easily translated into practical terms. Its essential instruction goes like this: when assessing the value of institutions, habits, conventions, manners, rules, and laws, and also when considering the merits of individual actions or policies, turn your attention to the actual or probable states of mind of the persons who are, or will be, affected by them. That is all you need to consider in your assessments. In a final analysis, nothing counts but the states of mind, and perhaps, more narrowly, the states of feeling, of persons; or, more generously in Bentham and G.E. Moore, of sentient creatures. Anything else that one might consider, in the indefinite range of natural and man-made things, is to be reckoned as mere machinery, as only a possible instrument for producing the all-important — literally all-important — states of feeling. From this moral standpoint the whole machinery of the natural order, other than states of mind, is just machinery, useful or harmful in proportion as it promotes or prevents desired states of feeling.

For a utilitarian, the moral standpoint, which is to govern all our actions, places men at the very centre of the universe, with their states of feeling as the source of all value in the world. If the species perished to the last man, or if the last men became impassible and devoid of feeling, things would become cold and indifferent and neutral, from the moral point of view; whether this or that other unfeeling species survived or perished, plants, stars and galaxies, would then be of no consequence. Destruction of things is evil only in so far as it is, or will be, felt as a loss by sentient beings; and the creation of things, and the preservation of species, are to be aimed at and commended only in so far as human beings are, or will be, emotionally and sentimentally interested in the things created and preserved.

This doctrine may reasonably be criticized in two contrary ways. First, as involving a kind of arrogance in the face of nature, an arrogance that is intelligible only if the doctrine is seen as a residue of the Christian account of this species' peculiar relation to the Creator. Without the Christian story it seems to entail a strangely arbitrary narrowing of moral interest. Is the destruction, for instance, of a species of animal to be avoided, as a great evil, only or principally because of the loss of the pleasure that human beings may derive from the species? May the natural order be farmed by human beings for their comfort and pleasure without any restriction other than the comfort and pleasure of future human beings? Perhaps there is no rational procedure for answering these questions. But it is strange to answer them with a confident 'yes'.

On the other hand, the doctrine that only human feelings are morally significant may be thought to belittle men; for it makes morality, the system of rights, duties, and obligations, a kind of psychical engineering, which shows the way to induce desired or valued states of mind. This suggests, as a corollary, that men might be trained, moulded, even bred, with a view to their experiencing the kinds of feeling that alone lend value to their morally neutral surroundings. With advancing knowledge, states of the soul might be controlled by chemical means, and the valuable experiences of the inner life may be best prolonged and protected by a medical technique. So the original sense of the sovereign importance of human beings, and of their feelings, has been converted by exaggeration into its opposite: a sense that these original ends of action are, or may soon become, comparatively manageable problems in applied science.

From the standpoint of philosophy, in a full, old-fashioned sense of that word, we have moved, slowly, stage by stage, in the years since 1914, into a different world of thought from that which most of Sidgwick's contemporaries inhabited; and by a 'world of thought' here I mean the set of conditioning assumptions which any European who thought in a philosophical way about morality would have in mind before he started to think, assumptions that he probably would not examine one by one, and that he would with difficulty make explicit to himself. One such assumption was that, even if the transcendental claims of Christianity have been denied, any serious thought about morality must acknowledge the absolute exceptionalness of men, the unique dignity and worth of this species among other-wise speechless, inattentive things, and their uniquely open future. How otherwise can morality have its overriding claims?

A second assumption, explicit in J.S. Mill, and unchallenged by his utilitarian successors, was that both emotional sensitiveness and intelligence in the calculation of consequences can be expected to multiply and increase, as moral enlightenment spreads and as standards of education improve, into an indefinite and open future. In this open future there will be less avoidable waste of human happiness, less unconsidered destruction of positive and valued feelings, as the human sciences develop and superstitions become weaker and softer. The story of the past — this is the assumption — is essentially the story of moral waste, of a lack of clear planning and contrivance, of always repeated losses of happiness because no one methodically added the emotional gains and losses with a clear head and undistracted by moral prejudices. The modern utilitarian policy makers will be careful social economists, and their planning mistakes will be progressively corrigible ones, so there is no reason why there should not be a steadily rising balance of positive over negative feelings in all societies that have a rational computational morality. A new era of development is possible, the equivalent in morality of high technology in production.

This implicit optimism has been lost, not so much because of philosophical arguments but perhaps rather because of the hideous face of political events. Persecutions, massacres, and wars have been coolly justified by calculations of long-range benefit to mankind; and political pragmatists in the advanced countries, using cost benefit analyses prepared for them by gifted professors, continue to burn and destroy. The utilitarian habit of mind has brought with it a new abstract cruelty in politics, a dull, destructive political righteousness: mechanical, quantitative thinking, leaden academic minds setting out their moral calculations in leaden abstract prose, and more civilized and more superstitious people destroyed because of enlightened calculations that have proved wrong.

Suppose a typical situation of political decision, typical, that is, of the present, and likely to be typical of the immediate future: an expert adviser has to present a set of possible policies among which a final choice has to be made: advantages and disadvantages of various outcomes are to be calculated, and a balance is to be struck. The methods of calculation may be quite sophisticated, and very disparate items may appear in the columns of gain and loss. The death of groups of persons may, for example, be balanced as a loss against a very considerable gain in amenity to be handed down to posterity; or a loss of liberty among one group may be balanced against a very great relief from poverty for another. Such calculations are the everyday stuff of political decision, and they seem to require a common measure that enables qualitatively unrelated effects to be held in balance. The need to calculate in this manner, and to do so convincingly, plainly becomes greater as the area of government decision is widened, and as the applied social sciences render remote effects more computable.

Given that the vast new powers of government are in any case going to be used, and given that remote and collateral effects of policies are no longer utterly calculable, and therefore to be neglected, a common measure to strike a balance is certain to be asked for and to be used; and apparently incommensurable interests will be brought together under this common measure. The utilitarian doctrine, insisting that there is a common measure of those gains and losses, which superficially seem incommensurable, is in any case called into being by the new conditions of political calculation. Any of the original defects in the doctrine will now be blown up, as a photograph is blown up, and made clearly visible in action.

For Machiavelli and his contemporaries, a political calculation was still a fairly simple computation of intended consequences, not unlike the strategems of private intrigue. He and his contemporaries had no thought that a political calculation might issue in a plan for the future of a whole society or nation, with all kinds of dissimilar side effects allowed for and fed into the computation. Computation by a common measure now seems the most orthodox way to think in politics, although this kind of computation had originally been almost scandalous. At first the scandal and surprise lingered around the notion that moral requirements, and moral outrages, could be represented as commensurable gains and losses along a single scale. Yet now those who talk about being responsible in political decision believe that the moral issues must be represented on a common scale, if they are to be counted at all. How can the future of an advanced society be reasonably discussed and planned, if not on this assumption?

To others, and particularly to many of the young in America and in Europe, who would not quote Burke, it now seems obvious that the large-scale computations in modern politics and social planning bring with them a coarseness and grossness of moral feeling, a blunting of sensibility, and a suppression of individual discrimination and gentleness, which are a price that they will not pay for the benefits of clear calculation. Their point is worth considering: perhaps it can be given a philosophical basis.

II

Allow me to go back to the beginnings of moral theory. As a noncommittal starting point, it may be agreed that we all assess ourselves, and other people, as having behaved well or badly on a particular occasion, or for a tract of time, or taking a lifetime as a whole. We similarly assess courses of action, and even whole ways of life, that are open to us before we make a decision. The more fundamental and overriding assessments, in relation to which all other assessments of persons are subsidiary and conditional, we call moral assessments, just because we count them as unconditional and overriding. The goodness or badness imputed may be imputed as a characteristic of persons, or of their actions, their decisions and their policies, or of their characters and their dispositions, or of their lives and ways of life.

Let me take the assessment of persons as the starting point. When we assess ourselves or others in some limited role or capacity, as performing well or ill in that role or capacity, the assessment is not fundamental and unconditional; the assessment gives guidance only to someone who wants to have that role or to act in that capacity, or who wants to make use of someone who does. But if we assess persons as good or bad without further qualification or limitation, merely as human beings, and similarly also their decisions, policies, characters, dispositions, ways of life, as being good or bad without qualification, then our assessments have unconditional implications in respect of what should and should not be done, and of what people should and should not be like, of their characters, dispositions, and ways of life. A human being has the power to reflect on what kind of person he wants to be, and to try to act accordingly, within the limits of his circumstances. His more considered practical choices, and the conflicts that accompany them, will show what he holds to be intrinsically worth pursuing and will therefore reveal his fundamental moral beliefs.

I believe that all I have so far said about this starting point of moral philosophy does not commit me to any one of the competing theories and begs no questions, and will be, or ought to be, accepted by moral philosophers of quite different persuasions, including the utilitarians. I believe this because the various classical moral philosophies can all be formulated within this noncommittal framework.

Each moral philosophy singles out some ultimate ground or grounds for unconditional praise of persons and prescribes the ultimate grounds for preferring one way of life to another.

This is no less true of a utilitarian ethics than of any other. The effectively beneficent and happy man is accounted by a utilitarian more praiseworthy and admirable than any other type of man, and his useful life is thought the best kind of life that anyone could have, merely in virtue of its usefulness, and apart from any other characteristics it may have. The utilitarian philosophy picks out its own essential virtues, very clearly, and the duties of a utilitarian are not hard to discern, even though they may on occasion involve difficult computations.

But there is one feature of familiar moralities which utilitarian ethics famously repudiates, or at least makes little of. There are a number of different moral prohibitions, apparent barriers to action, which a man acknowledges and which he thinks of as more or less insurmountable, except in abnormal, painful, and improbable circumstances. One expects to meet these prohibitions, barriers to action, in certain quite distinct and clearly marked areas of action; these are the taking of human life, sexual relations, family duties and obligations, and the administration of justice according to the laws and customs of a given society.

There are other areas in which strong barriers are to be expected; but these are, I think, the central and obvious ones. A morality is, at the very least, the regulation of the taking of life and the regulation of sexual relations, and it also includes rules of distributive and corrective justice, family duties, almost always duties of friendship, also rights and duties in respect of money and property. When specific prohibitions in these areas are probed and challenged by reflection, and the rational grounds for them looked for, the questioner will think that he is questioning a particular morality specified by particular prohibitions. But if he were to question the validity of any prohibitions in these areas, he would think of himself as challenging the claims of morality itself; for the notion of morality requires that there be some strong barriers against the taking of life, against some varieties of sexual and family relations, against some forms of trial and punishment, some taking of property, and against some distributions of rewards and benefits.

Moral theories of the philosophical kind are differentiated in part by the different accounts that they give of these prohibitions: whether the prohibitions are to be thought of as systematically connected or not, whether they are absolute prohibitions or to be thought of as conditional. Utilitarians always had, and still have, very definite answers. First, they *are* systematically connected, and, second, they are to be thought of as not absolute, but conditional, being dependent for their validity as prohibitions upon the beneficial consequences of observing them. Plainly there is no possibility of proof here, since this is a question in ethics, and not in logic or in the experimental sciences. But various reasons for rejecting the utilitarian position can be given.

All of us sometimes speak of things that cannot be done, or that must not be done, and that are ruled out as impossible by the nature of the case; also there are things that one must do, that one cannot not do, because of the nature of the case. The signs of necessity in such contexts mark the unqualified, unweakened barrier to action, while the word 'ought', too much discussed in philosophical writing, conveys a weakened prohibition or instruction. The same contrast appears in the context of empirical statements, as in the judgments, 'The inflation ought to stop soon' and 'The inflation must stop soon'.

The modal words 'must' and 'ought' preserve a constant relation in a number of different types of discourse, of which moral discourse is only one, not particularly conspicuous, example. He who in a shop says to the salesman, 'The coat must cover my knees', alternatively, 'The coat ought to cover my knees', speaks of a need or requirement and of something less. He who, looking at a mathematical puzzle, says, 'This must be the way to solve it', alternatively, 'This ought to be the way to solve it', speaks of a kind of rational necessity, and of something less. Examples of 'ought' as the weaker variant of 'must' could be indefinitely prolonged into other types of contexts. 'He must help him' is the basic, unmodified judgment in the context of moral discussion or reflection, and 'He ought to help him' is the weakened variant, as it is in other contexts. To learn what a man's moral beliefs are entails learning what he thinks that he must do, at any cost or at almost any cost.

The range of the utterly forbidden types of conduct among Mill's or Sidgwick's friends would differ significantly, but not greatly, from the range of the forbidden and the impossible that would be acknowledged by most of us now. Social anthropologists may record fairly wide variations in the range of the morally impossible, and also, I believe, some barriers that are very general, though not quite universal; and historians similarly. For example, in addition to certain fairly specific types of killing, certain fairly specific types of sexual promiscuity, certain takings of property, there are also types of disloyalty and of cowardice, particularly disloyalty to friends, which are very generally, almost universally, forbidden and forbidden absolutely. They are forbidden as being intrinsically disgraceful and unworthy, and as being, just for these reasons, ruled out: ruled out because they would be disgusting or disgraceful, or shameful, or brutal, or inhuman, or base, or an outrage.

In arguing against utilitarians I must dwell a little on these epithets usually associated with morally impossible action — on a sense of disgrace, of outrage, of horror, of baseness, of brutality, and, most important, a sense that a barrier, assumed to be firm and almost insurmountable, has been knocked over, and a feeling that, if this horrible, or outrageous, or squalid, or brutal action is possible, then anything is possible and nothing is forbidden, and all restraints are threatened.

Evidently these ideas have often been associated with impiety, and with a belief that God, or the gods, have been defied, and with a fear of divine anger. But they need not have these associations with the supernatural, and they may have, and often have had, a secular setting. In the face of the doing of something that must not be done and that is categorically excluded and forbidden morally, the fear that one may feel is fear of human nature. A relapse into a state of nature seems a real possibility, or perhaps seems actually to have occurred, unless an alternative morality with new restraints is clearly implied when the old barrier is crossed. This fear of human nature, and sense of outrage, when a barrier is broken down, is an aspect of respect for morality itself rather than for any particular morality and for any particular set of prohibitions.

The notion of the morally impossible — 'I cannot leave him now; it would be quite impossible. Surely you understand that I *must* help him' — is distinct. A course of conduct is ruled out ('You cannot do that') because it would be inexcusably unjust, or dishonest, or humiliating, or treacherous, or cruel, or ungenerous, or harsh. These epithets, specifying why the conduct is impossible, mark the vices characteristically recognized in a particular morality. In other societies, at other places and times, other specific epithets might be more usually associated with outrage and with morally impossible conduct; but the outrage or shock, and the recognition of impossibility, will be the same in cases where the type of conduct rejected, and the reasons for the rejection, are rather different.

The utilitarian will not deny these facts, but he will interpret them differently. Shock, he will say, is the primitive, prerational reaction; after rational reflection the strength of feeling associated with a prohibition can be, and ought to be, proportional to the estimated harm of the immediate and remote consequences; and he will find no more in the signs of necessity and impossibility than an emphasis on the moral rules which have proved to be necessary protections against evil effects. The signs of necessity are signs that there is a rule. But the rational justification of there being a rule is to be found in the full consequences of its observance, and not in non-rational reactions of horror, disgust, shame, and other emotional repugnances.

But I believe that critical reflection may leave the notion of absolutely forbidden, because absolutely repugnant, conduct untouched. There may in many cases be good reflective reasons why doing such things, assuming such a character, may be abhorrent, and excluded from the range of possible conduct; there may be reflective reasons, in the sense that one is able to say why the conduct is impossible as destroying the ideal of a way of life that one aspires to and respects, as being, for example, utterly unjust or cruel or treacherous or corruptly dishonest. To show that these vices are vices, and unconditionally to be avoided, would take one back to the criteria for the assessment of persons as persons, and therefore to the whole way of life that one aspires to as the best way of life. A reflective, critical scrutiny of moral claims is compatible, both logically and psychologically, with an overriding concern for a record of unmonstrous and respectworthy conduct, and of action that has never been mean or inhuman; and it may follow an assessment of the worth of persons which is not to be identified only with a computation of consequences and effects.

There is a model of rational reflection which depends upon a contrast between the primitive moral response of an uneducated man, and of an uneducated society, and the comparatively detached arguments of the sophisticated moralist, who discounts his intuitive responses as being prejudices inherited from an uncritical past. Conspicuous in the philosophical radicals, in John Stuart Mill, and in the Victorian freethinkers generally, this model in turn depended upon the idea that primitive, prescientific men are usually governed by strict moral taboos, and that in future intellectually evolved and scientifically trained men will be emancipated from these bonds, and will start again with clear reasoning about consequences. The word 'taboo', so often used in these contexts, shows the assumption of moral progress from primitive beginnings, and suggests a rather naïve contrast between older moralities and the open morality of the future; empirical calculation succeeds *a priori* prejudice, and the calculation of consequences is reason.

But reflection may discover a plurality of clear and definite moral injunctions; injunctions about the taking of life, about sexual relations, about the conduct of parents toward children and of children toward parents, about one's duties in times of war, about the conditions under which truth must be told and under which it may be concealed, about rights to property, about duties of friendship, and so on over the various aspects and phases of a normal span of life. Such injunctions need not be inferrable from a few basic principles, corresponding to the axioms of a theory. The pattern that they form can have a different type of unity.

Taken together, a full set of such injunctions, prohibiting types of conduct in types of circumstances, describes in rough and indeterminate outline an attainable and recognizable way of life, aspired to, respected, and admired — or at least the minimum general features of a respectworthy way of life. And a way of life is not identified and characterized by one distinct purpose, such as the increase of general happiness, or even by a set of such distinct purposes. The connection upon which a reasonable man reflects, is to be found in the coherence of a single way of life, distinguished by the characteristic virtues and vices recognized within it.

III

A way of life is a complicated thing, marked out by many details of style and of manner, and also by particular activities and interests, which a group of people of similar dispositions in a similar social situation may share; consequently the group may become an imitable human type who transmits many of its habits and ideals to its descendants, provided that social change is not too rapid.

In rational reflection one may justify an intuitively accepted and unconditional prohibition as a common, expected feature of a recognizable way of life that on other grounds one values and finds admirable, or as a necessary preliminary condition of this way of life. There are rather precise grounds in experience and in history for the reasonable man to expect that certain virtues, which he admires and values, can only be attained at the cost of certain others, and that the virtues typical of several different ways of life cannot be freely combined, as he might wish. Therefore a reasonable and reflective person will review the separate moral injunctions, which intuitively present themselves as having force and authority, as making a skeleton of an attainable, respectworthy, and preferred way of life. He will reject those that seem likely in practice to conflict with others that seem more closely part of, or conditions of, the way of life that he values and admires, or that seem irrelevant to this way of life.

One must not exaggerate the degree of connectedness that can be claimed for the set of injunctions that constitute the skeleton of a man's morality. For example, it is a loose, empirical connection that reasonably associates certain sexual customs with the observation of certain family duties, and certain loyalties to the state or country with the recognition of certain duties in respect of property, and in time of war.

The phrase 'way of life' is vague and is chosen for its vagueness. The unity of a single way of life, and the compatibility in practice of different habits and dispositions, are learned from observation, direct experience, and from psychology and history. We know that human nature naturally varies, and is deliberately variable, only within limits, and that not all theoretically compatible achievements and enjoyments are compatible in normal circumstances. A reasonable man may envisage a way of life, which excludes various kinds of conduct as impossible, without excluding a great variety of morally tolerable ways of life within this minimum framework. The moral prohibitions constitute a kind of grammar of conduct, showing the elements out of which any fully respectworthy conduct, as one conceives it, must be built.

The plurality of absolute prohibitions, and the looseness of their association with any one way of life that stresses a certain set of virtues, is to be contrasted with the unity and simplicity of utilitarian ethics. One might interpret the contrast in this way: to the utilitarian it is certain that all reasonable purposes are parts of a single purpose in a creature known to be governed by the pleasure principle or by a variant of it. The anti-utilitarian replies: nothing is certain in the *theory* of morality, but, at a pre-theoretical level, some human virtues fit together as virtues to form a way of life aspired to, and some monstrous and brutal acts are certainly vicious in the sense that they undermine and corrupt this way of life; and we can explain why they are, and what makes them so, provided that we do not insist upon either precision or certainty or simplicity in the explanation.

The absolute moral prohibitions, which I am defending, are not to be identified with Kant's categorical moral injunctions; for they are not to be picked out by the logical feature of being universal in form. Nor are they prescriptions that must be affirmed, and that cannot be questioned or denied, just because they are principles of rationality and because any contrary principles would involve a form of contradiction. They are indeed judgments of unconditional necessity, in the sense that they imply that what must be done is not necessary because it is a means to some independently valued end, but because the action is a necessary part of a way of life and ideal of conduct. The necessity resides in the nature of the action itself, as specified in the fully explicit moral judgment. The principal and proximate grounds for claiming that the action must, or must not, be performed are to be found in the characterization of the action offered within the prescription; and if the argument is pressed further, first a virtue or vice and then a whole way of life will have to be described.

But still a number of distinctions are needed to avoid misunderstandings. First, he who says, for example, 'You must not give a judgment about this until you have heard the evidence', or, 'I must stand by my friend in this crisis', claiming an absolute, and unconditional, necessity to act just so on this occasion, is not claiming an overriding necessity to act in this way in all circumstances. He has so far not generalized at all, as he would have generalized if he were to add 'always' or 'in all circumstances'. The immediate grounds for the necessity of the action or abstention are indicated in the judgment itself. These particular actions, which are cases of the general type 'respecting evidence' and 'standing by friends', are said to be necessary on this occasion in virtue of having just this character, and in virtue of their being this type of action. In other painful circumstances, and on other occasions, other unconditional necessities, with other grounds, might be judged to have overriding claims.

In a situation of conflict, the necessities may be felt to be stringent, and even generally inescapable, and the agent's further reflection may confirm his first feeling of their stringency. Yet in the circumstances of conflict he has to make a choice, and to bring himself to do one of the normally forbidden things in order to avoid doing the other. He may finally recognize one overriding necessity, even though he would not be ready to generalize it to other circumstances. The necessity that is associated with such types of action — e.g., not to betray one's friends — is absolute and unconditional, in the sense that it is not relative to, or conditional upon, some desirable external end; but it is liable occasionally to conflict with other necessities.

A second distinction must be drawn. From the fact that a man thinks that there is nothing other than X that he can do in a particular situation, it does not follow that it is intuitively obvious to him that he must do X. Certainly he may have reached the conclusion immediately and without reflection; but he might also have reached the very same conclusion after weighing a number of arguments for and against. A person's belief that so-and-so must be done, and that he must not act in any other way, may be the outcome of the calculation of the consequences of not doing the necessary thing, always provided that he sees the avoidance of bringing about these consequences as something that is imposed on him as a necessity in virtue of the character of the action. The reason for the necessity of the action sometimes is to be found in its later consequences rather than in the nature and quality of the action evident at the time of action. In every case there will be a description of the action that shows the immediate ground for the necessity, usually by indicating the virtue or vice involved.

Different men, and different social groups, recognize rather different moral necessities in the same essential areas of moral concern. This is no more surprising, or philosophically disquieting, than the fact that different men, and different social groups, will order the primary virtues of men, and the features of an admirable way of life, differently. That the poverty-stricken and the destitute must be helped, just because they suffer, and that a great wrong does not demand a great punishment as retribution, are typical modern opinions about what must be done. Reasoning is associated with these opinions, as it is also with the different orderings of essential virtues; there are no conclusive proofs, or infallible intuitions, which put a stop to the adducing of new considerations. One does not expect that everyone should recognize the same moral necessities; but rather that everyone should recognize some moral necessities, and similar and overlapping ones, in the same, or almost the same, areas of moral concern.

A man's morality, and the morality of a social group, can properly be seen as falling into two parts: first, a picture of the activities necessary to an ideal way of life which is aspired to, and, second, the unavoidable duties and necessities without which even the elements of human worth, and of a respectworthy way of life, are lacking. The two parts are not rationally unconnected. To take the obvious classical examples: a betrayal of friends in a moment of danger, and for the sake of one's own safety, is excluded from the calculation of possibilities; one may lose perhaps everything else, but this cannot be done; the stain would be too great. And one may take public examples: an outrage of cruelty perpetrated upon undefended civilians in war would constitute a stain that would not be erased and would not be balanced against political success.

IV

How would a philosophical friend of the utilitarians respond to these suggestions? Among other objections he would certainly say that I was turning the clock back, suggesting a return to the moral philosophies of the past: absolute prohibitions, elementary decencies and recognition of a plurality of prohibitions which do not all serve a single purpose — and with nothing more definite behind them than a form of life aspired to. This is the outline of an Aristotelian ethics: ancient doctrine. Modern utilitarians thought that men have the possibility of indefinite improvement in their moral thinking, and that they were confined and confused by their innate endowments of moral repugnances and emotional admirations. There was a sense of the open future in all their writing.

But hope of continuing improvement, if it survives at all, is now largely without evidence. Lowering the barriers of prohibition and making rational calculation of consequences the sole foundation of public policies have so far favoured, and are still favouring, a new callousness in policy, a dullness of sensibility, and sometimes moral despair, at least in respect of public affairs. When the generally respected barriers of impermissible conduct are once crossed, and when no different unconditional barriers, within the same areas of conduct, are put in their place, then the special, apparently superstitious, value attached to the preservation of human life will be questioned. This particular value will no longer be distinguished by an exceptionally solemn prohibition; rather it will be assessed on a common scale alongside other desirable things. Yet it is not clear that the taking of lives can be marked and evaluated on a common scale on which increases of pleasure and diminutions of suffering are also measured. This is the suggested discontinuity which a utilitarian must deny.

Moral prohibitions in general, and particularly those that govern the taking of life, the celebration of the dead, and that govern sexual relations and family relations, are artifices that give human lives some distinctive, peculiar, even arbitrary human shape and pattern. They make human the natural phases of experience and lend them a distinguishing sense and direction, one among many possible ones. It is normal for men to expect these artificialities, without which their lives would seem to them inhuman. Largely for this reason a purely naturalistic and utilitarian interpretation of duties and obligations, permissions and prohibitions, in these areas, and particularly in the taking of human life, leaves uneasiness. The idea of morality is connected with the idea that taking human life is a terrible act, one which has to be regulated by some set of overriding constraints that constitute a morality; and the connection of ideas alleged here is not a vague one.

If there were a people who did not recoil from killing, and, what is a distinguishable matter, who seemed to attach no exceptionable value to human life, they would be accounted a community of the subhuman; or, more probably, we would doubt whether their words and practices had been rightly interpreted and whether their way of life had been understood.

Yet the taking of life does not have any exceptional importance in utilitarian ethics, that is, in an ethics that is founded exclusively on the actual, ascertained desires and sentiments of men (unlike J.S. Mill's); the taking of life is morally significant in so far as it brings other losses with it. For a strict utilitarian (which J.S. Mill was not) the horror of killing is only the horror of causing other losses, principally of possible happiness; in cases where there are evidently no such losses, the horror of killing becomes superstition. And such a conclusion of naturalism, pressed to its limits, does produce a certain vertigo after reflection. It seems that the mainspring of morality has been taken away.

This vertigo is not principally the result of looking across a century of cool political massacres, undertaken with rational aims; it is also a sentiment with a philosophical thought behind it. A consistent naturalism displaces the pre-reflective moral emphasis upon respect for life, and for the preservation of life, on to an exclusive concern for one or other of the expected future products of being alive — happiness, pleasure, the satisfaction of desires. Respect for human life, independent of the use made of it, may seem to utilitarians a survival of a sacramental consciousness, or at least a survival of a doctrine of the soul's destiny, or of the unique relation between God and man. It had been natural to speak of the moral prohibitions against the taking of life as being respect for the sacredness of an individual life; and this phrase has no proper place, it is very reasonably assumed, in the thought of anyone who has rejected belief in supernatural sanctions.

But the situation may be more complicated. The sacredness of life, so called, and the absolute prohibitions against the taking of life, except under strictly defined conditions, may be admitted to be human inventions. Once the human origin of the prohibitions has been recognized, the prohibition against the taking of life, and respect for human life as such, may still be reaffirmed as absolute. They are reaffirmed as complementary to a set of customs, habits, and observances, which are understood by reference to their function, and which are sustained, partly because of, partly in spite of, this understanding: I mean sexual customs; family observances; ceremonial treatment of the dead; gentle treatment of those who are diseased and useless, and of the old and senile; customs of war and treatment of convicted criminals; political and legal safeguards for the rights of individuals; and some customary rituals of respect and gentleness in personal dealings.

This complex of habits, and the rituals associated with them, are carried over into a secular morality which makes no existential claims that a naturalist would dispute, and which still rejects the utilitarian morality associated with naturalism. The error of the optimistic utilitarian is that he carries the deritualization of trans-actions between men to a point at which men not only can, but ought to, use and exploit each other as they use and exploit any other natural objects, as far as this is compatible with general happiness. And at this point, when the mere existence of an individual person by itself has no value, apart from the by-products and uses of the individual in producing and enjoying desirable states of mind, there is no theoretical barrier against social surgery of all kinds. Not only is there no such barrier in theory, but, more important the non-existence of the barriers is explicitly recognized.

The draining of moral significance from ceremonies, rituals, manners, and observances that imaginatively express moral atti-tudes and prohibitions leaves morality incorporated only in a set of propositions and computations: thin and uninteresting proposi-tions, when so isolated from their base in the observances, and manners, which govern ordinary relations with people, and which always manifest implicit moral attitudes and opinions. The compu-tational morality, on which optimists rely, dismisses the non-propositional and unprogrammed elements in morality altogether, falsely confident that these elements can all be ticketed and brought into the computations.

One may object that I now seem to be arguing for the truth of a doctrine by pointing to the evil consequences of its being disbelieved. This is not my meaning. I have been assuming that prohibitions against killing are primary moral prohibitions; secondly, that the customs and rituals that govern, in different societies, relations between the sexes, marriage, property rights, family relationships, and the celebration of the dead are primary moral customs; they always disclose the peculiar kind of respect for human life, and occasions for disrespect, that a particular people or society recognizes, and therefore their more fundamental moral beliefs and attitudes.

Ordinarily a cosmology, or metaphysics, is associated with morality, and, for Europeans, it has usually been a supernatural cosmology. When the supernatural cosmology is generally rejected, or no longer is taken seriously, the idea that human life has a unique value has to be recognized as a human invention. But it is not an invention from nothing at all. The rituals and manners that govern behaviour and respect for persons already express a complex set of moral beliefs and attitudes, and embody a particular way of life. Affirmations of particular rights, duties, and obligations, the propositions of a morality, are a development and a correction of this inexplicit morality of ritual and manners.

Each society, each generation within it, and, in the last resort, each reflective individual, accepts and amends an established morality expressed in rituals and manners, and in explicit prohibitions; and an individual will do this in determining what kind of person he aspires to be and what are the necessary features of a desirable and admirable way of life as he conceives it. If these prohibitions, whatever they are, were no longer observed, and the particular way of life that depends on them was lost, and not just amended or replaced, no particular reason would be left to protect human life more than any other natural phenomenon.

The different manners of different societies provide, as an element in good manners, for the recognition of differences; so among the more serious moral constraints — serious in the sense that they regulate killing and sexuality and family relationships, and so the conditions of survival of the species — may be the requirement to respect moral differences, at least in certain cases. Provided that there are absolute prohibitions in the same domains with the same function, and provided that their congruence with a desired way of life is grasped, we may without irrationality accept the differences; and there may sometimes be a duty to avoid conflict or to look for compromise in cases of conflict.

Consider the intermediate case between manners in the restricted sense and absolute moral principles: a code of honour of a traditional kind. The different prohibitions of different codes are still recognized as codes of honour; and dishonour incurred in the breach of different disciplines is in each case recognizably dishonour, in virtue of the type of ideal behaviour, and the way of life, that has been betrayed. Prohibitions in other moralities, very different from the moralities of honour, may be similarly diverse in content.

The question cannot be evaded: what is the rational basis for acting as if human life has a peculiar value, quite beyond the value of any other natural things, when one can understand so clearly how different people, for quite different reasons, have come to believe that it has a particular value and to affirm this in their different moralities? Is one not rationally compelled to follow the utilitarians in denying the autonomy of ethics, and the absoluteness of moral prohibitions, if one once comes to understand the social, psychological, and other functions which the prohibitions serve? If one reflectively adopts and reaffirms one or other of these moralities, together with its prohibitions, then it may seem that one must be accepting the morality for the sake of its uses and function, rather than for the reasoning associated with it; and this concedes the utilitarian's case.

The conclusion is not necessary. A morality, with its ordering of virtues and its prohibitions, provides a particular ideal of humanity in an ideal way of life; and this moral ideal explains where and why killing is allowed and also for what purposes a man might reasonably give his life; and in this sense it sets its own peculiar value on human life. One cannot doubt that there are causes, largely unknown, that would explain why one particular ideal has a hold upon men at a particular time and place, apart from the reasoning that they would use to defend it. And it seems certain that the repugnances and horror surrounding some moral prohibitions are sentiments that have both a biological and a social function.

But the attitude of a reflective man to these repugnances and prohibitions does not for this reason have to be a utilitarian one. One may on reflection respect and reaffirm the prohibitions, and the way of life that they protect, for reasons unconnected with their known or presumed functions — just as one may respect and adopt a code of manners, or a legal system, for reasons that are unconnected with the known functions of such codes and systems, in general; and for reasons unconnected also with the known causes that brought these particular codes and systems into existence.

The reasons that lead a reflective man to prefer one code of manners, and one legal system, to another must be moral reasons;

that is, he must find his reasons in some order of priority of interests and activities in the kind of life that he praises and admires and that he aspires to have, and in the kind of person that he wants to become. Reasons for the most general moral choices, which may sometimes be choices among competing moralities, must be found in philosophical reasoning, if they are found at all: that is, in considerations about the relation of men to the natural, or to the supernatural, order.

V

I will mention one inclining philosophical reason, which has in the past been prominent in moral theories, particularly in those of Aristotle and of Spinoza, and which influences me. One may on reflection find a particular set of prohibitions and injunctions, and a particular way of life protected by them, acceptable and respect-worthy partly because this specifically conceived way of life, with its accompanying prohibitions, has in history appeared natural, and on the whole still feels natural, both to oneself and to others. If there are no countervailing reasons for rejecting this way of life, or for rejecting some distinguishing features of it, its felt and proven naturalness is one reason among others for accepting it.

This reason is likely to influence particularly those who, unlike utilitarians, cannot for other reasons believe that specific states of mind of human beings are the only elements of value in the universe: who, on the contrary, believe that the natural order as a whole is the fitting object of that kind of unconditional interest and respect that is called moral; that the peculiar value to be attached to human life, and the prohibitions against the taking of life, are not dependent on regarding and treating human beings as radically different from other species in some respects that cannot be specified in plain, empirical statements; that the exceptional value attached both to individual lives, and to the survival of the species as a whole, resides in the power of the human mind to begin to understand, and to enjoy, the natural order as a whole, and to reflect upon this understanding and enjoyment; and that, apart from this exceptional power, the uncompensated destruction of any species is always a loss to be avoided.

George Eliot and George Henry Lewes accepted a variant of Spinozistic naturalism close to the doctrine that I have been suggesting. But they still believed in the probability of future moral improvements, once superstitions had gone. Their ethics was still imbued with an optimism that was certainly not shared by Spinoza, and with a sense of an open and unconfined future for the species.

Spinoza's own naturalism was quite free from optimism about the historical future. He does not suggest that advanced, highly educated societies will for the first time be governed largely by the dictates of reason, and that human nature will radically change, and that the conflict between reason and the incapacitating emotions will be largely resolved. Rather he suggests an opposing view of history and of the future: that moral progress, in the proper sense of the increasing dominance of gentleness and of reason, is not to be expected except within very narrow limits. He thought he knew that as psycho-physical organisms people are so constructed that there must always in most men be recurrences of unreason alongside reason, and that in this respect social and historical change would be superficial in their consequences.

This pessimism, or at least lack of optimism, is compatible with a secular doctrine, akin to that of natural law, that represents many of the seemingly natural prohibitions of noncomputational morality as more likely to be endorsed than to be superseded by reflection. A moralist of this persuasion does not foresee a future in which rational computation will by itself replace the various imaginations, unconscious memories and habits, rituals and manners, which have lent substance and content to men's moral ideas, and which have partly formed their various ways of life.

Some of these ways of life, and certainly their complexity and variety, may be respected as an aspect of natural variety; and, like other natural phenomena, they may over the years be studied and explained, at least to some degree explained. From this point of view, that of natural knowledge, the species, if it survives, may perhaps make interesting advances. But this was not the utilitarians' hope; they looked for an historical transformation of human nature through new moral reasoning, and this has not occurred and is now not to be reasonably expected.

POSTSCRIPT

Editors' Note: The following remarks are taken from a reply by Stuart Hampshire to critics of his essay in *The New York Review of Books*, Vol. XX, No. 4 (20 September 1973). © NYRB Inc. 1973.

Stuart Hampshire replies:

(1) On at least one point criticisms received from readers of *The New York Review of Books* have convinced me that I was wrong on a point of historical fact: particularly Professor Goldworth's quotation from the Bentham manuscripts is decisive. For Bentham 'the sensitive creation' is the section of nature to which moral injunctions should exclusively refer. Mere sensitiveness is both necessary and sufficient to give occasion for the distinction between good and evil and to call for moral consideration. So much is true for Bentham: he did not restrict himself to sensitiveness to pain and pleasure as an object of reflection, or as something that is valued in some way by the subject, or that is made explicitly the target of his interests and plans.

Bentham apparently drew the line that divides the morally insignificant from the morally relevant at the precise point where anatomical and behavioural evidence, in the setting of theory, allows us to attribute sensation to a creature. In other moralities at other times, the line of division has been drawn either higher or lower in the natural scale of creatures. Theorists have argued, or they have asserted, that all and only thinking beings are of original moral interest, or they have asserted or assumed that all and only living things are objects of moral concern. Many different reasons, and different kinds of reasons, have been given for making the cut in nature at one level rather than another: reasons from religious cosmology, from pre-Christian or Christian doctrines of the soul, from various religious teachings about the immortality of the soul, or about the destiny of all living things: from reverence for reason or reverence for life.

Bentham's position is distinct and surprising. In several passages he repeats that we cannot consistently be morally concerned about the sufferings of men, unless we are equally concerned about the sufferings of all other sentient beings, and specifically of animals.* We may make allowances for their presumed lesser degree of sensitiveness; but the evil of their suffering, and also the value of their pleasure, are in no way affected by their status as animals and not persons. The questions of how we can know about the degrees of animal suffering, and of how we can compare the experiences of different creatures, did not trouble or detain Bentham. Nor was he detained by the truly philosophical question of the status and origin of his intuitive certainty, as it appears, that the distinction between

---

*Passages from Bentham quoted to me by Professor H.L.A. Hart.

good and evil is identical with the distinction between pleasure and pain.

Limitations of the scope of moral concern should be considered as disputable features of a particular morality, just as the stress on one range of duties or obligations rather than another is a feature of a particular morality; there is no logic, or 'logic of moral discourse', that tells one where the limits of moral concern are to be drawn, and where the cut in nature is to be made. I particularly wish to stress this point, which I believe most philosophers would now accept, because the relation between the natural order as a whole and the human species within it is a crucial part of the approach to morality that I was sketching in 'Morality and pessimism'. Not only that: but I would argue that different moralities, and different moral outlooks, are in part to be discriminated by how they construe this relation between one species and nature as a whole. Bentham's naturalism was absolutely uncompromising: there is no peculiar feature of human beings, among all other natural kinds, that makes them exclusively interesting from the moral point of view.

It was therefore unjust to represent classical utilitarians as anthropocentric. One cannot use animals for their pleasure without consideration of the suffering of animals, discussed recently in *The New York Review* by Peter Singer (5 April). Sentient creatures can only use the unfeeling natural environment for their pleasure without limits.

(2) The other principal criticisms seem to me either misunderstandings, or they call for a full statement of the moral foundations of the moral position that I was advocating: perhaps I may answer both together. The foundations are as stated in a paper of mine, 'Ethics: A Defence of Aristotle', which was republished in a volume of my essays entitled *Freedom of Mind*. Thinking about a moral question entails thinking about what way of life is the best way of life and about what dispositions and character the best men must have. The distinctive powers of human beings, and the complex of their known interests and desires, set a limit to what can be counted as intelligible answers to this question. But within limits there have always been differences of opinion, to be argued for and against, about the relative priorities to be given to different, and sometimes conflicting, human interests and activities. Different orderings of interests and activities, and of the matching dispositions, produce different ways of life.

Plainly it is only a pardonable philosopher's pretence that individuals, in most places and at most times, have a very wide choice of different ways of life, of different orderings of virtues and vices. One is born into, educated in, and formed for a certain way of life, or for a certain range of ways, and the range of later choice is usually narrow, and the opportunities for re-ordering are for most people not great. But both political decisions and the upbringing of children do raise the issues, at least for the more fortunate. Secondly, decisions made in difficult situations, and in situations of conflict, do unavoidably raise questions about the priority of one duty, and of one virtue, and of one valued part of a way of life relative to another.

So much for a way of life; it is a notion that is no more and no less vague than that of the character and dispositions of a man, which are manifested in his way of life, in the socially recognized pattern of his activities. Any way of life has a basic grammar of strict injunctions and prohibitions which regulate basic interests: some basic areas of regulation are the taking of life, the risking of one's life, sexuality, family relationships, justice in distribution of advantages and disadvantages, local loyalties and so on. The strict injunctions and prohibitions vary with the way of life, and the way of life varies as they are varied.

The common core is that some injunctions and prohibitions in these areas are always solemn and strict: these interests are always untrivial, unless practical reasoning is abandoned altogether and everything is possible and nothing is necessary. The strictest injunctions sometimes conflict, and an ordering is necessary, a decision about priorities. I was arguing that calculation, as the utilitarians imagine it, does not invariably resolve such a conflict, unless nothing in the world counts except pleasure and pain, or some clearly identifiable states of mind. But reasoning about human nature, and about the limits of our knowledge of it, and about the compatibility and incompatibility of different virtues and valued activities does have a place, and always has had, in situations of conflict.

(3) Critics ask what is the relevance of 'nature' and 'natural' to moral questions. What does the naturalness of a way of life prove? Did not the Nazis feel their slaughtering and lying and injustice to be natural, while they lasted? Two points have to be made in reply: First, it was not suggested that naturalness was a sufficient condition of a way of life being desirable, but only that it was prominent among the necessary conditions. Second, the intended sense of the notoriously slippery word 'natural' needs to be fixed: the word is to be understood as qualifying patterns of behaviour and activities

which human beings generally tend to prefer and to strive after, unless prevented, and the absence of which generally causes frustration and suffering: and both the striving and the frustration can be explained by causes in the deep-seated physical or psychological structure of human beings. The statement that something is natural to men is a highly theoretical statement, as I used it, implying not only that there are known or presumed causes for an activity being strongly desired, but also causes of an internal, structural kind.

The space of a separate essay would be needed to explain why a way of life will not be in the long run desirable unless it is also to a high degree also natural, and unless it feels natural. The references to Spinoza, on which I relied, perhaps condensed the reasons to the point of unintelligibility. The underpinning of morality by the conception of some reality external to it is usually dismissed when the supernatural is dismissed: or the qualification of the autonomy of morality, which underpinning implies, is considered as a betrayal of the moral point of view. But I doubt that we do justice either to our own institutions, or to the evidence of anthropology and of history, if the incompleteness of morality, and the need of an underpinning, are not acknowledged, together with the sense of a gap, and of arbitrariness, when a system of prohibitions and prescriptions stands alone, unexplained.

'Why particularly this way of life, these conventions and restraints rather than the many others that have been known?' is a question that is ordinarily asked and is thought to have an answer. The answer is expected to specify a reality external to the species which justifies or requires a certain way of life among men because of their crucial relation to this reality. Spinoza was self-consciously and deliberately substituting a conception of this reality as God or Nature for the conception of it as transcendent God; the crucial relation became for him one of understanding and dependence in place of the old relation of obedience and dependence. This was the ground of his prescription of a way of life, characterized as that of the free man who cultivates understanding of the whole of reality and of his place within it.

There was another over-condensed reference in the paragraphs about naturalness and nature in 'Morality and pessimism': to the fact that artificiality and naturalness are equal and contrary aspects of morality as they are of manners; and to the fact that the theory of ethics, from Greek writing onward, has usually alternated between a too exclusive stress on one of them at the expense of the other. It is natural to men to devise artificial restraints upon their impulses, particularly sexual and aggressive impulses, and to invent a great variety of systems of restraint. The diversity of these restraints and of the ways of life of which they are part suggest their artificiality, because the natural is usually associated with the universal. But it is still natural that some conventions of an artificial kind should operate, more or less universally, upon certain kinds of natural impulse. The artificiality is natural in the sense that the specific moral injunctions and prohibitions, parts of a way of life, seem to reflective men one of an open set of possibilities; and it is necessary only that some selection of them should be recognized, and recognized in certain determinate areas of action and of feeling.

Lastly, the Nazis, and the criticism that this outline account of the nature of morality provides no hard proof that evil is evil, and no unanswerable reason why evil should be counted as such. In an article published in 1949 called 'Fallacies in Moral Philosophy' (republished in *Freedom of Mind and Other Essays*), I argued that Aristotle was right in his claim that moral conclusions are not proved conclusions, and that no moral theory brings valid proofs to strengthen our intuitions. A moral theory suggests a way of unifying and explaining our moral intuitions by exhibiting some very unspecific principle, or principles, of which they seem to be specifications; then one can see, in place of an apparently unrelated heap of moral intuitions, an intelligible structure behind them.

The fit between general structure and specific intuitions will probably not be complete and perfect, and each is liable to be amended by reference to the other; a man thinks about his moral beliefs as he lives and applies them. Therefore the degradation of men who were Nazis, their brutality and evilness, the contempt and disgust that they evoke, might in principle be made the matter of argument and debate; there is no logical barrier to admiring and imitating the Nazis, and to adopting their moral attitudes, any more than there is a logical barrier to thinking Mickey Spillane a better writer than Shakespeare. The part of moral theory, as opposed to pretheoretical intuitions, is to explain our judgments of good and evil by revealing the connections between them.

My essay was not a systematic treatise on ethics, like Rawls's 'Theory of Justice'. But judgments of priority in viciousness and in the degradation and perversion of humanity can be as well, and in some respects better, explained within the modified form of Aristotelianism that I was advocating as within any comparable theory. The purpose of bringing historical pessimism into the discussion of moral theory was to suggest that the morality of strict prohibitions, protecting a specific way of life with a specific ideal of character, allows for the expected recurrence of vileness, injustice, and degradation in the natural history of the species. Such a morality does not presuppose some special law of development for men, governing the succession of social forms and of ways of life.

About respect for life, my meaning was that any morality worthy of the name implies a generally overwhelming respect for human life; but most moralities prescribe very precisely the various conditions (as in war) when the taking of life is licensed, and when the general prohibition is overridden: different moralities, different conditions. Utilitarianism does not give a plausible account of this generally overwhelming respect and of this general prohibition.

Secondly, the connection between recognizing understanding as a supreme virtue and also justice, and not 'squandering the lives of many for the cultivation of the few': the classical case for the incompatibility between injustice and understanding has been made on *a priori* grounds by Aristotle, Spinoza, and many other philosophers; but Mr Brumm is apparently saying that the facts are against them, because squandering lives has been justified by appeals to the cultivation of the few. But justifications prove nothing to the point: men may say anything in defence of their actions. He needs to show that a man aiming at the way of life, and the ordering of activities, skills and virtues, and also the social arrangements that a high priority given to intelligence requires might reasonably also permit or encourage the squandering of lives; he needs to show that a man who aims at a certain kind of understanding as the most desirable, though of course not the only desirable, disposition to have might also rationally dismiss prohibitions against squandering lives and might suppress any sentiments about injustice.

3

Understanding a primitive society

H. O. MOUNCE

In recent times Wittgenstein's work in logic has had an influence on other branches of philosophy. I am thinking, in particular, of social philosophy and the philosophy of religion. In these branches, Wittgenstein's followers have made much use of his notion of a language game. It has been argued, for example, that religion forms a language game of its own, having its own standards of reason, and is therefore not subject to criticism from outside. This argument has given rise to controversy, some seeing it as a subtle attempt by the religious to evade criticism. I have come myself to feel that the notion of a language game has been put to uses with which Wittgenstein himself might not have agreed, or, if he had, would have been wrong to do so. In order to explain what I mean I should like to look closely at the opening section of Peter Winch's article 'Understanding a Primitive Society'[1].

Winch is concerned in this section with an account given by Evans-Pritchard of certain magical practices found among the Azande, an account with which Winch partly agrees and partly disagrees. He agrees with Evans-Pritchard in dismissing a view of primitive practices put forward by Lévy-Bruhl. According to Lévy-Bruhl primitive peoples have practices which differ from our own, because, unlike ourselves, they have minds the structure of which is

Reprinted from Philosophy, *Vol. 48, No. 186 (October 1973), pp. 347-62, by permission of the author and the Editor.*

not suited to logical thought. Against this, Evans-Pritchard argues that primitive peoples do not, in one sense, think any differently from ourselves. Where they differ from ourselves is not so much in thinking differently as in appealing to different principles of explanation. If I were asked, say, to explain the occurrence of rainfall I should naturally seek to do so by referring to physical causes. A savage would do so by referring to the influence of certain magical practices. It is not that I have investigated the matter and have discovered that rainfall does indeed depend on natural causes. It is just that within my society this is the form that an explanation of rainfall would take and I therefore naturally turn to it. The explanation of rainfall within a primitive community would take a different form, and any particular savage would therefore appeal to different considerations. What this shows, however, is that the savage differs from ourselves not because his brain has a different structure, but because he lives in a different form of society.

So far Winch and Evans-Pritchard are in agreement. A difference emerges, however, when Evans-Pritchard goes on to make a comment on the different forms of explanation themselves. He is not content merely to say that the savages have their forms of explanation and we have ours. He wishes to maintain that our forms of explanation are superior to those of the savage. This is because our forms of explanation, unlike those of the savage, are 'in accord with the objective facts'. As Evans-Pritchard puts it, this is a matter not of logic but of what is the case. A savage is not being illogical in explaining the occurrence of rainfall by referring, say, to the activity of witches. This is because logic has to do with the validity of inference and not with the truth or falsity of premises. A valid inference is one in which the conclusion would be true were the premises true, the truth of the premises being irrelevant. Now if one holds that there are beings such as witches who are responsible for producing rainfall, one is being perfectly logical in explaining a particular occurrence of rainfall by referring to their activity. The only difficulty with this form of explanation is that it is based on a premise which is not in fact true. There are no such beings as witches. The form of explanation adopted by the savage is to be criticized, therefore, not because it is illogical but because it is not in accord with reality.

In opposition to Evans-Pritchard, Winch puts forward the following argument. When Evans-Pritchard says that scientific, as opposed to magical, explanations are in accord with reality, his assertion has sense only if he can specify a notion of reality which is independent of both the practices to which he refers. But this notion is not an intelligible one. Reality is not something which underlies language and gives it sense, but rather, 'what is real and what is unreal shows itself *in* the sense that language has'. Moreover within a language one will find not one but a great number of ways of distinguishing between the real and the unreal. Consequently there need be no common measure of reality by which both magic and science may be assessed. The notion of what is real that is found in science may be different from the notion of what is real that is found in magic. Evans-Pritchard's procedure seems plausible because his appeal to the concept of reality is only apparently an appeal to something which is independent of the practices he is considering. What he does, in fact, is to use the scientific notion of reality as a standard by which to assess magic. But this would be justified only if he had first shown that magic is a kind of science.

This argument seems to me sound. What it proves, however, is not that the magical practices of the Azande contain a genuine concept of reality but simply that they may do so. We have still to consider the practices themselves, to see whether they do in fact make sense.

Winch himself is quite aware of this. He points out, for example, that he is not committed to accepting the rationality of magical practices as such. There are some magical practices, he says, that he would not accept as rational and he mentions, as an example, the magical practices of our own society. These practices are irrational because they are parasitic on, and perversions of, other practices, such as Christianity and science.

Now certainly a practice which is a perversion of another may be said to be irrational. The difficulty is, however, that Winch seems to allow of no other possibility. What he implies is that a practice which is not a perversion of another cannot be irrational. This is why, in discussing the magical practices of our own society, he makes a point of saying that they, unlike the magical practices of the Azande, are not one of the principal foundations of a whole social life. Where a practice does have a fundamental place in a society, where it is not derived from another, the conclusion to be drawn is that one cannot raise doubts about its sense.

Now given this assumption it will be unnecessary even to consider what the magical practices of the Azande actually involve. Plainly these practices do have a fundamental place in the Azande society; plainly they are not parasitic on any other activity, such as science — the Azande do not even have a science. Doubts about the sense of these practices will therefore be ruled out beforehand.

It will be important, then to consider whether Winch's assumption is, in fact, sound. This will involve our first considering what has clearly had an influence on Winch's argument, namely, the use made by Wittgenstein in the *Investigations* of the notion of a language game. One of the reasons why Wittgenstein introduced this notion was to free us from the idea that logic constitutes what he called 'the *a priori* order of the world', the idea that logic is, as it were, 'prior to all experience'. He wished us to see, rather, that logic — the difference between sense and nonsense — is learnt when, through taking part in a social life, we come to speak a language. Logic is to be found not 'outside' language but only within the various language games themselves. This implies, as Winch says, that the sense of any language game cannot itself be questioned; for one could do so only on the assumption, which Wittgenstein rejects, that logic does lie 'outside' it[2].

It is important, however, to see what follows from this. It does not follow that one cannot question the sense of any *set of practices*. One can see this easily if one realizes that when Wittgenstein speaks of a language game he is not necessarily speaking of a kind of practice at all; he is often speaking, rather, of a set of concepts which run through many kinds of practices without belonging to any one in particular. The assumption that one cannot raise doubts about the sense of a practice which has a fundamental place in a society is based not on the notion of a language game but on a particular interpretation of that notion. The interpetation is that a language game consists of an independent practice or set of practices. This leads to the assumption that where one finds such a practice one also finds a language game and that the sense of this practice cannot be questioned.

In order to see that this interpretation is unsound it will be important to consider how Wittgenstein in the *Investigations* actually uses the notion of a language game. I have noticed that students when they are first reading the *Investigations* often have difficulty in knowing what the notion of a language game is meant to cover. At first they think that a difference between language games is simply a difference between kinds of activities. They soon learn, however, that this is not so. For example, needlework and cookery are perfectly distinct activities but they obviously do not constitute what Wittgenstein meant by different language games. Different activities constitute different language games only when they also involve what one might call important conceptual differences. Thus in order to understand what Wittgenstein meant by different language games the student has to distinguish not so much between different activities or practices as between different uses of concepts.

It is easy to illustrate this point further. Students usually find it easy to see that the statements 'the slip is in the box' and 'the pain is in his hand' belong to different language games. But what enables them to do so is not their having different activities or practices in mind. Indeed it is easy to show that these different statements may occur within one and the same activity. For example, a doctor, as part of his duties, might have to place a slip in a box whenever he is told that a patient has a pain in his hand. Here the two statements would occur within the same activity but they would still belong to different language games.

Moreover it is worth considering, in this connection, the examples of a language game that Wittgenstein himself gives in the *Investigations*. Most of them, one finds, could hardly be described as activities or practices at all, at least if by an activity or practice one means something like conducting scientific experiments or worshipping in church, or carrying out building operations. For example, one instance of a language game that Wittgenstein mentions is giving an order. Now if a person gives an order one may say that he is performing an action but hardly that he is engaged in an activity or practice. One may say, it is true, that an order can be given in the *course* of an activity. The point is, however, that in saying this, one does not have any particular activity in mind. Almost any activity can be the occasion for giving an order. Similar remarks apply to most of Wittgenstein's other examples. Thus he speaks at one point of the games we play with our words for colours, for sensations and for objects. When we speak of our certainty that another person is in pain, for example, we play a different game from when we speak of our certainty that there is a table in the next room. Now, once again, it would be difficult to suppose that what Wittgenstein here means by a language game is anything like a practice such as conducting scientific experiments or worshipping in church. For example, one may speak of people coming together to conduct a scientific experiment but hardly of their coming together to exercise the concept of pain; one may speak of a person giving up religious worship but not of his giving up the use of the notion of an object. What we here mean by a language game is not a practice or set of practices but a set of concepts which may enter into almost any practice we can imagine.

The point is, therefore, that whether something constitutes a language game cannot be determined simply by seeing whether it forms a distinctive practice. One has still to consider the details of the practice itself. It may be said that in order to raise doubts about the sense of a practice one is forced nevertheless to refer to something outside it. If the sense of a practice is distorted there must be something of which it is a distortion. This no doubt is true. But what is distorted need not be another *practice*; it may be certain concepts which enter into innumerable practices without belonging to any one in particular.

In order to make this point clearer let us look more closely at Winch's account of Azande witchcraft. One point that Winch emphasizes is that Azande witchcraft is not a form of science and, in particular, not a form of bad science. Thus when he speaks of the Azande practice of consulting oracles, he argues that what the oracle says is not to be taken as a prediction. In support of this view, he points out that the Azande will continue to consult their oracles whatever occurs in the future. Now this, certainly, is a reason for supposing his account to be correct. If one finds a practice in which the pronouncements made turn out to be false, one may conclude that the practice issues in false predictions. But if one finds later that the people continue with the practice though they know full well that the pronouncements are false, the obvious conclusion to draw is that the pronouncements were not intended as predictions in the first place.

If one looks more closely at the Azande practice, however, one finds that Winch's account is not as plausible as it may at first appear. In particular it is necessary to look closely at the attitude the Azande adopt when they find that a pronouncement has turned out to be false. If Winch's account were correct there would seem no reason why they should adopt any particular attitude towards it. Since the pronouncement was not intended in the first place as a true statement about the future, it would seem a matter of indifference if in the future it turns out not to be true. In fact, however, the Azande are not at all indifferent to such an occurrence but, on the contrary, take elaborate steps to explain it away. They will say, for example, that the *benge*, the special substance used in the ceremony, was bad, or that the operator of the ritual was unclean, or that the oracle was itself influenced by sorcery, and so on.

Now the question that arises in one's mind is, Why are these explanations necessary? Or, rather, What are they explanations of?

The obvious answer is that the Azande put forward these explanations because they are interested in showing why the oracle's pronouncement has turned out not to be true. But this is to imply that they do look on the oracle as a source of predictions.

I can illustrate this point further by referring to another of Winch's examples. One of the Azande may wish to know whether a particular person has placed bad medicine on his roof. 'At an oracular consultation benge is administered to a fowl, while a question is asked in a form permitting a yes or no answer. The fowl's death or survival is specified beforehand as giving the answer yes or no. The answer is then checked by administering benge to another fowl and asking the question the other way around. "Is Ndoruma responsible for placing bad medicines on the roof of my hut?"' If the fowl dies the answer is Yes. '"Did the oracle speak truly when it said that Ndoruma was responsible?"' This time if the fowl does not die the answer is Yes.

Now a question that may arise in one's mind is why a check should be needed in these circumstances. What is it that is being checked? Why are the Azande not content to say that just in so far as the oracle answers 'Yes' on the first occasion, Ndoruma is necessarily responsible for having cast a spell on his neighbour's hut? The only plausible answer to this question is that the Azande wish to know whether Ndoruma did *in fact* perform those actions which they would describe as casting a spell on his neighbour's hut. In other words, what they hope will be revealed is exactly what might have been revealed by adopting other, and, to us, more normal procedures, if these procedures had been available. Thus if one had been available, they might have tried to ascertain Ndoruma's guilt by consulting a witness. There is indeed a striking parallel between the procedures involved in consulting a witness and those involved in consulting an oracle. For example, in order to discover whether Ndoruma cast a spell on his neighbour's hut, one might consult a person who would have been in a position to witness this event if it had really occurred. The person tells one that Ndoruma did in fact cast a spell on his neighbour's hut. This is strong evidence but one might hesitate to think it conclusive. Might not the witness be unreliable? Might he not have some reason for lying? The prudent course would be to adopt a second check, this time in order to ascertain the reliability of the witness. This process of double checking is what characterizes the procedure of consulting the oracle. It makes sense only on the assumption that there is something independent of the oracle which the oracle will enable us to ascertain.

But perhaps the best way to reveal the nature of the Azande practice is to contrast it with practices which are clearly of a different kind. For example, in one of Tolstoy's novels there is a description of a death ceremony carried out by certain Caucasian tribesmen. The tribesmen have been surprised by a group of Russian cavalry. Heavily outnumbered they attempt to escape but are soon cornered. As the Russian cavalry prepares to move in, the tribesmen begin to sing a death lament; they then take leather thongs and bind themselves to one another. This ceremony is plainly not intended either to reveal or to influence the future in any way whatsoever. For example, it is obviously not intended as a charm which would help to extricate them from a difficult situation. The tribesmen know full well they are going to their death; their ceremony is simply their way of expressing that they are prepared for it and will meet it together. If one places this ceremony alongside the practice of consulting an oracle one will see that they belong in quite different categories.

Supposing one accepted, however, that the Azande practices are of the kind I suggest, there would still remain certain difficult questions. For example, how is it possible for anyone to believe in such practices? How is it possible for anyone to believe that a person's guilt can be established by administering poison to a fowl? The mistake, one feels, is just too big to be a mistake at all. No one can believe, one is inclined to say, what is hardly even intelligible. This inclination should, I believe, be resisted. People certainly can believe not only what is mistaken or foolish but even what is hardly intelligible. In case anyone should suppose that I am here thinking solely of primitive people let me illustrate the point by choosing examples from our own society.

Married couples often feel upset at the loss of a wedding ring. This feeling, so far as I can see, is neither rational nor irrational. It is just the way that many people, at least, happen to feel. There can come a point however at which the feeling passes into what is plainly absurd. For example, one can find oneself thinking 'This is a bad sign. If we don't find that ring soon I'm sure something is going to go wrong with our marriage.' I suppose that very many people, living in our own society, have had this feeling, if only momentarily, but it is just as absurd as anything held by the Azande.

Let me give a second example. Suppose a person gives one a sheet of paper and asks one to stick a pin into it. This might strike one as a strange request but one would have little difficulty in complying with it. Suppose he now draws on the paper an excellent likeness of one's mother and asks one to repeat one's action, this time taking special care to aim at one of the eyes. There is hardly anyone, I suppose, who would not find it very difficult to comply with this request. This reaction, again, so far as I can see, is neither rational nor irrational; it is just the way most people would happen to react. Suppose, however, that one does comply with the request and then discovers, a short time later, that one's mother has developed an affliction in the eye and is in danger of going blind. I wonder how many people would resist feeling, if only momentarily, that there was some connection between the two events. But this belief, once again, is just as absurd as anything held by the Azande. If one can believe that one's mother's eyesight may be affected by sticking a pin in a drawing one should have little difficulty with the belief that a person's guilt can be ascertained by administering poison to a fowl.

In any case it seems to me clear that it is to beliefs of the kind contained in these examples that one should turn if one wishes to have a proper understanding of Azande witchcraft. There remain, of course, considerable difficulties in attempting to characterize these beliefs. For example, I mentioned earlier that the 'mistake' involved in the Azande practice seems too big to be properly described as a mistake at all. Similarly, one feels reluctant to say of the belief that one's mother's eyesight has been affected by sticking a pin in a drawing that it is simply mistaken. The reason for this seems to me the following. If one says that these beliefs are mistaken one seems to imply that they might not have been mistaken, that one's mother's eyesight, for example, *might* have been affected by sticking a pin in a drawing, though in fact it was not. But this inadequately expresses one's objection to the belief. What one feels is that there is a certain craziness in this whole way of thinking; what is believed is not a real possibility at all. This is why, if one catches oneself thinking in this way, one tells oneself not that one is mistaken but that one is being absurd. This too, is why Evans-Pritchard seems to me misguided in supposing that the Azande are simply in error when they speak about witches. To say, for example, 'There are no witches' is inadequate because it commits one, at least, to going along with that way of speaking; it commits one to the view that although there are no witches, at least there might have been. But it is precisely the way of speaking to which one wishes to object. Just to speak in this way about witches, one feels, is to be involved in a distortion.

This leads to the question of what precisely is the nature of the distortion contained in a belief of this kind. In order to answer this question let us consider how a belief of the kind we are considering might arise. How can a man feel, if only momentarily, that someone's eyesight has been affected by his sticking a pin in a drawing? One thing at least seems to me quite clear: no one arrives at the belief through having subjected a hypothesis to controlled experiment, i.e. the belief does not arise through an application of anything remotely resembling, even in a distorted form, the methods of Western science. This indeed is clear on other grounds. If beliefs of this kind were parasitic on science, one would not expect with the development of science since the sixteenth century to find them declining. But this is in fact what has occurred. What one finds is that someone in our society will hold such a belief only momentarily, will soon say to himself 'Come now. Don't be stupid.' This is because such a belief will not fit into the network of beliefs about the physical world which has been developed by Western science and which has been taught to us since childhood; or, rather, it does not even qualify as something which could possibly fit into such a network of beliefs.

Given this, however, how do the beliefs still arise at all, even momentarily? One can begin to answer this question by considering certain human reactions which arise quite independently of any kind of rational or irrational consideration. For example, as I have just mentioned, if a man is asked to mutilate a picture of his mother, he will be reluctant to do so; or, alternatively, if he is asked to mutilate the picture of an enemy, he will do so with pleasure. He reacts to mutilating the picture as he might were he asked to inflict an injury on the person pictured. Now it is necessary to state this matter with some precision. I do not mean that he reacts in this way because he believes that he really is inflicting an injury on the person. On the contrary, it is of the greatest importance to see that he holds no belief on the matter whatsoever; this is simply the way he reacts. Indeed it is not the belief which gives rise to the reaction but rather the reaction which gives rise to the belief, or, rather, can do so in certain circumstances. For example, the man has stuck a pin into a drawing of his mother, taking care to aim at one of the eyes, and has reacted rather as he might were he actually to inflict an injury on her. Then his mother suffers an affliction of the eye. In these circumstances the idea that he has actually injured her comes irresistibly to mind.

What we have here is a belief which is crazy, when considered in itself, but which can nevertheless be understood in the sense that one can see how, given certain circumstances, it might arise irresistibly. Moreover it is important to see that if this belief arises, this is not because it is a distortion of some previously existing activity. On the contrary, it is rooted in reactions that are as primitive as almost any and are capable of giving rise to independent activities, particularly in societies which have no developed science. It seems to me, for example, that the practice of destroying effigies which is found in many primitive societies is of a comparable character. It is true, of course, that neither this practice nor indeed any other could have arisen unless certain concepts were already in use. For example, the practice of destroying effigies presupposes that people are already familiar with the notion of an effigy. Moreover in destroying an effigy in order, say, to injure an enemy there is obviously presupposed some idea of causal efficacy, if only the idea that by doing one thing something else may be brought about. But this idea is so primitive as to belong to any activity whatsoever. It depends in no way, for example, on the sophisticated notion of causal law which has been developed by Western science. It belongs no more to Western science than it does to Western cookery or, indeed, Azande cookery.

I should like now to develop these points further by looking more generally at the way in which people have sought to understand primitive societies. During the last 100 years there have been two predominant approaches, the second arising as a reaction to the first. The first approach may be represented by Frazer, whose tendency was to treat primitive practices as if they were rudimentary forms of science or technology. The second approach may be represented by Wittgenstein in his 'Remarks on Frazer', though I might also have chosen Collingwood, or Chesterton, two people, writing at about the same time as Wittgenstein, who adopted a similar approach.

Wittgenstein in his remarks on Frazer had the aim of showing that primitive practices can be understood in ways other than those adopted by Frazer. For example, among primitive peoples there is the practice of destroying an effigy of one's enemy. Frazer would have said that this practice rests on a mistaken scientific belief. The people who take part in the practice mistakenly believe that one may harm one's enemy by destroying his image. Wittgenstein gives a number of examples to show that this need not be the only interpretation. Sometimes in a philosophical discussion when I wish someone to stop talking I enact my wish by pressing my lips together. Do I believe that closing my lips is causally related to getting him to close his? Clearly not. My action does not have a purpose in the sense of bringing something about; it is merely the expression of what I wish. Now why should there not be a similar explanation of the practice we are considering? If one man is angry with another we can see why he would wish to stick pins in his effigy. He does not have to believe that he is causing the other harm. Sometimes if I am very angry I may lash at a tree with my stick. I do not have to believe that I am hurting the tree. Another example of this approach is provided by G. K. Chesterton. Certain anthropologists had explained the Egyptian practice of placing food in a tomb by saying that according to the Ancient Egyptians, the dead were still able to eat. This, said Chesterton, is like saying that we, in our country, place flowers on a grave because we believe that the dead are still able to see and smell.

It seems to me obvious that the latter approach is the more profound of the two, and there are many primitive myths and practices for which, in my view, it is wholly adequate. I think in this connection, for example, of the myth of Orpheus's descent into the underworld. Orpheus was allowed to lead Eurydice from the underworld providing only that he did not once look back. At the very last moment, however, he could not resist turning to see if she was following, thereby losing her for ever. This myth does not merely give expression to certain human feelings but rather, as in a true work of art, portrays these feelings in a memorable form so that we might understand them the better. The feelings portrayed are perhaps the bitterest in human experience. They arise not simply when one has lost what one wants but when one knows that it was because one wanted it that one lost it. Orpheus would not have lost Eurydice if he had not turned but he would not have turned if he had not loved and wanted her.

A myth of this kind can be appreciated only if one forgets that one is a scientist and remembers one is a man. G.K. Chesterton once expressed this point by telling a story which is found among very primitive people, about a giant frog who swallowed all the waters of the world. Confronted by the prospect of a terrible drought, the people searched about for some means of getting the frog to disgorge the waters, and they hit on the idea of making him laugh. This they attempted to do by parading before him the funniest creatures they could find. Creature after creature paraded before this monstrous frog but he remained unmoved until an eel stood up on its tail and did a little dance. The frog laughed and water flowed once more in the land. There is this resemblance, said Chesterton, between our anthropologists and the frog: in both cases there is a difficulty in making them laugh. There is, however, this difference: the frog did laugh eventually, but the anthropologists never laugh at all.

Nevertheless, this approach, it seems to me, though it is adequate for some practices is not adequate for them all. I can best explain what I mean by giving an example. I once saw a film about an Australian Aborigine who had committed a crime and had been cursed by the tribal witch doctor. In the meantime he had been captured by the police and he lay against the prison wall as if paralysed. He refused any food offered him and had, it was said, no desire whatever to go on living. His life was saved when the prison authorities called in a rival witch doctor who, he believed, had the power to remove the curse. This witch doctor performed a complicated ritual which involved sucking and spitting out the so-called bad blood from the man's body and removing a piece of glass from his leg, all of this being done without a mark appearing on the man's skin. It was explained that the witch doctor achieved this by biting his own tongue in order to produce the blood and by concealing the glass in the palm of his hand. But, whatever the explanation, once the ritual had been performed, the man believed himself to be free of the curse and resumed his normal activities.

I do not know the method by which the first witch doctor put the man under a curse. We may imagine, for the present purpose, that he did so by destroying his effigy. Now if one wished to explain magic as an expression of wishes or feelings, one might argue that the witch doctor in destroying the man's effigy was expressing the anger of the community at the man's crime and that the man suffered when the spell was cast on him because of his fear or shame at what the community thought of him. There are, however, difficulties in this argument. The spell was removed by a witch doctor provided by the prison authorities, the community the man had offended being totally ignorant of what occurred. The man himself therefore knew that the attitude of his community had not changed. Nevertheless he believed that the spell had been removed. Consequently he cannot have thought the spell merely an expression of the attitude of his community.

This practice can be properly understood, it seems to me, only by comparing it with the beliefs I mentioned earlier, i.e. with the beliefs that the loss of a ring may affect one's marriage and that the destruction of a drawing may affect a person's eyesight. What all these have in common is that they rest on ideas which are absurd, but which, for all their absurdity, can nevertheless, in certain circumstances, affect us deeply. Perhaps I can illustrate this further by mentioning the two sentences that G.K. Chesterton produced as a kind of test case for those who wish to write on these matters.

(a) Pluck this flower and a princess will die in a castle beyond the sea.

(b) In the hour when the king extinguished the candle his ships were wrecked far away on the coast of the Hebrides.

The test involving these sentences consists simply in whether or not one responds to them. If one does respond one may write on these matters but not otherwise. It is not easy to explain why one should find these sentences fascinating. What one can do quite easily, however, is explain how their fascination might be destroyed. This consists simply in making them reasonable. Suppose I say 'Plucking a flower killed a princess because it was a signal to a band of assassins who immediately rode off to see to her death.' Or suppose I say 'There was, of course, no connection between extinguishing the candle and the destruction of the fleet. It's just that this is what the king happened to be doing when his fleet was destroyed.' These sentences, which formerly had a kind of magic, are now merely commonplace. This is because their fascination depended in some way on their being an expression of what is impossible. It is impossible that the life of a princess should depend directly on our not plucking a flower, or that the existence of a fleet should depend directly on our keeping a candle alight. The point is, however, that if we alter these sentences, even slightly, in order to make them less impossible, their magic or fascination is destroyed.

It is this loss of fascination which many people experience, I believe, when they hear a primitive practice explained by a philosopher. Suppose we are told that in a foreign land someone has fashioned an image of another man and that in this image there lies the power of life and death. If that image is touched, the man feels pain; if it is torn, the man is injured; if it is destroyed, he dies instantly. What a terrible yet strangely fascinating idea! Someone then tells us we are confused. The image cannot harm the man in any way whatsoever. The man in constructing and destroying the image was merely giving vent to his anger. This is reasonable, but are we not slightly let down? It is true that the idea of an anger which finds expression in the destruction of an effigy is also in its way frightening. But this was not the fear of the man who lay as if paralysed against the prison wall. His was the fear of another, impossible, idea.

It will be significant, in this connection, to consider what Wittgenstein said about philosophical, or, rather, metaphysical beliefs, namely, that these beliefs are conjured up by the forms of our language. This remark has been misunderstood. Wittgenstein has been taken to be saying that when metaphysical philosophers put forward views about time or about physical objects, these views are not so much to do with time or with physical objects as with the language in which we talk about these things.

This, however, is to misunderstand what Wittgenstein took to be the relation between a metaphysical belief and the forms of language which give rise to it. Wittgenstein never suggested that the beliefs of the metaphysician are conclusions which he has drawn from an explicit consideration of language. For example, if someone holds that we can never know what is in another's mind, this belief has arisen, in Wittgenstein's view, because of certain resemblances and differences between the ways in which we speak of minds and the ways in which we speak of objects. But if the belief is suggested to the metaphysician by certain forms of language, this is not because he has himself taken these forms of language into account and based his belief on them. On the contrary, he is able to hold his belief just because he never does take these forms of language into account. Had he a better understanding of how his belief has arisen he would no longer hold it, or, rather, he would see that what he had was hardly a belief at all. Seen properly his belief vanishes, not because it is false but because it lacks substance, because it is not even something to which the notions of truth and falsity can apply.

There is here an analogy with what has been said about the belief that a person's eyesight may be affected by sticking a pin in a drawing. I have suggested that in certain circumstances this belief may come to mind because of certain reactions which arise quite independently of rational or irrational considerations. But I do not mean that these reactions stand to the belief in the relation of evidence to conclusion. No one would say 'Because I have these reactions to destroying a drawing *therefore* my mother's eyesight will be affected.' Put in this form the belief is transparently absurd. In other words, the reactions will suggest this belief to one's mind, the belief will be the result of the reactions, only to the extent that one is not reflecting on them. As with a metaphysical belief, in arriving at some understanding of how this belief arises, one is already beginning to free oneself from it.

Now my reason for mentioning metaphysical beliefs is that they seem to me to resemble in important ways not simply the belief I have just mentioned but the whole range of beliefs that we are here considering. Thus I have said of Chesterton's sentences, for example, that if they are altered so as to appear reasonable, they immediately lose their fascination. Much the same might be said of metaphysical beliefs. This is why the man who holds a metaphysical view usually objects vigorously to having it translated into something which, whether true or false, is at least clearly intelligible. Those who hold that we can never know what is in another person's mind will not relish being told that they are really speaking about the ways in which our talk about minds differs from our talk about objects. Or, again, compare the proposition 'Statements about physical objects can be analysed into statements about sense impressions' with the proposition 'Physical objects do not exist'. Both propositions, it is true, may be interesting but they are not interesting in the same way. The special aura that metaphysical beliefs have about them, the sense one has of their revealing something extraordinary, depends on their retaining a certain incoherence. The metaphysician himself, of course, would not put the matter in that way. The reason why he objects when one of his beliefs is translated into a statement about language is simply that the translation seems more commonplace than his own belief. He misses that sense of being confronted by an extraordinary revelation.

My argument, then, is that many of the practices one finds amongst primitive peoples are comparable in certain respects with metaphysical beliefs. Perhaps I should emphasize, however, that the analogy is intended to be a limited one. I am not suggesting that these primitive practices are really kinds of philosophy. What is missing in these practices, and what is essential to philosophy, is the spirit of inquiry. The witchcraft beliefs of the Azande are not put forward as solutions to problems and are not thought to be subject to criticism and discussion. Nevertheless the ideas which enter into a practice of this kind arise in ways which are similar in important respects to the ways in which metaphysical beliefs arise.

I should like to give a final illustration of this point. Among many primitive peoples one finds the belief that there are certain men who can see into other men's minds. In case, once again, there is the idea that a belief of this kind could occur only amongst primitive societies let me give an example of how the belief might arise in our own. Suppose a man is thinking to himself of someone he fears and dislikes, going through in his mind the other's various faults, when suddenly lifting his head he notices that the other man is opposite him and is looking at him intently. Instinctively the man might think to himself, 'He knows what I am thinking. He can see into my mind'.

Now one thing that is interesting about this belief is that the man who holds it has no clear idea of what he believes. If we were to ask him, for example, how precisely the other sees into his mind, what it is precisely that he sees, he would be at a loss for a reply, the reason being that the belief he holds has in fact no clear sense. This, however, raises the question of how, if the belief has no clear sense, it could appear to have one in the given circumstance. There are a number of factors to which one could refer in answering this question, but one essential factor consists in a natural, though confused, analogy between different forms of language. There is a tendency for us to think of thoughts and feelings in language which is appropriate to speaking about objects. What we feel is that our thoughts and feelings are special kinds of objects which are hidden within us. Now what is hidden may be hidden badly; one may think something or someone hidden and be mistaken about it. For example, someone who wishes to avoid another ducks behind a wall. After having proceeded for some time in a crouching fashion so as not to be seen on the other side, he turns, looks more closely at his own side of the wall, and discovers that the person he wishes to avoid has been there all the time watching him. The man who feels that his enemy can see into his mind has feelings of a comparable kind. What has happened is that he has treated his thoughts as objects which are hidden but not as well as he had believed. When he sees his enemy looking it is as if a wall has disappeared and he is exposed to the other's gaze.

Now I mention the analogy or picture which has given rise to this man's belief because it is identical with what gives rise in philosophy to the so-called problem of other minds. Both derive their force from certain apparent similarities between the ways in which we speak of thoughts and feelings and the ways in which we speak of objects. It would be wrong, perhaps, to say that the man who feels that another can see into his mind is holding a metaphysical belief, but what he feels can be properly understood only by seeing how much in certain important respects it resembles such a belief.

One of the features of Frazer's writings to which Collingwood and Wittgenstein particularly objected was the air of superiority which pervades them. Frazer accepted without question that primitive peoples were to be judged by the standards of his own time, as if the practices of these peoples were rudimentary forms of the practices which flourished in England during the nineteenth century. Wittgenstein, on the other hand, argued that a man who was familiar only with the standards of Frazer's time was in fact at a disadvantage in understanding these peoples, that practices which appeared trivial or foolish when judged by the standards of Victorian England may appear deeply impressive when seen for what they really were.

Now it may appear that the approach I have adopted in this paper is itself open to the kind of charge that Wittgenstein brought against Frazer, or, at least, that I, too, am open to the charge of having adopted a position of superiority in discussing certain primitive practices. For example, in saying that the ideas which enter into many primitive practices are comparable in certain respects with metaphysical beliefs, it may seem that I am dismissing these ideas as trivial or foolish. But this would be so only if I also held that metaphysical beliefs are trivial or foolish. In this connection it is necessary to remind ourselves of something further that Wittgenstein said about metaphysical beliefs. He argued that a belief of this kind, though in a sense the product of confusion, had nevertheless to be taken seriously and, in particular, that it must never be identified with a foolish mistake, such as one might find in, say, mathematics. A foolish mistake in mathematics can be explained by referring to some deficiency in the person who makes it — his attention has wandered or he simply lacks the intelligence to deal with this kind of problem. What gives rise to a metaphysical belief, however, is not some deficiency belonging to this man rather than that but certain tendencies which lie in the language and which are likely to mislead anyone, or, rather, are likely to mislead anyone who has attempted to think seriously about certain topics. A similar point can be made about the beliefs we have been considering. What gives rise to these beliefs is not, for example, a deficiency in intellect, but certain tendencies or reactions which in connection with certain deep human emotions such as love of a friend or fear of an enemy are likely to mislead us all. This is why in discussing some of the beliefs which occur in primitive societies I have tried constantly to show how they may also occur in our own. This, too, is why it is wrong to suppose that in discussing these beliefs I have been adopting a position of superiority. A man is not being superior in attributing certain beliefs to a particular set of people if he is anxious to point out that he is attracted to these beliefs himself[3].

Notes

1 *American Philosophical Quarterly*, vol.I (1964), 307-24.
2 The 'cannot', of course, is logical. I do not mean that if one tried one would fail, but that it would be senseless to try.
3 In writing this paper I have been helped by the discussions I have had with my colleagues in the philosophy department of the University College of Swansea. I want, in particular, to thank Mr C. Williamson and Mr M. Weston.

Social reality and social inquiry

PART II

Social reality and social inquiry

Introduction

RODGER BEEHLER

What sort of thing *is* 'human society'? What is going on in what we call 'social life'?

From the time of the Greeks the question 'what is human society' has been answered in different ways. By Hobbes, by Montesquieu, by Hegel, by Marx, by Durkheim, a different answer is given. Hobbes (and Locke after him) saw social relations and shared ways of life as conceivably arising out of the decisions and projects of individuals who in the beginning are outside society. Vico, Rousseau, and Hegel later all denied this view, holding that decisions, deliberations, and projects are inconceivable apart from social life. The view of these three is that the peculiar activities, attachments and achievements of human beings are possible only within social ways of life. The *human* world, *human* reality, is not given; it is created. But its creation could not conceivably proceed from individuals acting alone. For the reality which is this world is logically tied to social interaction, to human agreement and shared ways of living.

Since Hegel's time, and especially as a result of the influence of Bentham, Marx, and others, inquiry into social life has become more and more empirical. The intention, as before, is to describe and explain. But the task is now conceived somewhat differently. This, as we shall see, has not always been a gain.

In social as in any other kind of inquiry we seek understanding. We seek explanations. Now the expression 'to understand what someone is doing' sometimes means only 'to be able to give a correct description of what he or she is doing'. However the understanding we seek as social inquirers is not merely to be able to give the appropriate description of some action or practice. We seek to understand why the act is done or the practice followed; what explains persons' doing it. We signal the difference between these two by the expression 'to understand a person, or a people'. If we understand someone, we understand *why* he acts as he does.

To most social theorists and investigators it has seemed obvious that to understand correctly a particular action or social practice, in the sense in which we are capable of explaining it, is not necessarily to understand it as those whose action or practice it is to understand it. What the members of a society understand themselves to be doing may not be the correct understanding of what they do. It follows then that the explanation, perhaps even the description, which the members of a society will give of an action or custom or institution is not what the social investigator seeks. He seeks for the correct explanation of that action or practice. And he does not expect this always to be identical with the explanation which those whose society he is studying will describe it as having. For just as an individual may misunderstand the motives, intentions, or prejudices behind his own actions and judgments, and may come in time to learn that these are different from what he thought them to be, so the members of a society may misunderstand or mistake — may even deceive themselves about — the character of their social life together. Hence the judgments of the members of a society are not, merely because they are their judgments, entitled to any special hearing when descriptions and explanations are being offered of the institutions and ways of life of their society. The historian, the political scientist, the sociologist, may give an explanation different from theirs of a practice or event or social evil. And his account, not theirs, may be the truth.

However when certain social theorists and investigators assert that the correct explanation of social practices may be expected to differ from the explanations proferred by those whose social practices they are, these theorists and investigators mean something different from what has just been said. They mean that their theoretical explanations, which give a correct understanding of that social life, will be *cast in different terms* from those in which the society's members are accustomed to think of their actions and ways of life.

Human actions, like anything else, call for their own categories of explanation. It will be inappropriate to seek to explain them as if they were something else. The question is, of course, what *are* they? Everything will turn on how this question is answered. If human actions and ways of social life are not, for example, merely physical happenings or processes, but involve consciousness, deliberation, intentions, purposes, and choice, then (provided these are not themselves mere physical events or processes) any attempt even to identify an action or social practice, let alone explain it, must involve appeal to the intentions, reasons, and purposes of the person by whom the action is done. The question 'what action is being performed here?', as much as the question 'what explains its being done?', can be answered only by appeal to what enters (or could enter) into the sense or purport the action has for those whose action or practice it is.

It is true that when some social theorists or investigators have said that their explanations of social life will be different from those whose social life is being studied, they have meant only that the investigator's explanations will make no appeal to anything that could be described as 'values'. But some have gone further than this, and claimed that the correct explanation of social phenomena must not only eschew ideals, attachments, loyalties, allegiances, and condemnations, etc.; it must as well involve no appeal to intentions, reasons, motives, deliberations, or decisions. The conviction common to these two positions, which explains each, is a determination to admit as evidence only what are *observable phenomena*. For only what is observable is, it is claimed, a proper object for the title of 'data' in science, and so in social science. And what is observable in human societies is: behaviour.

'Behaviourism' is the name given this methodological and philosophical position in social science which stems from the influence exerted upon the social studies by the achievement and prestige of the natural sciences. The behaviourist is emphatically the practitioner of social *science*. He seeks quite deliberately to fashion his practice as a social inquirer according to the canons (as he understands them) of the natural sciences. The achievements of the natural sciences, he tells us, proceed from confining scientific attention to what is *knowable*; that is, to what can be observed, measured, and confirmed by other observers. There is no place in science for anything but facts. And facts are perceivable, datable, describable, measurable, confirmable, and so indisputable — especially the last. Furthermore the natural scientist aims at dis- covering what is going on. He does this by attending *to* what is going on; to what *is* the case. Science does not inquire into what *ought* to be the case, or into what people desire or wish were the case. Science, as science, does not bring before its attention human valuations of what is going on in the world.

The social scientist too wishes to know, and not merely to have opinions. He wishes to uncover by investigation the indisputable truth about the social goings-on of human communities. And it has seemed to him that while some things are capable of being indisputably established, others are not. Those things can, he believes, be indisputably established which involve only observation. But disputes are both unavoidable and unresolvable where any sort of evaluation of what is observed is involved. To confine oneself therefore to what can be observed is to confine oneself to fact, which can be confirmed by others as fact, and so to remove one's inquiry from the realm of mere opinion.

The difficulties which attach to such a view are not small in number. One of the most serious concerns the presupposition that everything which is explanatory of human social life can be collected by the probing scrutiny of the observer, where the model of observation at work is that of *vision*. The idea appears to be that everything which the investigator needs to discover will be there and perceivable in the form of colours, shapes, movements, etc. — i.e., as physical happenings. But it is a commonplace that we observe countless things where our observations are not of this sort at all. We observe (to name just a few) acts of generosity, acts of treachery, looks of tender regard, hateful wrongs, sorrow, joy, fear, concentration, impatience, grace, skill, humility, shame, anticipation, courage, eagerness, beauty, pain, defeat, dishonesty, despair, regret, enthusiasm, concern, respect, admiration, cowardice, meanness, greed, ambition, the passage of time, that something is to the left of some other thing, that someone has forgotten, that we are mistaken, that someone is apprehensive, that you are afraid[1]. Are any of these observations which the strict behaviourist is able to allow?

Consider the description of even the most trivial social fact. If I move a certain piece of wood or ivory on a surface which is marked into squares, the correct description of what I did may be that I put your king in check. But this description involves appeal to the rules of chess, and to the concepts 'play', 'move', 'entitled', 'opponent', 'king', 'victory', and so on. It cannot be read off from a consideration only of physical masses, movements or positions. Observing a victory at chess is not a matter simply of being confronted by pieces of ivory or wood. Even if our behaviourist investigator is completely indifferent to chess, or to the question who won this game of chess, for him tc see and understand what did go on here must involve observation on his part of a very sophisticated sort, in which use is made of the very concepts which enter into the actions he is observing. (Even in seeing just the wooden pieces, and not the game, the question arises whether this too does not require something which is an interpretation of what is 'brutely' perceived or 'sensed'.)

Strictly to keep to the behaviourist canon one must, as we have just seen, confine oneself to observing and recording correlations between physical events such as 'bodily movements'. There will be no possibility of introducing into one's descriptions or explanations of social practices the concepts in terms of which we ordinarily understand and appreciate our lives. John Cook, in his paper 'Behaviouralism in political science', considers two criticisms of the behaviourist position in social science, and he shows that while each criticism is right to repudiate behaviourist methodology, one does so for the wrong reason. Cook goes on to show that the correct reason for rejecting the behaviourist position is that it rules out, not only any illuminating comment upon, but even any understanding of, the phenomena the social investigator is purporting to study and explain.

This consequence of behaviourism is especially obvious in the work of B.F. Skinner, which Noam Chomsky considers in his essay 'Psychology and ideology'. According to Skinner, science has revealed that the conception most of us presently have of human beings is untenable, and thus our traditional attitudes and beliefs about human life need to be altered. On Skinner's view, to understand human beings and their actions correctly is to see that questions of freedom, for example, or the integrity of human action, do not arise. Science has carried us beyond these questions, to questions of determination and control. It is the truth and coherence of opinions such as these that Noam Chomsky examines in his paper. He is able to show that these pronouncements issue, not from science, but from its malpractice and misuse.

It is a central tenet of Skinner's social 'science' that the goal of a behaviourist social technology is to 'design a world in which behaviour likely to be punished seldom or never occurs'. This claim, while it may seem at first glance fairly innocuous, and even perhaps acceptable, in fact is neither. For it leaves entirely out of account the consideration that in certain all too possible conditions of social life the triumph of such a technology would be the death of all that is humane and worth living for. There have been, and there exist now, actual human societies in which 'behaviour likely to be punished' is precisely the behaviour that all who are humane and decent (and courageous) would wish to see done, and seek to encourage. The criterion of success of Skinner's technology is that behaviour that is likely to be punished seldom or never occurs. But could the category 'likely to be punished' ever tell us enough about a kind of behaviour to enable us (on that basis alone) to applaud its successful repression?

A second thing to notice about Skinner's proposal is his peculiarly narrow notion of what is to count as punishment. The real issue in social design, Skinner tells us, 'is the effectiveness of techniques of control'. It is not putting it too simply to say that Skinner's aim is to eliminate punishment by achieving total control. The way he proposes we do this is by distinguishing between control through 'reinforcement' and control through punishment. An example Chomsky uses may help to bring this out. Suppose we wish to bring it about that no one ever utters an opinion contrary to the teaching of the governing party. We can do this in two ways. We can reward — i.e. 'reinforce' — those who do not utter such opinions (rewarding even more generously, perhaps, those who utter pro-regime opinions); or, we can punish those who utter anti-regime opinions. Skinner's idea is that it is a better state of affairs where we bring about what we want by the first method of control rather than the second. That this is not obviously a better way to proceed is so plain, surely, as to be incontrovertible. For in the first place, control through reinforcement and deprivation involves an overwhelmingly greater intervention in and regulation of the lives of individuals than the method of punishment requires. (And furthermore *am I not*, in fact, *punished* if I am systematically denied certain things because I act in the 'discouraged' fashion?) In the second place, the method of punishment has the very important advantage that it makes patently visible which individuals are being made to suffer (and for what reason) deliberately inflicted deprivations; which the first method does not.

The drift of Skinner's teaching about social design is powerfully reminiscent of one of the more menacing dictums of Hobbes:

[I]t is annexed to the Soveraignty, to be Judge of what Opinions and Doctrines are averse, and what conducing to Peace; and consequently, on what occasions, how farre, and what, men are to be trusted withall, in speaking to Multitudes of people; and who shall examine the Doctrines of all bookes before they be

published. For the Actions of men proceed from their Opinions;
and in the well governing of Opinions, consisteth the well
governing of mens Actions, in order to their Peace, and
Concord. And though in matter of Doctrine, nothing ought to
be regarded but the Truth; yet this is not repugnant to
regulating of the same by Peace. For Doctrine repugnant to
Peace, can no more be True, than Peace and Concord can be
against the Law of Nature.[2]

The menace in this idea, as well as its (apparent) specious plausibility, proceeds from an equivocation on the word 'Peace'. Peace, as
Hobbes means it, is nothing more than the absence of conflict; or
more specifically the obedience of citizens. It ought then to be
immediately obvious that all manner of doctrines may be true which
are repugnant to peace, so understood. Any true doctrine which
calls for individuals to cease complying with and to begin struggling
against an unjust *status quo* is so. — Of course the word 'Peace' also
has for us a different, *moral* connotation: of brotherhood, the
absence of want, justice to all, social and human grace. ('Peace on
Earth.') Of this state of peace we may well judge that no doctrine
repugnant to it can be true. But this surely gives us one more reason
for repudiating Skinner's views on social design[3].

The singular oddness of Skinner's notion of a better system of
social control comes out especially forcefully in a remark which
Chomsky calls attention to.

A state *which converts all its citizens into spies* ... makes escape
from the punisher practically impossible, and punitive contingencies are then maximally effective. People behave well
although there is no visible supervision. [My emphasis.]

'No *visible* supervision'! This is perhaps the *reductio ad absurdum* of
the behaviourist preoccupation with 'observable data'.

Returning from social control to inquiry: sometimes we may
understand an event, and yet not be able to explain it to another. We
may not be able to articulate the understanding we have. Or we may
be able to, but others do not grasp the explanation. We have
explained, but they do not understand. How is this possible?

This issue is one of many illuminated by Charles Taylor in his
essay 'Interpretation and the sciences of man'. Taylor's is perhaps
the most difficult paper collected in this book. Its difficulty is
connected to the depth of a *fundamental* exploration which Taylor
seeks to take us to.

Imagine a people who inhabit a rain forest, and who live by hunting. This people continually reject the entreaties of a neighbouring and kindred people for help against a third, alien group who periodically maraud and plunder them. A number of things might explain the resistance of the forest people to ally with those whose language and physiognomy mark them out as kindred descendants of a common race. For one thing, they may not appreciate that this is what these facts indicate. They have no knowledge of race or linguistics. Another reason might be that the people of the rain forest look with contempt upon the ways of life of the kindred people, who live on the plains, and who sow seed and husband animals. They would feel themselves disgraced were they to involve themselves in these people's affairs. Another reason might be a cunning stratagem on the part of the forest people to keep their own domain untroubled by leaving the weaker and more vulnerable people of the plains to occupy the restless alien aggressors. A fourth explanation might be that the people of the rain forest look upon the inability of the farmers and herdsmen to defend themselves as like the weakness of the dove or the antelope: something which it is natural that others should prey upon. Perhaps all of these reasons contribute to explain their refusal to treat or ally. One could invent other possible explanations as well.

Let us suppose that what explains the refusal of the forest people to ally is their contempt for the ways of life of the agrarian people, and their untroubled acceptance that whatever is weak or isolated must almost certainly suffer at the hands of what is stronger and wants what the weaker has to give.

Now the forest people *agree* in looking with contempt upon the plains people. They also agree in the way they regard and react to the others' weakness. It is this agreement in judgments and reactions which explains their immovability in the face of the entreaties of the plains people. This common agreement in judgments and reactions is something these people have 'made'. (And make anew in each generation.) What we are confronted with here is a common *meaning* which the predicament and ways of life of the plains people have for the forest people. Their way of life is something contemptible, their predicament natural and unsurprising. This common reaction of the forest people to the plains people is a part of what Charles Taylor calls their 'self-definition'. 'We are they for whom such a way of life is contemptible.' This common reaction is not a collection of isolated reactions, but a shared, mutually fostered and sustained apprehension of the plains people and their situation. The significance which these things meet with in the forest people is, as Taylor terms it, *intersubjective*. It is a social meaning, shaping, with other such meanings, their society together; their 'human world'[4].

To study these, or any, people must therefore involve taking the meaning which things have for them. There can be no 'uninterpretive observing' of what explains what people do. One must rather interpret the significance which natural phenomena or ways of living have for them. For most of human behaviour is *action*: it is *meant* behaviour. And what any human being does may change through time, in relation to his recognition of what he has done, or in response to a failure to find a desired or intended meaning in what he does. Human beings are self-defining and self-interpreting creatures, whose lives are shaped, and change, in relation to this flow of meaning and self-interpretation. Charles Taylor argues that to know what human beings are doing, and what explains their doing it — to understand what is going on in this part of 'reality' — involves reading these meanings. Moreover, because our task is to arrive at the correct reading of such a 'text' (in this case the 'complex' of inter-subjectively shared meanings and meant-behaviour which confronts us), 'what we can appeal to as ground for [our] reading can only be other readings'. There can be no escaping to a point where one can check one's interpretation or reading by means of 'direct observations' which involve no interpretation or reading of what confronts one. For as meanings (judgments, appreciations, attachments, responses, reactions and so on) are involved, any attempt to step out of the circle of 'the meaning-things-have-for-them' is an attempt to step out of the circle of understanding. You cannot escape the task of *comprehending* the lives of these people. You cannot uninterpretively 'look to see' what is going on here. You have to make out the sense of what these human beings do. This is what 'looking to see' is here.

It is this that Taylor refers to as a 'hermeneutical' component in the sciences of man. Hermeneutics is the business of interpreting what a text or statement, what an expressed meaning, says. The hermeneutical task is the task of grasping what the meaning is. It is to be contrasted with exegesis, which is 'exposing' the meaning; stating what it is. To be capable even of the correct 'exposition' of a people's social reality together one has first to apprehend that reality, that *social life*. This is a matter of comprehending a meaning or meanings; not 'perceiving what is there brutely on the surface'.

Notes

1 This catalogue (as I have remarked) is not meant to be exhaustive. My point is only that none of these things is explicable in terms simply of a 'direct, uninterpretive sensory perception'.

2 *Leviathan*, part II, chapter 18.

3 See also pp. 103-4 of John Cook's essay. Perhaps it is worth noting that certain of Herrnstein's assumptions, which Noam Chomsky examines in his essay, are also reminiscent of Hobbes. See p. 138; and compare: '[M]en are continually in competition for Honour and Dignity, ... and consequently amongst men there ariseth on that ground, Envy and Hatred, and finally Warre' (*Leviathan*, part II, chapter 17).

4 Looking at these paragraphs in proof I am aware that here is one place where the effort to be elementary has led to distortion. Strictly: the common meanings I discuss here are termed by Taylor *non*-subjective; the term '*inter-subjective* meanings' he reserves for those meanings which are constitutive of the social practices and institutions of a people — the ways of interacting with and apprehending one another on the part of members of a society which constitute their society's distinctive 'structure' and reality. Taylor gives some very effective examples of these in his paper. A further one might be the transactions that comprise property in Western societies. That these transactions are 'meanings' becomes apparent when one notes that they are internally connected to what we identify as 'harm' and 'interference'. It is undeniable that being poor can harm persons and interfere with the satisfaction of their needs. But if a bank forecloses on a mortgage, with the result that a family is homeless, is this identified by us as someone interfering with or harming someone? The poverty of most persons is the consequence of institutions which *could* be different from what they are. And these institutions are nothing more than ways of acting of other men. Yet when we look about to identify acts of harming and ways in which persons are interfered with in our society, do we count the preponderant wealth of the few, and the relative wealth of the many, and the property transactions that produce these disparities, acts of *harm*, cases of *interference*?

4

Behaviouralism in political science

JOHN COOK

Behaviouralism in political science has come under attack from both conservative and radical members of the profession. One of the common targets of these critics is the behaviouralists' 'value-neutrality', their insistence on distinguishing between facts and values. It is important, however, to recognize that these two types of critics have in mind very different diagnoses of the ills brought on by value-neutrality. The chief complaint of the conservatives is that the fact-value distinction undermines the possibility of political *philosophy* and thereby undermines any ultimate justification of political decisions and institutions[1]. The radical critics, on the other hand, have argued that the fact-value distinction distorts or impairs the very project that the behaviouralists are purportedly engaged in: the empirical study of political phenomena[2]. In the present essay I shall explore these criticisms with the aim of discovering which, if either, of them is sound.

I

It will be useful to begin by considering the conservatives' criticism of value-neutrality, for this will take us through a bit of the history of the issue. These critics appear to identify the problem in terms of the question: 'Can values (or first principles) be discovered or proved either by science or by some other means, e.g., by theological or philosophical reasoning?' These critics, then, think of their affirmative answer to this question as what most sharply distinguishes them from the behaviouralists. Moreover, the question itself is understood in such a way that to give a negative answer to it is to embrace moral nihilism[3]. On the other hand, affirmative answers to the question have taken various forms. Social Darwinism, I suppose, was one kind of affirmative answer; another kind was the philosophical idea of moral intuitions, and still another kind of affirmative answer is the idea that God is the source of 'values' and communicates knowledge of these to men in revelation[4].

We can see something of how this question still exercises certain political scientists by considering the following passages from an article by Russell Kirk in which he is concerned to attack behaviouralism in political science. He writes:

> To what lengths the dedicated behaviourist may carry his notion of a value-free science was borne in upon me during the course of a debate in which I was engaged before the Ethical Culture Society, in New York, late in 1961. The subject was 'Values in a World of Change', and the other speaker was a young behaviourist scholar. When the question was put to him, the behaviourist declared that he could discern no means for determining whether Jesus or Nero was the better person: each man had his own value system, and what one enjoyed, the other did not. Who can judge?[5]

Kirk's own view of the matter is summed up in these words:

> The 'great tradition' of politics — to employ Leo Strauss's phrase — has been normative; that is, the political philosopher has sought what T.S. Eliot calls 'the enduring things', the standards for order and justice and freedom. And these political norms have been rooted in transcendent insights — in religious belief and in transcendent philosophical systems like that of Plato. Even the rationalistic political scientists of the eighteenth and nineteenth centuries endeavoured to establish a solid moral foundation — though divorced from religious authority — for the good society. What, in effect, amounts to moral nihilism has been reserved for twentieth-century political science.[6]

What is at issue here can perhaps be seen a bit more clearly from a passage that Kirk quotes with approval from an article by Francis Graham Wilson:

> The rise of the behavioural sciences could mean the disintegration

of political science ... such a science of politics is destructive because it cannot support the proof of values. In time of crisis it must either desert its [value-neutral] position or it must become silent while lesser figures propound the truth.[7]

The idea seems to be that values stand in need of proof and that the behavioural political scientists, because they disdain such proofs, are thereby committed to a kind of moral nihilism. Just what these values are that stand in need of proof is not quite clear. Kirk speaks, in the second of the above passages, of 'the standards for order and justice and freedom', but this doesn't help much. Is the idea this: that we ought to be able to prove that order, justice, and freedom are good? Or perhaps that the good society is one that will have order, freedom, and justice for all? I suppose that it is some such idea that Kirk has in mind. The trouble is that even this much of an explanation leaves us still in the dark. For it is not at all clear what we are to do with these proofs if and when we manage to produce them. Nor is it clear how we are worse off for having no such proofs. Does Kirk think that in the absence of such proofs we may all wonder whether perhaps we should work towards disorder, injustice and slavery? Or is he perhaps thinking that there are men in the world today — and that there were others in the recent past — whose designs have filled the rest of the world with the fear of slavery and injustice? Is Kirk thinking that we should have proofs ready at hand with which to confront the next Stalin or the next Hitler or their would-be followers?

It does appear that the spectre of the unscrupulous, tyrannical, or maniacal ruler and his servile minions provides the central motive for insisting on a proof of values[8]. But this, if one stops to think about it, is quite a strange idea. I cannot resist the temptation to quote here a passage from Arthur Murphy's review of Brand Blanshard's book *Reason and Goodness*:

> Blanshard objects to the emotivist that on their theory 'one can never give relevant *reasons* for or against an ethical judgement' and [he] gives an example to show how his own view, which he here identifies with that of 'modern man', is in a better situation. In this matter,
>
>> Modern man would claim some advance over ancient Assyria in respect to the treatment of prisoners of war. Suppose that he could catch an ancient Assyrian by the beard and expostulate with him about the practice of torturing prisoners of war

for his own pleasure. Could he offer any relevant *arguments* to
show that the Assyrian practice was wrong? He would have no
doubt that he could. He could say that to act in this way was
to produce gratuitous pain, or at least pain that was far
greater than any pleasure it produced; and that this was
wrong; he could show that it was to indulge one's impulses to
hatred and to satisfaction in others' misery, and that this too
was wrong. If then he was asked why these should be called
wrong, could he continue the argument? He could say that to
produce intense pain was wrong because such pain was evil. If
he was asked to give reasons for these judgements again, he
would probably be nonplussed. He has arrived here at judgements that he would be content to regard as self-evident. But
at any rate he has offered an ethical argument.

And surely it is one of the strangest arguments on record. I know
little about the reasoning processes of the ancient Assyrian, but
recalling that he came down like a wolf on the fold, I should
question this as a prudent approach even to the most ancient of
the breed.[9]

Murphy's point is not merely, of course, that Blanshard's hedonistic
'argument' is ludicrous; even more absurd is the idea of setting out
to dissuade people from torturing prisoners of war by trying to
'prove' to them, by *any* sort of argument, that 'torture is wrong'.
The idea that people act cruelly for lack of 'proof' should strike us as
a thoroughly silly idea. Hence, if it is for some such purpose that
Kirk wants his 'proof' of values, I can only shake my head in despair:
poor man, what has addled his brain?

Now sometimes when it is said that political science must observe
a distinction between facts and values, or that it must regard values
as relative, what is meant is (in part, at least) that political science,
when it tends to its proper business and doesn't dabble in metaphysics, does not come up with 'arguments' like Blanshard's. This
seems to be Arnold Brecht's understanding of the issue in his book
*Political Theory: The Foundations of Twentieth-Century Political
Thought*. Consider his remarks about August Comte:

The need for a scientific distinction between facts and values did
not worry Comte. It never occurred to him that ultimate value
judgements could not be verified by science; on the contrary, he
blamed Condorcet for his exclusion of moral questions from
scientific efforts. His own value judgements were quite explicit,

and they were closely interwoven with his entire work. Abolition of war, for example, was to Comte both, an 'inevitable' result of progress, i.e., the final outcome of the law of progress, and a desirable aim, i.e., a high value, superior or the opposite. Scientific Value Relativism would reject the first proposition as non-scientific, and refrain even from the second whenever it competed with other value judgements...[10]

Brecht's criticism, I suppose, is that, since 'progress' is a word used in contrast with 'regress' or 'degenerate', Comte was mistaken in thinking that it is somehow within the province of science to determine whether mankind is, on the whole, progressing rather than degenerating. (The same criticism would no doubt be made of Herbert Spencer, who explained that 'My ultimate purpose, lying behind all proximate purposes, has been that of finding for the principles of right and wrong, in conduct at large, a scientific basis'[11].) This idea of Comte's is a piece of pseudo-science, according to Brecht's Scientific Value Relativist. Brecht gives us some further examples when he tells us that if the Relativist is an aggressive type, he

enters the political arena in a fighting spirit that pits him against all those who try to sell their own value systems under the false flag of science, whether they be religious organizations who claim their religious dogmas to be scientifically established or verified, or political movements, such as Marxism, based on a pseudo-scientific prediction of the course of history; or old-fashioned monarchism, based on quasi-scientific theories of natural law and divine rights; or National Socialism, based on quasi-scientific doctrines of the superiority of violence and of racial prerogatives. The aggressive relativist is, in principle, militant against adherents of democracy who absolutize democratic values as if the latter could be scientifically established beyond [merely] a comparative examination of risks and consequences.[12]

Elsewhere Brecht gives a further insight into the sort of thing that present-day political scientists avoid. Discussing 'the logical gulf between is and ought', he writes:

Far into the nineteenth century, and in part even into the twentieth, writers on ethical and legal questions derived their doctrines of what ought to be, or what ought to be done, from the factual data on what is. Human beings are, therefore they ought to be; they ought not to be killed. They have a natural impulse to preserve their lives; therefore they ought to have the right of self-defense. They are born equal; therefore they ought to be treated as equal. Society exists, and is useful to the maintenance of life; therefore there ought to be society.[13]

This, no doubt, is a caricature, but perhaps we can see why political scientists would want to avoid, in the future, anything that even remotely resembled the above examples of reasoning. Thus Brecht's Scientific Value Relativist might appear to be nothing more than the champion of clear-headed reasoning and the stubborn foe of pseudo-science.

The trouble is that Brecht, or his Scientific Value Relativist, is not content merely to discard such dubious pieces of reasoning as we were entertained with in the above quotations. Like Kirk, he thinks he understands those propositions that Kirk was anxious to see proved, such as 'Torture is wrong' and 'Justice is good'. We can see this from the following remark:

> According to Scientific Value Relativism, 'ultimate', 'highest', or 'absolute' values or 'standards of values' are 'chosen' by mind or will, or possibly ... 'grasped' by faith, intuition, or instinct; but they are not 'proven' by science....[14]

What Brecht appears to be saying here is that philosophers have held various meta-ethical theories about propositions like 'Torture is wrong', 'Justice is good', 'Men ought not to be murdered', etc.: some have held that such propositions are 'chosen' by will (emotivists and existentialists, I suppose) and others that they are 'grasped' by faith, intuition, or instinct. And Scientific Value Relativists, Brecht seems to be saying, take no part in this dispute, except to deny that such propositions are scientifically verifiable. Now this would be a salutary indifference to philosophical issues, but unfortunately Brecht has in mind something more than what he says here. Because Brecht thinks he *understands* those propositions (I think that's the word) which state (or express) 'ultimate values', he is inevitably led into the following piece of reasoning: 'Since science can't prove that murder is wrong, that justice is good, or that war is bad, a political scientist, if his work is to remain untainted by unscientific elements, must avoid in his work any suggestion that some course of action that leads unnecessarily to war is wrong or any suggestion that its perpetrators are callous or corrupt. Similarly, one can't judge a man to be corrupt on the grounds that he is unjust, unless one holds that injustice is wrong. And since science can't prove that injustice is wrong, no scientist, in his purely scientific work, is entitled to draw the consequences of this proposition.' This seems to be the moral of his discussion of Comte. Brecht's complaint against Comte seems to be not merely that Comte thought that *science* could tell us what constitutes progress; he also deplores Comte's thinking that if we manage to abolish war we will certainly have made some progress. This thought, Brecht clearly implies, has no place in a piece of scientific writing.

My point here is that Brecht, who appears to be opposing people like Strauss and Kirk, really shares with them a certain highly questionable philosophical idea, namely, that behind people's particular judgments (evaluations) of men and events there lie certain unspoken 'value premises', such as 'Murder is wrong', 'Justice is good', and so on. That this is the guiding idea of Kirk's position can be seen from his remark that

...human action and social operation are impelled by belief, even though the believer may be aware only vaguely of his intellectual premises....[15]

From this remark it is evident why Kirk is so violently antagonistic toward the behaviouralists: he thinks that without the proper 'intellectual premises', men's actions will be corrupted. Perhaps we could put the matter thus: Kirk is concerned to dispute Hume's claim that reason is, and must always be, the slave of the passions, and he can see no way to dispute this save by claiming that men's actions are 'impelled' by certain 'intellectual premises'. Thus the behaviouralist, who, unlike earlier philosophers and theologians, disdains the discussion of — and the attempt to prove — these intellectual premises, must be willing to accept Hume's view that men can be nothing but the creatures of their passions, or at least the behaviouralist is willing that men should behave as if they could be nothing but the creatures of their passions. This, then, is really the source of the conservatives' criticism of the behaviouralists. The conservative critic is one who has a certain philosophical conception of human actions, namely, as being 'impelled' by 'intellectual premises'. And my criticism of Brecht's analysis of the problem is that, not only does he fail to recognize this aspect of the problem, but he seems to allow that he at least *understands* those 'premises' which Kirk insists on regarding as intellectual. Brecht, by allowing that these 'premises' may be, so far as *he* knows, either 'chosen by the will' or 'grasped by intuition', must appear to Kirk to have

side-stepped the whole issue. For Kirk the real question is this: are
the principles (or the 'springs') of our actions rational, intellectual
premises, or are they, as Hume thought, merely our passions, which
our reason cunningly subserves? The question for *us* must be
whether these are really the only alternatives: must we side with
either Hume or Kirk? And this comes to much the same question as
whether we must side with either Hume or Kirk in their accounts of
'propositions' like 'Murder is wrong', 'Justice is good', and so on.
Perhaps the right course to follow here is to call a plague on both
these houses.

By returning to Brecht for a moment we can see more clearly
what is at issue here. In a passage quoted above he deplores those
writers on ethical and legal questions who 'derived their doctrines of
what ought to be, or what ought to be done, from the factual data
on what is'. Now Brecht's disapproval of this may strike us as odd
unless we take proper notice of the word 'doctrines'. For surely there
is no difficulty in practice in concluding what ought to be done
'from the factual data on what is'. For example, there is surely no
difficulty in reasoning that if there are children going hungry and
severely malnourished in the Mississippi delta region, then the
government ought to get food to them as quickly as possible. Here is
a perfectly familiar, unproblematic sort of reasoning which no one
would baulk at, were it not for misguided philosophical scruples. So
if we think of examples of this sort, we may well wonder why Brecht
imagines that there is a problem about inferring what ought to be
done from what is. In fact, however, this is not the sort of example
that Brecht has in mind. If he were to consider this example at all,
he would say that his concern is with the 'doctrine' or 'premise'
behind this example. That is, he would say that behind this example
lies some such premise as 'Children ought not to suffer malnutrition'
and that the problem is about this premise, i.e. about using 'the
factual data on what is' to prove that this premise is true. In one
place he states his point as follows:

> ...as long as scholars continued to infer what ought to be done
> from what is and to accept judgements on ultimate values as
> scientific, they necessarily transgressed on institutional and
> metaphysical grounds beyond the boundaries of a science based
> on observation and logical reasoning.[16]

Here we find Brecht saying both that (1) scholars cannot infer what
ought to be from what is, and that (2) scholars ought not to think
that judgments on 'ultimate values' are scientifically verifiable. Now

evidently he thinks that these are two ways of saying the same thing, so we may infer that the 'ought' which cannot be inferred from 'what is' is the 'ought' of an 'ultimate value judgment', such as 'Children ought not to suffer from malnutrition when it can be prevented' or (to use one of his own examples) 'There ought to be society.' Thus it is misleading for Brecht to say that scholars cannot infer what ought to be from what is and to say that there is a 'logical gulf between is and ought'. The 'logical gulf' does not exist in someone's reasoning that there are children starving in Mississippi so we ought to get food to them right away; the 'logical gulf' appears only if we try to reason from what is to the 'ought' of some 'ultimate value judgment'. But this should make us see that the problem lies, not in reasoning from what is to what ought to be (or ought to be done); the problem, rather, lies in those odd sentences called 'ultimate value judgments'. In other words, we can reason cogently from what is to what ought to be so long as 'ought' is playing its familiar role and is not buried in what Kirk calls an 'intellectual premise'.

It would appear, then, that these 'premises' are superfluous: not only can we reason cogently without them, but they appear ludicrous, as we saw earlier, when cast in the role of saving us from Assyrian torturers and other miscreants. Moreover, since these 'premises' are also what Kirk means by 'values', I think we may say that values, thus understood, are a fiction, an invention of the philosophical mind. But if so, then there is no sense in demanding, as Kirk does, that political scientists or philosophers should come up with 'proofs' of values. There is nothing to *be* proved. The point, then, is not that values *cannot* be proved or that they *lack* proofs or that (as emotivists maintain) they merely express emotions (or feelings or preferences), but rather that we are only imagining that there is something here that we should like to see proved.

Where, then, does this leave the conservatives' criticism of behaviouralism? Well, pretty clearly political scientists have done well in not yielding to these criticisms. Political science can only be the better off for refusing to accept Kirk's notion of 'ultimate value judgments' or the 'intellectual premises' of actions. And if the ideal of a value-free social science meant nothing more than the eschewing of these fictitious notions, we could applaud this ideal. Unfortunately, behaviouralists (or some of them) understand their value-neutrality in a rather different way, and this is what has led to criticism from the radical members of the profession. Let us now turn to this second kind of criticism.

II

At the end of the previous section I quoted a passage from Brecht in which we found him saying that (1) scholars cannot infer what ought to be from what is, and also that (2) scholars must reject the idea that ultimate value judgments are scientifically verifiable. Moreover, Brecht appears to think that these are two ways of saying the same thing. The trouble is that (1) appears to exclude, not only the kind of pseudo-science that Brecht rightly opposes, but also our perfectly familiar, non-metaphysical ways of reasoning about what ought (or ought not) to be (or be done). Now the question to ask ourselves is whether behaviouralists (or some of them) have begun, rightly enough, by opposing pseudo-science and 'ultimate value judgments', then expressed their opposition, as Brecht does, in the vague and misleading slogan 'You can't infer what ought to be from what is', and, finally, had the idea, from this slogan, that there is something improper (or at least 'unscientific') in our familiar, non-metaphysical kind of reasoning about what ought to be (or ought to be done). In other words, are behaviouralists proceeding on the mistaken idea that because they must avoid 'ultimate value judg-ments', it is also necessary for the true political scientist to avoid identifying and describing the political phenomena he studies in 'moral' or critical terms, such as 'injustice', 'exploitation', 'inequal-ity', 'oppression', 'demagoguery', 'deception', 'manipulation', 'repression', and so on? The point is, of course, that if the *a priori* exclusion of these terms is the kind of value-neutrality invoked by the behaviouralists, then their studies cannot provide us with an understanding of *political* phenomena, since political phenomena cannot be properly (i.e., without distortion) identified and des-cribed without the use of these 'moral' or critical terms. (In future I shall refer to these as political terms.) Now this is, in fact, the kind of criticism that radical political scientists have levelled at the behaviouralists.

In assessing this criticism, it is necessary to make a distinction between the behaviouralists' theory and their practice, for it may be that although in their theoretical moments they make pronounce-ments which leave them open to this criticism, their practice does not coincide with their theoretical pronouncements and is not open to this criticism. In what follows I make no claim to have thoroughly surveyed their practice, and accordingly I want to avoid any suggestion that all behaviouralists are to be tarred with the same brush. I want to confine my remarks, then, to behaviouralist theory, and in only one case will I try to illustrate how this theory adversely affects practice.

Let us begin, then, by considering a behaviouralist's own theoretical (or methodological) pronouncements on those aspects of behaviouralism that have drawn fire from its radical critics. For this purpose I have chosen a leading figure, David Easton. His essay, 'The Current Meaning of "Behavioralism" in Political Science', provides, if only in a rather sketchy form, those elements of the view that concerns us. The first point to notice is that behaviouralism aims at providing a better *understanding* of man's political actions. This is a repeated theme of Easton's essay. For example, he tells us that:

> In its broadest sweep, adoption of the label 'behavioral sciences' symbolizes the hope that, ultimately, some common labels may be discovered, variables that will stand at the core of a theory useful for the better understanding of human behavior in all fields.[17]

> The behavioral aspects of the new movement in political research involves more than method; it reflects the inception in our discipline of a theoretical search for stable units for understanding human behavior in its political aspects.[18]

Behaviouralism, then, seeks to provide a 'better understanding' of human behaviour in its 'political aspects', and moreover it proposes to do this by discovering relevant variables (or 'stable units'), presumably for the purpose of formulating generalizations about political behaviour.

This is the first point to bear in mind. The second point concerns the behaviouralists' value-neutrality. Easton explains that 'unlike the great traditional theories of past political thought, new theory tends to be analytic, not substantive, general rather than particular, and explanatory rather than ethical'[19]. The source of this last distinction becomes evident when Easton tells us that the behaviouralist is one who holds that 'ethical evaluation and empirical explanation involve two different kinds of propositions'[20]. The idea, apparently, is that 'ethical evaluations' are not empirical, and since a science must concern itself only with what is empirical, it must dispense with ethical evaluation.

Now if we put this together with the two earlier quotations, it becomes evident that Easton is saying that the variables (or 'stable units') that the behaviouralist seeks to identify for achieving a better understanding of political behaviour are to be identified without introducing any ethical evaluations. According to behaviouralism, then, it should be possible for anyone, whatever his moral understanding may be, i.e., whether he be wise or foolish, insightful or obtuse, to identify these variables, provided he makes suitable use of scientific method. To put the matter in another way, identifying these variables does not require, according to the behaviouralist, that the political scientist make distinctions between, for example, just and unjust policies, repressive and non-repressive institutions or practices, and so on. The behaviouralists' claim, then, is to be able to provide explanations and understanding of political behaviour without bringing in, at a fundamental level of inquiry, ethical (i.e. political) evaluations.

It is this claim, then, that has encountered criticism from radical members of the profession. H.R.G. Greaves summarizes the criticism as follows: 'It has been insufficiently understood how far description in this field is dependent for significance upon analysis and explanation into which values enter'[21]. What needs to be shown in defence of this criticism is, then, why relevant or significant description (or the identification of 'variables') is dependent on evaluation. Or to put the matter in another way, the task is to show that if we proceed as the behaviouralists would have us proceed, then we cannot achieve the kind of understanding we rightly seek of political phenomena. Now perhaps the best way to try to show this is to begin with a particular instance of this kind of criticism. For this purpose I turn to Christian Bay's essay, 'The Cheerful Science of Dismal Politics', and his criticism there of the analysis of 'interest articulation' by Almond and Powell in *Comparative Politics*.

Before quoting at length the relevant passage from Bay's essay, I should observe that this criticism is introduced to illustrate the following more general complaint against Almond and Powell: 'I object', says Bay, 'not to a functional approach, but to a functional approach that has no normative reference beyond the range of data it seeks to order and make use of. The range of data is simply called "the political system". The trouble with this theoretical framework is that it has little bearing on politics as distinct from pseudopolitics; for it has little bearing on the problem of man and his needs, as distinct from ... his manipulated propensities as consumer of political output and contributor of inputs'[22]. Another way of putting this is to say that Almond and Powell fail to make a distinction between legitimate and illegitimate, or justified and unjustified, political demands. For instance, they explain their term 'interest articulation' as follows: 'the process by which individuals and groups make demands upon political decision makers we call interest articulation'[23], but they appear to treat all demands alike, as if, for their 'scientific' purposes, it is irrelevant to consider the nature of the demands. It is with this in mind that we must read the following criticism of Almond and Powell:

> Last year I had my students in a graduate seminar read Frantz Fanon's *The Wretched of the Earth* alongside Almond and Powell's book. The work of Almond and Powell is far superior in its conceptual clarity and sophistication; the romantic revolutionary Fanon is more concerned with exhortation than with analysis. Yet the fact that we inhabit a world filled with desperation and explosive indignation is a manifest reality, eloquently described, perhaps exaggerated, but hardly conjured up by Fanon. Where is this reality accounted for, or even acknowledged, in the Almond-Powell scheme of analysis? It appears as 'anomic interest groups': 'Political systems may be marked by a high frequency of such violence and spontaneous group formation (as in France of the Fourth Republic, Italy, and the Arab nations), or notable for its absence.' In less than a page the 'wretched of the earth' are disposed of; the implied norm appears to be that the more the state is able to monopolize violence the better, while the state of wretchedness is at best a secondary issue. Which is perhaps a suitable value premise for those hardy professionals who wish to justify the American warfare in Vietnam; but it hardly contributes a realistic approach toward understanding the political behaviour of such 'anomic interest groups' (what an anaemic phrase!) as, for example, South Vietnam's National Liberation Front.[24]

The nature of Bay's criticism is not entirely clear from this passage, but I take him to be making the following points. First, by indiscriminately lumping together under the heading 'anomic interest groups' all kinds of violent intrusions into the 'political system', these authors blur certain normative distinctions which are essential for understanding the political actions of those whom Fanon calls 'the wretched of the earth'. In particular, this lumping together prevents Almond and Powell from treating differently the justified uprisings of exploited peoples and, for example, the irrational fears that lead the ultra-rightwing Minute Men to establish a para-military organization and carry out attacks on meetings of peace groups in upstate New York[25]. Secondly, it is irrelevant to be told, as Almond and Powell tell us, that some political systems are marked by a high frequency of such violence and that others are 'notable for its absence', for this does not distinguish between those systems in which such violence is absent because the system adequately allows for the fulfilment of human needs and those systems which have managed to crush justified uprisings.

Let us now connect this particular criticism with the more general form of the criticism stated earlier. Easton tells us that the behaviouralists propose to enlarge our understanding of political behaviour and to do this without introducing 'ethical evaluations' into the selection of variables. Now Almond and Powell's term 'anomic interest group' is an instance of this: a variable selected without concern for the difference between the desperate resort to violence by exploited (or otherwise oppressed) peoples and the merely irrational ventures of fanatics. Now the general criticism is that the behaviouralists' value-neutral stance positively interferes with our reaching the understanding we seek of political phenomena. Is this true of Almond and Powell's term 'anomic interest group'? Well, surely it is. For, first of all, there are very different things to be explained in the two kinds of cases mentioned. In the case of irrational fanatics, the explanation will not be that the system failed to accommodate the demands of these people, but will refer, perhaps, to the speeches of demagogues and to other factors that lead to this kind of disorientation. In the case of exploited or otherwise oppressed peoples (think of the Watts riots, for instance), what is needed for understanding these is precisely an account of the system's failure. Hence, to neglect the difference between these cases, as is inevitable with the behaviouralists' kind of value-neutrality, is to describe political behaviour in such a way that we do not know which kind of explanation is called for. Moreover, and this seems to be the point which Bay is emphasizing, if a variety of cases are lumped together under the heading 'anomic' violence, and if these are treated alike as 'penetrations into the political system', there will be a tendency, at least, to treat all these cases as undesirable, as something to be suppressed by the system. This leads Bay to claim that the behaviouralists' purported neutrality is really a bias toward conservatism. Whether or not one accepts this last point, there is at least the following important point to be made. It is surely essential to any claim to understand political phenomena that we be able to make a distinction between information and education, on the one hand, and indoctrination and propaganda, on the other. One place that this distinction is important is in characterizing the way in which political systems may deal with violence or the threat of violence. Attempts at dealing with violence by getting people to give up their demands and to accept the system as it is will amount to indoctrination or propaganda if the demands are justified demands, for if the demands are justified, then the people who threaten the system must be dealt with falsely if they are to be persuaded to abandon their demands and accept the *status quo*. On the other hand, if the demands themselves are misguided, then attempts to make this clear to the complaining citizens will be, not indoctrination, but education or information. Now there is all the difference in the world, politically speaking, between a government that must rely on indoctrination (in either overt or covert forms) in order to stay in power or 'keep the peace' and a government that has no need of indoctrination (or other suppressive techniques). Even if governments differ only in degree in this matter, still this difference is as important as any that could be regarded as *political* in nature. Hence, we could not rightly claim to be working towards a better understanding of *political* behaviour (or institutions or policies or practices) if we are wedded to some notion of value-neutrality which requires us to lump together all demands of 'anomic interest groups' without regard to their merit. A variable of this sort not only does not give us the kind of understanding we seek; it positively obscures a difference that is essential for such understanding.

We have considered this particular criticism by Bay in order to illustrate a more general criticism of the behaviouralists by their radical colleagues, and I think we can now see the point of that more general criticism. If the understanding or the explanations that we seek are to be *politically* relevant, if they are to illuminate *political* actions, institutions, policies, or whatnot, then we cannot be satisfied to describe the phenomena to be explained in an apolitical terminology. Only when actions, policies, and so on are described in politically relevant terms can we ask the right sorts of questions about them and begin to seek the kind of understanding that is relevant here. Hence that version of value-neutrality which would require political scientists to eschew (evaluative) political terms at the outset must lead to a sterile political science.

At this point it may be objected that this criticism *cannot* be a sound one since the actual work of behaviouralists (voting studies and so on) have been of very real and unquestionable significance. Now in answer to this rejoinder, I need only point out a qualification already introduced. I said above that behaviouralists' practice may not (or not always) reflect the defects of their methodological pronouncements. And in fact there is good reason to expect that their practice would be sounder than their theory. For there is no reason to suppose that behaviouralists as a group are any less politically astute than their non-behaviouralist colleagues nor is there any reason to suppose that they have any less interest in genuine political problems and issues. If they disguise this astuteness and this interest behind a 'value-neutral' or behaviouristic terminology, it does not follow that their findings, formulated in this terminology, cannot be translated back into politically relevant terms. It only follows that this terminological manoeuvre was an unnecessary shuffle.

But even in those cases (few or many) in which the foregoing qualification of the general criticism is appropriate, there is another criticism that may be unavoidable. For even in these cases there is something potentially misleading in the use of apolitical terms for the description of political activities and processes. Christian Bay, once again, has called attention to this point. He writes:

> My quarrel is not with research on pseudopolitics *per se*, but with the way findings are reported and interpreted. I object to the tendency in much of the behaviour literature to deal with the pseudopolitical aspects of behaviour almost exclusively, and to imply that the prevalence of pseudopolitics is and always will be the natural or even the desirable state of affairs in a democracy.[26]

Bay's point, then, is that the behaviouralists' way of reporting their findings (and I take this to mean: the language in which their findings are couched) has unfortunate and misleading implications. Leaving aside for the moment the question of what these implications are, let us ask: how can a *way* of reporting something (or the choice of a special terminology) have implications of any sort? Well let us consider for a moment a particular case. How are we to talk about, or theorize about, voting? Should we say that voters go to the polls to 'express their attitudes' and 'register their opinions'? Suppose that this *were* our chosen terminology. What would it imply? Well, notice that people who are very ill-informed can be said to have expressed an attitude or registered an opinion. Notice also that someone who was venting his outrage against college students by voting against a measure that would give nineteen-year-olds the vote could be said to be expressing his attitude. But this use of the vote, surely, is a degenerate use of it, and is to be distinguished from someone's voting for or against a measure after thinking through the issues and reaching a reasoned decision. Accordingly, if we choose to describe voters exclusively in terms of 'expressing attitudes' and 'registering opinions', we have chosen to describe voting in a way that implies that voters have no responsibility to be well-informed and to think about the issues and reach reasoned decisions. Why is this implied? Well, simply because our terminology is intended to be 'value-neutral', to carry no criticism, and yet it describes voters *as if* the most that could be expected of them is what we rightly expect in the case of ill informed and prejudiced voters. Bay's criticism of the behaviouralists, then, could perhaps be stated as follows: the terminology in which they state their findings is intended to be non-critical, value-neutral, and yet the terminology they use, and apply wholesale to political behaviour, is in fact the language appropriate for describing certain degenerate forms of political behaviour, and in this way they tacitly imply that pseudo-politics is the natural (not to be criticized) state of affairs in a democracy.

This, I think, illustrates Bay's criticism. The point is that the use of apolitical terminology does not achieve some kind of desirable objectivity but creates, instead, an undesirable distortion. To see whether in their actual research and writing behaviouralists are really guilty of this kind of distortion, one would have to look carefully at particular cases of behaviouralist research and see whether they turned out to share the relevant features of the example discussed above. I gladly leave this job to the political scientists themselves.

If there is a common theme to the criticisms voiced by the conservative and radical critics of behaviouralism, it is that which Leo Strauss states as follows:

> A man who refuses to distinguish between great statesmen, mediocrities, and insane imposters may be a good biblio-grapher; he cannot say anything relevant about politics and political history. A man who cannot distinguish between a pro-found religious thought and a languishing superstition may be a good statistician; he cannot say anything relevant about the sociology of religion. Generally speaking, it is impossible to understand thought or action or work without evaluating it. If we are unable to evaluate adequately, as we frequently are, we have not yet succeeded in understanding adequately.[27]

This statement seems to me to be exactly right, and my only quarrel with Strauss and his fellow conservatives is that they hold the view that in order to evaluate adequately one must have proofs of 'ultimate value premises'. In so far as the behaviouralists eschew proofs of 'ultimate value premises', I have no quarrel with them, but unfortunately they seem to have concluded that without these proofs and these premises one cannot make sound and objective evaluations, and it is this conclusion of theirs that I regard as profoundly mistaken.

Notes

1 See, for example, Leo Strauss, *What is Political Philosophy?* (New York, 1959), pp. 10-19.
2 There is, for example, the charge reiterated in several articles by Christian Bay that the behaviouralists fail to make the crucial distinction between political and pseudo-political decisions or actions.
3 Leo Strauss insists that 'the contemporary rejection of natural right leads to nihilism — nay, it is identical with nihilism.' *Natural Right and History* (Chicago, 1953), pp. 4-5.
4 Emil Brunner, for example, holds that 'if there is no sacred, eternal, divine, absolute law, there is no possibility of denouncing any form of law or policy or national act as unjust.' *Justice and the Social Order*, trans. Mary Hottinger (New York, 1945), p. 8.
5 'Segments of Political Science not Amenable to Behavioristic Treatment' in James C. Charlesworth (ed.), *The Limits of Behavioralism in Political Science* (Philadelphia, 1962), p. 55.
6 Ibid., p. 54.
7 From 'The Behaviorist's Persuasion', *Modern Age*, vol. 3 (Summer 1959), p. 316. Quoted by Kirk in Charlesworth, op. cit., p. 52.
8 This is sometimes made quite explicit, as for example in F.S.C. Northrop, *The Logic of the Sciences and the Humanities* (New York, 1949), p. 282, and in Brunner, op. cit., p. 7.
9 'Blanshard on Goodness in General', *The Philosophical Review*, vol. LXXII (1963), pp. 327-8.
10 Arnold Brecht, *Political Theory* (Princeton, 1959), p. 172.
11 *Data of Ethics* (New York, 1901), p. vii.
12 Ibid., pp. 134-5.
13 Ibid., p. 126.
14 Ibid., p. 118.
15 Op. cit., p. 53. Strauss seems to be voicing much the same idea when he says that 'To judge soundly one must know the true standards. If political philosophy wishes to do justice to its subject matter, it must strive

for genuine knowledge of these standards' (*What is Political Philosophy?*, p. 12).

16 Op. cit., p. 166.

17 'The Current Meaning of "Behavioralism" in Political Science' in Charlesworth, op. cit., p. 18.

18 Ibid., p. 19.

19 Ibid., p. 25.

20 Ibid., p. 8.

21 'Political Theory Today' in Charles A. McCoy and John Playford (eds.), *Apolitical Politics: A Critique of Behavioralism* (New York, 1967), p. 235.

22 Christian Bay, 'The Cheerful Science of Dismal Politics', in Theodore Roszak (ed.), *The Dissenting Academy* (New York, 1968), p. 216.

23 Gabriel A. Almond and G. Bingham Powell, Jr, *Comparative Politics: A Developmental Approach* (Boston, 1966), p. 73.

24 Christian Bay, op. cit., pp. 218-19.

25 Almond and Powell explain that 'anomic interest groups [are] the more or less spontaneous penetrations into the political system from the society, such as riots, demonstrations, assassinations, and the like ... [P]articularly in the cases where explicitly organized groups are not present, or where they have failed to obtain adequate representation of their interests in the political system, latent discontent ... may suddenly impinge upon the political system in unpredictable and uncontrollable ways.' Op. cit., pp. 75-6.

26 'Politics and Pseudopolitics: A Critical Evaluation of Some Behavioral Literature' in McCoy and Playford, op. cit., p. 16.

27 *What is Political Philosophy?*, p. 21.

5

Psychology and ideology

NOAM CHOMSKY

I

A century ago, a voice of British liberalism described the 'China-man' as 'an inferior race of malleable orientals'[1]. During the same years, anthropology became professionalized as a discipline, 'inti-mately associated with the rise of raciology'[2]. Presented with the claims of nineteenth-century racist anthropology, a rational person will ask two sorts of questions: What is the scientific status of the claims? and, What social or ideological needs do they serve? The questions are logically independent, but those of the second sort naturally come to the fore as scientific pretensions are undermined. In the case of nineteenth-century racist anthropology, the question of its scientific status is no longer seriously at issue, and it is not difficult to perceive its social function. If the Chinaman is malleable by nature, then what objection can there be to controls exercised by a superior race?

Consider now a generalization of the pseudoscience of the twentieth century: it is not merely the heathen Chinese who are malleable by nature, but rather all people. Science has revealed that it is an illusion to speak of 'freedom' and 'dignity'. What a person does is fully determined by his genetic endowment and history of reinforcement. Therefore we should make use of the best behavioural technology to shape and control behaviour in the common interest.

Again, we may inquire into the exact meaning and scientific status of the claim, and the social functions it serves. Again, if the scientific status of whatever is clear is slight, then it is particularly interesting to consider the climate of opinion within which the claim is taken seriously.

II

In his speculations on human behaviour, which are to be clearly distinguished from his experimental investigation of operant conditioning, B.F. Skinner offers a particular version of the theory of human malleability. The public reception is a matter of some interest. Skinner has been condemned as a trail blazer of totalitarian thinking and lauded for his advocacy of a tightly managed social environment. He is accused of immorality and praised as a spokesman for science and rationality in human affairs. He appears to be attacking fundamental human values, demanding control in place of the defence of freedom and dignity. There seems something scandalous in this, and since Skinner invokes the authority of science, some critics condemn science itself, or 'the scientific view of man', for supporting such conclusions, while others assure us that science will 'win out' over mysticism and irrational belief.

A close analysis shows that the appearance is misleading. Skinner is saying nothing about freedom and dignity, though he uses the words 'freedom' and 'dignity' in some odd and idiosyncratic sense. His speculations are devoid of scientific content and do not even hint at general outlines of a possible science of human behaviour. Furthermore, Skinner imposes certain arbitrary limitations on scientific research which virtually guarantee continued failure.

As to its social implications, Skinner's science of human behaviour, being quite vacuous, is as congenial to the libertarian as to the fascist. If certain of his remarks suggest one or another interpretation, it must be stressed that these do not follow from his 'science' any more than their negations do. I think it would be more accurate to regard Skinner's *Beyond Freedom and Dignity* as a kind of Rorschach test. The fact that it is widely regarded as pointing the way to 1984 is, perhaps, a suggestive indication of certain tendencies in modern industrial society. There is little doubt that a theory of human malleability might be put to the service of totalitarian doctrine. If, indeed, freedom and dignity are merely the relics of outdated mystical beliefs, then what objection can there be to narrow and effective controls instituted to ensure 'the survival of a culture'?

Given the prestige of science and the tendencies towards centralized authoritarian control that can easily be detected in modern industrial society, it is important to investigate seriously the claim that the science of behaviour and a related technology provide the rationale and the means for control of behaviour. What in fact has been demonstrated, or even plausibly suggested, in this regard?

Skinner assures us repeatedly that his science of behaviour is advancing mightily and that there exists an effective technology of control. It is, he claims, a 'fact that all control is exerted by the environment'[3]. Consequently, 'When we seem to turn control over to a person himself, we simply shift from one mode of control to another' (p. 97). The only serious task, then, is to design less 'aversive' and more effective controls, an engineering problem. 'The outlines of a technology are already clear' (p.149). 'We have the physical, biological, and behavioural technologies needed "to save ourselves"; the problem is how to get people to use them' (p. 158).

It is a fact, Skinner maintains, that 'behaviour is shaped and maintained by its consequences' and that as the consequences contingent on behaviour are investigated, more and more 'they are taking over the explanatory functions previously assigned to personalities, states of mind, feelings, traits of character, purposes, and intentions' (p. 18).

> As a *science of behaviour* adopts the strategy of physics and biology, the autonomous agent to which behaviour has traditionally been attributed is replaced by the environment — the environment in which the species evolved and in which the behaviour of the individual is shaped and maintained. (p.184)

A 'behavioural analysis' is thus replacing the 'traditional appeal to states of mind, feelings, and other aspects of the autonomous man', and 'is in fact much further advanced than its critics usually realize' (p. 160). Human behaviour is a function of 'conditions, environmental or genetic', and people should not object 'when a scientific analysis traces their behaviour to external conditions' (p. 75), or when a behavioural technology improves the system of control.

Not only has all of this been demonstrated; furthermore, it *must be* that as the science of behaviour progresses, it will more fully establish these facts. 'It is in the nature of scientific progress that the functions of autonomous man be taken over one by one as the role of the environment is better understood' (p. 58). This is the 'scientific view', and 'it is in the nature of scientific inquiry' that the evidence should shift in its favour (p. 101). 'It is in the nature of an experimental analysis of human behaviour that it should strip away the functions previously assigned to autonomous man and transfer them one by one to the controlling environment' (p. 198). Furthermore, physiology someday 'will explain why behaviour is indeed related to the antecedent events of which it can be shown to be a function' (p. 195).

These claims fall into two categories. In the first are claims about what has been discovered; in the second, assertions about what science must discover in its inexorable progress. It is likely that the hope or fear or resignation induced by Skinner's proclamations results, in part, from such assertions about the inevitability of scientific progress towards the demonstration that all control is exerted by the environment, that the ability of 'autonomous man' to choose is an illusion.

Claims of the first sort must be evaluated in terms of the evidence presented for them. In the present instance, this is a simple task. No evidence is presented. In fact, as will become clear when we turn to more specific examples, the question of evidence is beside the point, since the claims dissolve into triviality or incoherence under analysis. Claims with regard to the inevitability of future discoveries are more ambiguous. Is Skinner saying that as a matter of necessity, science will show that behaviour is completely determined by the environment? If so, his claim can be dismissed as pure dogmatism, foreign to the 'nature of scientific inquiry'. It is quite conceivable that as scientific understanding advances, it will reveal that even with full details about genetic endowment and personal history, a Laplacean omniscience could predict very little about what an organism will do. It is even possible that science may someday provide principled reasons for this conclusion (if indeed it is true). But perhaps Skinner is suggesting merely that the term 'scientific understanding' be restricted to the prediction of behaviour from environmental conditions. If so, then science may reveal, as it progresses, that 'scientific understanding of human behaviour', in this sense, is inherently limited. At the moment, we have virtually no scientific evidence and not the germs of an interesting hypothesis as to how human behaviour is determined. Consequently, we can only express our hopes and guesses as to what some future science may demonstrate. In any event, the claims that Skinner puts forth in this category are either dogmatic or uninteresting, depending on which interpretation we give to them.

The dogmatic element in Skinner's thinking is further revealed when he states that 'the task of a scientific analysis is to explain how the behaviour of a person as a physical system is related to the conditions under which the human species evolved and the conditions under which the individual lives' (p. 14). Surely the task of a scientific analysis is to discover the facts and explain them. Suppose that in fact the human brain operates by physical principles (perhaps now unknown) that provide for free choice, appropriate to situations but only marginally affected by environmental contingencies. The task of scientific analysis is not — as Skinner believes — to demonstrate that the conditions to which he restricts his attention fully determine human behaviour, but rather to discover whether in fact they do (or whether they are at all significant), a very different matter. If they do not, as seems quite plausible, the 'task of a scientific analysis' will be to clarify the issues and discover an intelligible explanatory theory that will deal with the actual facts. Surely no scientist would follow Skinner in insisting on the *a priori* necessity that scientific investigation will lead to a particular conclusion, specified in advance.

In support of his belief that science will demonstrate that behaviour is entirely a function of antecedent events, Skinner notes that physics advanced only when it 'stopped personifying things' and attributing to them 'wills, impulses, feelings, purposes', and so on (p. 8). Therefore, he concludes, the science of behaviour will progress only when it stops personifying people and avoids reference to 'internal states'. No doubt physics advanced by rejecting the view that a rock's wish to fall is a factor in its 'behaviour', because in fact a rock has no such wish. For Skinner's argument to have any force, he must show that people have wills, impulses, feelings, purposes, and the like no more than rocks do. If people differ from rocks in this respect, then a science of human behaviour will have to take account of this fact.

Similarly, Skinner is correct in asserting that 'modern physics or most of biology' does not discuss such matters as 'a crisis of belief' or 'loss of confidence' (p. 10). Evidently, from this correct observation nothing follows with regard to the science of human behaviour. Physics and biology, Skinner observes, 'did not advance by looking more closely at the jubilance of a falling body, or ... the nature of vital spirits, and we do not need to try to discover what personalities, states of mind, feelings, traits of character, plans, purposes, intentions, or the other perquisites of autonomous man really are in order to get on with a scientific analysis of behaviour'; and we must neglect 'supposed mediating states of mind' (p. 15). This is true enough, if indeed there are no mediating states that can be characterized by an abstract theory of mind, and if personalities, etc., are not more real than the jubilance of a falling body. But if the factual assumptions are false, then we certainly do need to try to discover what the 'perquisites of autonomous man' really are and to determine the 'mediating states of mind' — at least this is so if we wish to develop a science of human behaviour with any intellectual content and explanatory force. Skinner might argue, more rationally, that his 'science' does not overlook these 'perquisites' and inner states but rather accounts in other ways for the phenomena discussed in these terms. We shall see directly what substance there is to such a claim.

It is hardly possible to argue that science has advanced only by repudiating hypotheses concerning 'internal states'. By rejecting the study of postulated inner states, Skinner reveals his hostility not only to 'the nature of scientific inquiry' but even to common engineering practice. For example, Skinner believes that 'information theory' ran into a 'problem when an inner "processor" had to be invented to convert input into output' (p. 18). This is a strange way of describing the matter; 'information theory' ran into no such 'problem'. Rather, the consideration of 'inner processors' in the mathematical theory of communication or its applications to psychology followed normal scientific and engineering practice. Suppose that an investigator is presented with a device whose functioning he does not understand, and suppose that through experiment he can obtain information about input-output relations for this device. He would not hesitate, if rational, to construct a theory of the internal states of the device and to test it against further evidence. He might also go on to try to determine the mechanisms that function in the ways described by his theory of internal states, and the physical principles at work — leaving open the possibility that new and unknown physical principles might be involved, a particularly important matter in the study of behaviour of organisms. His theory of internal states might well be the only useful guide to further research. By objecting, *a priori*, to this commonplace research strategy, Skinner merely condemns his strange variety of 'behavioural science' to continued ineptitude.

Skinner's antagonism to science is also revealed by his treatment of matters of fact. Psychologists concerned with the facts have argued that the child's acquisition of language and various concepts is in part a function of developmental age, that through maturational processes a child's language grows 'like an embryo', and that isolation interferes with certain growth processes. Skinner rejects these hypotheses (pp. 139, 141, 221), and asserts rather that verbal and other environmental contingencies explain all of the observed phenomena. Neither here nor elsewhere does he provide any evidence or rational argument to this effect; nor does he show some other fault in the perfectly intelligible, though possibly incorrect, theories that he summarily rejects. (He does, however, give irrelevant objections that for some reason seem to him to be applicable — see pages cited above.) His dogmatism in this regard is particularly curious, since he would surely not deny that genetically determined maturational processes are involved in other aspects of development. But in this area he insists that the explanation must lie elsewhere. Though his conclusion might, by sheer accident, be correct, still it would be difficult to imagine an attitude more basically opposed to 'the nature of scientific inquiry'.

We cannot specify, *a priori*, what postulates and hypotheses are legitimate. Skinner's apriorism in this regard is no more legitimate than the claim that classical physics is not 'science' because it appeals to the 'occult force of gravity'. If a concept or principle finds its place in an explanatory theory, it cannot be excluded on methodological grounds, as Skinner's discussion suggests. In general, Skinner's conception of science is very odd. Not only do his *a priori* methodological assumptions rule out all but the most trivial scientific theories; he is, furthermore, given to strange pronouncements such as the assertion that 'the laws of science are descriptions of contingencies of reinforcement' (p. 189) — which I happily leave to others to decode.

It is important to bear in mind that Skinner's strictures do not define the practice of behavioural science. In fact, those who call themselves 'behavioural scientists' or even 'behaviourists' vary widely in the kinds of theoretical constructions that they are willing to admit. W.V.O. Quine, who on other occasions has attempted to work within the Skinnerian framework, goes so far as to define 'behaviourism' simply as the insistence that conjectures and conclusions must eventually be verified in terms of observations[4]. As he points out, any reasonable person is a 'behaviourist' in this sense. Quine's proposal signifies the demise of behaviourism as a substantive point of view, which is just as well. Whatever function 'behaviourism' may have served in the past, it has become nothing more than a set of arbitrary restrictions on 'legitimate' theory construction, and there is no reason why someone who investigates man and society should accept the kind of intellectual shackles that physical scientists would surely not tolerate and that condemn any intellectual pursuit to insignificance.

Notice that what is at issue here is not 'philosophical behaviourism', a set of ideas about legitimate claims to knowledge, but rather behaviourism as a set of conditions imposed on legitimate theory construction in the study of mental abilities and achievements and human social organization. Thus a person might accept Quine's version of 'behaviourism' for scientific theory construction, thus in effect abandoning the doctrine, while still maintaining that the scientific theories constructed in accordance with the condition that hypotheses must eventually be verified in terms of observations do not truly constitute 'knowledge'. If consistent, such a person will also reject the natural sciences as not constituting 'true knowledge'. It is, of course, possible to impose conditions of arbitrary severity on the concept 'knowledge'. Whatever the interest of this enterprise may be, it is not what I am discussing here. Nor am I discussing the question whether the system of unconscious rules and principles that the mind constructs, or the innate schematism that provides the basis for such constructions, should properly be called 'knowledge', or perhaps be given some other name. In my opinion, no investigation of the concept of 'knowledge' in ordinary usage will provide an answer to these questions, since it is too vague and unclear at precisely the critical points. This, however, is not the question at issue in the present discussion, and I will pursue it no further here.

Let us consider more carefully what Skinner means when he asserts that all behaviour is externally controlled and that behaviour is a function of genetic and environmental conditions. Does he mean that full knowledge of such conditions would permit, in principle, specific predictions as to what a person will do? Surely not. Skinner means that genetic and environmental conditions determine 'probability of response'. But he is so vague about this notion that it is unclear whether his claims about determinism amount to anything at all. No one would doubt that the likelihood of my going to the beach depends on the temperature, or that the likelihood of my producing a sentence of English rather than Chinese is 'determined' by my past experience, or that the likelihood of my producing a sentence of a human language rather than of some imaginable but humanly inaccessible system is 'determined' by my genetic constitution. We hardly need behavioural science to tell us this. When we look for more specific predictions, however, we find virtually nothing. Worse, we discover that Skinner's *a priori* limitations on 'scientific' inquiry make it impossible for him even to formulate the relevant concepts, let alone investigate them.

Consider, for example, the notion 'likelihood of producing a sentence of English rather than Chinese'. Given a characterization of 'English' and 'Chinese' by an abstract theory of postulated internal states (mental states, if you like), it is possible to give some meaning to this notion — though the probabilities, being negligible under any known characterization of determining factors, will be of no interest for the prediction of behaviour[5]. But for Skinner, even this marginal achievement is impossible. For Skinner, what we call 'knowledge of French' is a 'repertoire acquired as a person learns to speak French' (p. 197). Therefore probabilities will be defined over such 'repertoires'. But what does it mean to say that some utterance of English that I have never heard or produced belongs to my 'repertoire', but not any utterance of Chinese (so that the former has a higher 'probability')? Skinnerians, at this point in the discussion, appeal to 'similarity' or 'generalization', always without characterizing the ways in which a new expression is 'similar' to familiar examples or 'generalized' from them. The reason for this failure is simple. So far as is known, the relevant properties can be expressed only in terms of abstract theories which can be taken as descriptions of postulated internal states of the organism, and such theories are excluded, *a priori*, from Skinner's 'science'. The immediate consequence is that the Skinnerian must lapse into mysticism (unexplained 'similarities' and 'generalization' of a sort that cannot be specified) as soon as the discussion touches the world of fact. While the situation is perhaps clearer in the case of language, there is no reason to suppose that other aspects of human behaviour will fall within the grasp of the 'science' constrained by *a priori* Skinnerian restrictions.

It is interesting, incidentally, to see how Skinner's defenders respond to this inability to deal with concrete factual questions. Aubrey Yates, for example, refers to a criticism by Breger and McGaugh[6], who argue that the Skinnerian approach to language learning and usage cannot handle facts that can be explained by postulating an abstract theory (a grammar) that is learned and used. Yates presents the following rebuttal, which he regards as 'devastating': 'the assertion that children learn and utilize a grammar is not ... a "fact" which Skinner has to explain, if his theory is to remain viable, but an *inference* or theoretical construct.' 'No one has ever observed a "grammar"' and the child would be unable to specify it; 'it is quite improper to set up a theoretical construct to account for complex verbal behaviour and then demand that Skinner explain this theoretical construct by means of his own theory'[7].

But Breger and McGaugh do not insist that Skinner explain the theoretical construct 'grammar' by means of his own theory (whatever this would mean); rather, they argue that by employing the theoretical construct 'grammar' it is possible to account for important facts that escape the limits of Skinner's system. A proper answer would be that the proposed explanation fails, or that Skinner can explain these facts in some other way, or that the facts are not important for his particular purposes. But Yates's 'devastating rebuttal', like Skinner's own refusal to face the problem, is merely an evasion. By similar logic a mystic could argue that his account of planetary motion is not to be rejected on grounds of its inability to deal with the phenomena explained by Newtonian physics, which is, after all, merely a theory designed to account for the facts. As to the remark that the grammar cannot be 'observed' or specified by the child, of course no theoretical construct is 'observed', and the insistence that abstract characterizations of internal mental states be accessible to introspection, by the child or anyone else, is again (despite its distinguished ancestry) mere dogmatism, to be dismissed in serious inquiry. The explanatory theory that Breger and McGaugh discuss may be quite wrong, but it is irrelevant to remark that it cannot be observed or described by the person whose behaviour is allegedly explained by use of this theory. Unfortunately, this kind of manoeuvre is all too typical.

Skinner's own response to criticism is no less illuminating. He believes that people attack him and argue against his 'scientific picture of man' because 'the scientific formulation has destroyed accustomed reinforcers' and causes 'behaviour previously reinforced by credit or admiration [to] undergo extinction', since 'a person can no longer take credit or be admired for what he does'. And extinction, he asserts, 'often leads to aggressive attack' (p. 212). Elsewhere, he accuses his critics of 'emotional instability', citing comments of Arthur Koestler and Peter Gay to the effect that behaviourism is 'a monumental triviality' marked by 'innate naïvete' and 'intellectual bankruptcy' (p. 165). Skinner does not attempt to meet this criticism by presenting some relevant results that are not a monumental triviality. He is quite unable to perceive that objection to his 'scientific picture of man' derives, not from extinction of certain behaviour or opposition to science, but from an ability to distinguish science from triviality and obvious error. Skinner does not comprehend the basic criticism: when his formulations are interpreted literally, they are trivially true, unsupported by evidence, or clearly false; and when these assertions are interpreted in his characteristically vague and metaphorical way, they are merely a poor substitute for ordinary usage. Such criticisms cannot be overcome by verbal magic, by mere reiteration that his approach is scientific and that those who do not see this are opposed to science or deranged.

Similarly, Skinner claims that Koestler's characterization of behaviourism is seventy years out of date, but does not indicate what great achievements of the past seventy years Koestler has neglected. In fact, the real achievements of behavioural science, so far as we know, in no way support Skinner's conclusions (in so far as these are nontrivial). It is for this reason, one must presume, that Skinner assures the reader that he has no 'need to know the details of a scientific analysis of behaviour' (p. 22), none of which are presented. It is not the depth or complexity of this theory that prevents Skinner from outlining it for the lay reader. For example, Jacques Monod, in his recent work on biology and human affairs[8], gives a rather detailed presentation of achievements of modern biology that he believes to be relevant to his (clearly identified) speculations. I should add, to make myself clear, that I am not criticizing Skinner for the relative lack of significant achievement in the behavioural sciences as compared to, say, biology, but rather for his irresponsible claims regarding the 'science of behaviour' which the reader need not know but which has allegedly produced all sorts of remarkable results concerning the control of behaviour.

III

Let us now turn to the evidence that Skinner provides for his extraordinary claims: as, that 'an analysis of behaviour' reveals that the achievements of artists, writers, statesmen, and scientists can be explained almost entirely in terms of environmental contingencies (p. 44); that it is the environment that makes a person wise or compassionate (p. 171); that 'all these questions about purposes, feelings, knowledge, and so on, can be restated in terms of the environment to which a person has been exposed' and that 'what a person "intends to do" depends on what he has done in the past and what has then happened' (p. 72); and so on.

According to Skinner, apart from genetic endowment, behaviour is determined entirely by reinforcement. To a hungry organism, food is a positive reinforcer. This means that 'anything the organism does that is followed by the receipt of food is more likely to be done again whenever the organism is hungry' (p. 27); but 'food is reinforcing only in a state of deprivation' (p.37). A negative reinforcer is a stimulus that increases the probability of behaviour that reduces the intensity of that stimulus; it is 'aversive', and roughly speaking, constitutes a threat (p. 27). A stimulus can become a conditioned reinforcer by association with other reinforcers. Thus money is 'reinforcing only after it has been exchanged for reinforcing things' (p. 33). The same is generally true of approval and affection. (The reader may attempt something that Skinner always avoids, namely, to characterize the 'stimuli' that constitute 'approval' — for example, why is the statement 'this article ought to appear in journal such-and-such' an instance of 'approval' when made by one person and of 'disapproval' when made by another?) Behaviour is shaped and maintained by the arrangement of such reinforcers. Thus, 'We change the relative strengths of responses by differential reinforcement of alternative courses of action' (pp. 94-5); one's repertoire of behaviour is determined by 'the contingencies of reinforcement to which he is exposed as an individual' (p. 127); 'an organism will range between vigorous activity and complete quiescence depending upon the schedules on which it has been reinforced' (p. 186). As Skinner realizes (though some of his defenders do not)[9] meticulous control is necessary to shape behaviour in highly specific ways. Thus, 'The culture ... teaches a person to make fine discriminations by making differential reinforcement more precise' (p. 194), a fact which causes problems when 'the verbal community cannot arrange the subtle contingencies necessary to teach fine distinctions among stimuli which are inaccessible to it'; 'as a result the language of emotion is not precise' (p. 106).

The problem in 'design of a culture' is to 'make the social environment as free as possible of aversive stimuli' (p. 42), 'to make life less punishing and in doing so to release for more reinforcing activities the time and energy consumed in the avoidance of punishment' (p. 81). It is an engineering problem, and we could get on with it if only we could overcome the irrational concern for freedom and dignity. What we require is the more effective use of the available technology, more and better controls. In fact, 'A technology of behaviour is available which would more successfully reduce the aversive consequences of behaviour, proximate or deferred, and maximize the achievements of which the human organism is capable'

(p. 125). But 'the defenders of freedom oppose its use', thus contributing to social malaise and human suffering. It is this irrationality that Skinner hopes to persuade us to overcome.

At this point an annoying though obvious question intrudes. If Skinner's thesis is false, then there is no point in his having written the book or our reading it. But if his thesis is true, then there is also no point in his having written the book or our reading it. For the only point could be to modify behaviour, and behaviour, according to the thesis, is entirely controlled by arrangement of reinforcers. Therefore reading the book can modify behaviour only if it is a reinforcer, that is, if reading the book increases the probability of the behaviour which led to reading the book (assuming an appropriate state of deprivation). At this point, we seem to be reduced to gibberish.

As a counterargument it might be claimed that even if the thesis is false, there is a point to writing and reading the book, since certain false theses are illuminating and provocative. But this escape is hardly available. In this case, the thesis is elementary and not of much interest in itself. Its only value lies in its possible truth. But if the thesis is true, then reading or writing the book would appear to be an entire waste of time, since it reinforces no behaviour.

Skinner would surely argue that reading the book, or perhaps the book itself, is a 'reinforcer' in some other sense. He wants us to be persuaded by the book, and, not to our surprise, he refers to persuasion as a form of behavioural control, albeit a weak and ineffective form. Skinner hopes to persuade us to allow greater scope to the behavioural technologists, and apparently believes that reading this book will increase the probability of our behaving in such a way as to permit them greater scope (freedom?). Thus reading the book, he might claim, reinforces this behaviour. It will change our behaviour with respect to the 'science of behaviour' (p. 124).

Let us overlook the problem, insuperable in his terms, of specifying the notion 'behaviour that gives greater scope to behavioural technologists', and consider the claim that reading the book might reinforce such behaviour. Unfortunately, the claim is clearly false, if we use the term 'reinforce' with anything like its technical meaning. Recall that reading the book reinforces the desired behaviour only if it is a consequence of the behaviour, and obviously putting our fate in the hands of behavioural technologists is not behaviour that led to (and hence can be reinforced by) reading Skinner's book. Therefore the claim can be true only if we deprive the term 'reinforce' of its technical meaning. Combining these observations, we see that there can be some point to reading the book or to Skinner's having written it only if the thesis of the book is divorced from the 'science of behaviour' on which it allegedly rests.

Let us consider further the matter of 'persuasion'. According to Skinner, we persuade ('change minds') 'by manipulating environmental contingencies', specifically, 'by pointing to stimuli associated with positive consequences' and 'making a situation more favourable for action, as by describing likely reinforcing consequences' (pp. 91-3). Even if we overlook that fact that persuasion, so characterized, is a form of control (a variety of 'reinforcement') unknown to Skinner's science, his argument is in no way advanced. Suppose Skinner were to claim that his book might persuade us by pointing to positive consequences of behavioural technology. But this will not do at all. It is not enough for him to point to those consequences (for example, to draw pictures of happy people); rather he must show that these are indeed *consequences* of the recommended behaviour. To persuade us, he must establish a connection between the recommended behaviour and the pleasant situation he describes. The question is begged by use of the term 'consequences'[10]. It is not enough merely to conjoin a description of the desired behaviour and a description of the 'reinforcing' state of affairs (overlooking, again, that not even these notions are expressible in Skinner's terms). Were that sufficient for 'persuasion', then we could 'persuade' someone of the opposite by merely conjoining a description of an unpleasant state of affairs with a description of the behaviour that Skinner hopes to produce.

If persuasion were merely a matter of pointing to reinforcing stimuli and the like, then any persuasive argument would retain its force if its steps were randomly interchanged, or if some of its steps were replaced by arbitrary descriptions of reinforcing stimuli. And the argument would lose its force if descriptions of unwelcome circumstances were randomly introduced. Of course, this is nonsense. For an argument to be persuasive, at least to a rational person, it must be coherent; its conclusions must follow from its premises. But these notions are entirely beyond the scope of Skinner's framework. When he states that 'deriving new reasons from old, the process of deduction' merely 'depends upon a much longer verbal history' (p. 96), he is indulging in hand waving of a most pathetic sort. Neither Skinner nor anyone else has offered the faintest hint that 'the process of deduction' can be characterized in his terms on the basis of 'verbal history', however long. An approach that cannot even formulate properly, let alone solve, the problem of why some new expression is intelligible, but not, say, a permutation of its component elements (see above, p. 118), cannot even begin to consider the notions 'coherent argument' or 'process of deduction'.

Consider Skinner's claim that 'we sample and change verbal behaviour, not opinions' (so a behavioural analysis reveals) (p. 95). Taken literally, this means that if, under a credible threat of torture, I force someone to say, repeatedly, that the Earth stands still, then I have changed his opinion. Comment is unnecessary, and we perceive at once the significance of the 'behavioural analysis' that yields this conclusion.

Skinner claims that persuasion is a weak method of control, and he asserts that 'changing a mind is condoned by the defenders of freedom and dignity because it is an ineffective way of changing behaviour, and the changer of minds can therefore escape from the charge that he is controlling people' (p. 97). Suppose that your doctor gives you a powerful and rational argument to the effect that if you continue to smoke, you will die a horrible death from lung cancer. Is it necessarily the case that this argument will be less effective in modifying your behaviour than any arrangement of true reinforcers? In fact, whether persuasion is effective or not depends on the content of the argument (for a rational person), a factor that Skinner cannot begin to describe. The problem becomes still worse if we consider other forms of 'changing minds'. Suppose that a description of a napalm raid on a Vietnamese village induces someone in an American audience to carry out an act of sabotage. In this case, the effective stimulus is not a reinforcer, the mode of changing behaviour may be quite effective, and the act that is performed (the behaviour 'reinforced') is entirely new (not in the 'repertoire') and may not even have been hinted at in the 'stimulus' that induced the change of behaviour. In every possible respect, then, Skinner's account is simply incoherent.

Since his William James lectures of 1947[11], Skinner has been sparring with these and related problems. The results are nil. It remains impossible for Skinner to formulate the relevant notions in his terms, let alone investigate them. What is more, no nontrivial scientific hypotheses with supporting evidence have been produced to substantiate the extravagant claims to which he is addicted[12]. Furthermore, this record of failure was predictable from the start, from an analysis of the problems and the means proposed to deal with them. It must be stressed that 'verbal behaviour' is the only aspect of human behaviour that Skinner has attempted to investigate in any detail. To his credit, he recognized quite early that only through a successful analysis of language could he hope to come to terms with human behaviour. By comparing the results that have been achieved in this twenty-five-year period with the claims that are still advanced, we gain a good insight into the nature of Skinner's science of behaviour. My impression is, in fact, that the claims are becoming more extreme and more strident as the inability to support them and the reasons for this failure become increasingly obvious.

It is unnecessary to labour the point any further. Evidently, Skinner has no way of dealing with the factors that are involved in persuading someone or changing his mind. The attempt to invoke 'reinforcement' merely leads to incoherence or pretence. The point is crucial. Skinner's discussion of persuasion and 'changing minds' is one of the few instances in which he tries to come to terms with what he calls the 'literature of freedom and dignity'. The libertarian whom he condemns distinguishes between persuasion and certain forms of control. He advocates persuasion and objects to coercion. In response, Skinner claims that persuasion is itself a (weak) form of control and that by using weak methods of control we simply shift control to other environmental conditions, not to the person himself (pp. 97, 99). Thus, Skinner claims, the advocate of freedom and dignity is deluding himself in his belief that persuasion leaves the matter of choice to 'autonomous man', and furthermore he poses a danger to society because he stands in the way of more effective controls. As we see, however, Skinner's argument against the 'literature of freedom and dignity' is without force. Persuasion is no form of control at all, in Skinner's sense; in fact, he is quite unable to deal with the concept in his terms.

But there is little doubt that persuasion can 'change minds' and affect behaviour, on occasion, quite drastically. Since persuasion cannot be coherently described in terms of arrangement of reinforcers, it follows that behaviour is not entirely determined by the specific contingencies to which Skinner arbitrarily restricts his attention, and that the major thesis of the book is false. Skinner can escape this conclusion only by claiming that persuasion *is* a matter of arranging reinforcing stimuli, but this claim is tenable only if the term 'reinforcement' is deprived of its technical meaning and used as a mere substitute for the detailed and specific terminology of ordinary language (similarly, the notion of 'arrangement or scheduling of reinforcement'). In any event, Skinner's 'science of behaviour' is irrelevant; the thesis of the book is either false (if we use terminology in its technical sense) or empty (if we do not). And the argument against the libertarian collapses entirely.

Not only is Skinner unable to uphold his claim that persuasion is a form of control, but he also offers not a particle of evidence to support his claim that the use of 'weak methods of control' simply shifts the mode of control to some obscure environmental factor rather than to the mind of autonomous man. Of course, from the thesis that all behaviour is controlled by the environment, it follows that reliance on weak rather than strong controls shifts control to other aspects of the environment. But the thesis, in so far as it is at all clear, is without empirical support, and in fact may even be quite empty, as we have seen in discussing 'probability of response' and persuasion. Skinner is left with no coherent criticism of the 'literature of freedom and dignity'.

The emptiness of Skinner's system is nicely illustrated in his treatment of more peripheral matters. He claims (p. 112) that the statement 'You should (you ought to) read *David Copperfield*' may be translated 'You will be reinforced if you read *David Copperfield*'. But what does this mean? Literally applying Skinner's definition (see above), it means that behaviour that is followed by reading *David Copperfield* is more likely to be done again if you are in need of reading. Or perhaps it means that the act of reading *David Copperfield* will be followed by some stimulus that will increase the probability of this act. When I tell someone that he ought to read *David Copperfield*, then, I am telling him something of this sort. Suppose, say, I told you that you should read *David Copperfield* because this would disabuse you of the notion that Dickens is worth reading, or show you what true boredom really is. In fact, no matter how we try to interpret Skinner's suggestion, giving the term 'reinforce' something like its literal sense, we fall into utter confusion.

Probably what Skinner has in mind in using the phrase 'You will be reinforced if you read *David Copperfield*' is that you will like it, enjoy it, or learn something useful, and thus be 'reinforced'. But this gives the game away. We are now using 'reinforce' in a sense quite different from that of the operant-conditioning paradigm. It would make no sense at all to try to apply results about scheduling of reinforcement, for example, to this situation. Furthermore, it is no wonder that we can 'explain' behaviour by using the nontechnical term 'reinforce' with the full range of meaning of 'like' or 'enjoy' or 'learn something from' or whatever. Similarly when Skinner tells us that a fascinating hobby is 'reinforcing' (p. 36), he is surely not claiming that the behaviour that leads to indulging in this hobby will be increased in probability. Rather, he means that we enjoy the hobby. A literal interpretation of such remarks yields gibberish, and a metaphorical interpretation merely replaces an ordinary term by a homonym of a technical term, with no gain in precision.

The system of Skinnerian translation is quite readily available to anyone and can indeed be employed with no knowledge of the theory of operant conditioning and its results, and with no information beyond normal observation, of the circumstances in which behaviour takes place or the nature of the behaviour itself. Recognizing this fact, we can appreciate the value of Skinner's 'science of behaviour' for the purposes at hand, and the insights it provides. But it is important to bear in mind that this system of translation leads to a significant loss of precision, for the simple reason that the full range of terms for the description and evaluation of behaviour, attitude, opinion, and so on must be translated into the impoverished system of terminology borrowed from the laboratory (and deprived of its meaning in transition)[13]. It is hardly surprising, then, that Skinnerian translation generally misses the point, even with the metaphorical use of such terms as 'reinforce'. Thus Skinner asserts that 'a person wants something if he acts to get it when the occasion raises' (p. 37). It follows that it is impossible to act to get something, given the opportunity, but not to want it — say, to act thoughtlessly, or out of a sense of duty (we can, as usual, reduce Skinner's assertion to triviality by saying that what the person wants is to do his duty, and so on). It is clear from the context that Skinner means 'if' as 'if and only if'. Thus it follows from his definition of 'want' that it is impossible for a person to want something but not to act to get it when the occasion arises, say for reasons of conscience (again, we can escape to triviality by assigning such reasons to the 'occasion'). Or consider the claim that 'we are likely to admire behaviour more as we understand it less' (p. 53). In a strong sense of 'explain', it follows that we admire virtually all behaviour, since we can explain virtually none. In a looser sense, Skinner is claiming that if Eichmann is incomprehensible to us but we understand why the Vietnamese fight on, then we are likely to admire Eichmann but not the Vietnamese resistance.

The real content of Skinner's system can be appreciated only by examining such cases, for example, as the following.

'Except when physically restrained, a person is least free or dignified when he is under threat of punishment' (p. 60). Thus someone who refuses to bend to authority in the face of severe threat has lost all dignity.

'We read books which help us say things we are on the verge of saying anyway but cannot quite say without help', and thus 'we understand the author' (p. 86). Is the point supposed to be that we do not read books that we expect to disagree with, and would not be able to understand what they say? If not, the claim is empty. If so, it is absurd.

Things we call 'good' are positive reinforcers and things we call 'bad' are negative reinforcers (pp. 104, 107); we work to achieve positive reinforcers and avoid negative reinforcers (p. 107)[14]. This explains why people, by definition, always seek good and avoid evil. Furthermore, 'Behaviour is called good or bad ... according to the way it is usually reinforced by others' (p. 109). As long as Hitler was being 'reinforced' by events and by those around him, his behaviour was good. On the other hand, the behaviour of Dietrich Bonhoeffer and Martin Niemoeller was, by definition, bad. In the Biblical tale, it was self-contradictory to seek ten good men in Sodom. Recall that the study of operant reinforcement, the conclusions of which we are now reviewing, is 'a science of values' (p. 104).

'A person acts intentionally ... in the sense that his behaviour has been strengthened by consequences' (p. 108) — as in the case of a person who intentionally commits suicide.

The hero who has killed a monster is reinforced by praise 'precisely to induce him to take on other monsters' (p. 111) — and thus is never praised on his deathbed or at his funeral.

The statement 'You should (you ought to) tell the truth' means, in this science of value, 'If you are reinforced by the approval of your fellow men, you will be reinforced when you tell the truth' (p. 112). In a subculture so cynical that telling the truth is regarded as absurd and not approved, one who is reinforced by approval ought not to tell the truth. Or to be more precise, the statement 'You ought to tell the truth' is false. Similarly, it is wrong to tell someone not to steal if he is almost certain to get away with it, since 'You ought not to steal' can be translated 'If you tend to avoid punishment, avoid stealing' (p. 114).

'Scientific discoveries and inventions are improbable; that is what is meant by discovery and invention' (p. 155). Thus by arranging mathematical formulas in some novel and improbable way, I succeed (by definition) in making a mathematical discovery.

Stimuli attract attention because they have been associated with important things and have figured in contingencies of reinforcement (p. 187). Thus if a cat with two heads walked into a room, only those to whom cats were important would notice it; others would pay no attention. An entirely new stimulus — new to the species or the individual — would be entirely ignored.

A person may derive his rules of behaviour 'from an analysis of punitive contingencies' (p. 69), and a person may be reinforced 'by the fact that the culture will long survive him' (p. 210). Thus something imagined can be a 'reinforcing stimulus'. (Try to apply to this example the fanciful discussion of 'condition reinforcers' that 'usurp' the reinforcing effort of deferred consequences — pp. 120-2.)

A person 'behaves bravely when environmental circumstances induce him to do so' (p. 197). Since, as noted earlier, we act to achieve positive reinforcers, we can conclude that no one behaves bravely when punishment or death is a likely consequence (unless he is 'reinforced' by 'stimuli' that impinge on him after his death).

A young man who is dissatisfied, discouraged, frustrated, has no sense of purpose, and so on is simply one who is not properly reinforced (pp. 146-7). Therefore no one has such feelings if he can attain wealth and the positive reinforcers it can buy.

Notice that in most of these cases, perhaps all, we can convert error to tautology by relying on the vagueness of the Skinnerian terminology, for example, by using 'reinforcement' as a cover term for whatever is liked, wanted, intended, and so on.

We can get a taste of the explanatory force of Skinner's theory from such (quite typical) examples as these: a pianist learns to play a scale smoothly because 'smoothly played scales are reinforcing' (p. 204); 'A person can know what it is to fight for a cause only after a long history during which he has learned to perceive and to know that state of affairs called fighting for a cause' (p. 190); and so on.

Similarly, we can perceive the power of Skinner's behavioural technology by considering the useful observations and advice he offers: 'Punishable behaviour can be minimized by creating circumstances in which it is not likely to occur' (p. 64); if a person 'is strongly reinforced when he sees other people enjoying themselves ... he will design an environment in which children are happy' (p. 150); if overpopulation, nuclear war, pollution, and depletion of resources are a problem, 'we may then change practices to induce people to have fewer children, spend less on nuclear weapons, stop polluting the environment, and consume resources at a lower rate, respectively' (152).

The reader may search for more profound thoughts than these. He may seek, but he will not find.

In his book, Skinner alludes more frequently to the role of genetic endowment than in his earlier speculations about human behaviour and society. One would think that this would lead to some modification in his conclusion, or to new conclusions. It does not. The reason is that Skinner is as vague and uninformative about genetic endowment as he is about control by contingencies of reinforcement. Unfortunately, zero plus zero still equals zero.

According to Skinner, 'The ease with which mentalistic explanations can be invented on the spot is perhaps the best gauge of how little attention we should pay to them' (p. 160). We can turn this into a true statement by replacing 'mentalistic' with 'Skinnerian'. In fact, a Skinnerian translation is always available for any description of behaviour — we can always say that an act is performed because it is 'reinforcing' or 'reinforced' or because the contingencies of reinforcement shaped behaviour in this way, and so on. There is a handy explanation for any eventuality, and given the vacuity of the system, we can never be proved wrong.

But Skinner's comment on 'mentalistic explanations' is surely incorrect, given his usage of this term. Consider, for example, the expressions (1)-(4):

(1) The two men promised their wives to kill each other
(2) The two men persuaded their wives to kill each other
(3) The two men promised me to kill each other
(4) The two men persuaded me to kill each other

We understand these sentences (even if they are new in our experience) in the following way: (1) is a close paraphrase of 'Each of the two men promised his wife to kill the other' and means that the men are to kill each other; (2) is a close paraphrase of 'The two men persuaded their wives each to kill the other' and means that the wives are to kill each other; (3) is a close paraphrase of 'Each of the two men promised me to kill the other'; but (4) cannot be paraphrased in any of these ways, and in fact is not a sentence of our 'repertoire' at all. One can propose an explanation for such facts as these within an abstract theory of language, a theory that Skinner would (quite legitimately) call 'mentalistic'. It is, however, not at all easy to invent a satisfactory 'mentalistic explanation' for these and many related facts[15], that is, a system of general principles that will explain these facts and will not be refuted by other facts. To construct a theory of 'internal (mental) states' is no easy task, contrary to what Skinner believes; though in this case too a Skinnerian explanation, employing the mystical notions 'similar' and 'generalize', can of course be invented on the spot, no matter what the facts may be. Skinner's failure to understand this results from his unwillingness to attempt to construct explanatory theories that have empirical content in the domain of human thought and action. Because of this unwillingness, there is also no discernible progress — today's formulations in this domain are hardly different from those of fifteen or twenty years ago — and no convincing refutation, for those who are untroubled by the fact that explanations can be invented on the spot, whatever the facts may be, within a system that is devoid of substance.

IV

We have so far been considering the scientific status of Skinner's claims. Let us now turn to the matter of 'design of a culture'. The principles of Skinner's 'science' tell us nothing about designing a culture (since they tell us virtually nothing), but that is not to say that Skinner leaves us completely in the dark as to what he has in mind. He believes that 'the control of the population as a whole must be delegated to specialists — to police, priests, owners, teachers, therapists, and so on, with their specialized reinforcers and their codified contingencies' (p. 155). The controller and the designer of a culture should be members of the group that is controlled (p.172). When the technology of behaviour is 'applied to the design of a culture, the survival of the culture functions as a value'. If our culture 'continues to take freedom or dignity, rather than its own survival, as its principal value, then it is possible that some other culture will make a greater contribution to the future'. The refusal to exercise available controls may be 'a lethal cultural mutation'. 'Life, liberty, and the pursuit of happiness are basic rights ... [but] they have only a minor bearing on the survival of a culture' (pp. 180-3); one might wonder, then, what importance they have for the behavioural technologist who takes the survival of the culture as a value. These and similar observations, to which we turn directly, may be what lead some readers to suspect that Skinner is advocating a form of totalitarian control.

There is no doubt that in his specific recommendations, vague though they are, Skinner succeeds in differentiating his position from the 'literature of freedom'. Skinner claims that the latter has 'overlooked ... control which does not have aversive consequences at any time' (p. 41) and has encouraged opposition to all control, whereas he is proposing a much more extensive use of controls that have no aversive consequences. The most obvious form of control of this benign type is differential wages. It is, of course, incorrect to say that the 'literature of freedom' has overlooked such controls. Since the industrial revolution, it has been much concerned with the problems of 'wage slavery' and the 'benign' forms of control that rely on deprivation and reward rather than direct punishment. This concern clearly distinguishes the literature of freedom from Skinner's social concepts. Or consider freedom of speech. Skinner's approach suggests that control of speech by direct punishment should be avoided, but that it is quite appropriate for speech to be controlled, say, by restricting good jobs to people who say what is approved by the designer of the culture. In accordance with Skinner's ideas, there would be no violation of academic freedom if promotions were granted only to those who conform, in their speech and writings, to the rules of the culture, though it would be wrong to go farther and punish those who deviate by saying what they believe to be true. Such deviants will simply remain in a state of deprivation. In fact, by giving people strict rules to follow, so that they know just what to say to be 'reinforced' by promotion, we will be 'making the world safer' and thus achieving the ends of behavioural technology (pp. 74, 81). The literature of freedom would, quite properly, reject and abhor such controls.

In fact, there is nothing in Skinner's approach that is incompatible with a police state in which rigid laws are enforced by people who are themselves subject to them and the threat of dire punishment hangs over all. Skinner argues that the goal of a behavioural technology is to 'design a world in which behaviour likely to be punished seldom or never occurs' — a world of 'automatic goodness' (p. 66). The 'real issue', he explains, 'is the effectiveness of techniques of control' which will 'make the world safer'. We make the world safer for 'babies, retardates, or psychotics' by arranging matters so that punishable behaviour rarely occurs. If only all people could be treated in this way, 'much time and energy would be saved' (pp. 66, 74). Skinner even offers, perhaps unintentionally, some indications as to how this benign environment might be brought into being:

> A state which converts all its citizens into spies or a religion which promotes the concept of an all-seeing God makes escape from the punishers practically impossible, and punitive contingencies are then maximally effective. People behave well although there is no visible supervision. (pp. 67-8)

Elsewhere, we learn that 'of course' freedom 'waxes as visible control wanes' (p. 70). Therefore the situation just described is one of maximal freedom, since there is no visible control; for the same reason, it is a situation of maximal dignity. Furthermore, since 'our task' is simply 'to make life less punishing' (p. 81), the situation just described would seem ideal. Since people behave well, life will be minimally punishing. In this way, we can progress 'toward an environment in which men are automatically good' (p. 73).

Extending these thoughts, consider a well-run concentration camp with inmates spying on one another and the gas ovens smoking in the distance, and perhaps an occasional verbal hint as a reminder of the meaning of this reinforcer. It would appear to be an almost perfect world. Skinner claims that a totalitarian state is morally wrong because of its deferred aversive consequences (p. 174). But in the delightful culture we have just designed, there should be no aversive consequences, immediate or deferred. Unwanted behaviour will be eliminated from the start by the threat of the crematoria and the all-seeing spies. Thus all behaviour would be automatically 'good', as required. There would be no punishment. Everyone would be reinforced — differently, of course, in accordance with ability to obey the rules. Within Skinner's scheme there is no objection to this social order. Rather, it seems close to ideal. Perhaps we could improve it still further by noting that 'the release from threat becomes more reinforcing the greater the threat' (as in mountain climbing; p. 111). We can, then, enhance the total reinforcement and improve the culture by devising a still more intense threat, say, by introducing occasional screams, or by flashing pictures of hideous torture as we describe the crematoria to our fellow citizens. The culture might survive, perhaps for a thousand years.

Though Skinner's recommendations might be read in this way, nevertheless it would be improper to conclude that Skinner is advocating concentration camps and totalitarian rule (though he also offers no objection). Such a conclusion overlooks a fundamental property of Skinner's science, namely, its vacuity. Though Skinner seems to believe that 'survival of a culture' is an important value for the behavioural technologist, he fails to consider the questions that arise at once. When the culture changes, has it survived, or died? Suppose that it changes in such a way as to extend the basic individual rights that Skinner personally regards as outdated (pp. 180-3). Is this survival, or death? Do we want the thousand-year Reich to survive? Why not, if survival of the culture functions as a value for the behavioural technologist? Suppose that in fact people are 'reinforced' by (that is, prefer) reduction of both sanctions and differential reinforcement. Do we then design the culture so as to lead to this result, thus diminishing effective controls rather than extending them, as Skinner urges? Suppose that humans happen to be so constructed that they desire the opportunity for freely undertaken productive work. Suppose that they want to be free from the meddling of technocrats and commissars, bankers and tycoons, mad bombers who engage in psychological tests of will with peasants defending their homes, behavioural scientists who can't tell a pigeon from a poet, or anyone else who tries to wish freedom and dignity out of existence or beat them into oblivion. Do we then 'design our culture' to achieve these ends (which, of course, can be given an appropriate Skinnerian translation)? There are no answers to any of these questions in Skinner's science, despite his claim that it accommodates (fully, it seems) consideration of 'values'. It is for this reason that his approach is as congenial to an anarchist as to a Nazi, as already noted[16].

V

Skinner's treatment of the notions 'leisure' and 'work' gives an interesting insight into the behaviourist system of beliefs (in so far as an identifiable doctrine still exists — see p. 117 above). Recall his assertion that the level of an organism's activity depends on its 'environmental history of reinforcement' and that 'an organism will range between vigorous activity and complete quiescence depending upon the schedules on which it has been reinforced' (p. 186). Weakening of controls, then, might induce passivity or random behaviour, particularly under conditions of affluence (low deprivation). People are 'at leisure', Skinner notes, if they 'have little to do', for example, people who 'have enough power to force or induce others to work for them', children, the retarded and mentally ill, members of affluent and welfare societies, and so on. Such people 'appear to be able to "do as they please".' This, Skinner continues, 'is a natural goal of the libertarian' (pp. 177-80). But leisure 'is a condition for which the human species has been badly prepared', and therefore a dangerous condition.

Evidently, a distinction must be made between having nothing to do and being able to do as one pleases. Both states presuppose lack of compulsion, but being able to do as one pleases requires the availability of opportunities as well. Under Skinnerian assumptions, it is difficult to distinguish properly between having nothing to do and being able to do as one pleases, since there is no reason to expect anyone to take the opportunity to work without deprivation and reinforcement. Thus it is not surprising that Skinner slips easily from the definition of 'leisure' as the state in which one appears to be able to do as one pleases, to the assertion that leisure (that is, having nothing to do) is a dangerous condition, as in the case of a caged lion or an institutionalized person.

Being able to do as one pleases is a natural goal of the libertarian, but having nothing to do is not. While it may be correct to say that the human species is badly prepared for having nothing to do, it is quite a different matter to say that it is badly prepared for the freedom to do as one pleases. People who are able to do as they please may work very hard, given the opportunity to do interesting work. Similarly a child who is 'at leisure' in Skinner's sense may not have to be 'reinforced' to expend energy in creative activities, but may eagerly exploit the opportunity to do so. Skinner's loose usage of the term 'leisure', while understandable under his assumptions, nevertheless obscures the fundamental difference between freedom to do as one wishes (for Skinner, the appearance of this, since he believes there is no such thing) and having nothing to do, as in an institution or on welfare, when there is no interesting work available. Skinner's remarks thus convey the impression that it might be dangerous, perhaps another 'lethal cultural mutation', to create social arrangements in which people are free to choose their work and to absorb themselves in satisfying work. A further comment that 'specific cultural conditions' (not further specified) are necessary to enable those with leisure to engage in 'artistic, literary, and scientific productivity' contributes as much to clarifying the issues as his other remarks about 'contingencies of reinforcement'.

Running through the discussion is a vague background assumption that unless 'reinforcements' are provided, individuals will vegetate. That there may be an intrinsic human need to find productive work, that a free person may, given the opportunity, seek such work and pursue it with energy, is a possibility that is never faced — though of course the vacuous system of Skinnerian translation would permit us to say that such work is 'reinforcing' (and undertaken for this reason), if we happen to enjoy tautologies.

The lingering background assumption in Skinner's discussion of leisure and liberty also arises in work that is somewhat more serious than his, in that it at least has the form of an argument and is based on some evidence. There is, at the moment, considerable controversy over a recent article by Harvard psychologist Richard

Herrnstein[17] which purports to show that American society is drifting towards a stable hereditary meritocracy, with social stratification by inborn differences and a corresponding distribution of 'rewards'. The argument is based on the hypothesis that differences in mental abilities are inherited and that people close in mental ability are more likely to marry and reproduce[18], so that there will be a tendency towards long-term stratification by mental ability, which Herrnstein takes to be measured by IQ. Secondly, Herrnstein argues that 'success' requires mental ability and that social rewards 'depend on success'. This step in the argument embodies two assumptions: first, it is so in fact; and second, it must be so for society to function effectively. The conclusion is that there is a tendency towards hereditary meritocracy, with 'social standing (which reflects earnings and prestige)' concentrated in groups with higher IQ. The tendency will be accelerated as society becomes more egalitarian, that is, as artificial social barriers are eliminated, defects in prenatal (e.g., nutritional) environment are overcome, and so on, so that natural ability can play a more direct role in attainment of social reward. Therefore, as society becomes more egalitarian, social rewards will be concentrated in a hereditary meritocratic elite.

Herrnstein has been widely denounced as a racist for this argument, a conclusion which seems to me unwarranted. There is, however, an ideological element in his argument that is absolutely critical to it. Consider the second step, that is, the claim that IQ is a factor in attaining reward and that this must be so for society to function effectively. Herrnstein recognizes that his argument will collapse if, indeed, society can be organized in accordance with the 'socialist dictum, "From each according to his ability, to each according to his needs."' His argument would not apply in a society in which 'income (economic, social, and political) is unaffected by success'.

Actually, Herrnstein fails to point out that his argument not only requires the assumption that success must be rewarded, but that it must be rewarded in quite specific ways. If individuals are rewarded for success only by prestige, then no conclusions of any importance follow. It will only follow (granting his other assumptions) that children of people who are respected for their achievements will be more likely to be respected for their own achievements, an innocuous result even if true. It may be that the child of two Olympic swimmers has a greater than average chance of achieving the same success (and the acclaim for it), but no dire social consequences from this hypothesis.

Though the point seems obvious, it has been misunderstood (by Herrnstein, in particular) and therefore perhaps merits an additional comment. Assume, with Herrnstein, that ability 'expresses itself in labour only for gain' and that such ability is partially heritable. Consider two parents with greater than average ability who attain thereby an increment R of reward beyond the average. By hypothesis, their child is likely to have higher than average ability, though less so than the parents, because of regression towards the mean, as Herrnstein notes. Thus the child will be expected to attain, by virtue of his own ability, an increment R' of reward beyond the average, where R' is less than R. Suppose that reward is wealth. Then the child's total increment, given the characteristics of this reward in our society, will be $R' + R_1 + R_2 + R_3$, where R_1 is that part of R transmitted to the child, R_2 is the increment resulting from the fact that R_1 itself generates additional wealth, and R_3 is the increment attained by the child beyond R' by virtue of the initial advantages afforded him by R_1. In our society, R_1, R_2, and R_3 are substantial, and of course cumulative over generations. Thus if social reward is wealth, there may indeed be a significant tendency for reward to concentrate in family lines over time. If, on the other hand, social reward and its effects are nontransmittable, then the child's total increment is R', in general less than R; there is nothing corresponding to the substantial and cumulative increment $R_1 + R_2 + R_3$. Thus if prestige and acclaim suffice as a motivating social reward, there will be no significant tendency for rewards to be concentrated in a 'hereditary meritocracy' as Herrnstein predicts, and his 'most troubling' conclusion vanishes. Whatever slight tendencies might exist in this direction are further diminished by the fact that matching in the kind of ability that brings 'reward' is at best a partial factor in selecting mates. Finally, whatever tendency there might be for prestige to persist along family lines has none of the large-scale social effects of concentration of wealth.

Furthermore, prestige and acclaim differ from wealth in that by granting more of this 'reward' to one individual, we do not correspondingly deprive another of it. Still accepting Herrnstein's assumption that individuals labour only for gain, if the reward is prestige, then performance can be assured generally by granting prestige to each individual to the extent that he achieves in accordance with his abilities, whatever his task. (Observe also that there is no reason to grant more prestige to those with more ability, so that from still another point of view Herrnstein's beliefs about the inevitability of a hereditary meritocracy are groundless, on the assumption that reward is prestige or acclaim.) Of course, it is conceivable that some individual will work only if his reward in prestige is not only greater than what he would attain by not working or working less well, but also greater than the prestige given to others for their accomplishments. Such a person would also, presumably, feel deprived or punished if others are successful; say, if someone else writes an outstanding novel or makes a scientific discovery or does a fine job of carpentry, and is respected for his achievement. Rather than take pleasure in this fact, this unfortunate creature would be pained by it. For such a person, 'differential prestige' would be a source of pain or pleasure and a necessary condition for undertaking any effort. There is, however, no reason to suppose that this form of psychic malady is characteristic of the human race.

It is interesting to note that Herrnstein does believe humans are so constituted by nature that this malady is characteristic of them. He argues that if prestige were sufficiently potent to 'sustain work no less well than do the rewards in our society, including money and power', then lack of prestige would cause 'sadness and regret' and society would be 'stratified by a mortal competition for prestige' in the 'hereditary meritocracy' he regards as unavoidable. As already noted, he is in error in assuming long-term stratification, even granting his assumptions, if reward is prestige. What of his further assumption that humans require 'differential reward' in his special sense: that is, not merely more prestige than they would attain by not working or working less well, but more than their fellows? If it is true, then we can anticipate that people will suffer 'painful psychic deprivations' if others achieve and are respected, and that they will find themselves in a 'mortal competition for prestige'. Though this is surely imaginable, the assumption seems to me even more curious and implausible than others that Herrnstein makes, to which we turn next. But whatever the status of this strange belief about human nature, it should be clear that it has no bearing on Herrnstein's central and 'most troubling' conclusion. To repeat: if prestige and respect suffice to motivate labour (on Herrnstein's assumption that ability expresses itself in labour only for gain), there is no reason to expect a long-term tendency of any significance towards a stable hereditary 'meritocracy', nor will such a tendency be enhanced by the realization of 'contemporary political and social goals', nor is there any reason to accept Herrnstein's 'extrapolation' that in any viable society a stable 'hereditary meritocracy' will arise. Nothing is left, in short, of his central and 'most troubling' conclusion.

The conclusion that Herrnstein and others find disturbing is that wealth and power will tend to concentrate in a hereditary meritocracy. But this follows only on the assumption that wealth and power (not merely respect) must be the rewards of successful achievement and that these (or their effects) are transmitted from parents to children. The issue is confused by Herrnstein's failure to isolate the specific factors crucial to his argument, and his use of the phrase 'income (economic, social, and political)' to cover 'rewards' of all types, including respect as well as wealth. It is confused further by the fact that he continually slips into identifying 'social standing' with wealth. Thus he writes that if the social ladder is tapered steeply, the obvious way to rescue the people at the bottom is 'to increase the aggregate wealth of society so that there is more room at the top' — which is untrue, if 'social standing' is a matter of acclaim and respect. (We overlook the fact that even on his tacit assumption, redistribution of income would appear to be an equally obvious strategy.)

Consider then the narrower assumption that is crucial to his argument: transmittable wealth and power accrue to mental ability, and must, for society to function effectively. If this assumption is false and society can be organized more or less in accordance with the 'socialist dictum', then nothing is left of Herrnstein's argument (except that it will apply to a competitive society in which his other factual assumptions hold). But the assumption is true, Herrnstein claims. The reason is that ability 'expresses itself in labor only for gain' and people 'compete for gain — economic and otherwise'. People will work only if they are rewarded in terms of 'social and political influence or relief from threat'. All of this is merely asserted; no justification is given for these assertions. Note again that the argument supports the disturbing conclusions he draws only if we identify the 'gain' for which people allegedly compete as transmittable wealth and power.

What reason is there to believe the crucial assumption that people will work only for gain in (transmittable) wealth and power, so that society cannot be organized in accordance with the socialist dictum? In a decent society everyone would have the opportunity to find interesting work, and each person would be permitted the fullest possible scope for his talents. Would more be required, in particular, extrinsic reward in the form of wealth and power? Only if we assume that applying one's talents in interesting and socially useful work is not rewarding in itself, that there is no intrinsic satisfaction in creative and productive work, suited to one's abilities, or in helping others (say, one's family, friends, associates, or simply fellow members of society). Unless we suppose this, then even granting all of Herrnstein's other assumptions, it does not follow that there should be any concentration of wealth or power or influence in a hereditary elite.

The implicit assumption is the same as Skinner's, in effect. For Herrnstein's argument to have any force at all, we must assume that people labour only for gain, and that the satisfaction in interesting or socially beneficial work or in work well done or in the respect shown to such activities is not a sufficient 'gain' to induce anyone to work. The assumption, in short, is that without material reward, people will vegetate. For this crucial assumption, no semblance of an argument is offered. Rather, Herrnstein merely asserts that if bakers and lumberjacks 'got the top salaries and the top social approval'[19], in place of those now at the top of the social ladder, then 'the scale of I.Q.'s would also invert', and the most talented would strive to become bakers and lumberjacks. This, of course, is no argument, but merely a reiteration of the claim that, necessarily, individuals work only for extrinsic reward. Furthermore, it is an extremely implausible claim. I doubt very much that Herrnstein would become a baker or lumberjack if he could earn more money that way.

Similar points have been made in commentary on Herrnstein's article[20], but in response he merely reiterates his belief that there is no way 'to end the blight of differential rewards'. Continued assertion, however, is not to be confused with argument. Herrnstein's further assertion that history shows ... in effect concedes defeat. Of course, history shows concentration of wealth and power in the hands of those able to accumulate it. One thought Herrnstein was trying to do more than merely put forth this truism. By reducing his argument finally to this assertion, Herrnstein implicitly concedes that he has no justification for the crucial assumption on which his argument rests, the unargued and unsupported claim that the talented must receive higher rewards.

If we look more carefully at what history and experience show, we find that if free exercise is permitted to the combination of ruthlessness, cunning, obsequiousness, and whatever other qualities provide 'success' in competitive societies, then those who have these qualities will rise to the top and will use their wealth and power to preserve and extend the privileges they attain. They will also construct ideologies to demonstrate that this result is only fair and just. We also find, contrary to capitalist ideology and behaviourist doctrine (of the nontautological variety), that many people often do not act solely, or even primarily, so as to achieve material gain, or even so as to maximize applause. As for the argument (if offered) that 'history shows' the untenability of the 'socialist dictum' that Herrnstein must reject for his argument to be valid, this may be assigned the same status as an eighteenth-century argument to the effect that capitalist democracy is impossible, as history shows.

One sometimes comes across arguments to the effect that people are 'economic maximizers', as we can see from the fact that given the opportunity, some will accumulate material reward and power[21]. By similar logic we could prove that people are psychopathic criminals, since given social conditions under which those with violent criminal tendencies were free from all restraint, they might very well accumulate power and wealth while nonpsychopaths suffered in servitude. Evidently, from the lessons of history we can reach only the most tentative conclusions about basic human tendencies.

Suppose that Herrnstein's unargued and crucial claim is incorrect. Suppose that there is in fact some intrinsic satisfaction in employing one's talents in challenging and creative work. Then, one might argue, this should compensate even for a diminution of extrinsic reward; and 'reinforcement' should be given for the performance of unpleasant and boring tasks. It follows, then, that there should be a concentration of wealth (and the power that comes from wealth) among the less talented. I do not urge this conclusion, but merely observe that it is more plausible than Herrnstein's if his fundamental and unsupported assumption is false.

The belief that people must be driven or drawn to work by 'gain' is a curious one. Of course, it is true if we use the vacuous Skinnerian scheme and speak of the 'reinforcing quality' of interesting or useful work; and it may be true, though irrelevant to Herrnstein's thesis, if the 'gain' sought is merely general respect and prestige. The assumption necessary for Herrnstein's argument, namely, that people must be driven or drawn to work by reward of wealth or power, does not, obviously, derive from science, nor does it appear to be supported by personal experience. I suspect that Herrnstein would exclude himself from the generalization, as already noted. Thus I am not convinced that he would at once apply for a job as a garbage collector if this were to pay more than his present position as a teacher and research psychologist. He would say, I am sure, that he does his work not because it maximizes

wealth (or even prestige) but because it is interesting and challenging, that is, intrinsically rewarding; and there is no reason to doubt
that this response would be correct. The statistical evidence, he
points out, suggests that 'if *very* high income is your goal, and you
have a high IQ, do not waste your time with formal education
beyond high school'. Thus if you are an economic maximizer, don't
bother with a college education, given a high IQ. Few follow this
advice, quite probably because they prefer interesting work to mere
material reward. The assumption that people will work only for
gain in wealth and power is not only unargued but quite probably
false, except under extreme deprivation. But this degrading and
brutal assumption, common to capitalist ideology and the behaviourist view of human beings (excepting, again, the tautological
behaviourism of Skinner), is fundamental to Herrnstein's argument.

There are other ideological elements in Herrnstein's argument,
more peripheral but still worth noting. He invariably describes the
society he sees evolving as a 'meritocracy', thus expressing the value
judgment that the characteristics that yield reward are a sign of
merit, that is, positive characteristics. He considers specifically IQ,
but of course recognizes that there might very well be other factors
in the attainment of 'social success'. One might speculate, rather
plausibly, that wealth and power tend to accrue to those who are
ruthless, cunning, avaricious, self-seeking, lacking in sympathy and
compassion, subservient to authority and willing to abandon principle for material gain, and so on. Furthermore, these traits might
very well be as heritable as IQ, and might outweigh IQ factors in
gaining material reward. Such qualities might be just the valuable
ones for a war of all against all. If so, then the society that results
(applying Herrnstein's 'syllogism') could hardly be characterized as
a 'meritocracy'. By using the word 'meritocracy' Herrnstein begs
some interesting questions and reveals implicit assumptions about
our society that are hardly self-evident.

Teachers in ghetto schools commonly observe that students who
are self-reliant, imaginative, energetic, and unwilling to submit to
authority are often regarded as troublemakers and punished, on
occasion even driven out of the school system. The implicit assumption that in a highly discriminatory society, or one with tremendous
inequality of wealth and power, the 'meritorious' will be rewarded is
a curious one indeed.

Consider further Herrnstein's assumption that in fact social
rewards accrue to those who perform beneficial and needed services.
He claims that the 'gradient of occupations' is 'a natural measure of

value and scarcity', and that 'the ties among IQ, occupation, and social standing make practical sense'. This is his way of expressing the familiar theory that people are automatically rewarded in a just society (and more or less in our society) in accordance with their contribution to social welfare or 'output'. The theory is familiar, and so are its fallacies. Given great inequalities of wealth, we will expect to find that the 'gradient of occupations' by pay is a natural measure of service to wealth and power — to those who can purchase and compel — and only by accident 'a natural measure of value'. The ties among IQ, occupation, and social standing that Herrnstein notes make 'practical sense' for those with wealth and power, but not necessarily for society or its members in general[22].

The point is quite obvious. Herrnstein's failure to notice it is particularly surprising given the data on which he bases his observations about the relation between social reward and occupation. He bases these judgments on a ranking of occupations which shows, for example, that accountants, specialists in public relations, auditors, and sales managers tend to have higher IQs (hence, he would claim, receive higher pay, as they must if society is to function effectively) than musicians, riveters, bakers, lumberjacks, and teamsters. Accountants were ranked highest among seventy-four listed occupations, with public relations fourth, musicians thirty-fifth, riveters fiftieth, bakers sixty-fifth, truck drivers sixty-seventh, and lumberjacks seventieth. From such data, Herrnstein concludes that society is wisely 'husbanding its intellectual resources'[23] and that the gradient of occupation is a natural measure of value and makes practical sense. Is it obvious that an accountant helping a corporation to cut its tax bill is doing work of greater social value than a musician, riveter, baker, truck driver, or lumberjack? Is a lawyer who earns a $100,000 fee to keep a dangerous drug on the market worth more to society than a farm worker or a nurse? Is a surgeon who performs operations for the rich doing work of greater social value than a practitioner in the slums, who may work much harder for much less extrinsic reward? The gradient of occupations that Herrnstein uses to support his claims with regard to the correlation between IQ and social value surely reflects, in part at least, the demands of wealth and power; a further argument is needed to demonstrate Herrnstein's claim that those at the top of the list are performing the highest service to 'society', which is wisely husbanding its resources by rewarding accountants and public-relations experts and engineers (e.g., designers of antipersonnel weapons) for their special skills. Herrnstein's failure to notice what his data immediately suggest is another indication of his uncritical and apparently unconscious acceptance of capitalist ideology in its crudest form.

Notice that if the ranking of occupations by IQ correlates with ranking by income, then the data that Herrnstein cites can be interpreted in part as an indication of an unfortunate bias in material reward towards occupations that serve the wealthy and powerful and away from work that might be more satisfying and socially useful. At least, this would certainly seem a plausible assumption, one that Herrnstein never discusses, given his unquestioning acceptance of the prevailing ideology.

There is, no doubt, some complex of characteristics conducive to material reward in a state capitalist society. This complex may include IQ and quite possibly other more important factors, perhaps those noted earlier. To the extent that these characteristics are heritable (and a factor in choosing mates) there will be a tendency towards stratification in terms of these qualities. This much is obvious enough.

Furthermore, people with higher IQs will tend to have more freedom in selection of occupation. Depending on their other traits and opportunities, they will tend to choose more interesting work or more remunerative work, these categories being by no means identical. Therefore one can expect to find some correlation between IQ and material reward, and some correlation between IQ and an independent ranking of occupations by their intrinsic interest and intellectual challenge. Were we to rank occupations by social utility in some manner, we would probably find at most a weak correlation with remuneration or with intrinsic interest, and quite possibly a negative correlation. Unequal distribution of wealth and power will naturally introduce a bias towards greater remuneration for services to the privileged, thereby causing the scale of remuneration to diverge from the scale of social utility in many instances.

From Herrnstein's data and arguments, we can draw no further conclusions about what would happen in a just society, unless we add the assumption that people labour only for material gain, for wealth and power, and that they do not seek interesting work suited to their abilities — that they would vegetate rather than do such work. Since Herrnstein offers no reason why we should believe any of this (and there is certainly some reason why we should not), none of his conclusions follow from his factual assumptions, even if these are correct. The crucial step in his 'syllogism' in effect amounts to the claim that the ideology of capitalist society expresses universal traits of human nature, and that certain related implicit assumptions of behaviourist psychology are correct. Conceivably, these unsupported assumptions are true. But once it is recognized how critical their role is in his argument and what empirical support they in fact have, any further interest in this argument would seem to evaporate.

I have assumed so far that prestige, respect and so on might be factors in causing people to work (as Herrnstein implies). This seems to me by no means obvious, though even if it is true, Herrnstein's conclusions clearly do not follow. In a decent society, socially necessary and unpleasant work would be divided on some egalitarian basis, and beyond that people would have, as an inalienable right, the widest possible opportunity to do work that interests them. They might be 'reinforced' by self-respect, if they do their work to the best of their ability, or if their work benefits those to whom they are related by bonds of friendship and sympathy and solidarity. Such notions are commonly an object of ridicule — as it was common, in an earlier period, to scoff at the absurd idea that a peasant has the same inalienable rights as a nobleman. There always have been and no doubt always will be people who cannot conceive of the possibility that things could be different from what they are. Perhaps they are right, but again, one awaits a rational argument.

In a decent society of the sort just described — which, one might think, becomes increasingly realizable with technological progress — there should be no shortage of scientists, engineers, surgeons, artists, craftsmen, teachers, and so on, simply because such work is intrinsically rewarding. There is no reason to doubt that people in these occupations would work as hard as those fortunate few who can choose their own work generally do today. Of course, if Herrnstein's assumptions, borrowed from capitalist ideology and behaviourist belief, are correct, then people will remain idle rather than do such work unless there is deprivation and extrinsic reward. But no reason is offered to explain why we should accept this strange and demeaning doctrine.

Lurking in the background of the debate over Herrnstein's syllogism is the matter of race, though he himself barely alludes to it. His critics are disturbed, and rightly so, by the fact that his argument will surely be exploited by racists to justify discrimination, much as Herrnstein may personally deplore this fact. More generally, Herrnstein's argument will be adopted by the privileged to justify their privilege on grounds that they are being rewarded for their ability and that such reward is necessary if society is to function properly. The situation is reminiscent of nineteenth-century racist anthropology, discussed at the outset. Marvin Harris notes:

> Racism also had its uses as a justification for class and caste hierarchies; it was a splendid explanation of both national and class privilege. It helped to maintain slavery and serfdom; it smoothed the way for the rape of Africa and the slaughter of the American Indian; it steeled the nerves of the Manchester captains of industry as they lowered wages, lengthened the working day, and hired more women and children.[24]

We can expect Herrnstein's arguments to be used in a similar way, and for similar reasons. When we discover that his argument is without force, unless we adopt unargued and implausible premises that happen to incorporate the dominant ideology, we quite naturally turn to the question of the social function of his conclusions and ask why the argument is taken seriously, exactly as in the case of nineteenth-century racist anthropology.

Since the issue is often obscured by polemic, it is perhaps worth stating again that the question of the validity and scientific status of a particular point of view is of course logically independent from the question of its social function; each is a legitimate topic of inquiry, and the latter becomes of particular interest when the point of view in question is revealed to be seriously deficient, on empirical or logical grounds.

The nineteenth-century racist anthropologists were no doubt quite often honest and sincere. They may have believed that they were simply dispassionate investigators, advancing science, following the facts where they led. Conceding this, we might nevertheless question their judgment, and not merely because the evidence was poor and the arguments fallacious. We might take note of the relative lack of concern over the ways in which these 'scientific investigations' were likely to be used. It would have been a poor excuse for the nineteenth-century racist anthropologist to plead, in Herrnstein's words, that 'a neutral commentator ... would have to say that the case is simply not settled' (with regard to racial inferiority) and that the 'fundamental issue' is 'whether inquiry shall (again) be shut off because someone thinks society is best left in ignorance'. The nineteenth-century racist anthropologist, like any other person, was responsible for the effects of what he did, in so far as they could be clearly foreseen. If the likely consequences of his 'scientific work' were those that Harris describes, he had the responsibility to take this likelihood into account. This would be true even if the work had real scientific merit — more so, in fact, in this case.

Similarly, imagine a psychologist in Hitler's Germany who thought he could show that Jews had a genetically determined tendency towards usury (like squirrels bred to collect too many nuts) or a drive towards antisocial conspiracy and domination, and so on. If he were criticized for even undertaking these studies, could he merely respond that 'a neutral commentator ... would have to say that the case is simply not settled' and that the 'fundamental issue' is 'whether inquiry shall (again) be shut off because someone thinks society is best left in ignorance'? I think not. Rather, I think that such a response would have been met with justifiable contempt. At best, he could claim that he is faced with a conflict of values. On the one hand, there is the alleged scientific importance of determining whether in fact Jews have a genetically determined tendency towards usury and domination (an empirical question, no doubt). On the other, there is the likelihood that even opening this question and regarding it as a subject for scientific inquiry would provide ammunition for Goebbels and Rosenberg and their henchmen. Were this hypothetical psychologist to disregard the likely social consequences of his research (or even his undertaking of research) under existing social conditions, he would fully deserve the contempt of decent people. Of course, scientific curiosity should be encouraged (though fallacious argument and investigation of silly questions should not), but it is not an absolute value.

The extravagant praise lavished on Herrnstein's flimsy argument and the widespread failure to note its implicit bias and unargued assumptions[25] suggest that we are not dealing simply with a question of scientific curiosity. Since it is impossible to explain this acclaim on the basis of the substance or force of the argument, it is natural to ask whether the conclusions are so welcome to many commentators that they lose their critical faculties and fail to perceive that certain crucial and quite unsupported assumptions happen to be nothing other than a variant of the prevailing ideology. This failure is disturbing — more so, perhaps, than the conclusions Herrnstein attempts to draw from his flawed syllogism.

Turning to the question of race and intelligence, we grant too much to the contemporary investigator of this question when we see him as faced with a conflict of values: scientific curiosity versus social consequences. Given the virtual certainty that even the undertaking of the inquiry will reinforce some of the most despicable features of our society, the seriousness of the presumed moral dilemma depends critically on the scientific significance of the issue that he is choosing to investigate. Even if the scientific significance were immense, we should certainly question the seriousness of the dilemma, given the likely social consequences. But if the scientific interest of any possible finding is slight, then the dilemma vanishes.

In fact, it seems that the question of the relation, if any, between race and intelligence has little scientific importance (as it has no social importance, except under the assumptions of a racist society). A possible correlation between mean IQ and skin colour is of no greater scientific interest than a correlation between any two other arbitrarily selected traits, say, mean height and colour of eyes. The empirical results, whatever they might be, appear to have little bearing on any issue of scientific significance. In the present state of scientific understanding, there would appear to be little scientific interest in the discovery that one partly heritable trait correlates (or not) with another partly heritable trait. Such questions might be interesting if the results had some bearing, say, on some psychological theory, or on hypotheses about the physiological mechanisms involved, but this is not the case. Therefore the investigation seems of quite limited scientific interest, and the zeal and intensity with which some pursue or welcome it cannot reasonably be attributed to a dispassionate desire to advance science. It would, of course, be foolish to claim, in response, that 'society should not be left in ignorance'. Society is happily 'in ignorance' of insignificant matters of all sorts. And with the best of will, it is difficult to avoid questioning the good faith of those who deplore the alleged 'anti-intellectualism' of the critics of scientifically trivial and socially malicious investigations. On the contrary, the investigator of race and intelligence might do well to explain the intellectual significance of the topic he is studying, and thus enlighten us as to the moral dilemma he perceives. If he perceives none, the conclusion is obvious, with no further discussion.

As to social importance, a correlation between race and mean IQ (were this shown to exist) entails no social consequences except in a racist society in which each individual is assigned to a racial category and dealt with not as an individual in his own right, but as a representative of this category. Herrnstein mentions a possible correlation between height and IQ. Of what social importance is that? None, of course, since our society does not suffer under discrimination by height. We do not insist on assigning each adult to the category 'below six feet in height' or 'above six feet in height' when we ask what sort of education he should receive or where he should live or what work he should do. Rather, he is what he is, quite independent of the mean IQ of people of his height category. In a nonracist society, the category of race would be of no greater significance. The mean IQ of individuals of a certain racial background is irrelevant to the situation of a particular individual, who is what he is. Recognizing this perfectly obvious fact, we are left with little, if any, plausible justification for an interest in the relation between mean IQ and race, apart from the 'justification' provided by the existence of racial discrimination.

The question of heritability of IQ might conceivably have some social importance, say, with regard to educational practice. However, even this seems dubious, and one would like to see an argument. It is, incidentally, surprising to me that so many commentators should find it disturbing that IQ might be heritable, perhaps largely so[26]. Would it also be disturbing to discover that relative height or musical talent or rank in running the one-hundred-yard dash is in part genetically determined? Why should one have preconceptions one way or another about these questions, and how do the answers to them, whatever they may be, relate either to serious scientific issues (in the present state of our knowledge) or to social practice in a decent society?

VI

Returning to Skinner, we have noted that his 'science' neither justifies nor provides any rational objection to a totalitarian state or even a well-run concentration camp. The libertarians and humanists whom Skinner scorns object to totalitarianism out of respect for freedom and dignity. But, Skinner argues, these notions are merely the residue of traditional mystical beliefs and must be replaced by the stern scientific concepts of behavioural analysis. However, there exists no behavioural science incorporating nontrivial, empirically supported propositions that apply to human affairs or support a behavioural technology. It is for this reason that Skinner's book contains no clearly formulated substantive hypotheses or proposals. We can at least begin to speculate coherently about the acquisition of certain systems of knowledge and belief on the basis of experience and genetic endowment, and can outline the general nature of some device that might duplicate aspects of this achievement. But as to how a person who has acquired systems of knowledge and belief then proceeds to use them in his daily life, we are entirely in the dark, at the level of scientific inquiry. If there were some science capable of treating such matters, it might well be concerned precisely with freedom and dignity and might suggest possibilities for enhancing them. Perhaps, as the classical literature of freedom and dignity sometimes suggests, there is an intrinsic human inclination towards free creative inquiry and productive work, and humans are not merely dull mechanisms shaped by a history of reinforcement and behaving predictably with no intrinsic needs apart from the need for physiological satiation. Then humans are not fit subjects for manipulation, and we will seek to design a social order accordingly. But we cannot, at present, turn to science for insight into these matters. To claim otherwise is pure fraud. For the moment, an honest scientist will admit at once that we understand virtually nothing, at the level of scientific inquiry, with regard to human freedom and dignity.

There is, of course, no doubt that behaviour can be controlled, for example, by threat of violence or a pattern of deprivation and reward. This much is not at issue, and the conclusion is quite consistent with a belief in 'autonomous man'. If a tyrant has the power to demand certain acts, whether by threat of punishment or by allowing only those who perform these acts to escape from deprivation (e.g., by restricting employment to such people), his subjects may choose to obey — though some may have the dignity to refuse. They will be aware that they are submitting under compulsion. They will understand the difference between this compulsion and the laws that govern falling bodies. Of course, they are not free. Sanctions backed by force restrict freedom, as does differential reward. An increase in wages, in Marx's phrase 'would be nothing more than a better *remuneration of slaves*, and would not restore, either to the worker or to the work, their human significance and worth'. But it would be absurd to conclude, merely from the fact that freedom is limited, that 'autonomous man' is an illusion, or to overlook the distinction between a person who chooses to conform in the face of threat, or force, or deprivation and differential reward and a person who 'chooses' to obey Newtonian principles as he falls from a high tower. The inference remains absurd even where it is possible to predict the course of action that most 'autonomous men' would select, under conditions of duress and limited opportunity for survival. The absurdity merely becomes more obvious when we consider the real social world, in which determinable 'probabilities of response' are so slight as to have virtually no predictive value. And it would be not absurd, but grotesque, to argue that since circumstances can be arranged under which behaviour is quite predictable — as in a prison, for example, or the concentration-camp society 'designed' above — therefore there need be no concern for the freedom and dignity of 'autonomous man'. When such conclusions are taken to be the result of a 'scientific analysis', one can only be amazed at human gullibility.

Skinner confuses science with terminology. He apparently believes that if he rephrases commonplace 'mentalistic' expressions with terminology drawn from the laboratory study of behaviour, but deprived of its precise content, then he has achieved a scientific analysis of behaviour. It would be hard to conceive of a more striking failure to comprehend even the rudiments of scientific thinking. The public may well be deceived, given the prestige of science and technology. It may even choose to be misled into agreeing that concern for freedom and dignity must be abandoned. Perhaps it will choose this course out of fear and insecurity with regard to the consequences of a serious concern for freedom and dignity. The tendencies in our society that lead towards submission to authoritarian rule may prepare individuals for a doctrine that can be interpreted as justifying it.

The problems that Skinner discusses — it would be more proper to say 'circumvents' — are often real enough. Despite his curious belief to the contrary, his libertarian and humanist opponents do not object to 'design of a culture', that is, to creating social forms that will be more conducive to the satisfaction of human needs, though they differ from Skinner in the intuitive perception of what these needs truly are. They would not, or at least should not, oppose scientific inquiry or, where possible, its applications, though they will no doubt dismiss the travesty that Skinner presents.

If a physical scientist were to assure us that we need not concern ourselves over the world's sources of energy because he has demonstrated in his laboratory that windmills will surely suffice for all future human needs, he would be expected to produce some evidence, or other scientists would expose this pernicious nonsense. The situation is different in the behavioural sciences. A person who claims that he has a behavioural technology that will solve the world's problems and a science of behaviour that supports it and reveals the factors that determine human behaviour is required to demonstrate nothing. One waits in vain for psychologists to make clear to the general public the actual limits of what is known. Given the prestige of science and technology, this is a most unfortunate situation.

Notes

This chapter is expanded from an essay published in *Cognition*, vol. 1, no. 1 (1972). Parts appeared, in a slightly different form, as a review of B.F. Skinner, *Beyond Freedom and Dignity*, in *The New York Review of Books* (30 December 1972). The discussion of Herrnstein's work appeared in part in *Social Policy*, vol. 3, no. 1 (1972), and in *Ramparts* (July 1972). For Herrnstein's response, with further comments of mine (in part incorporated here), see *Cognition*, vol. 1, nos. 2-3, 4 (1972).

1 *Economist* (31 October 1862). Cited by Frederick F. Clairmonte in his review of Ronald Segal, *The Race War, Journal of Modern African Studies*, forthcoming.

2 Marvin Harris, *The Rise of Anthropological Theory* (New York, 1968), pp. 100-1. By the 1860s, he writes, 'anthropology and racial determinism had become almost synonyms'.

3 B.F. Skinner, *Beyond Freedom and Dignity* (New York, 1971), p. 82. Subsequent references will be to page number only.

4 W.V.O. Quine, 'Linguistics and Philosophy', in Sidney Hook (ed.), *Language and Philosophy* (New York, 1969), p. 97.

5 We can, of course, design circumstances under which behaviour can be predicted quite closely, as any military interrogator in the field is aware. And we can reduce the issue to triviality by regarding a person's wishes, intentions, purposes, and so on as part of the circumstances that elicit behaviour. If we are really intent on deluding ourselves, we might go on to 'translate' wishes, intentions, and purposes into the terminology of operant conditioning theory, along the lines that we will explore in a moment.

6 L. Breger and J.L. McGaugh, 'Critique and Reformulation of "Learning-Theory" Approaches to Psychotherapy and Neurosis', *Psychological Bulletin* (May 1965), pp. 63, 338-58.

7 Aubrey J. Yates, *Behavior Therapy* (New York, 1970), p. 396. Skinner also points out, irrelevantly to any rational consideration, that 'the speaker does not feel the *grammatical rules* he is said to apply in composing sentences, and men spoke grammatically for thousands of years before anyone knew there were rules' (p. 16).

8 Jacques Monod, *Choice and Necessity* (New York, 1971).

9 See, e.g., Kenneth MacCorquodale, 'On Chomsky's Review of Skinner's *'Verbal Behavior'*, *Journal of the Experimental Analysis of Behavior*, vol. 13, no. 1 (1970), pp. 83-99.

10 As Koestler points out, in remarks Skinner quotes, Skinner's approach represents 'question-begging on a heroic scale' (p. 165). It will not do to respond, as Skinner does, by claiming that this is 'name-calling' and a sign of emotional instability. Rather it will be necessary to show that this is not the literal and obvious truth (as indeed it is).

11 See his *Verbal Behavior* (New York, 1957), which incorporates and extends these lectures.

12 In reviewing Skinner's *Verbal Behavior* (*Language*, vol. 35, no. 1, 1959, pp. 26-58), I stated that there did appear to be one result, namely, with regard to modifying certain aspects of the speaker's behaviour (say, production of plural nouns) by 'reinforcement' with such expressions as 'right' and 'good', without the speaker's awareness. The result is at best of marginal interest, since evidently the speaker's behaviour in such respects could be far more 'effectively' modified by a simple instruction, a fact that cannot be incorporated into the Skinnerian system, if the latter is interpreted at all strictly. Of course, if the subject is aware of what the experimenter is doing, the result is of no interest at all. It turns out that this may very well be the case. See D. Dulany, 'Awareness, Rules and Propositional Control: A Confrontation with S-R Behavior Theory', in Theodore R. Dixon and David Horton (eds), *Verbal Behavior and General Behavior Theory* (Englewood Cliffs, NJ, 1968). Therefore it seems that there are no clear nontrivial results that have been achieved in the study of normal human speech by application of the operant-conditioning paradigm.

Interesting reading, in this connection, is MacCorquodale, op. cit. I cannot take the space here to correct the many errors (such as his misunderstanding of the notion of 'function', which leads to much confusion). The major confusion in the article is this: MacCorquodale assumes that I was attempting to disprove Skinner's theses, and he points out that I present no data to disprove them. But my point was, rather, to demonstrate that when Skinner's assertions are taken literally, they are false on the face of it (MacCorquodale discusses none of these examples accurately) or else quite vacuous (as when we say that the response 'Mozart' is under the control of a subtle stimulus), and that many of his false statements can be converted into uninteresting truths by employing such terms as 'reinforce' with the full imprecision of 'like', 'want', 'enjoy', and so on (with a loss of accuracy in transition, of course, since a rich and detailed terminology is replaced by a few terms that are divorced entirely from the setting in which they have some precision). Failing to understand this, MacCorquodale 'defends' Skinner by showing that quite often it is possible to give a vacuous interpretation to his pronouncements; exactly my point. The article is useful, once errors are eliminated, in revealing the bankruptcy of the operant-conditioning approach to the study of verbal behaviour.

13 See MacCorquodale, op. cit., for a revealing example of complete inability to understand this point.

14 Note the shift in Skinner's account from the discussion of things that taste good to value judgments about things that we call good (pp. 103-5).

15 One way out would be to deny that these are facts. This is the approach taken by Patrick Suppes, in remarks that MacCorquodale quotes.

Suppes refers to several books that contain a variety of facts such as these and explore the problem of accounting for them by an explanatory theory, and he asserts simply that these books contain no data. Apparently, Suppes would have us believe that these facts become 'data' only when someone conducts an experiment in which he 'proves' that the facts are what we know them to be, on a moment's thought. It would, of course, be a straightforward matter to devise such experiments (adjusting them, in the typical fashion of such experimental work, until they give what we antecedently know to be the right results), were anyone willing to waste his time in such ways. Then the books would contain 'data', in Suppes' sense.

16 Libertarian thinkers have often been 'radical environmentalists', mistakenly so, in my opinion, for reasons discussed elsewhere (see my *Problems of Knowledge and Freedom*, New York, 1971).

17 Richard Herrnstein, 'IQ', *Atlantic Monthly* (September 1971).

18 He does not specifically mention this assumption, but it is necessary to the argument. I will not discuss here two factual matters central to Herrnstein's argument: heritability of IQ, and the significance of IQ as a factor in determining economic reward. On the former, see Christopher Jencks *et al.*, *Inequality* (New York, 1972), app. A; this extensive analysis suggests that Herrnstein accepts an estimate of heritability that is far too high. On IQ as a factor in determining 'social reward', Herrnstein presents no serious evidence for his claim that it is a major factor, but the matter has been carefully investigated by others (see Jencks *et al.*, and Samuel Bowles and Herbert Gintis, 'I.Q. in the U.S. Class Structure', mimeographed, Harvard University, July 1972). Bowles and Gintis conclude that IQ, social class, and education 'contribute independently to economic success, but that IQ is by far the least important'; 'a perfect equalization of IQs across social classes would reduce the intergenerational transmission of economic status by a negligible amount'. Jencks *et al.* give as their 'best estimate' that there is 'about three per cent less income inequality in genetically homogeneous subpopulations than in the entire American population' (p. 221). In short, empirical investigations indicate that IQ is a minor factor determining income, and the genetic component in IQ a negligible factor. Thus there is nothing to support Herrnstein's belief that in a society like ours, a genetic component in IQ will tend to produce a stable hereditary 'meritocracy'. These observations suffice to dismiss Herrnstein's rather careless discussion. But my concern here is not its empirical inadequacies but rather its ideological assumptions, and in particular, the question why there has been such interest in and acclaim for work so lacking in substance.

19 Note again Herrnstein's failure to distinguish remuneration from social approval, though the argument collapses if the only reward is approval.

20 *Atlantic Monthly* (November 1971). See p. 110, first paragraph, for his rejoinder.

21 See, e.g., Harry W. Blair, 'The Green Revolution and "economic man": Some Lessons for Community Development in South Asia', *Pacific Affairs*, vol. 44, no. 3 (1971), pp. 353-67.

22 To assume that society tends to reward those who perform a social service is to succumb to essentially the same fallacy (among others) that undermines the argument that a free market, in principle, leads to optimal satisfaction of wants — whereas when wealth is badly distributed, the system will tend to produce luxuries for the few who can pay rather than necessities for the many who cannot.

23 Misleadingly, Herrnstein states that 'society is, in effect, husbanding its intellectual resources by holding engineers in greater esteem and paying them more'. But if he really wants to claim this on the basis of the ties between IQ and social standing that his data reveal, then he should conclude as well that society is husbanding its intellectual resources by holding accountants and PR men in greater esteem and paying them more. Quite apart from this, it is not so obvious as he apparently believes that society is wisely husbanding its intellectual resources by employing most of its scientists and engineers in military and space R-and-D.

24 Op. cit., p. 106.

25 See the correspondence in the *Atlantic Monthly* (November 1971).

26 An advertisement in the *Harvard Crimson* (29 November 1971), signed by many faculty members, refers to the 'disturbing conclusion that "intelligence" is largely genetic, so that over many, many years society might evolve into classes marked by distinctly different levels of ability'. Since the conclusion does not follow from the premise, as already noted, it may be that what disturbs the signers is the 'conclusion that "intelligence" is largely genetic'. Why this should seem disturbing remains obscure.

6

Interpretation and the sciences of man

CHARLES TAYLOR

I

(i)

Is there a sense in which interpretation is essential to explanation in the sciences of man? The view that it is, that there is an unavoidably 'hermeneutical' component in the sciences of man, goes back to Dilthey. But recently the question has come again to the fore, for instance, in the work of Gadamer[1], in Ricoeur's interpretation of Freud[2], and in the writings of Habermas[3].

Interpretation, in the sense relevant to hermeneutics, is an attempt to make clear, to make sense of an object of study. This object must, therefore, be a text, or a text-analogue, which in some way is confused, incomplete, cloudy, seemingly contradictory — in one way or another, unclear. The interpretation aims to bring to light an underlying coherence or sense.

This means that any science which can be called 'hermeneutical,' even in an extended sense, must be dealing with one or another of the confusingly interrelated forms of meaning. Let us try to see a little more clearly what this involves.

Reprinted from The Review of Metaphysics, *Vol. XXV, No. 1 (1971), by permission of the author and Editor.*

(1) We need, first, an object or field of objects, about which we can speak in terms of coherence or its absence, of making sense or nonsense.

(2) Second, we need to be able to make a distinction, even if only a relative one, between the sense or coherence made, and its embodiment in a particular field of carriers or signifiers. For otherwise, the task of making clear what is fragmentary or confused would be radically impossible. No sense could be given to this idea. We have to be able to make for our interpretations claims of the order: the meaning confusedly present in this text or text-analogue is clearly expressed here. The meaning, in other words, is one which admits of more than one expression, and, in this sense, a distinction must be possible between meaning and expression.

The point of the above qualification, that this distinction may be only relative, is that there are cases where no clear, unambiguous, non-arbitrary line can be drawn between what is said and its expression. It can be plausibly argued (I think convincingly although there isn't space to go into it here) that this is the normal and fundamental condition of meaningful expression, that exact synonymy, or equivalence of meaning, is a rare and localized achievement of specialized languages or uses of civilization. But this, if true (and I think it is), doesn't do away with the distinction between meaning and expression. Even if there is an important sense in which a meaning re-expressed in a new medium cannot be declared identical, this by no means entails that we can give no sense to the project of expressing a meaning in a new way. It does of course raise an interesting and difficult question about what can be meant by expressing it in a clearer way: what is the 'it' which is clarified if equivalence is denied? I hope to return to this in examining interpretation in the sciences of man.

Hence the object of a science of interpretation must be describable in terms of sense and nonsense, coherence and its absence and must admit of a distinction between meaning and its expression.

(3) There is also a third condition it must meet. We can speak of sense or coherence, and of their different embodiments in connection with such phenomena as gestalts, or patterns in rock formations, or snow crystals, where the notion of expression has no real warrant. What is lacking here is the notion of a subject for whom these meanings are. Without such a subject, the choice of criteria of sameness and difference, the choice among the different forms of coherence which can be identified in a given pattern, among the

different conceptual fields in which it can be seen, is arbitrary.

In a text or text-analogue, on the other hand, we are trying to make explicit the meaning expressed, and this means expressed by or for a subject or subjects. The notion of expression refers us to that of a subject. The identification of the subject is by no means necessarily unproblematical, as we shall see further on; it may be one of the most difficult problems, an area in which prevailing epistemological prejudice may blind us to the nature of our object of study. I think this has been the case, as I will show below. And moreover, the identification of a subject does not assure us of a clear and absolute distinction between meaning and expression as we saw above. But any such distinction, even a relative one, is without any anchor at all, is totally arbitrary, without appeal to a subject.

The object of a science of interpretation must thus have: sense, distinguishable from its expression, which is for or by a subject.

(ii)

Before going on to see in what way, if any, these conditions are realized in the sciences of man, I think it would be useful to set out more clearly what rides on this question, why it matters whether or not we think of the sciences of man as hermeneutical, what the issue is at stake here.

The issue here is at the root an epistemological one. But it is inextricable from an ontological one, and, hence, cannot but be relevant to our notions of science and of the proper conduct of inquiry. We might say that it is an ontological issue which has been argued ever since the seventeenth century in terms of epistemological considerations which have appeared to some to be unanswerable.

The case could be put in these terms: what are the criteria of judgment in a hermeneutical science? A successful interpretation is one which makes clear the meaning originally present in a confused, fragmentary, cloudy form. But how does one know that this interpretation is correct? Presumably because it makes sense of the original text: what is strange, mystifying, puzzling, contradictory is no longer so, is accounted for. The interpretation appeals throughout to our understanding of the 'language' of expression, which understanding allows us to see that this expression is puzzling, that it is in contradiction to that other, etc., and that these difficulties are cleared up when the meaning is expressed in a new way.

But this appeal to our understanding seems to be crucially

inadequate. What if someone does not 'see' the adequacy of our interpretation, does not accept our reading? We try to show him how it makes sense of the original non- or partial sense. But for him to follow us he must read the original language as we do, he must recognize these expressions as puzzling in a certain way, and hence be looking for a solution to our problem. If he does not, what can we do? The answer, it would seem, can only be more of the same. We have to show him through the reading of other expressions why this expression must be read in the way we propose. But success here requires that he follow us in these other readings, and so on, it would seem, potentially forever. We cannot escape an ultimate appeal to a common understanding of the expressions, of the 'language' involved. This is one way of trying to express what has been called the 'hermeneutical circle'. What we are trying to establish is a certain reading of text or expressions, and what we appeal to as our grounds for this reading can only be other readings. The circle can also be put in terms of part-whole relations: we are trying to establish a reading for the whole text, and for this we appeal to readings of its partial expressions; and yet because we are dealing with meaning, with making sense, where expressions only make sense or not in relation to others, the readings of partial expressions depend on those of others, and ultimately of the whole.

Put in forensic terms, as we started to do above, we can only convince an interlocutor if at some point he shares our understanding of the language concerned. If he does not, there is no further step to take in rational argument; we can try to awaken these intuitions in him, or we can simply give up; argument will advance us no further. But of course the forensic predicament can be transferred into my own judging: if I am this ill-equipped to convince a stubborn interlocutor, how can I convince myself? How can I be sure? Maybe my intuitions are wrong or distorted, maybe I am locked into a circle of illusion.

Now one, and perhaps the only sane response to this would be to say that such uncertainty is an ineradicable part of our epistemological predicament. That even to characterize it as 'uncertainty' is to adopt an absurdly severe criterion of 'certainty', which deprives the concept of any sensible use. But this has not been the only or even the main response of our philosophical tradition. And it is another response which has had an important and far-reaching effect on the sciences of man. The demand has been for a level of certainty which can only be attained by breaking beyond the circle.

There are two ways in which this break-out has been envisaged.

The first might be called the 'rationalist' one and could be thought to reach a culmination in Hegel. It does not involve a negation of intuition, or of our understanding of meaning, but rather aspires to attainment of an understanding of such clarity that it would carry with it the certainty of the undeniable. In Hegel's case, for instance, our full understanding of the whole in 'thought' carries with it a grasp of its inner necessity, such that we see how it could not be otherwise. No higher grade of certainty is conceivable. For this aspiration the word 'break-out' is badly chosen; the aim is rather to bring understanding to an inner clarity which is absolute.

The other way, which we can call 'empiricist', is a genuine attempt to go beyond the circle of our own interpretations, to get beyond subjectivity. The attempt is to reconstruct knowledge in such a way that there is no need to make final appeal to readings or judgments which cannot be checked further. That is why the basic building block of knowledge on this view is the impression, or sense-datum, a unit of information which is not the deliverance of a judgment, which has by definition no element in it of reading or interpretation, which is a brute datum. The highest ambition would be to build our knowledge from such building blocks by judgments which could be anchored in a certainty beyond subjective intuition. This is what underlies the attraction of the notion of the association of ideas, or if the same procedure is viewed as a method, induction. If the original acquisition of the units of information is not the fruit of judgment or interpretation, then the constatation that two such elements occur together need not either be the fruit of interpretation, of a reading or intuition which cannot be checked. For if the occurrence of a single element is a brute datum, then so is the co-occurrence of two such elements. The path to true knowledge would then repose crucially on the correct recording of such co-occurrences.

This is what lies behind an ideal of verification which is central to an important tradition in the philosophy of science, whose main contemporary protagonists are the logical empiricists. Verification must be grounded ultimately in the acquisition of brute data. By 'brute data', I mean here and throughout data whose validity cannot be questioned by offering another interpretation or reading, data whose credibility cannot be founded or undermined by further reasoning[4]. If such a difference of interpretation can arise over given data, then it must be possible to structure the argument so as to distinguish the basic, brute data from the inferences made on the basis of them.

The inferences themselves, of course, to be valid must similarly be beyond the challenge of a rival interpretation. Here the logical empiricists added to the armoury of traditional empiricism which set great store by the method of induction, the whole domain of logical and mathematical inference which had been central to the rationalist position (with Leibniz at least, although not with Hegel), and which offered another brand of unquestionable certainty.

Of course, mathematical inference and empirical verification were combined in such a way that two theories or more could be verified of the same domain of facts. But this was a consequence to which logical empiricism was willing to accommodate itself. As for the surplus meaning in a theory which could not be rigorously co-ordinated with brute data, it was considered to be quite outside the logic of verification.

As a theory of perception, this epistemology gave rise to all sorts of problems, not least of which was the perpetual threat of scepticism and solipsism inseparable from a conception of the basic data of knowledge as brute data, beyond investigation. As a theory of perception, however it seems largely a thing of the past, in spite of a surprising recrudescence in the Anglo-Saxon world in the thirties and forties. But there is no doubt that it goes marching on, among other places, as a theory of how the human mind and human knowledge actually function.

In a sense, the contemporary period has seen a better, more rigorous statement of what this epistemology is about in the form of computer-influenced theories of intelligence. These try to model intelligence as consisting of operations on machine-recognizable input which could themselves be matched by programmes which could be run on machines. The machine criterion provides us with our assurance against an appeal to intuition or interpretations which cannot be understood by fully explicit procedures operating on brute data — the input[5].

The progress of natural science has lent great credibility to this epistemology, since it can be plausibly reconstructed on this model, as for instance has been done by the logical empiricists. And, of course, the temptation has been overwhelming to reconstruct the sciences of man on the same model; or rather to launch them in lines of inquiry that fit this paradigm, since they are constantly said to be in their 'infancy'. Psychology, where an earlier vogue of behaviourism is being replaced by a boom of computer-based models, is far from the only case.

The form this epistemological bias — one might say obsession — takes is different for different sciences. Later I would like to look at a particular case, the study of politics, where the issue can be followed out. But in general, the empiricist orientation must be hostile to a conduct of inquiry which is based on interpretation, and which encounters the hermeneutical circle as this was characterized above. This cannot meet the requirements of intersubjective, non-arbitrary verification which it considers essential to science. And along with the epistemological stance goes the ontological belief that reality must be susceptible to understanding and explanation by science so understood. From this follows a certain set of notions of what the sciences of man must be.

On the other hand, many, including myself, would like to argue that these notions about the sciences of man are sterile, that we cannot come to understand important dimensions of human life within the bounds set by this epistemological orientation. This dispute is of course familiar to all in at least some of its ramifications. What I want to claim is that the issue can be fruitfully posed in terms of the notion of interpretation as I began to outline it above.

I think this way of putting the question is useful because it allows us at once to bring to the surface the powerful epistemological beliefs which underlie the orthodox view of the sciences of man in our academy, and to make explicit the notion of our epistemological predicament implicit in the opposing thesis. This is in fact rather more way-out and shocking to the tradition of scientific thought than is often admitted or realized by the opponents of narrow scientism. It may not strengthen the case of the opposition to bring out fully what is involved in a hermeneutical science as far as convincing waverers is concerned, but a gain in clarity is surely worth a thinning of the ranks — at least in philosophy.

(iii)

Before going on to look at the case of political science, it might be worth asking another question: why should we even pose the question whether the sciences of man are hermeneutical? What gives us the idea in the first place that men and their actions constitute an object or a series of objects which meet the conditions outlined above?

The answer is that on the phenomenological level or that of ordinary speech (and the two converge for the purposes of this argument) a certain notion of meaning has an essential place in the characterization of human behaviour. This is the sense in which we speak of a situation, an action, a demand, a prospect having a certain meaning for a person.

Now it is frequently thought that 'meaning' is used here in a sense which is a kind of illegitimate extension from the notion of linguistic meaning. Whether it can be considered an extension or not is another matter; it certainly differs from linguistic meaning. But it would be very hard to argue that it is an illegitimate use of the term.

When we speak of the 'meaning' of a given predicament, we are using a concept which has the following articulation. (a) Meaning is for a subject: it is not the meaning of the situation *in vacuo*, but its meaning for a subject, a specific subject, a group of subjects, or perhaps what its meaning is for the human subject as such (even though particular humans might be reproached with not admitting or realizing this). (b) Meaning is of something; that is, we can distinguish between a given element — situation, action, or whatever — and its meaning. But this is not to say that they are physically separable. Rather we are dealing with two descriptions of the element, in one of which it is characterized in terms of its meaning for the subject. But the relations between the two descriptions are not symmetrical. For, on the one hand, the description in terms of meaning cannot be unless descriptions of the other kind apply as well; or put differently, there can be no meaning without a substrate. But on the other hand, it may be that the same meaning may be borne by another substrate — e.g., a situation with the same meaning may be realized in different physical conditions. There is a necessary role for a potentially substitutable substrate; or all meanings are of something.

And thirdly, (c) things only have meaning in a field, that is, in relation to the meanings of other things. This means that there is no such thing as a single, unrelated meaningful element; and it means that changes in the other meanings in the field can involve changes in the given element. Meanings cannot be identified except in relation to others, and in this way resemble words. The meaning of a word depends, for instance, on those words with which it contrasts, on those which define its place in the language (e.g. those defining 'determinable' dimensions, like colour, shape), on those which define the activity or 'language game' it figures in (describing, invoking, establishing communion), and so on. The relations between meanings in this sense are like those between concepts in a semantic field.

Just as our colour concepts are given their meaning by the field of contrast they set up together, so that the introduction of new concepts will alter the boundaries of others, so the various meanings that a subordinate's demeanour can have for us, as deferential, respectful, cringing, mildly mocking, ironical, insolent, provoking, downright rude, are established by a field of contrast; and as with finer discrimination on our part, or a more sophisticated culture, new possibilities are born, so other terms of this range are altered. And as the meaning of our terms 'red', 'blue', 'green' is fixed by the definition of a field of contrast through the determinable term 'colour', so all these alternative demeanours are only available in a society which has, among other types, hierarchical relations of power and command. And corresponding to the underlying language game of designating coloured objects is the set of social practices which sustain these hierarchical structures and are fulfilled in them.

Meaning in this sense — let us call it experiential meaning — thus is for a subject, of something, in a field. This distinguishes it from linguistic meaning which has a four and not three-dimensional structure. Linguistic meaning is for subjects and in a field, but it is the meaning of signifiers and it is about a world of referents. Once we are clear about the likenesses and differences, there should be little doubt that the term 'meaning' is not a misnomer, the product of an illegitimate extension into this context of experience and behaviour.

There is thus a quite legitimate notion of meaning which we use when we speak of the meaning of a situation for an agent. And that this concept has a place is integral to our ordinary consciousness and hence speech about our actions. Our actions are ordinarily characterized by the purpose sought and explained by desires, feelings, emotions. But the language by which we describe our goals, feelings, desires is also a definition of the meaning things have for us. The vocabulary defining meaning — words like 'terrifying', 'attractive' — is linked with that describing feeling — 'fear', 'desire' — and that describing goals — 'safety', 'possession'.

Moreover, our understanding of these terms moves inescapably in a hermeneutical circle. An emotion term like 'shame', for instance, essentially refers us to a certain kind of situation, the 'shameful', or 'humiliating', and a certain mode of response, that of hiding oneself, of covering up, or else 'wiping out' the blot. That is, it is essential to this feeling's being identified as shame that it be related to this situation and give rise to this type of disposition. But this situation in its turn can only be identified in relation to the feelings which it provokes; and the disposition is to a goal which can similarly not be understood without reference to the feelings experienced: the 'hiding' in question is one which will cover up my shame; it is not the same as hiding from an armed pursuer; we can only understand what is meant by 'hiding' here if we understand what kind of feeling and situation is being talked about. We have to be within the circle.

An emotion term like 'shame' can only be explained by reference to other concepts which in turn cannot be understood without reference to shame. To understand these concepts we have to be in on a certain experience, we have to understand a certain language, not just of words, but also a certain language of mutual action and communication, by which we blame, exhort, admire, esteem each other. In the end we are in on this because we grow up in the ambit of certain common meanings. But we can often experience what it is like to be on the outside when we encounter the feeling, action, and experiential meaning language of another civilization. Here there is no translation, no way of explaining in other, more accessible concepts. We can only catch on by getting somehow into their way of life, if only in imagination. Thus if we look at human behaviour as action done out of a background of desire, feeling, emotion, then we are looking at a reality which must be characterized in terms of meaning. But does this mean that it can be the object of a hermeneutical science as this was outlined above?

There are, to remind ourselves, three characteristics that the object of a science of interpretation has: it must have sense or coherence; this must be distinguishable from its expression, and this sense must be for a subject.

Now in so far as we are talking about behaviour as action, hence in terms of meaning, the category of sense or coherence must apply to it. This is not to say that all behaviour must 'make sense', if we mean by this be rational, avoid contradiction, confusion of purpose, and the like. Plainly a great deal of our action falls short of this goal. But in another sense, even contradictory, irrational action is 'made sense of', when we understand why it was engaged in. We make sense of action when there is a coherence between the actions of the agent and the meaning of his situation for him. We find his action puzzling until we find such a coherence. It may not be bad to repeat that this coherence in no way implies that the action is rational: the meaning of a situation for an agent may be full of confusion and contradiction; but the adequate depiction of this contradiction makes sense of it.

Making sense in this way through coherence of meaning and action, the meanings of action and situation, cannot but move in a

hermeneutical circle. Our conviction that the account makes sense
is contingent on our reading of action and situation. But these
readings cannot be explained or justified except by reference to
other such readings, and their relation to the whole. If an interlocutor does not understand this kind of reading, or will not accept it as
valid, there is nowhere else the argument can go. Ultimately, a good
explanation is one which makes sense of the behaviour; but then to
appreciate a good explanation, one has to agree on what makes
good sense; what makes good sense is a function of one's readings;
and these in turn are based on the kind of sense one understands.

But how about the second characteristic, that sense should be
distinguishable from its embodiment? This is necessary for a science
of interpretation because interpretation lays a claim to make a
confused meaning clearer; hence there must be some sense in which
the 'same' meaning is expressed, but differently.

This immediately raises a difficulty. In talking of experiential
meaning above, I mentioned that we can distinguish between a
given element and its meaning, between meaning and substrate.
This carried the claim that a given meaning *may* be realized in
another substrate. But does this mean that we can *always* embody
the same meaning in another situation? Perhaps there are some
situations, standing before death, for instance, which have a
meaning which cannot be embodied otherwise.

But fortunately this difficult question is irrelevant for our purposes. For here we have a case in which the analogy between text
and behaviour implicit in the notion of a hermeneutical science of
man only applies with important modifications. The text is replaced
in the interpretation by another text, one which is clearer. The text-
analogue of behaviour is not replaced by another such text-
analogue. When this happens we have revolutionary theatre, or
terroristic acts designed to make propaganda of the deed, in which
the hidden relations of a society are supposedly shown up in a
dramatic confrontation. But this is not scientific understanding,
even though it may perhaps be based on such understanding, or
claim to be.

But in science the text-analogue is replaced by a text, an account.
Which might prompt the question, how we can even begin to talk of
interpretation here, of expressing the same meaning more clearly,
when we have two such utterly different terms of comparison, a text
and a tract of behaviour? Is the whole thing not just a bad pun?

This question leads us to open up another aspect of experiential
meaning which we abstracted from earlier. Experiential meanings

are defined in fields of contrast, as words are in semantic fields.

But what was not mentioned above is that these two kinds of definition are not independent of each other. The range of human desires, feelings, emotions, and hence meanings is bound up with the level and type of culture, which in turn is inseparable from the distinctions and categories marked by the language people speak. The field of meanings in which a given situation can find its place is bound up with the semantic field of the terms characterizing these meanings and the related feelings, desires, predicaments.

But the relationship involved here is not a simple one. There are two simple types of models of relation which could be offered here, but both are inadequate. We could think of the feeling vocabulary as simply describing pre-existing feelings, as marking distinctions which would be there without them. But this is not adequate because we often experience in ourselves or others how achieving, say, a more sophisticated vocabulary of the emotions makes our emotional life more sophisticated and not just our descriptions of it. Reading a good, powerful novel may give me the picture of an emotion which I had not previously been aware of. But we cannot draw a neat line between an increased ability to identify and an altered ability to feel emotions which this enables.

The other simple inadequate model of the relationship is to jump from the above to the conclusion that thinking makes it so. But this clearly will not do either, since not just any new definition can be forced on us, nor can we force it on ourselves; and some which we do gladly take up can be judged inauthentic, or in bad faith, or just wrong-headed by others. These judgments may be wrong, but they are not in principle illicit. Rather we make an effort to be lucid about ourselves and our feelings, and admire a man who achieves this.

Thus, neither the simple correspondence view is correct, nor the view that thinking makes it so. But both have prima facie warrant. There is such a thing as self-lucidity, which points us to a correspondence view; but the achievement of such lucidity means moral change, that is, it changes the object known. At the same time, error about oneself is not just an absence of correspondence; it is also in some form inauthenticity, bad faith, self-delusion, repression of one's human feelings, or something of the kind; it is a matter of the quality of what is felt just as much as what is known about this, just as self-knowledge is.

If this is so, then we have to think of man as a self-interpreting animal. He is necessarily so, for there is no such thing as the structure of meanings for him independently of his interpretation of them; for one is woven into the other. But then the text of our interpretation is not that heterogeneous from what is interpreted: for what is interpreted is itself an interpretation; a self-interpretation which is embedded in a stream of action. It is an interpretation of experiential meaning which contributes to the constitution of this meaning. Or to put it in another way: that of which we are trying to find the coherence is itself partly constituted by self-interpretation.

Our aim is to replace this confused, incomplete, partly erroneous self-interpretation by a correct one. And in doing this we look not only to the self-interpretation but to the stream of behaviour in which it is set; just as in interpreting a historical document we have to place it in the stream of events which it relates to. But of course the analogy is not exact, for here we are interpreting the interpretation and the stream of behaviour in which it is set together, and not just one or the other.

There is thus no utter heterogeneity of interpretation of what it is about; rather there is a slide in the notion of interpretation. Already to be a living agent is to experience one's situation in terms of certain meanings; and this in a sense can be thought of as a sort of proto-'interpretation'. This is in turn interpreted and shaped by the language in which the agent lives these meanings. This whole is then at a third level interpreted by the explanation we proffer of his actions.

In this way the second condition of a hermeneutical science is met. But this account poses in a new light the question mentioned at the beginning whether the interpretation can ever express the same meaning as the interpreted. And in this case, there is clearly a way in which the two will not be congruent. For if the explanation is really clearer than the lived interpretation then it will be such that it would alter in some way the behaviour if it came to be internalized by the agent as his self-interpretation. In this way a hermeneutical science which achieves its goal, that is, attains greater clarity than the immediate understanding of agent or observer, must offer us an interpretation which is in this way crucially out of phase with the explicandum.

Thus, human behaviour seen as action of agents who desire and are moved, who have goals and aspirations, necessarily offers a purchase for descriptions in terms of meaning — what I have called 'experiential meaning'. The norm of explanation which it posits is one which 'makes sense' of the behaviour, which shows a coherence of meaning. This 'making sense of' is the profferring of an interpretation; and we have seen that what is interpreted meets the conditions of a science of interpretation: first, that we can speak of its sense or coherence; and second, that this sense can be expressed in another form, so that we can speak of the interpretation as giving clearer expression to what is only implicit in the explicandum. The third condition, that this sense be for a subject, is obviously met in this case, although who this subject is is by no means an unproblematical question as we shall see later on.

This should be enough to show that there is a good prima facie case to the effect that men and their actions are amenable to explanation of a hermeneutical kind. There is, therefore, some reason to raise the issue and challenge the epistemological orientation which would rule interpretation out of the sciences of man. A great deal more must be said to bring out what is involved in the hermeneutical sciences of man. But before getting on to this, it might help to clarify the issue with a couple of examples drawn from a specific field, that of politics.

II

(i)

In politics, too, the goal of a verifiable science has led to the concentration on features which can supposedly be identified in abstraction from our understanding or not understanding experiential meaning. These — let us call them brute data identifications — are what supposedly enable us to break out from the hermeneutical circle and found our science four square on a verification procedure which meets the requirements of the empiricist tradition.

But in politics the search for such brute data has not gone to the lengths which it has in psychology, where the object of science has been thought of by many as behaviour qua 'colourless movement', or as machine-recognizable properties. The tendency in politics has been to stop with something less basic, but — so it is thought — the identification of which cannot be challenged by the offering of another interpretation or reading of the data concerned (pp. 159*ff*. above). This is what is referred to as 'behaviour' in the rhetoric of political scientists, but it has not the rock bottom quality of its psychological homonym.

Political behaviour includes what we would ordinarily call actions, but ones that are supposedly brute data identifiable. How can this be so? Well, actions are usually described by the purpose or end-state realized. But the purposes of some actions can be specified in what might be thought to be brute data terms; some actions, for instance, have physical end-states, like getting the car in the garage or climbing the mountain. Others have end-states which are closely tied by institutional rules to some unmistakable physical movement; thus, when I raise my hand in the meeting at the appropriate time, I am voting for the motion. The only questions we can raise about the corresponding actions, given such movements or the realization of such end-states, are whether the agent was aware of what he was doing, was acting as against simply emitting reflex behaviour, knew the institutional significance of his movement, etc. Any worries on this score generally turn out to be pretty artificial in the contexts political scientists are concerned with; and where they do arise they can be checked by relatively simple devices, e.g., asking the subject: did you mean to vote for the motion?

Hence, it would appear that there are actions which can be identified beyond fear of interpretative dispute; and this is what gives the foundation for the category of 'political behaviour'. Thus, there are some acts of obvious political relevance which can be specified thus in physical terms, such as killing, sending tanks into the streets, seizing people and confining them to cells; and there is an immense range of others which can be specified from physical acts by institutional rules, such as voting for instance. These can be the object of a science of politics which can hope to meet the stringent requirements of verification. The latter class particularly has provided matter for study in recent decades — most notably in the case of voting studies.

But of course a science of politics confined to such acts would be much too narrow. For on another level these actions also have meaning for the agents which is not exhausted in the brute data descriptions, and which is often crucial to understanding why they were done. Thus, in voting for the motion I am also saving the honour of my party, or defending the value of free speech, or vindicating public morality, or saving civilization from breakdown. It is in such terms that the agents talk about the motivation of much of their political action, and it is difficult to conceive a science of politics which does not come to grips with it.

Behavioural political science comes to grips with it by taking the meanings involved in action as facts about the agent, his beliefs, his affective reactions, his 'values', as the term is frequently used. For it can be thought verifiable in the brute data sense that men will agree to subscribe or not to a certain form of words (expressing a belief, say); or express a positive or negative reaction to certain events, or symbols; or agree or not with the proposition that some act is right or wrong. We can thus get at meanings as just another form of brute data by the techniques of the opinion survey and content analysis.

An immediate objection springs to mind. If we are trying to deal with the meanings which inform political action, then surely interpretative acumen is unavoidable. Let us say we are trying to understand the goals and values of a certain group, or grasp their vision of the polity; we might try to probe this by a questionnaire asking them whether they assent or not to a number of propositions, which are meant to express different goals, evaluations, beliefs. But how did we design the questionnaire? How did we pick these propositions? Here we relied on our understanding of the goals, values, vision involved. But then this understanding can be challenged, and hence the significance of our results questioned. Perhaps the finding of our study, the compiling of proportions of assent and dissent to these propositions is irrelevant, is without significance for understanding the agents or the polity concerned. This kind of attack is frequently made by critics of mainstream political science, or for that matter social science in general.

To this the proponents of this mainstream reply with a standard move of logical empiricism: distinguishing the process of discovery from the logic of verification. Of course, it is our understanding of these meanings which enables us to draw up the questionnaire which will test people's attitudes in respect to them. And, of course, interpretative dispute about these meanings is potentially endless; there are no brute data at this level, every affirmation can be challenged by a rival interpretation. But this has nothing to do with verifiable science. What is firmly verified is the set of correlations between, say, the assent to certain propositions and certain behaviour. We discover, for instance, that people who are active politically (defined by participation in a certain set of institutions) are more likely to consent to certain sets of propositions supposedly expressing the values underlying the system[6]. This finding is a firmly verified correlation no matter what one thinks of the reasoning, or simple hunches, that went into designing the research which established it. Political science as a body of knowledge is made up of such correlations; it does not give a truth value to the background reasoning or hunch. A good interpretative nose may be useful in hitting on the right correlations to test, but science is never called on to arbitrate the disputes between interpretations.

Thus, in addition to those overt acts which can be defined

physically or institutionally, the category of political behaviour can include assent or dissent to verbal formulae, or the occurrence or not of verbal formulae in speech, or expressions of approval or rejection of certain events or measures as observed in institutionally-defined behaviour (for instance, turning out for a demonstration).

Now there are a number of objections which can be made to this notion of political behaviour; one might question in all sorts of ways how interpretation-free it is in fact. But I would like to question it from another angle. One of the basic characteristics of this kind of social science is that it reconstructs reality in line with certain categorial principles. These allow for an intersubjective social reality which is made up of brute data, identifiable acts and structures, certain institutions, procedures, actions. It allows for beliefs, affective reactions, evaluations as the psychological properties of individuals. And it allows for correlations between these two orders or reality: e.g., that certain beliefs go along with certain acts, certain values with certain institutions, etc.

To put it another way, what is objectively (intersubjectively) real is brute data identifiable. This is what social reality *is*. Social reality described in terms of its meaning for the actors, such that disputes could arise about interpretation which could not be settled by brute data (e.g., are people rioting to get a hearing, or are they rioting to redress humiliation, out of blind anger, because they recover a sense of dignity in insurrection?), this is given subjective reality, that is, there are certain beliefs, affective reactions, evaluations which individuals make or have about or in relation to social reality. These beliefs or reactions can have an effect on this reality; and the fact that such a belief is held is a fact of objective social reality. But the social reality which is the object of these attitudes, beliefs, reactions can only be made up of brute data. Thus any description of reality in terms of meanings which is open to interpretative question is only allowed into this scientific discourse if it is placed, as it were, in quotes and attributed to individuals as their opinion, belief, attitude. That this opinion, belief, etc. is held is thought of as a brute datum, since it is redefined as the respondents giving a certain answer to the questionnaire.

This aspect of social reality which concerns its meanings for the agents has been taken up in a number of ways, but recently it has been spoken of in terms of political culture. Now the way this is defined and studied illustrates clearly the categorial principles above. For instance, political culture is referred to by Almond and Powell[7] as the 'psychological dimension of the political system'

(p. 23). Further on they state: 'Political culture is the pattern of individual attitudes and orientations towards politics among the members of a political system. It is the subjective realm which underlies and gives meaning to political actions' (p. 50). The authors then go on to distinguish three different kinds of orientations, cognitive (knowledge and beliefs), affective (feelings), and evaluative (judgments and opinions).

From the point of view of empiricist epistemology, this set of categorical principles leaves nothing out. Both reality and the meanings it has for actors are coped with. But what it in fact cannot allow for are intersubjective meanings, that is, it cannot allow for the validity of descriptions of social reality in terms of meanings, hence not as brute data, which are not in quotation marks and attributed as opinion, attitude, etc. to individual(s). Now it is this exclusion that I would like to challenge in the name of another set of categorical principles, inspired by a quite other epistemology.

(ii)

We spoke earlier about the brute data identification of acts by means of institutional rules. Thus, putting a cross beside someone's name on a slip of paper and putting this in a box counts in the right context as voting for that person; leaving the room, saying or writing a certain form of words, counts as breaking off the negotiations; writing one's name on a piece of paper counts as signing the petition, etc. But what is worth looking at is what underlies this set of identifications. These identifications are the application of a language of social life, a language which marks distinctions among different possible social acts, relations, structures. But what underlies this language?

Let us take the example of breaking off negotiations above. The language of our society recognizes states or actions like the following: entering into negotiation, breaking off negotiations, offering to negotiate, negotiating in good (bad) faith, concluding negotiations, making a new offer, etc. In other more jargon-infested language, the semantic 'space' of this range of social activity is carved up in a certain way, by a certain set of distinctions which our vocabulary marks; and the shape and nature of these distinctions is the nature of our language in this area. These distinctions are applied in our society with more or less formalism in different contexts.

But of course this is not true of every society. Our whole notion of negotiation is bound up for instance with the distinct identity and

autonomy of the parties, with the willed nature of their relations; it
is a very contractual notion. But other societies have no such conception. It is reported about the traditional Japanese village that the
foundation of its social life was a powerful form of consensus, which
put a high premium on unanimous decision[8]. Such a consensus
would be considered shattered if two clearly articulated parties were
to separate out, pursuing opposed aims and attempting either to
vote down the opposition or push it into a settlement on the most
favourable possible terms for themselves. Discussion there must be,
and some kind of adjustment of differences. But our idea of bargaining, with the assumption of distinct autonomous parties in willed
relationship, has no place there; nor does a series of distinctions, like
entering into and leaving negotiation, or bargaining in good faith
(i.e. with the genuine intention of seeking agreement).

Now the difference between our society and one of the kind just
described could not be well expressed if we said we have a
vocabulary to describe negotiation which they lack. We might say,
for instance, that we have a vocabulary to describe the heavens that
they lack, viz., that of Newtonian mechanics; for here we assume
that they live under the same heavens as we do, only understand it
differently. But it is not true that they have the same kind of
bargaining as we do. The word, or whatever word of their language
we translate as 'bargaining', must have an entirely different gloss,
which is marked by the distinctions their vocabulary allows in
contrast to those marked by ours. But this different gloss is not just a
difference of vocabulary, but also one of social reality.

But this still may be misleading as a way of putting the difference.
For it might imply that there is a social reality which can be
discovered in each society and which might exist quite independently of the vocabulary of that society, or indeed of any vocabulary, as the heavens would exist whether men theorized about them
or not. And this is not the case; the realities here are practices; and
these cannot be identified in abstraction from the language we use
to describe them, or invoke them, or carry them out. That the
practice of negotiation allows us to distinguish bargaining in good
or bad faith, or entering into or breaking off negotiations, presupposes that our acts and situation have a certain description for us,
e.g., that we are distinct parties entering into willed relations. But
they cannot have these descriptions for us unless this is somehow
expressed in our vocabulary of this practice; if not in our descriptions of the practices (for we may as yet be unconscious of some of
the important distinctions) in the appropriate language for carrying

them on. (Thus, the language marking a distinction between public and private acts or contexts may exist even where these terms or their equivalents are not part of this language; for the distinction will be marked by the different language which is appropriate in one context and the other, be it perhaps a difference of style, or dialect, even though the distinction is not designated by specific descriptive expressions.)

The situation we have here is one in which the vocabulary of a given social dimension is grounded in the shape of social practice in this dimension; that is, the vocabulary would not make sense, could not be applied sensibly, where this range of practices did not prevail. And yet this range of practices could not exist without the prevalence of this or some related vocabulary. There is no simple one-way dependence here. We can speak of mutual dependence if we like, but really what this points up is the artificiality of the distinction between social reality and the language of description of that social reality. The language is constitutive of reality, is essential to its being the kind of reality it is. To separate the two and distinguish them as we quite rightly distinguish the heavens from our theories about them is forever to miss the point.

This type of relation has been recently explored, e.g., by John Searle, with his concept of a constitutive rule. As Searle points out[9], we are normally induced to think of rules as applying to behaviour which could be available to us whether or not the rule existed. Some rules are like this, they are regulative like commandments: don't take the goods of another. But there are other rules, e.g., that governing the Queen's move in chess, which are not so separable. If one suspends these rules, or imagines a state in which they have not yet been introduced, then the whole range of behaviour in question, in this case, chess playing, would not be. There would still, of course, be the activity of pushing a wood piece around on a board made of squares eight by eight; but this is not chess any longer. Rules of this kind are constitutive rules. By contrast again, there are other rules of chess, such as that one says 'j'adoube' when one touches a piece without intending to play it, which are clearly regulative[10].

I am suggesting that this notion of the constitutive be extended beyond the domain of rule-governed behaviour. That is why I suggest the vaguer word 'practice'. Even in an area where there are no clearly defined rules, there are distinctions between different sorts of behaviour such that one sort is considered the appropriate form for one action or context, the other for another action or context; e.g. doing or saying certain things amounts to breaking off negotiations, doing or saying other things amounts to making a new offer. But just as there are constitutive rules, i.e. rules such that the behaviour they govern could not exist without them, and which are in this sense inseparable from that behaviour, so I am suggesting that there are constitutive distinctions, constitutive ranges of language which are similarly inseparable, in that certain practices are not without them.

We can reverse this relationship and say that all the institutions and practices by which we live are constituted by certain distinctions and hence a certain language which is thus essential to them. We can take voting, a practice which is central to large numbers of institutions in a democratic society. What is essential to the practice of voting is that some decision or verdict be delivered (a man elected, a measure passed), through some criterion of preponderance (simple majority, two-thirds majority, or whatever) out of a set of micro-choices (the votes of the citizens, MPs, delegates). If there is not some such significance attached to our behaviour, no amount of marking and counting pieces of paper, raising hands, walking out into lobbies amounts to voting. From this it follows that the institution of voting must be such that certain distinctions have application; e.g., that between someone being elected, or a measure passed, and their failing of election, or passage; that between a valid vote and an invalid one which in turn requires a distinction between a real choice and one which is forced or counterfeited. For no matter how far we move from the Rousseauian notion that each man decide in full autonomy, the very institution of the vote requires that in some sense the enfranchised choose. For there to be voting in a sense recognizably like ours, there must be a distinction in men's self-interpretations between autonomy and forced choice.

This is to say that an activity of marking and counting papers has to bear intentional descriptions which fall within a certain range before we can agree to call it voting, just as the intercourse of two men or teams has to bear descriptions of a certain range before we will call it negotiation. Or in other words, that some practice is voting or negotiation has to do in part with the vocabulary established in a society as appropriate for engaging in it or describing it.

Hence implicit in these practices is a certain vision of the agent and his relation to others and to society. We saw in connection with negotiation in our society that it requires a picture of the parties as in some sense autonomous, and as entering into willed relations.

And this picture carries with it certain implicit norms, such as that of good faith mentioned above, or a norm of rationality, that agreement correspond to one's goals as far as attainable, or the norm of continued freedom of action as far as attainable. These practices require that one's actions and relations be seen in the light of this picture and the accompanying norms, good faith, autonomy, and rationality. But men do not see themselves in this way in all societies, nor do they understand these norms in all societies. The experience of autonomy as we know it, the sense of rational action and the satisfactions thereof, are unavailable to them. The meaning of these terms is opaque to them because they have a different structure of experiential meaning open to them.

We can think of the difference between our society and the simplified version of the traditional Japanese village as consisting in this, that the range of meaning open to the members of the two societies is very different. But what we are dealing with here is not subjective meaning which can fit into the categorial grid of behavioural political science, but rather intersubjective meanings. It is not just that the people in our society all or mostly have a given set of ideas in their heads and subscribe to a given set of goals. The meanings and norms implicit in these practices are not just in the minds of the actors but are out there in the practices themselves, practices which cannot be conceived as a set of individual actions, but which are essentially modes of social relation, of mutual action.

The actors may have all sorts of beliefs and attitudes which may be rightly thought of as their individual beliefs and attitudes, even if others share them; they may subscribe to certain policy goals or certain forms of theory about the polity, or feel resentment at certain things, and so on. They bring these with them into their negotiations, and strive to satisfy them. But what they do not bring into the negotiations is the set of ideas and norms constitutive of negotiation themselves. These must be the common property of the society before there can be any question of anyone entering into negotiation or not. Hence they are not subjective meanings, the property of one or some individuals, but rather intersubjective meanings, which are constitutive of the social matrix in which individuals find themselves and act.

The intersubjective meanings which are the background to the social action are often treated by political scientists under the heading 'consensus'. By this is meant convergence of beliefs on certain basic matters, or of attitude. But the two are not the same. Whether there is consensus or not, the condition of there being either one or the other is a certain set of common terms of reference. A society in which this was lacking would not be a society in the normal sense of the term, but several. Perhaps some multi-racial or multi-tribal states approach this limit. Some multinational states are bedevilled by consistent cross-purposes, e.g., my own country. But consensus as a convergence of beliefs or values is not the opposite of this kind of fundamental diversity. Rather the opposite of diversity is a high degree of intersubjective meanings. And this can go along with profound cleavage. Indeed, intersubjective meanings are a condition of a certain kind of very profound cleavage, such as was visible in the Reformation, or the American Civil War, or splits in left wing parties, where the dispute is at fever pitch just because both sides can fully understand the other.

In other words, convergence of belief or attitude or its absence presupposes a common language in which these beliefs can be formulated, and in which these formulations can be opposed. Much of this common language in any society is rooted in its institutions and practices; it is constitutive of these institutions and practices. It is part of the intersubjective meanings. To put the point another way, apart from the question of how much people's beliefs converge is the question of how much they have a common language of social and political reality in which these beliefs are expressed. This second question cannot be reduced to the first; intersubjective meaning is not a matter of converging beliefs or values. When we speak of consensus we speak of beliefs and values which could be the property of a single person, or many, or all; but intersubjective meanings could not be the property of a single person because they are rooted in social practice.

We can perhaps see this if we envisage the situation in which the ideas and norms underlying a practice are the property of single individuals. This is what happens when single individuals from one society interiorize the notions and values of another, e.g., children in missionary schools. Here we have a totally different situation. We *are* really talking now about subjective beliefs and attitudes. The ideas are abstract, they are mere social 'ideals'. Whereas in the original society, these ideas and norms are rooted in their social relations, and are that on the basis of which they can formulate opinions and ideals.

We can see this in connection with the example we have been using all along, that of negotiations. The vision of a society based on negotiation is coming in for heavy attack by a growing segment of modern youth, as are the attendant norms of rationality and the definition of autonomy. This is a dramatic failure of 'consensus'. But this cleavage takes place in the ambit of this intersubjective meaning, the social practice of negotiation as it is lived in our society. The rejection would not have the bitter quality it has if what is rejected were not understood in common, because it is part of a social practice which we find it hard to avoid, so pervasive is it in our society. At the same time there is a reaching out for other forms which have still the 'abstract' quality of ideals which are subjective in this sense, that is, not rooted in practice; which is what makes the rebellion look so 'unreal' to outsiders, and so irrational.

(iii)

Intersubjective meanings, ways of experiencing action in society which are expressed in the language and descriptions constitutive of institutions and practices, do not fit into the categorial grid of mainstream political science. This allows only for an intersubjective reality which is brute data identifiable. But social practices and institutions which are partly constituted by certain ways of talking about them are not so identifiable. We have to understand the language, the underlying meanings, which constitute them.

We can allow, once we accept a certain set of institutions or practices as our starting point and not as objects of further questioning, that we can easily take as brute data that certain acts are judged to take place or certain states judged to hold within the semantic field of these practices. For instance, that someone has voted Liberal, or signed the petition. We can then go on to correlate certain subjective meanings — beliefs, attitudes, etc. — with this behaviour or its lack. But this means that we give up trying to define further just what these practices and institutions are, what the meanings are which they require and hence sustain. For these meanings do not fit into the grid; they are not subjective beliefs or values, but are constitutive of social reality. In order to get at them we have to drop the basic premise that social reality is made up of brute data alone. For any characterization of the meanings under-lying these practices is open to question by someone offering an alternative interpretation. The negation of this is what was meant as brute data. We have to admit that intersubjective social reality has to be partly defined in terms of meanings; that meanings as subjective are not just in causal interaction with a social reality made up of brute data, but that as intersubjective they are constitutive of this reality.

We have been talking here of intersubjective meanings. And earlier I was contrasting the question of intersubjective meaning with that of consensus as convergence of opinions. But there is another kind of non-subjective meaning which is also often inadequately discussed under the head of 'consensus'. In a society with a strong web of intersubjective meanings, there can be a more or less powerful set of common meanings. By these I mean notions of what is significant which are not just shared in the sense that everyone has them, but are also common in the sense of being in the common reference world. Thus, almost everyone in our society may share a susceptibility to a certain kind of feminine beauty, but this may not be a common meaning. It may be known to no one, except perhaps market researchers, who play on it in their advertisements. But the survival of a national identity as francophones is a common meaning of *Québecois*; for it is not just shared, and not just known to be shared, but its being a common aspiration is one of the common reference points of all debate, communication, and all public life in the society.

We can speak of a shared belief, aspiration, etc. when there is convergence between the subjective beliefs, aspirations, of many individuals. But it is part of the meaning of a common aspiration, belief, celebration, etc. that it be not just shared but part of the common reference world. Or to put it another way, its being shared is a collective act, it is a consciousness which is communally sustained, whereas sharing is something we do each on his own as it were, even if each of us is influenced by the others.

Common meanings are the basis of community. Intersubjective meaning gives a people a common language to talk about social reality and a common understanding of certain norms, but only with common meanings does this common reference world contain significant common actions, celebrations, and feelings. These are objects in the world that everybody shares. This is what makes community.

Once again, we cannot really understand this phenomenon through the usual definition of consensus as convergence of opinion and value. For what is meant here is something more than convergence. Convergence is what happens when our values are shared. But what is required for common meanings is that this shared value be part of the common world, that this sharing be shared. But we could also say that common meanings are quite other than consensus, for they can subsist with a high degree of cleavage; this is what happens when a common meaning comes to be lived and understood differently by different groups in a society. It remains a common meaning, because there is the reference point which is the common purpose, aspiration, celebration. Such is for example the American Way, or freedom as understood in the USA. But this common meaning is differently articulated by different groups. This is the basis of the bitterest fights in a society, and this we are also seeing in the US today. Perhaps one might say that a common meaning is very often the cause of the most bitter lack of consensus. It thus must not be confused with convergence of opinion, value, attitude.

Of course, common meanings and intersubjective meanings are closely interwoven. There must be a powerful net of intersubjective meanings for there to be common meanings; and the result of powerful common meanings is the development of a greater web of intersubjective meanings as people live in community.

On the other hand, when common meanings wither, which they can do through the kind of deep dissensus we described earlier, the groups tend to grow apart and develop different languages of social reality, hence to share less intersubjective meanings.

Hence, to take our above example again, there has been a powerful common meaning in our civilization around a certain vision of the free society in which bargaining has a central place. This has helped to entrench the social practice of negotiation which makes us participate in this intersubjective meaning. But there is a severe challenge to this common meaning today, as we have seen. Should those who object to it really succeed in building up an alternative society, there would develop a gap between those who remain in the present type of society and those who had founded the new one.

Common meanings, as well as intersubjective ones, fall through the net of mainstream social science. They can find no place in its categories. For they are not simply a converging set of subjective reactions, but part of the common world. What the ontology of mainstream social science lacks is the notion of meaning as not simply for an individual subject; of a subject who can be a 'we' as well as an 'I'. The exclusion of this possibility, of the communal, comes once again from the baleful influence of the epistemological tradition for which all knowledge has to be reconstructed from the impressions imprinted on the individual subject. But if we free ourselves from the hold of these prejudices, this seems a wildly implausible view about the development of human consciousness; we are aware of the world through a 'we' before we are through an

'I'. Hence we need the distinction between what is just shared in the sense that each of us has it in our individual worlds, and that which is in the common world. But the very idea of something which is in the common world in contradistinction to what is in all the individual worlds is totally opaque to empiricist epistemology. Hence it finds no place in mainstream social science. What this results in must now be seen.

III

(i)

Thus, to sum up the last pages: a social science which wishes to fulfil the requirements of the empiricist tradition naturally tries to reconstruct social reality as consisting of brute data alone. These data are the acts of people (behaviour) as identified supposedly beyond interpretation either by physical descriptions or by descriptions clearly defined by institutions and practices; and secondly, they include the subjective reality of individuals' beliefs, attitudes, values, as attested by their responses to certain forms of words, or in some cases their overt non-verbal behaviour.

What this excludes is a consideration of social reality as characterized by intersubjective and common meanings. It excludes, for instance, an attempt to understand our civilization, in which negotiation plays such a central part both in fact and in justificatory theory, by probing the self-definitions of agent, other and social relatedness which it embodies. Such definitions which deal with the meaning for agents of their own and others' action, and of the social relations in which they stand, do not in any sense record brute data, in the sense that this term is being used in this argument; that is, they are in no sense beyond challenge by those who would quarrel with our interpretations of these meanings.

Thus, I tried to adumbrate above the vision implicit in the practice of negotiation by reference to certain notions of autonomy and rationality. But this reading will undoubtedly be challenged by those who have different fundamental conceptions of man, human motivation, the human condition; or even by those who judge other features of our present predicament to have greater importance. If we wish to avoid these disputes, and have a science grounded in verification as this is understood by the logical empiricists, then we have to avoid this level of study altogether and hope to make do with a correlation of behaviour which is brute data identifiable.

A similar point goes for the distinction between common meanings and shared subjective meanings. We can hope to identify the subjective meanings of individuals if we take these in the sense in which there are adequate criteria for them in people's dissent or assent to verbal formulae or their brute data identifiable behaviour. But once we allow the distinction between such subjective meanings which are widely shared and genuine common meanings, then we can no longer make do with brute data identification. We are in a domain where our definitions can be challenged by those with another reading.

The profound option of mainstream social scientists for the empiricist conception of knowledge and science makes it inevitable that they should accept the verification model of political science and the categorial principles that this entails. This means in turn that a study of our civilization in terms of its intersubjective and common meanings is ruled out. Rather this whole level of study is made invisible.

On the mainstream view, therefore, the different practices and institutions of different societies are not seen as related to different clusters of intersubjective or common meanings, rather, we should be able to differentiate them by different clusters of 'behaviour' and/or subjective meaning. The comparison between societies requires on this view that we elaborate a universal vocabulary of behaviour which will allow us to present the different forms and practices of different societies in the same conceptual web.

Now present day political science is contemptuous of the older attempt at comparative politics via a comparison of institutions. An influential school of our day has therefore shifted comparison to certain practices, or very general classes of practices, and proposes to compare societies according to the different ways in which these practices are carried on. Such are the 'functions' of the influential 'developmental approach'[11]. But it is epistemologically crucial that such functions be identified independently of those intersubjective meanings which are different in different societies; for otherwise, they will not be genuinely universal; or will be universal only in the loose and unilluminating sense that the function-name can be given application in every society but with varying, and often widely varying meaning — the same term being 'glossed' very differently by different sets of practices and intersubjective meanings. The danger that such universality might not hold is not even suspected by mainstream political scientists since they are unaware that there is such a level of description as that which defines intersubjective

meanings and are convinced that functions and the various structures which perform them can be identified in terms of brute data
behaviour.

But the result of ignoring the difference in intersubjective
meanings can be disastrous to a science of comparative politics, viz.,
that we interpret all other societies in the categories of our own.
Ironically, this is what seems to have happened to American
political science. Having strongly criticized the old institution-
focused comparative politics for its ethnocentricity (or Western
bias), it proposes to understand the politics of all society in terms of
such functions, for instance, as 'interest articulation' and 'interest
aggregation' whose definition is strongly influenced by the bargaining culture of our civilization, but which is far from being guaranteed appropriateness elsewhere. The not surprising result is a theory
of political development which places the Atlantic-type polity at the
summit of human political achievement.

Much can be said in this area of comparative politics (interestingly explored by Alasdair MacIntyre in a recently published
paper)[12]. But I would like to illustrate the significance of these two
rival approaches in connection with another common problem area
of politics. This is the question of what is called 'legitimacy'[13].

(ii)

It is an obvious fact, with which politics has been concerned since at
least Plato, that some societies enjoy an easier, more spontaneous
cohesion which relies less on the use of force than others. It has been
an important question of political theory to understand what
underlies this difference. Among others, Aristotle, Machiavelli,
Montesquieu, de Tocqueville have dealt with it.

Contemporary mainstream political scientists approach this question with the concept 'legitimacy'. The use of the word here can be
easily understood. Those societies which are more spontaneously
cohesive can be thought to enjoy a greater sense of legitimacy
among their members. But the application of the term has been
shifted. 'Legitimacy' is a term in which we discuss the authority of
the state or polity, its right to our allegiance. However we conceive
of this legitimacy, it can only be attributed to a polity in the light of
a number of surrounding conceptions — e.g., that it provides men
freedom, that it emanates from their will, that it secures them
order, the rule of law, or that it is founded on tradition, or
commands obedience by its superior qualities. These conceptions

are all such that they rely on definitions of what is significant for men in general or in some particular society or circumstances, definitions of paradigmatic meaning which cannot be identifiable as brute data. Even where some of these terms might be given an 'operational definition' in terms of brute data — a term like 'freedom' for instance, can be defined in terms of the absence of legal restriction, *à la* Hobbes — this definition would not carry the full force of the term, and in particular that whereby it could be considered significant for men.

According to the empiricist paradigm, this latter aspect of the meaning of such a term is labelled 'evaluative' and is thought to be utterly heterogeneous from the 'descriptive' aspect. But this analysis is far from firmly established; no more so in fact than the empiricist paradigm of knowledge itself with which it is closely bound up. A challenge to this paradigm in the name of a hermeneutical science is also a challenge to the distinction between 'descriptive' and 'evaluative' and the entire conception of *'Wertfreiheit'* which goes with it.

In any case, whether because it is 'evaluative' or can only be applied in connection with definitions of meaning, 'legitimate' is not a word which can be used in the description of social reality according to the conceptions of mainstream social science. It can only be used as a description of subjective meaning. What enters into scientific consideration is thus not the legitimacy of a polity but the opinions or feelings of its member individuals concerning its legitimacy. The differences between different societies in their manner of spontaneous cohesion and sense of community are to be understood by correlations between the beliefs and feelings of their members towards them on one hand and the prevalence of certain brute data identifiable indices of stability in them on the other.

Thus Robert Dahl in *Modern Political Analysis*[14] (pp. 31-2) speaks of the different ways in which leaders gain 'compliance' for their policies. The more citizens comply because of 'internal rewards and deprivations', the less leaders need to use 'external rewards and deprivations'. But if citizens believe a government is legitimate, then their conscience will bind them to obey it; they will be internally punished if they disobey; hence government will have to use less external resources, including force.

Less crude is the discussion of Seymour Lipset in *Political Man*[15] (Chapter 3). But it is founded on the same basic ideas, viz. that legitimacy defined as subjective meaning is correlated with stability. 'Legitimacy involves the capacity of the system to engender and maintain the belief that the existing political institutions are the most appropriate ones for the society' (p. 64).

Lipset is engaged in a discussion of the determinants of stability in modern politics. He singles out two important ones in this chapter, effectiveness and legitimacy. 'Effectiveness means actual perform-ance, the extent to which the system satisfies the basic functions of government as most of the population and such powerful groups within it as big business or the armed forces see them' (loc. cit.). Thus we have one factor which has to do with objective reality, what the government has actually done; and the other which has to do with subjective beliefs and 'values'. 'While effectiveness is primarily instrumental, legitimacy is evaluative' (loc. cit.). Hence from the beginning the stage is set by a distinction between social reality and what men think and feel about it.

Lipset sees two types of crisis of legitimacy that modern societies have affronted more or less well. One concerns the status of major conservative institutions which may be under threat from the development of modern industrial democracies. The second con-cerns the degree to which all political groups have access to the political process. Thus, under the first head, some traditional groups, such as landed aristocracy or clericals, have been roughly handled in a society like France, and have remained alienated from the democratic system for decades afterwards; whereas in England the traditional classes were more gently handled, themselves were willing to compromise and have been slowly integrated and trans-formed into the new order. Under the second head, some societies managed to integrate the working class or bourgeoisie into the political process at an early stage, whereas in others they have been kept out till quite recently, and consequently, have developed a deep sense of alienation from the system, have tended to adopt extremist ideologies, and have generally contributed to instability. One of the determinants of a society's performance on these two heads is whether or not it is forced to affront the different conflicts of democratic development all at once or one at a time. Another important determinant of legitimacy is effectiveness.

This approach which sees stability as partly the result of legiti-macy beliefs, and these in turn as resulting partly from the way the status, welfare, access to political life of different groups fare, seems at first blush eminently sensible and well designed to help us understand the history of the last century or two. But this approach has no place for a study of the intersubjective and common meanings which are constitutive of modern civilization. And we may doubt whether we can understand the cohesion of modern societies or their present crisis if we leave these out of account.

Let us take the winning of the allegiance of the working class to the new industrial regimes in the nineteenth and early twentieth century. This is far from being a matter simply or even perhaps most significantly of the speed with which this class was integrated into the political process and the effectiveness of the regime. Rather the consideration of the granting of access to the political process as an independent variable may be misleading.

It is not just that we often find ourselves invited by historians to account for class cohesion in particular countries in terms of other factors, such as the impact of Methodism in early nineteenth-century England (Elie Halévy)[16] or the draw of Germany's newly successful nationalism. These factors could be assimilated to the social scientist's grid by being classed as 'ideologies' or widely-held 'value-systems' or some other such concatenations of subjective meaning.

But perhaps the most important such 'ideology' in accounting for the cohesion of industrial democratic societies has been that of the society of work, the vision of society as a large-scale enterprise of production in which widely different functions are integrated into interdependence; a vision of society in which economic relations are considered as primary, as it is not only in Marxism (and in a sense not really with Marxism) but above all with the tradition of Classical Utilitarianism. In line with this vision there is a fundamental solidarity between all members of society that labour (to use Arendt's language)[17], for they are all engaged in producing what is indispensable to life and happiness in far-reaching interdependence.

This is the 'ideology' which has frequently presided over the integration of the working class into industrial democracies, at first directed polemically against the 'unproductive' classes, e.g., in England with the Anti-Corn-Law League, and later with the campaigns of Joseph Chamberlain ('when Adam delved and Eve span/who was then the gentleman'), but later as a support for social cohesion and solidarity.

But, of course, the reason for putting 'ideology' in quotes above is that this definition of things, which has been well integrated with the conception of social life as based on negotiation, cannot be understood in the terms of mainstream social science, as beliefs and 'values' held by a large number of individuals. For the great interdependent matrix of labour is not just a set of ideas in people's heads but is an important aspect of the reality which we live in modern society. And at the same time, these ideas are embedded in this matrix in that they are constitutive of it; that is, we wouldn't be able to live in this type of society unless we were imbued with these ideas or some others which could call forth the discipline and voluntary co-ordination needed to operate this kind of economy. All industrial civilizations have required a huge wrench from the traditional peasant populations on which they have been imposed; for they require an entirely unprecedented level of disciplined, sustained, monotonous effort, long hours unpunctuated by any meaningful rhythm, such as that of seasons or festivals. In the end this way of life can only be accepted when the idea of making a living is endowed with more significance than that of just avoiding starvation; and this it is in the civilization of labour.

Now this civilization of work is only one aspect of modern societies, along with the society based on negotiation and willed relations (in Anglo-Saxon countries), and other common and intersubjective meanings which have different importance in different countries. My point is that it is certainly not implausible to say that it has some importance in explaining the integration of the working class in modern industrial democratic society. But it can only be called a cluster of intersubjective meaning. As such it cannot come into the purview of mainstream political science; and an author like Lipset cannot take it into consideration when discussing this very problem.

But, of course, such a massive fact does not escape notice. What happens rather is that it is re-interpreted. And what has generally happened is that the interdependent productive and negotiating society has been recognized by political science, but not as one structure of intersubjective meaning among others, rather as the inescapable background of social action as such. In this guise it no longer need be an object of study. Rather it retreats to the middle distance, where its general outline takes the role of universal framework, within which (it is hoped) actions and structures will be brute data identifiable, and this for any society at any time. The view is then that the political actions of men in all societies can be understood as variants of the processing of 'demands' which is an important part of our political life. The inability to recognize the specificity of our intersubjective meanings is thus inseparably linked with the belief in the universality of North Atlantic behaviour types or 'functions' which vitiates so much of contemporary comparative politics.

The notion is that what politics is about perennially is the adjustment of differences, or the production of symbolic and effective 'outputs' on the basis of demand and support 'inputs'. The rise of the intersubjective meaning of the civilization of work is seen as the increase of correct perception of the political process at the expense of 'ideology'. Thus Almond and Powell introduce the concept of 'political secularization' to describe 'the emergence of a pragmatic, empirical orientation' to politics[18]. A secular political culture is opposed not only to a traditional one, but also to an 'ideological' culture, which is characterized by 'an inflexible image of political life, closed to conflicting information' and 'fails to develop the open, bargaining attitudes associated with full secularization' (p. 61). The clear understanding here is that a secularized culture is one which essentially depends less on illusion, which sees things are they are, which is not infected with the 'false consciousness' of traditional or ideological culture (to use a term which is not in the mainstream vocabulary).

(iii)

This way of looking at the civilization of work, as resulting from the retreat of illusion before the correct perception of what politics perennially and really is, is thus closely bound up with the epistemological premises of mainstream political science and its resultant inability to recognize the historical specificity of this civilization's intersubjective meanings. But the weakness of this approach, already visible in the attempts to explain the rise of this civilization and its relation to others, becomes even more painful when we try to account for its present malaise, even crisis.

The strains in contemporary society, the breakdown of civility, the rise of deep alienation, which is translated into even more destructive action, tend to shake the basic categories of our social science. It is not just that such a development was quite unpredicted by this science, which saw in the rise of affluence the cause rather of a further entrenching of the bargaining culture, a reduction of irrational cleavage, an increase of tolerance, in short 'the end of ideology'. For prediction, as we shall see below, cannot be a goal of social science as it is of natural science. It is rather that this mainstream science has not the categories to explain this breakdown. It is forced to look on extremism either as a bargaining gambit of the desperate, deliberately raising the ante in order to force a hearing. Or, alternatively, it can recognize the novelty of the rebellion by accepting the hypothesis that heightened demands are being made on the system owing to a revolution of 'expectations', or else to the eruption of new desires or aspirations which hitherto had no place in the bargaining process. But these new desires or aspirations must be in the domain of individual psychology, that is, they must be such that their arousal and satisfaction is to be understood in terms of states of individuals rather than in terms of the intersubjective meanings in which they live. For these latter have no place in the categories of the mainstream, which thus cannot accommodate a genuine historical psychology.

But some of the more extreme protests and acts of rebellion in our society cannot be interpreted as bargaining gambits in the name of any demands, old or new. These can only be interpreted within the accepted framework of our social science as a return to ideology, and hence as irrational. Now in the case of some of the more bizarre and bloody forms of protest, there will be little disagreement; they will be judged irrational by all but their protagonists. But within the accepted categories this irrationality can only be understood in terms of individual psychology; it is the public eruption of private pathology; it cannot be understood as a malady of society itself, a malaise which afflicts its constitutive meanings[19].

No one can claim to begin to have an adequate explanation for these major changes which our civilization is undergoing. But in contrast to the incapacity of a science which remains within the accepted categories, a hermeneutical science of man which has a place for a study of intersubjective meaning can at least begin to explore fruitful avenues. Plainly the discipline which was integral to the civilization of work and bargaining is beginning to fail. The structures of this civilization, interdependent work, bargaining, mutual adjustment of individual ends, are beginning to change their meaning for many, and are beginning to be felt not as normal and best suited to man, but as hateful or empty. And yet we are all caught in these intersubjective meanings in so far as we live in this society, and in a sense more and more all-pervasively as it progresses. Hence the virulence and tension of the critique of our society which is always in some real sense a self-rejection (in a way that the old socialist opposition never was).

Why has this set of meanings gone sour? Plainly, we have to accept that they are not to be understood at their face value. The free, productive, bargaining culture claimed to be sufficient for man. If it was not, then we have to assume that while it did hold our allegiance, it also had other meanings for us which commanded this allegiance and which have now gone.

This is the starting point of a set of hypotheses which attempt to redefine our past in order to make our present and future intelligible. We might think that the productive, bargaining culture offered in the past common meanings (even though there was no place for them in its philosophy), and hence a basis for community, which were essentially linked with its being in the process of building. It linked men who could see themselves as breaking with the past to build a new happiness in America, for instance. But in all essentials that future is built; the notion of a horizon to be attained by future greater production (as against social transformation) verges on the absurd in contemporary America. Suddenly the horizon which was essential to the sense of meaningful purpose has collapsed, which would show that like so many other Enlightenment-based dreams the free, productive, bargaining society can only sustain man as a goal, not as a reality.

Or we can look at this development in terms of identity. A sense of building their future through the civilization of work can sustain men as long as they see themselves as having broken with a millenial past of injustice and hardship in order to create qualitatively different conditions for their children. All the requirements of a humanly acceptable identity can be met by this predicament, a relation to the past (one soars above it but preserves it in folkloric memory), to the social world (the interdependent world of free, productive men), to the earth (the raw material which awaits shaping), to the future and ones own death (the everlasting monument in the lives of prosperous children), to the absolute (the absolute values of freedom, integrity, dignity).

But at some point the children will be unable to sustain this forward thrust into the future. This effort has placed them in a private haven of security, within which they are unable to reach and recover touch with the great realities: their parents have only a negated past, lives which have been oriented wholly to the future; the social world is distant and without shape; rather one can only insert oneself into it by taking one's place in the future-oriented productive juggernaut. But this now seems without any sense; the relation to the earth as raw material is therefore experienced as empty and alienating, but the recovery of a valid relation to the earth is the hardest thing once lost; and there is no relation to the absolute where we are caught in the web of meanings which have gone dead for us. Hence past, future, earth, world, and absolute are in some way or another occluded; and what must arise is an identity crisis of frightening proportions.

These two hypotheses are mainly focused on the crisis in US civilization, and they would perhaps help account for the fact that the US is in some sense going first through this crisis of all Atlantic nations; not, that is, only because it is the most affluent, but more because it has been more fully based on the civilization of work than European countries who retained something of more traditional common meanings.

But they might also help us to understand why alienation is most severe among groups which have been but marginal in affluent bargaining societies. These have had the greatest strain in living in this civilization while their identity was in some ways antithetical to it. Such are blacks in the US, and the community of French-speaking Canadians, each in different ways. For many immigrant groups the strain was also great, but they forced themselves to surmount the obstacles, and the new identity is sealed in the blood of the old, as it were.

But for those who would not or could not succeed in thus transforming themselves, but always lived a life of strain on the defensive, the breakdown of the central, powerful identity is the trigger to a deep turn-over. It can be thought of as a liberation but at the same time it is deeply unsettling, because the basic parameters of former life are being changed, and there are not yet the new images and definitions to live a new, fully acceptable identity. In a sense we are in a condition where a new social compact (rather the first social compact) has to be made between these groups and those they live with, and no one knows where to start.

In the last pages, I have presented some hypotheses which may appear very speculative; and they may indeed turn out to be without foundation, even without much interest. But their aim was mainly illustrative. My principal claim is that we can only come to grips with this phenomenon of breakdown by trying to understand more clearly and profoundly the common and intersubjective meanings of the society in which we have been living. For it is these which no longer hold us, and to understand this change we have to have an adequate grasp of these meanings. But this we cannot do as long as we remain within the ambit of mainstream social science, for it will not recognize intersubjective meaning, and is forced to look at the central ones of our society as though they were the inescapable background of all political action. Breakdown is thus inexplicable in political terms; it is an outbreak of irrationality which must ultimately be explained by some form of psychological illness.

Mainstream science may thus venture into the area explored by the above hypotheses, but after its own fashion, by forcing the psycho-historical facts of identity into the grid of an individual psychology, in short, by re-interpreting all meanings as subjective. The result might be a psychological theory of emotional maladjustment, perhaps traced to certain features of family background, analogous to the theories of the authoritarian personality and the California F-scale. But this would no longer be a political or social theory. We would be giving up the attempt to understand the change in social reality at the level of its constitutive intersubjective meanings.

IV

It can be argued, then, that mainstream social science is kept within certain limits by its categorial principles which are rooted in the traditional epistemology of empiricism; and secondly, that these restrictions are a severe handicap and prevent us from coming to grips with important problems of our day which should be the object of political science. We need to go beyond the bounds of a science based on verification to one which would study the intersubjective and common meanings embedded in social reality.

But this science would be hermeneutical in the sense that has been developed in this paper. It would not be founded on brute data; its most primitive data would be readings of meanings, and its object would have the three properties mentioned above: the meanings are for a subject in a field or fields; they are moreover meanings which are partially constituted by self-definitions, which are in this sense already interpretations, and which can thus be re-expressed or made explicit by a science of politics. In our case, the subject may be a society or community; but the intersubjective meanings, as we saw, embody a certain self-definition, a vision of the agent and his society, which is that of the society or community.

But then the difficulties which the proponents of the verification model foresee will arise. If we have a science which has no brute data, which relies on readings, then it cannot but move in a hermeneutical circle. A given reading of the intersubjective meanings of a society, or of given institutions or practices, may seem well founded, because it makes sense of these practices or the development of that society. But the conviction that it does make sense of this history itself is founded on further related readings. Thus, what I said above on the identity-crisis which is generated by our society makes sense and holds together only if one accepts this reading of the intersubjective meanings of our society, and if one accepts this reading of the rebellion against our society by many young people (i.e. the reading in terms of identity-crisis). These two readings make sense together, so that in a sense the explanation as a whole reposes on the readings, and the readings in their turn are strengthened by the explanation as a whole.

But if these readings seem implausible, or even more, if they are not understood by our interlocutor, there is no verification procedure which we can fall back on. We can only continue to offer interpretations; we are in an interpretative circle.

But the ideal of a science of verification is to find an appeal beyond differences of interpretation. Insight will always be useful in discovery, but should not have to play any part in establishing the truth of its findings. This ideal can be said to have been met by our natural sciences. But a hermeneutic science cannot but rely on insight. It requires that one have the sensibility and understanding necessary to be able to make and comprehend the readings by which we can explain the reality concerned. In physics we might argue that if someone does not accept a true theory, then either he has not been shown enough (brute data) evidence (perhaps not enough is yet available), or he cannot understand and apply some formalized language. But in the sciences of man conceived as hermeneutical, the non-acceptance of a true or illuminating theory may come from neither of these, indeed is unlikely to be due to either of these, but rather from a failure to grasp the meaning field in question, an inability to make and understand readings of this field.

In other words, in a hermeneutical science, a certain measure of insight is indispensable, and this insight cannot be communicated by the gathering of brute data, or initiation in modes of formal reasoning or some combination of these. It is unformalizable. But this is a scandalous result according to the authoritative conception of science in our tradition, which is shared even by many of those who are highly critical of the approach of mainstream psychology, or sociology, or political science. For it means that this is not a study in which anyone can engage, regardless of their level of insight; that some claims of the form: 'if you do not understand, then your intuitions are at fault, are blind or inadequate', some claims of this form will be justified; that some differences will be non-arbitrable by further evidence, but that each side can only make appeal to deeper insight on the part of the other. The superiority of one position over another will thus consist in this, that from the more adequate position one can understand one's own stand and that of one's opponent, but not the other way around. It goes without saying that this argument can only have weight for those in the superior position.

Thus, a hermeneutical science encounters a gap in intuitions, which is the other side, as it were, of the hermeneutical circle. But the situation is graver than this; for this gap is bound up with our divergent options in politics and life.

We speak of a gap when some cannot understand the kind of self-definition which others are proposing as underlying a certain society or set of institutions. Thus some positivistically-minded thinkers will find the language of identity-theory quite opaque; and some thinkers will not recognize any theory which does not fit with the categorial presuppositions of empiricism. But self-definitions are not only important to us as scientists who are trying to understand some, perhaps distant, social reality. As men we are self-defining beings, and we are partly what we are in virtue of the self-definitions which we have accepted, however we have come by them. What self-definitions we understand and what ones we do not understand, is closely linked with the self-definitions which help to constitute what we are. If it is too simple to say that one only understands an 'ideology' which one subscribes to, it is nevertheless hard to deny that we have great difficulty grasping definitions whose terms structure the world in ways which are utterly different from or incompatible with our own.

Hence the gap in intuitions does not just divide different theoretical positions, it also tends to divide different fundamental options in life. The practical and the theoretical are inextricably joined here. It may not just be that to understand a certain explanation one has to sharpen one's intuitions, it may be that one has to change one's orientation — if not in adopting another orientation, at least in living one's own in a way which allows for greater comprehension of others. Thus, in the sciences of man, in so far as they are hermeneutical there can be a valid response to 'I don't understand' which takes the form, not only 'develop your intuitions', but more radically 'change yourself'. This puts an end to any aspiration to a value-free or 'ideology-free' science of man. A study of the science of man is inseparable from an examination of the options between which men must choose.

This means that we can speak here not only of error, but of illusion. We speak of 'illusion' when we are dealing with something of greater substance than error, error which in a sense builds a counterfeit reality of its own. But errors of interpretation of meaning, which are also self-definitions of those who interpret and hence inform their lives, are more than errors in this sense: they are sustained by certain practices of which they are constitutive. It is not implausible to single out as examples two rampant illusions in our present society. One is that of the proponents of the bargaining society who can recognize nothing but either bargaining gambits or madness in those who rebel against this society. Here the error is sustained by the practices of the bargaining culture, and given a semblance of reality by the refusal to treat any protests on other terms; it hence acquires the more substantive reality of illusion. The second example is provided by much 'revolutionary' activity in our society which in desperate search for an alternative mode of life purports to see its situation in that of an Andean guerilla or Chinese peasants. Lived out, this passes from the stage of laughable error to tragic illusion. One illusion cannot recognize the possibility of human variation, the other cannot see any limits to man's ability to transform itself. Both make a valid science of man impossible.

In face of all this, we might be so scandalized by the prospect of such a hermeneutical science, that we will want to go back to the verification model. Why can we not take our understanding of meaning as part of the logic of discovery, as the logical empiricists suggest for our unformalizable insights, and still found our science on the exactness of our predictions? Our insightful understanding of the intersubjective meanings of our society will then serve to elaborate fruitful hypotheses, but the proof of these puddings will remain in the degree they enable us to predict.

The answer is that if the epistemological views underlying the science of interpretation are right, such exact prediction is radically impossible. This, for three reasons of ascending order of fundamentalness.

The first is the well-known 'open system' predicament, one shared by human life and meteorology, that we cannot shield a certain domain of human events, the psychological, economic, political, from external interference; it is impossible to delineate a closed system.

The second, more fundamental, is that if we are to understand men by a science of interpretation, we cannot achieve the degree of fine exactitude of a science based on brute data. The data of natural science admit of measurement to virtually any degree of exactitude. But different interpretations cannot be judged in this way. At the same time different nuances of interpretation may lead to different predictions in some circumstances, and these different outcomes may eventually create widely varying futures. Hence it is more than easy to be wide of the mark.

But the third and most fundamental reason for the impossibility of hard prediction is that man is a self-defining animal. With changes in his self-definition go changes in what man is, such that he has to be understood in different terms. But the conceptual mutations in human history can and frequently do produce conceptual webs which are incommensurable, that is, where the terms can't be defined in relation to a common stratum of expressions. The entirely different notions of bargaining in our society and in some primitive ones provide an example. Each will be glossed in terms of practices, institutions, ideas in each society which have nothing corresponding to them in the other.

The success of prediction in the natural sciences is bound up with the fact that all states of the system, past and future, can be described in the same range of concepts, as values, say, of the same variables. Hence all future states of the solar system can be characterized, as past ones are, in the language of Newtonian mechanics. This is far from being a sufficient condition of exact prediction, but it is a necessary one in this sense, that only if past and future are brought under the same conceptual net can one understand the states of the latter as some function of the states of the former, and hence predict.

This conceptual unity is vitiated in the sciences of man by the fact of conceptual innovation which in turn alters human reality. The very terms in which the future will have to be characterized if we are to understand it properly are not all available to us at present. Hence we have such radically unpredictable events as the culture of youth today, the Puritan rebellion of the sixteenth and seventeenth centuries, the development of Soviet society, etc.

And thus, it is much easier to understand after the fact than it is to predict. Human science is largely *ex post* understanding. Or often one has the sense of impending change, of some big reorganization, but is powerless to make clear what it will consist in: one lacks the vocabulary. But there is a clear assymetry here, which there is not (or not supposed to be) in natural science, where events are said to be predicted from the theory with exactly the same ease with which one explains past events and by exactly the same process. In human science this will never be the case.

Of course, we strive *ex post* to understand the changes, and to do this we try to develop a language in which we can situate the incommensurable webs of concepts. We see the rise of Puritanism, for instance, as a shift in man's stance to the sacred; and thus, we have a language in which we can express both stances — the earlier mediaeval Catholic one and the Puritan rebellion — as 'glosses' on this fundamental term. We thus have a language in which to talk of the transition. But think how we acquired it. This general category of the sacred is acquired not only from our experience of the shift which came in the Reformation, but from the study of human religion in general, including primitive religion, and with the detachment which came with secularization. It would be conceivable, but unthinkable, that a mediaeval Catholic could have this conception — or for that matter a Puritan. These two protagonists only had a language of condemnation for each other: 'heretic', 'idolator'. The place for such a concept was pre-empted by a certain way of living the sacred. After a big change has happened, and the trauma has been resorbed, it is possible to try to understand it, because one now has available the new language, the transformed meaning world. But hard prediction before just makes one a laughing stock. Really to be able to predict the future would be to have explicited so clearly the human condition that one would already have pre-empted all cultural innovation and transformation. This is hardly in the bounds of the possible.

Sometimes men show amazing prescience: the myth of Faust, for instance, which is treated several times at the beginning of the modern era. There is a kind of prophesy here, a premonition. But what characterizes these bursts of foresight is that they see through a glass darkly, for they see in terms of the old language: Faust sells his soul to the devil. They are in no sense hard predictions. Human science looks backward. It is inescapably historical.

There are thus good grounds both in epistemological arguments and in their greater fruitfulness for opting for hermeneutical sciences of man. But we cannot hide from ourselves how greatly this option breaks with certain commonly held notions about our scientific tradition. We cannot measure such sciences against the requirements of a science of verification: we cannot judge them by their predictive capacity. We have to accept that they are founded on intuitions which all do not share, and what is worse that these intuitions are closely bound up with our fundamental options. These sciences cannot be *'wertfrei'*; they are moral sciences in a more radical sense than the eighteenth century understood. Finally, their successful prosecution requires a high degree of self-knowledge, a freedom from illusion, in the sense of error which is rooted and expressed in one's way of life; for our incapacity to understand is rooted in our own self-definitions, hence in what we are. To say this is not to say anything new: Aristotle makes a similar point in Book I of the *Ethics*. But it is still radically shocking and unassimilable to the mainstream of modern science.

Notes

1 Cf. e.g., H.G. Gadamer, *Wahrheit und Methode* (Tübingen, 1960).
2 Cf. Paul Ricoeur, *De l'interprétation* (Paris, 1965).
3 Cf. e.g. J. Habermas, *Erkenninis und Interesse* (Frankfurt, 1968).
4 The notion of brute data here has some relation to, but is not at all the same as the 'brute facts' discussed by Elizabeth Anscombe, 'On Brute Facts', *Analysis,* vol. 18 (1957-8), pp. 69-72, and John Searle, *Speech Acts* (Cambridge, 1969), pp. 50-3. For Anscombe and Searle, brute facts are contrasted to what may be called 'institutional facts', to use Searle's term, i.e., facts which presuppose the existence of certain institutions. Voting would be an example. But, as we shall see below in part II, some institutional facts, such as X's having voted Liberal, can be verified as brute data in the sense used here, and thus find a place in the category of political behaviour. What cannot as easily be described in terms of brute data are the institutions themselves. Cf. the discussion below in part II.
5 Cf. discussion in M. Minsky, *Computation* (Englewood Cliffs, NJ, 1967), pp. 104-7, where Minsky explicitly argues that an effective procedure, which no longer requires intuition or interpretation, is one which can be realized by a machine.
6 Cf. II. McClosky, 'Consensus and Ideology in American Politics', *American Political Science Review,* vol. 58 (1964), pp. 361-82.
7 Gabriel A. Almond and G. Bingham Powell, *Comparative Politics: a Developmental Approach* (Boston and Toronto, 1966). Page references in my text here and below are to this work.
8 Cf. Thomas C. Smith, *The Agrarian Origins of Modern Japan* (Stanford, 1959), chapter 5. This type of consensus is also found in other traditional societies. Cf. for instance, the *desa* system of the Indonesian village.
9 J. Searle, *Speech Acts: an Essay in the Philosophy of Language* (Cambridge, 1969), pp. 33-42.
10 Cf. the discussion in Stanley Cavell, *Must We Mean What We Say?* (New York, 1969), pp. 21-31.
11 Cf. Almond and Powell, op. cit.

12 'How is a Comparative Science of Politics Possible?', in Alasdair MacIntyre, *Against the Self-Images of the Age* (London, 1971).

13 MacIntyre's article also contains an interesting discussion of 'legitimacy' from a different, although I think related, angle.

14 (Englewood Cliffs, NJ, 1963). Foundation of Modern Political Science Series.

15 (New York, 1963). Page references are to this edition.

16 *Histoire du Peuple anglais au* xixe *siècle* (Paris, 1913).

17 *The Human Condition* (New York, 1959).

18 Op. cit.

19 Thus Lewis Feuer in *The Conflict of Generations* (New York, 1969) attempts to account for the 'misperception of social reality' in the Berkeley student uprising in terms of a generational conflict (pp. 466-70), which in turn is rooted in the psychology of adolescence and attaining adulthood. Yet Feuer himself in his first chapter notes the comparative recency of self-defining political generations, a phenomenon which dates from the post-Napoleonic era (p. 33). But an adequate attempt to explain this historical shift, which after all underlies the Berkeley rising and many others, would I believe have to take us beyond the ambit of individual psychology to psycho-history, to a study of the intrication of psychological conflict and intersubjective meanings. A variant of this form of study has been adumbrated in the work of Erik Erikson.

PART III

Social institutions and social change

Introduction

ALAN R. DRENGSON

That there is social change is incontrovertible. How this change comes about, and whether change can be managed as a result of careful planning, are both matters of controversy. During the nineteenth century a number of thinkers attempted to construct theories that would explain the change and development of societies. As Europeans, they concentrated their efforts on European societies. The elaborate theories they constructed explained social change in terms of what were supposed to be historical laws governing the development of human societies. Just as processes of the natural world are governed by natural laws that can be discovered by the scientist, likewise, it was thought, human societies must be governed by similar laws. The emphasis was, for the most part, on development and not mere change. 'Development' emphasizes change in a progressive direction. For example, an organism develops, from the moment of conception, from a single cell to a multi-cellular being. Humans are born as helpless babes and develop finally into mature adults. In contrast, 'mere change' means an alteration in the state of an organism that is not part of a series of changes leading to maturity, or to some other realized state. The deepening of the male voice, the growth of body hair and beard, these are some of the changes that are part of the development of male sexual maturity. They are not separate, unrelated events. If I, as a mature male, grow a beard, I have changed or altered my appearance. This change is not, however, part of a pattern of development in me as an organism.

I have concentrated on organic entities in my discussion above since nineteenth-century thinkers often used analogies between society and such entities in order to explain social change as development. Darwin's kind of thinking was very much in the air, and the faith that man's history is the story of progress captured and captivated the imagination of many of these philosophers. A number of thinkers thus tried to do for whole societies what they thought Darwin had done for natural species. Society was often conceived as a large organism, and organic analogies and metaphors were used to explain how various significant changes come about. Once we know the direction of development and the governing forces, it was reasoned, we should be able to predict the state of society we can expect in the future. This is not easy to do. In fact, the difficulty of accurately predicting the course of social development has been the reef upon which many an enterprising and hopeful social theorist has come to grief. For, unless these predictions are cast in the most general terms, the hope of their realization is usually a forlorn one.

'Development' usually implies change as growth that leads to some end; in the case of an organism, this end might be maturity. The overall development of an organism, while not rigid in detail, nevertheless follows a predictable pattern. Individual organisms may, for various reasons, fail to develop or might develop in aberrant ways. None the less, we are inclined to think of their development as determined by an interaction between the environment and their own inner make-up. Today we refer to their genetic make-up as that which plays a major role, in concert with the environment, in determining what they will become. Many of these things were not as well understood in the nineteenth century and the emphasis was either on a rather crude sort of mechanistic determinism or, on the other hand, on voluntarism or vitalism[1]. Those nineteenth-century theorists who were keen to predict the future of human societies usually came down hard on the side of determinism. They did not, for the most part, allow that men have control over the destiny or shape of the societies they inhabit. At the same time, many of these theorists, such as Marx, were highly critical of the social and economic organization of the societies of Western Europe. Marx was certain that capitalism would eventually be overthrown; his certainty was based on his belief that capitalism contains intrinsic features that will inevitably lead to its demise. None the less, he writes in places to encourage us to abet the change and transformation necessary to create a society free of the alienation and injustices which are, in his view, characteristic of capitalist society.

In Marx's writings — given their scope — it is not clear to what degree acceptance of the theories would commit us to determinism. If, however, we insist that both the rate and the direction of social change are determined by impersonal forces, then recommendations are pointless. A moment's reflection should tell us that we cannot have it both ways. Either our actions can affect the course of history, and, therefore, no events in human history are inevitable in the sense that they are incapable of being affected by human decisions deliberately made, or else the course of history is truly inevitable and what social and economic organizations appear is independent of our decisions and actions. Social and economic organizations, in a rigid determinist view, are not influenced in their growth by free human decisions and deliberation, but rather are the result of the operation of certain inherent and inevitable forces.

In contrast to the rigid determinist conception of social change, social activists and many governments have conceived of human societies as amenable to human control. Change can be managed and managed for human benefit. However, the facts are anything but clear here. When we look at the state of human societies, we are confronted with the question of whether or not anything we now plan and do will have the sort of effects at which we are aiming. Is it possible to bring about social changes that will solve the various problems we face today in our highly industrialized, urbanized societies? Are we capable of controlling pollution, eliminating poverty and injustice, etc.? For a long time the American experiment involved the belief that one could develop a just society partly through universal, compulsory education. Education was viewed as a means to social equality and equal opportunity. Through education, it was thought, everyone can be brought up to a certain minimum level and from there he is free to go as far as his ability and ambition will allow. It was believed that this approach would, to a certain extent, solve problems thought to result from the older privileged class structures of European nations. These experiments did not, however, realize many of their aims.

During recent years federal administrations in the United States have attempted to correct deficiencies in the education system by developing special programmes aimed at those children thought to be underprivileged as a result of race discrimination, poverty and other conditions. A number of expensive programmes were developed during the Johnson administration aimed at solving these problems. This type of social tinkering, which could in the spirit of Karl Popper be called piecemeal social engineering, has gone on in the US in a major way since the first administration of Franklin D. Roosevelt. Recently, the Brookings Institute, a prestigious think-tank in Washington, DC, published a carefully documented study of government programmes which are aimed at solving various social problems. Their main conclusion, which surprised no one, was that these programmes on the whole have not been very successful. More importantly, they also went on to argue that we do not seem to know how to solve these problems. In contrast to this view, some theorists argue that it is the character of government programmes that keeps them from being successful. What needs doing is nothing short of a complete revolution of the political, economic and social systems. What is called for is a complete restructuring of the society that finally breaks up existing power concentrations that create inequities. We must put political power in the hands of all the people instead of a few. The slogan, 'power to the people', carries this thought with it. Even if widespread change is necessary, we are still faced with the problem of whether we can do the specific and detailed things that need doing in order to realize this change; here slogans are of little help.

The problem is, then, can social change be realized so that growth is not destructive, so that various social problems can be solved, and so that life can be made somewhat less trying? Is there room for social engineering? Before, however, we even begin to attempt such intervention, we need to ask the difficult philosophical questions, 'What point change?', 'Where do we want to go?', 'Why do we want to get there?' These are questions which focus on values.

In order to focus more directly on our capacity to direct social change, let us take as an example one major social problem and see what we can learn from past attempts to deal with it. Recently, the United States and other Western nations have had costly social problems associated with drug abuse. In the case of the United States, problems associated with drug abuse have been amply documented. Not only are there large numbers of young people experimenting with harmful drugs, but there are large numbers of narcotics addicts in the United States who support a large black market system which distributes narcotic drugs to them. This black market system not only exploits the addict, it is also a source of capital which is used to finance other illicit activities. Moreover, black market costs lead drug addicts to steal, rob and mug in order to support a habit costing up to 100 dollars a day. In the case of narcotic drugs alone, the federal government in the United States has attempted to deal with these problems by the expenditure of vast sums of tax money, by the use of anti-drug propaganda, by passing ever more stringent laws and by creating a vast bureaucracy of law enforcement. The more money, time and effort the government has spent the more serious the problems have become and some studies have concluded that these problems are, in part, a result of government actions[2]. Now one might conclude that the problems associated with drug abuse are out of hand in the United States and that there is no way to bring about the needed social changes that will solve these problems: public education has failed; law enforcement approaches have failed; rehabilitation and special hospitals designed to treat addicts have failed. So far, nothing tried seems to have had much effect. As a result one might conclude from all this that there are forces at work here that cannot be controlled by human effort; one might say that trying to control these problems associated with drug abuse is rather like trying to control a hurricane. The only thing one can do when faced with the latter is take cover. Many people in large cities have done just this.

Perhaps this is the wrong conclusion to draw. Perhaps the whole approach of the United States government has been misguided and misconceived. We see, for example, that in Britain there is no *large scale* black market for opiates and, with respect to addicting drugs, in comparison to the United States, virtually no drug problem. The British approach has been based on the view that this is not a law enforcement problem, but a medical one. They have not as a result driven the addict to illicit sources for drugs, but rather have allowed him to get the drugs he needs from his physician. The American attitude, on the other hand, has been characterized by fear of the addict, belief that he could become non-addicted if he just had enough will power, and belief that the government should protect him from himself because heroin and other similar drugs are harmful, and that, after all, is the main reason for not dispensing them to him.

A review of the literature and research papers on this whole complex of problems clearly indicates that the American approach failed because it did not appreciate the nature of the problem with respect to addiction: addiction is primarily a medical problem and one cannot treat or prevent it by law enforcement alone. A similar approach to alcohol had earlier demonstrated that the government cannot successfully alter people's behaviour by simply passing laws and setting up an enforcement bureaucracy: unless people think that the behaviour sanctioned by those laws ought to be sanctioned they will generally ignore those laws. The evidence is clear from the

American experience with alcohol that the majority of Americans did not agree with their government that drinking is bad. Alcohol abuse is still the number one drug abuse problem in the United States and many authorities think this is in part a result of the earlier prohibition.

Now what is the point of all of these observations? The point is that we shall not be apt to be successful in any attempt at directed, planned social change unless we have a clear idea of what it is we are trying to accomplish and what the exact character of the problem is. It is understanding we need most of all. It is not clear just how we arrive at this understanding independent of making certain *value* judgments about what sorts of things are worth doing. A lot of people wish to make such judgments for others, and as a result they attempt to eliminate certain sorts of pursuits of a private character that involve no harm to others. These efforts invariably fail to alter peoples' behaviour, and they fail to bring about the desired social change. Also, it is easy to let ourselves think that we have more control over things than we in fact do. To this extent the nineteenth-century determinists were right: individual decisions do not directly determine the outcome of the social institutions that men have. As John Plamenatz observes:

> When we contemplate society and consider how we may improve it, we fall easily into the habit of speaking of institutions as if they were instruments devised for our convenience. And so, to a limited extent, they are, especially in sophisticated societies. When, however, we compare our own society with others very different from it and see how much we owe what is peculiar to us to our social environment, it is easy and natural to speak of society as if it consisted of processes independent of our wills. Just as we do not decide what will happen to our bodies as they come to maturity, so we do not choose how 'society' shall influence our minds. In neither case do we control the processes in which we are involved, and so we come to speak of them in the same way, as if the second were also a kind of growth. In one sense, social processes are very largely independent of our wills, for they are the ways in which we behave. When they change it is because people have either decided or been moved to behave differently. They are not what happens to us, as the growth of our bodies is; they are what we, as rational and wilful beings do.[3]

And again from Plamenatz:

In any case, it is no nearer the truth to speak of social institutions *growing* than to suggest that men have *made* them deliberately. They neither grow nor are made; they are largely the unforeseen consequences of deliberate actions.[4]

That is what we should realize: that there are often unforeseen consequences of our deliberate actions. The United States government embarked on a programme designed to curb and control drug addiction, and it has been convincingly argued in *Licit and Illicit Drugs* that these actions had the unforeseen consequences of creating a problem of epidemic proportions; the end result was not the result intended at all[5]. Both Karl Popper and Rush Rhees make much the same point in their articles. Popper's claim is that any attempt at large scale 'Utopian engineering' will be so disruptive and involve such extreme measures that the results invariably will not be the intended ones. What will be realized by large scale social engineering will not be Utopia. In fact, the end realized will usually be worse than what prevailed at the beginning. This leads Popper to favour small scale, piecemeal social engineering. It seems mainly the scale of the undertaking that bothers Popper, although he claims that Utopian schemes are inherently irrational, for they assume that a complete restructuring of our social order would lead at once to a workable system. This is not possible, he writes, because we can learn only by trial and error, and by making mistakes and improvements that can be checked by experience. We have no experience of such large scale social construction and, furthermore, we are not apt to gain any such experience. Society must continue to function during any reconstruction and this, according to Popper, is one of the main reasons we must reform its institutions little by little. In Popper's view, then, we introduce small changes here and there with the hope of improving our institutions and getting them to function more consistently with our purposes. Just as we gradually refine our techniques and materials in improving the functioning of an engine, so, in a like manner, should we improve our institutions.

Rhees takes issue with this claim. According to Rhees, the critical question for Popper is, how or by what standards do we judge that we have improved our society and its institutions? Popper rejects both the Utopian approach which attempts to improve society as a whole, and the 'inspired' vision of society that, he claims, lies behind such an approach. Yet, as Rhees points out, he favours the reform of institutions by means of piecemeal social engineering. How can he talk of reform and improvement without accepting some ideal of the society as a whole? According to Rhees, Popper does not seem to have escaped the same kind of difficulties he lays at the feet of the Utopian engineer. More importantly, according to Rhees, Popper thinks that many of our difficulties are amenable to a type of engineering that, by implication, must be capable of making value judgments that involve some measure of consensus. It is uncertain how any social science or social technology can, as a science or a technology, bring us to this end[6].

When our ideals conflict, as they often do, application of the methods of science is, by itself, not going to resolve them. Some of these conflicts might never be resolved, or, again, they might only be resolved as a result of the kind of long, hard, philosophical reflection that leads to a change in our own personal lives. Conflicts of ideals often give rise to fundamental philosophical problems that are not susceptible to scientific solutions. This brings me back to my earlier remark: if we actively seek social change, then we must be clear what it is we want to realize as a result of it. Conceptual confusions often underlie our thinking in these areas, and confused thinking rarely leads anywhere.

The two articles mentioned thus far only open up the discussion of social change. The last paper in this chapter canvasses the range of possibilities within the political sphere. When people in the West think of social change they often think first of political change and the political process. This is no doubt because some degree of participation is possible, and also because politicians are often viewed as having a central role in making crucial decisions that affect the future of our societies. It is not clear that politicians play the important role that is often attributed to them. In any case, a range of possibilities with respect to political action is open to us, as citizens of nations with free political institutions. This range of possibilities is surveyed and discussed by Clyde Frazier.

Notes

1 The different possibilities are nicely sorted out in Gaylord Simpson, *The Meaning of Evolution* (New Haven, Conn., 1949).

2 Edward Becker (ed.), *Licit and Illicit Drugs* (The Consumer's Union Report) (New York, 1972).
3 John Plamenatz, *The English Utilitarians* (Oxford, 1966), p. 172.
4 Ibid, p. 191.
5 Becker, op. cit.
6 This is not meant to imply that Popper favours such scientism. See the notes at the end of Popper's article in this volume, pp. 224-5, for example.

7

Aestheticism, perfectionism, Utopianism

KARL POPPER

'Everything's got to be smashed to start with.
Our whole damned civilization's got to go, before
we can bring any decency into the world.'
'Mourlan', in Roger Martin du Gard, *Les Thibaults*

Inherent in Plato's programme there is a certain approach towards politics which, I believe, is most dangerous. Its analysis is of great practical importance from the point of view of rational social engineering. The Platonic approach I have in mind can be described as that of *Utopian engineering*, as opposed to another kind of social engineering which I consider as the only rational one and which may be characterized by the name of *piecemeal engineering*.

The Utopian approach may be described as follows. Any rational action must have a certain aim. It is rational in the same degree as it pursues its aim consciously and consistently, and as it determines its means according to this end. To choose the end is therefore the first thing we have to do if we wish to act rationally; and we must be careful to determine our real or ultimate ends, from which we must distinguish clearly those intermediate or partial ends which actually are only means, or steps on the way, to the ultimate end. If we neglect this distinction, then we must also neglect to ask whether

Reprinted from K.R. Popper, The Open Society and Its Enemies, *Vol. 1, Chapter 9 (Princeton University Press and Routledge and Kegan Paul, 5th rev. edn 1966) by permission of the author and publishers.* © *1962, 1966 Karl Raimund Popper.*

these partial ends are likely to promote the ultimate end, and accordingly, we must fail to act rationally. These principles, if applied to the realm of political activity, demand that we must determine our ultimate political aim, or the Ideal State, before taking any practical action. Only when this ultimate aim is determined, in rough outlines at least, only when we are in the possession of something like a blueprint of the society at which we aim, only then can we begin to consider the best ways and means of its realization, and to draw up a plan for practical action. These are the necessary preliminaries of any practical political move that can be called rational, and especially of social engineering.

This, in brief, is the methodological approach which I call Utopian engineering[1]. It is convincing and attractive. In fact, it is just the kind of methodological approach to attract all those who are either unaffected by historicist prejudices or reacting against them. This makes it only the more dangerous, and its criticism the more imperative.

Before proceeding to criticize Utopian engineering in detail, I wish to outline another approach to social engineering, namely, that of piecemeal engineering. It is an approach which I think to be methodologically sound. The politician who adopts this method may or may not have a blueprint of society before his mind, he may or may not hope that mankind will one day realize an ideal state, and achieve happiness and perfection on earth. But he will be aware that perfection, if at all attainable, is far distant, and that every generation of men, and therefore also the living, have a claim; perhaps not so much a claim to be made happy, for there are no institutional means of making a man happy, but a claim not to be made unhappy, where it can be avoided. They have a claim to be given all possible help, if they suffer. The piecemeal engineer will, accordingly, adopt the method of searching for, and fighting against, the greatest and most urgent evils of society, rather than searching for, and fighting for, its greatest ultimate good[2]. This difference is far from being merely verbal. In fact, it is most important. It is the difference between a reasonable method of improving the lot of man, and a method which, if really tried, may easily lead to an intolerable increase in human suffering. It is the difference between a method which can be applied at any moment, and a method whose advocacy may easily become a means of continually postponing action until a later date, when conditions are more favourable. And it is also the difference between the only method of improving matters which has so far been really successful, at any time, and in any place (Russia included, as will be seen) and a method which, wherever it has been tried, has led only to the use of violence in place of reason, and if not to its own abandonment, at any rate to that of its original blueprint.

In favour of his method, the piecemeal engineer can claim that a systematic fight against suffering and injustice and war is more likely to be supported by the approval and agreement of a great number of people than the fight for the establishment of some ideal. The existence of social evils, that is to say, of social conditions under which many men are suffering, can be comparatively well established. Those who suffer can judge for themselves, and the others can hardly deny that they would not like to change places. It is infinitely more difficult to reason about an ideal society. Social life is so complicated that few men, or none at all, could judge a blueprint for social engineering on the grand scale; whether it be practicable; whether it would result in a real improvement; what kind of suffering it may involve; and what may be the means for its realization. As opposed to this, blueprints for piecemeal engineering are comparatively simple. They are blueprints for single institutions, for health and unemployed insurance, for instance, or arbitration courts, or antidepression budgeting[3] or educational reform. If they go wrong, the damage is not very great, and a readjustment not very difficult. They are less risky, and for this very reason less controversial. But if it is easier to reach a reasonable agreement about existing evils and the means of combating them than it is about an ideal good and the means of its realization, then there is also more hope that by using the piecemeal method we may get over the very greatest practical difficulty of all reasonable political reform, namely, the use of reason, instead of passion and violence, in executing the programme. There will be a possibility of reaching a reasonable compromise and therefore of achieving the improvement by democratic methods. ('Compromise' is an ugly word, but it is important for us to learn its proper use. *Institutions* are inevitably the result of a compromise with circumstances, interests, etc., though as *persons* we should resist influences of this kind.)

As opposed to that, the Utopian attempt to realize an ideal state, using a blueprint of society as a whole, is one which demands a strong centralized rule of a few, and which therefore is likely to lead to a dictatorship[4]. This I consider a criticism of the Utopian approach; for I have tried to show, in chapter 7 of *The Open Society*, that an authoritarian rule is a most objectionable form of government. Some points not touched upon in that chapter furnish us with even more direct arguments against the Utopian approach. One of the difficulties faced by a benevolent dictator is to find whether the effects of his measures agree with his good intentions. The difficulty arises out of the fact that authoritarianism must discourage criticism; accordingly, the benevolent dictator will not easily hear of complaints concerning the measures he has taken. But without some such check, he can hardly find out whether his measures achieve the desired benevolent aim. The situation must become even worse for the Utopian engineer. The reconstruction of society is a big undertaking which must cause considerable inconvenience to many, and for a considerable span of time. Accordingly, the Utopian engineer will have to be deaf to many complaints; in fact, it will be part of his business to suppress unreasonable objections. But with it, he must invariably suppress reasonable criticism also. Another difficulty of Utopian engineering is related to the *problem of the dictator's successor*. Utopian engineering raises a difficulty analogous to, but even more serious than, the one which faces the benevolent tyrant who tries to find an equally benevolent successor. The very sweep of such a Utopian undertaking makes it improbable that it will realize its ends during the lifetime of one social engineer, or group of engineers. And if the successors do not pursue the same ideal, then all the suffering of the people for the sake of the ideal may have been in vain.

A generalization of this argument leads to a further criticism of the Utopian approach. This approach, it is clear, can be of practical value only if we assume that the original blueprint, perhaps with certain adjustments, remains the basis of the work until it is completed. But that will take some time. It will be a time of revolutions, both political and spiritual, and of new experiments and experience in the political field. It is therefore to be expected that ideas and ideals will change. What had appeared the ideal state to the people who made the original blueprint, may not appear so to their successors. If that is granted, then the whole approach breaks down. The method of first establishing an ultimate political aim and then beginning to move towards it is futile if we admit that the aim may be considerably changed during the process of its realization. It may at any moment turn out that the steps so far taken actually lead away from the realization of the new aim. And if we change our direction according to the new aim, then we expose ourselves to the same risk again. In spite of all the sacrifices made, we may never get anywhere at all. Those who prefer one step towards a distant ideal to the realization of a piecemeal compromise should always remember that if the ideal is very distant, it may even become difficult to say whether the step taken was towards or away from it. This is especially so if the course should proceed by zigzag steps, or, in Hegel's jargon, 'dialectically', or if it is not clearly planned at all. (This bears upon the old and somewhat childish question of how far the end can justify the means. Apart from claiming that no end could ever justify all means, I think that a fairly concrete and realizable end may justify temporary measures which a more distant ideal never could[5].)

We see now that the Utopian approach can be saved only by the Platonic belief in one absolute and unchanging ideal, together with two further assumptions, namely (a) that there are rational methods to determine once and forever what this ideal is, and (b) what the best means of its realization are. Only such far-reaching assumptions could prevent us from declaring the Utopian methodology to be utterly futile. But even Plato himself and the most ardent Platonists would admit that (a) is certainly not true; that there is no rational method for determining the ultimate aim, but, if anything, only some kind of intuition. Any difference of opinion between Utopian engineers must therefore lead, in the absence of rational methods, to the use of power instead of reason, i.e. to violence. If any progress in any definite direction is made at all, then it is made in spite of the method adopted, not because of it. The success may be due, for instance, to the excellence of the leaders; but we must never forget that excellent leaders cannot be produced by rational methods, but only by luck.

It is important to understand this criticism properly; I do not criticize the ideal by claiming that an ideal can never be realized, that it must always remain a Utopia. This would not be a valid criticism, for many things have been realized which have once been dogmatically declared to be unrealizable, for instance, the establishment of corresponding institutions for the prevention of international crime, i.e. armed aggression or blackmail, though often branded as Utopian, is not even a very difficult problem[6]. What I criticize under the name Utopian engineering recommends the reconstruction of society as a whole, i.e. very sweeping changes whose practical consequences are hard to calculate, owing to our limited experiences. It claims to plan rationally for the whole of society, although we do not possess anything like the factual knowledge which would be necessary to make good such an ambitious claim. We cannot possess such knowledge since we have insufficient practical experience in this kind of planning, and knowledge of facts must be based upon experience. At present, the sociological knowledge necessary for large-scale engineering is simply nonexistent.

In view of this criticism, the Utopian engineer is likely to grant the need for practical experience, and for a social technology based upon practical experiences. But he will argue that we shall never know more about these matters if we recoil from making social experiments which alone can furnish us with the practical experience needed. And he might add that Utopian engineering is nothing but the application of the experimental method to society. Experiments cannot be carried out without involving sweeping changes. They must be on a large scale, owing to the peculiar character of modern society with its great masses of people. An experiment in socialism, for instance, if confined to a factory, or to a village, or even to a district, would never give us the kind of realistic information which we need so urgently.

Such arguments in favour of Utopian engineering exhibit a prejudice which is as widely held as it is untenable, namely, the prejudice that social experiments must be on a 'large scale', that they must involve the whole of society if they are to be carried out under realistic conditions. But piecemeal social experiments can be carried out under realistic conditions, in the midst of society, in spite of being on a 'small scale', that is to say, without revolutionizing the whole of society. In fact, we are making such experiments all the time. The introduction of a new kind of life insurance, of a new kind of taxation, of a new penal reform, are all social experiments which have their repercussions through the whole of society without remodelling society as a whole. Even a man who opens a new shop, or who reserves a ticket for the theatre, is carrying out a kind of social experiment on a small scale; and all our knowledge of social conditions is based on experience gained by making experiments of this kind. The Utopian engineer we are combating is right when he stresses that an experiment in socialism would be of little value if carried out under laboratory conditions, for instance, in an isolated village, since what we want to know is how things work out in society under normal social conditions. But this very example shows where the prejudice of the Utopian engineer lies. He is convinced that we must recast the whole structure of society, when we experiment with it; and he can therefore conceive a more *modest* experiment only as one that recasts the whole structure of a *small* society. But the kind of experiment from which we can learn most is the alteration of one social institution at a time. For only in this way can we learn how to fit institutions into the framework of other institutions, and how to adjust them so that they work according to our intentions. And only in this way can we make mistakes, and learn from our mistakes, without risking repercussions of a gravity that must endanger the will to future reforms. Furthermore, the Utopian method must lead to a dangerous dogmatic attachment to a blueprint for which countless sacrifices have been made. Powerful interests must become linked up with the success of the experiment. All this does not contribute to the rationality, or to the scientific value, of the experiment. But the piecemeal method permits repeated experiments and continuous readjustments. In fact, it might lead to the happy situation where politicians begin to look out for their own mistakes instead of trying to explain them away and to prove that they have always been right. This — and not Utopian planning or historical prophecy — would mean the introduction of scientific method into politics, since the whole secret of scientific method is a readiness to learn from mistakes[7].

These views can be corroborated, I believe, by comparing social and, for instance, mechanical engineering. The Utopian engineer will of course claim that mechanical engineers sometimes plan even very complicated machinery as a whole, and that their blueprints may cover, and plan in advance, not only a certain kind of machinery, but even the whole factory which produces this machinery. My reply would be that the mechanical engineer can do all this because he has sufficient experience at his disposal; i.e. theories developed by trial and error. But this means that he can plan because he has made all kinds of mistakes already; or in other words, because he relies on experience which he has gained by applying piecemeal methods. His new machinery is the result of a great many small improvements. He usually has a model first, and only after a great number of piecemeal adjustments to its various parts does he proceed to a stage where he could draw up his final plans for the production. Similarly, his plan for the production of his machine incorporates a great number of experiences, namely, of piecemeal improvements made in older factories. The wholesale or large-scale method works only where the piecemeal method has furnished us first with a great number of detailed experiences, and even then only within the realm of these experiences. Few manufacturers would be prepared to proceed to the production of a new engine on the basis of a blueprint alone, even if it were drawn up by by the greatest expert, without first making a model and 'developing' it by little adjustments as far as possible.

It is perhaps useful to contrast this criticism of Platonic Idealism in politics with Marx's criticism of what he calls 'Utopianism'. What is common to Marx's criticism and mine is that both demand more realism. We both believe that Utopian plans will never be realized in the way they were conceived, because hardly any social action ever produces precisely the result expected. (This does not, in my opinion, invalidate the piecemeal approach, because here we may learn — or rather, we ought to learn — and change our views, while we act.) But there are many differences. In arguing against Utopianism, Marx condemns in fact *all* social engineering — a point which is rarely understood. He denounces the hope in a rational planning of social institutions as altogether unrealistic, since society must grow according to the laws of history and not according to our rational plans. All we can do, he asserts, is to lessen the birthpangs of the historical processes. In other words, he adopts a radically historicist attitude, opposed to all social engineering. But there is one element within Utopianism which is particularly characteristic of Plato's approach and which Marx does not oppose, although it is perhaps the most important of those elements which I have attacked as unrealistic. It is the sweep of Utopianism, its attempt to deal with society as a whole, leaving nothing unturned. It is the conviction that one has to go to the very root of the social evil, that nothing short of a complete eradication of the offending social system will do if we wish to 'bring any decency into the world' (as Du Gard says). It is, in short, its uncompromising *radicalism*. (The reader will notice that I am using this term in its original and literal sense — not in the now customary sense of a 'liberal progressivism', but in order to characterize an attitude of 'going to the root of the matter'.) Both Plato and Marx are dreaming of the apocalyptic revolution which will radically transfigure the whole social world.

This sweep, this extreme radicalism of the Platonic approach (and of the Marxian as well) is, I believe, connected with its aestheticism, i.e. with the desire to build a world which is not only a little better and more rational than ours, but which is free from all its ugliness: not a crazy quilt, an old garment badly patched, but an entirely new coat, a really beautiful new world[8]. This aestheticism is a very understandable attitude; in fact, I believe most of us suffer a little from such dreams of perfection. But this aesthetic enthusiasm becomes valuable only if it is bridled by reason, by a feeling of responsibility, and by a humanitarian urge to help. Otherwise it is a dangerous enthusiasm, liable to develop into a form of neurosis or hysteria.

Nowhere do we find this aestheticism more strongly expressed than in Plato. Plato was an artist; and like many of the best artists, he tried to visualize a model, the 'divine original' of his work, and to 'copy' it faithfully. What Plato describes as dialectics is, in the main, the intellectual intuition of the world of pure beauty. His trained philosophers are men who 'have seen the truth of what is beautiful and just, and good'[9], and can bring it down from heaven to earth. Politics, to Plato, is the Royal Art. It is an art — not in a metaphorical sense in which we may speak about the art of treating men, or the art of getting things done, but in a more literal sense of the word. It is an art of composition, like music, painting, or architecture. The Platonic politician composes cities, for beauty's sake.

But here I must protest. I do not believe that human lives may be made the means for satisfying an artist's desire for self-expression. We must demand, rather, that every man should be given, if he wishes, the right to model his life himself, as far as this does not interfere too much with others. Much as I may sympathize with the aesthetic impulse, I suggest that the artist might seek expression in another material. Politics, I demand, must uphold equalitarian and individualistic principles; dreams of beauty have to submit to the necessity of helping men in distress, and men who suffer injustice; and to the necessity of constructing institutions to serve such purposes[10]

It is interesting to observe the close relationship between Plato's utter radicalism, the demand for sweeping measures, and his aestheticism. The following passages are most characteristic. Plato, speaking about 'the philosopher who has communion with the divine', mentions first that he will be 'overwhelmed by the urge... to realize his heavenly vision in individuals as well as in the city,' — a city which 'will never know happiness unless its draughtsmen are artists who have the divine as their model'. Asked about the details of their draughtsmanship, Plato's 'Socrates' gives the following striking reply: 'They will take as their canvas a city and the characters of men, and they will, first of all, *make their canvas clean* — by no means an easy matter. But this is just the point, you know, where they will differ from all others. They will not start work on a city nor on an individual (nor will they draw up laws) unless they are given a clean canvas, or have cleaned it themselves'[11].

The kind of thing Plato has in mind when he speaks of canvas cleaning is explained a little later. 'How can that be done?' asks Glaucon. 'All citizens above the age of ten', Socrates answers, 'must be expelled from the city and deported somewhere into the country; and the children who are now free from the influence of the mean character of their parents must be taken over. They must be educated in the ways of true philosophers, and in accordance with the laws we have described.' In the same spirit, Plato says in the *Statesman* of the royal rulers who rule in accordance with the Royal Science of Statesmanship: 'Whether they happen to rule by law or without law, over willing or unwilling subjects; ... and whether they purge the state for its good, by killing or by deporting some of its citizens ... so long as they proceed according to science and justice, and preserve ... the state and make it better than it was, this form of government must be described as the only one that is right.'

This is the way in which the artist-politician must proceed. This is what canvas cleaning means. He must eradicate the existing institutions and traditions. He must purify, purge, expel, deport, and kill. ('Liquidate' is the terrible modern term for it.) Plato's statement is indeed a true description of the uncompromising attitude of all forms of out-and-out political radicalism — of the aestheticist's refusal to compromise. The view that society should be beautiful like a work of art leads only too easily to violent measures. But all this radicalism and violence is both unrealistic and futile. (This has been shown by the example of Russia's development. After the economic breakdown to which the canvas cleaning of the so-called 'war communism' had led, Lenin introduced his 'New Economic Policy', in fact a kind of piecemeal engineering, though without the conscious formulation of its principles or of a technology. He started by restoring most of the features of the picture which had been eradicated with so much human suffering. Money, markets, differentiation of income, and private property — for a time even private enterprise in production — were reintroduced, and only after this basis was re-established began a new period of reform.)

In order to criticize the foundations of Plato's aesthetic radicalism, we may distinguish two different points.

The first is this. What some people have in mind who speak of our 'social system', and of the need to replace it by another 'system', is very similar to a picture painted on a canvas which has to be wiped clean before one can paint a new one. But there are some great differences. One of them is that the painter and those who co-operate with him as well as the institutions which make their life possible, his dreams and plans for a better world, and his standards of decency and morality, are all part of the social system, i.e. of the picture to be wiped out. If they were really to clean the canvas, they would have to destroy themselves, and their Utopian plans. (And what follows then would probably not be a beautiful copy of a Platonic ideal but chaos.) The political artist clamours, like Archimedes, for a place outside the social world on which he can take his stand, in order to lever it off its hinges. But such a place does not exist; and the social world must continue to function during any reconstruction. This is the simple reason why we must reform its institutions little by little, until we have more experience in social engineering.

This leads us to the more important second point, to the irrationalism which is inherent in radicalism. In all matters, we can only learn by trial and error, by making mistakes and improvements; we can never rely on inspiration, although inspirations may be most valuable as long as they can be checked by experience. Accordingly, *it is not reasonable to assume that a complete reconstruction of our social world would lead at once to a workable system*. Rather we should expect that, owing to lack of experience, many mistakes would be made, which could only be eliminated by a long and laborious process of small adjustments; in other words, by that rational method of piecemeal engineering whose application we advocate. But those who dislike this method as insufficiently radical would have again to wipe out their freshly constructed society, in order to start anew with a clean canvas; and since the new start, for the same reasons, would not lead to perfection either, they would have to repeat this process without ever getting anywhere. Those who admit this and are prepared to adopt our more modest method of piecemeal improvements, but only after the first radical canvas cleaning, can hardly escape the criticism that their first sweeping and violent measures were quite unnecessary.

Aestheticism and radicalism must lead us to jettison reason, and to replace it by a desperate hope for political miracles. This irrational attitude which springs from an intoxication with dreams of a beautiful world is what I call Romanticism[12]. It may seek its heavenly city in the past or in the future; it may preach 'back to nature' or 'forward to a world of love and beauty'; but its appeal is always to our emotions rather than to reason. Even with the best intentions of making heaven on earth it only succeeds in making it a hell — that hell which man alone prepares for his fellowmen.

Notes

The motto, from *Les Thibaults* by Roger Martin du Gard, is quoted from p. 575 of the English edition (*Summer 1914*, London 1940).

1 My description of Utopian social engineering seems to coincide with that kind of social engineering advocated by M. Eastman in *Marxism — Is it Science?*; see especially pp. 22*f*. I have the impression that Eastman's views represent the swing of the pendulum from historicism to Utopian engineering. But I may possibly be mistaken, and what Eastman really has in mind may be more in the direction of what I call piecemeal engineering. Roscoe Pound's conception of 'social engineering' is clearly 'piecemeal'.

2 I believe that there is, from the ethical point of view, no symmetry between suffering and happiness, or between pain and pleasure. Both the greatest happiness principle of the Utilitarians and Kant's principle, 'Promote other people's happiness…', seem to me (at least in their formulations) fundamentally wrong in this point, which is, however, not one for rational argument. (For the irrational aspect of ethical beliefs, see note 10 to the present chapter. In my opinion human suffering makes a direct moral appeal, namely, the appeal for help, while there is no similar call to increase the happiness of a man who is doing well anyway. (A further criticism of the Utilitarian formula 'Maximize pleasure' is that it assumes, in principle, a continuous pleasure-pain scale which allows us to treat degrees of pain as negative degrees of pleasure. But, from the moral point of view, pain cannot be outweighed by pleasure, and especially not one man's pain by another man's pleasure. Instead of the greatest happiness for the greatest number, one should demand, more modestly, the least amount of avoidable suffering for all; and further, that unavoidable suffering — such as hunger in times of unavoidable shortage of food — should be distributed as equally as possible.) I find that there is some kind of analogy between this view of ethics and the view of scientific methodology which I have advocated in my *Lugik der Forschung*. It adds to clarity in the field of ethics if we formulate our demands negatively, i.e. if we demand the elimination of suffering rather than the promotion of happiness. Similarly, it is helpful to formulate the task of scientific method as the elimination of false theories (from the various theories tentatively proffered) rather than the attainment of established truths.

3 A very good example of this kind of piecemeal engineering, or perhaps of the corresponding piecemeal technology, are C.G.F. Simkin's two articles on 'Budgetary Reform' in the Australian *Economic Record* (1941, pp. 192*ff*., and 1942, pp. 16*ff*.) I am glad to be able to refer to these two articles since they make conscious use of the methodological

principles which I advocate; they thus show that these principles are useful in the practice of technological research.

I do not suggest that piecemeal engineering cannot be bold, or that it must be confined to 'smallish' problems. But I think that the degree of complication which we can tackle is governed by the degree of our experience gained in conscious and systematic piecemeal engineering.

4 This view has recently been emphasized by F.A. von Hayek in various interesting papers (cf. for instance his *Freedom and the Economic System*, Public Policy Pamphlets, Chicago, 1939). What I call 'Utopian engineering' corresponds largely, I believe, to what Hayek would call 'centralized' or 'collectivist' planning. Hayek himself recommends what he calls 'planning for freedom'. I suppose he would agree that this would take the character of 'piecemeal engineering'. One could, I believe, formulate Hayek's objections to collectivist planning somewhat like this. If we try to construct society according to a blueprint, then we may find that we cannot incorporate individual freedom in our blueprint; or if we do, that we cannot realize it. The reason is that centralized economic planning eliminates from economic life one of the most important functions of the individual, namely his function as a chooser of the product, as a free consumer. In other words, Hayek's criticism belongs to the realm of social technology. He points out a certain technological impossibility, namely that of drafting a plan for a society which is at once economically centralized and individualistic.

[Readers of Hayek's *The Road to Serfdom* (1944) may feel puzzled by this note; for Hayek's attitude in this book is so explicit that no room is left for the somewhat vague comments of my note. But my note was printed before Hayek's book was published; and although many of his leading ideas were foreshadowed in his earlier writings, they were not yet quite as explicit as in *The Road to Serfdom*. And many ideas which, as a matter of course, we now associate with Hayek's name were unknown to me when I wrote my note.

In the light of what I know now about Hayek's position, my summary of it does not appear to me to be mistaken, although it is, no doubt, an understatement of his position. The following modifications may perhaps put the matter right.

Hayek would not himself use the word 'social engineering' for any political activity which he would be prepared to advocate. He objects to this term because it is associated with a general tendency which he has called 'scientism' — the naïve belief that the methods of the natural sciences (or, rather, what many people believe to be the natural sciences) must produce similarly impressive results in the social field. (Cf. Hayek's two series of articles *Scientism and the Study of Society*, *Economica*, ix-xi, 1942-4, and *The Counter-Revolution of Science*, ibid., viii, 1941.)

If, by 'scientism', we mean a tendency to ape, in the field of social science, what is supposed to be the methods of the natural sciences, then *historicism can be described as a form of scientism.* A typical and influential scientistic argument in favour of historicism is, in brief, this: 'We can predict eclipses; why should we not be able to predict revolutions'; or, in a more elaborate form: 'The task of science is to predict; thus the task of the social sciences must be to make social, i.e. historical predictions'. I have tried to refute this kind of argument (cf. my *Poverty of Historicism, Economica,* 1944-5, esp. part III, 1945, and *Prediction and Prophecy, and Their Significance for Social Theory,* Library of the Xth International Congress of Philosophy, Amsterdam, 1948); and in this sense I am opposed to scientism.

But if by 'scientism' we should mean the view that the methods of the social sciences are, to a very considerable extent, the same as those of the natural sciences, then I should be obliged to plead 'guilty' to being an adherent of 'scientism'; indeed, I believe that the similarity between the social and the natural sciences can even be used for correcting wrong ideas about the natural sciences by showing that these are much more similar to the social sciences than is generally supposed.

It is for this reason that I have continued to use Roscoe Pound's term 'social engineering' in Roscoe Pound's sense, which, as far as I can see, is free of that 'scientism' which, I think, must be rejected.

Terminology apart, I still think that Hayek's views can be interpreted as favourable to what I call 'piecemeal engineering'. On the other hand, Hayek has given a much clearer formulation of his views than my old outline indicates. The part of his views which corresponds to what I should call 'social engineering' (in Pound's sense) is his suggestion that there is an urgent need, in a free society, to reconstruct what he describes as its *'legal framework'.*]

5 The problem whether or not a good end justifies bad means seems to arise out of such cases as whether one should lie to a sick man in order to set his mind at rest; or whether one should keep a people in ignorance in order to make them happy; or whether one should begin a long and bloody civil war in order to establish a world of peace and beauty.

In all these cases the action contemplated is to bring about first a more immediate result (called 'the means') which is considered an evil, in order that a secondary result (called 'the end') may be brought about which is considered a good.

I think that in all such cases three different kinds of questions arise.

(a) How far are we entitled to assume that the means will in fact lead to the expected end? Since the means are the more immediate result, they will in most cases be the more certain result of the contemplated action, and the end, which is more remote, will be less certain.

The question here raised is a factual question rather than one of moral valuations. It is the question whether, as a matter of fact, the assumed causal connection between the means and the end can be relied upon; and one might say that, if the assumed causal connection does not hold, the case was not one of means and ends, and therefore should not really be considered under this heading.

This may be true. But in practice, the point here considered contains what is perhaps the most important moral issue. For although the question (whether the contemplated means will bring about the contemplated end) is a factual one, *our attitude towards this question raises some of the most fundamental moral problems* — the problem whether we ought to rely, in such cases, on our conviction that such a causal connection holds; or in other words, whether we ought to rely, dogmatically, on causal theories, or whether we should adopt a sceptical attitude towards them, especially where the immediate result of our action is, in itself, considered evil.

This question is perhaps not so important in the first of our three examples, but it is so in the two others. Some people may feel very certain that the causal connections assumed in these two cases hold; but the connection may be a very remote one; and even the emotional certainty of their belief may itself be the result of an attempt to suppress their doubts. (The issue, in other words, is that between the fanatic and the rationalist in the Socratic sense — the man who tries to know his intellectual limitations.) The issue will be the more important the greater the evil of 'the means'. However that may be, to educate oneself so as to adopt an attitude of scepticism towards one's causal theories, and one of intellectual modesty is, without doubt, one of the most important moral duties.

But let us assume that the assumed causal connection holds, or in other words, that there is a situation in which one can properly speak of means and ends. Then we have to distinguish between two further questions, (b) and (c).

(b) Assuming that the causal relation holds, and that we can be reasonably certain of it, the problem becomes, in the main, one of choosing the lesser of two evils — that of the contemplated means and that which must arise if these means are not adopted. In other words, the best of ends do not as such justify bad means, but the attempt to avoid worse results may justify actions which are in themselves producing bad results. (Most of us do not doubt that it is right to cut off a man's limb in order to save his life.)

In this connection it may become very important that we are not really able to assess the evils in question. Some Marxists, for example, believe that there would be far less suffering involved in a violent social revolution than in the chronic evils inherent in what they call 'Capitalism'. But even assuming that this revolution leads to a better state of affairs — how can they evaluate the suffering in the one state and in the other? Here, again, a factual question arises, and it is again our duty not to overestimate our factual knowledge. Besides, granted that the contemplated means will on balance improve the situation — have we ascertained whether other means would not achieve better results, at a lesser price?

But the same example raises another very important question. Assuming, again, that the sum total of suffering under 'Capitalism' would, if it continues for several generations, outweigh the suffering of civil war — can we condemn one generation to suffer for the sake of later generations? (There is a great difference between sacrificing oneself for the sake of others, and between sacrificing others — or oneself *and* others — for some such end.)

(c) The third point of importance is that we must not think that the so-called 'end', as a final result, is more important than the intermediate result, the 'means'. This idea which is suggested by such sayings as 'All is well that ends well' is most misleading. First, the so-called 'end' is hardly ever the end of the matter. Secondly, the means are not, as it were, superseded once the end is achieved. For example, 'bad' means, such as a new powerful weapon, used in war for the sake of victory may, after this 'end' is achieved, create new trouble. In other words, even if something can be correctly described as a means to an end, it is, very often, much more than this. It produces other results apart from the end in question; and what we have to balance is not the (past or present) means against (future) ends, but the total results, as far as they can be foreseen, of one course of action against those of another. These results spread over a period of time which includes intermediate results; and the contemplated 'end' will not be the last to be considered.

6   (1) I believe that the parallelism between the institutional problems of civil and of international peace is most important. Any international organization which has legislative, administrative, and judicial institutions *as well as an armed executive which is prepared to act* should be as successful in upholding international peace as are the analogous institutions within the state. But it seems to me important not to expect more. We have been able to reduce crime within the states to something comparatively unimportant, but we have not been able to stamp it out entirely. Therefore we shall, for a long time to come, need a police force which is ready to strike, and which sometimes does strike. Similarly, I believe that we must be prepared for the probability that we may not be able to stamp out international crime. If we declare that our aim is to make war impossible once and for all, then we may undertake too much, with the fatal result that we may not have a force which is ready to strike when these hopes are disappointed. (The failure of the League of Nations to take action against aggressors was, at least in the case of the attack on Manchukuo, due largely to the general feeling that the League had been established in order to end *all* wars and not to wage them. This shows that propaganda for ending *all* wars is self-defeating. We must end international anarchy, and be ready to go to war against any international crime. Cf. especially H. Mannheim, *War and Crime*, 1941; and A.D. Lindsay, 'War to End War', in

Background and Issues, 1940.)

But it is also important to search for the weak spot in the analogy between civil and international peace, that is to say, for the point where the analogy breaks down. In the case of civil peace, upheld by the state, there is the individual citizen to be protected by the state. The citizen is, as it were, a 'natural' unit or atom (although there is a certain 'conventional' element even in the conditions of citizenship). On the other hand, the members or units or atoms of our international order will be states. But a state can never be a 'natural' unit like the citizen; *there are no natural boundaries to a state.* The boundaries of a state change, and can be defined only by applying the principle of a *status quo*; and since every *status quo* must refer to an arbitrarily chosen date, the determination of the boundaries of a state is purely conventional.

The attempt to find some 'natural' boundaries for states, and accordingly, to look upon the state as a 'natural' unit, leads to the *principle of the national state* and to the romantic fictions of nationalism, racialism, and tribalism. But this principle is not 'natural', and the idea that there exist natural units like nations or linguistic or racial groups, is entirely fictitious. Here, if anywhere, we should learn from history; for since the dawn of history, men have been continually mixed, unified, broken up, and mixed again; and this cannot be undone, even if it were desirable.

There is a second point in which the analogy between civil and international peace breaks down. The state must protect the individual citizen, its units or atoms; but the international organization also must ultimately protect human individuals, and not its units or atoms, i.e. states or nations.

The complete renunciation of the principle of the national state (a principle which owes its popularity solely to the fact that it appeals to tribal instincts and that it is the cheapest and surest method by which a political who has nothing better to offer can make his way), and the recognition of the necessarily conventional demarcation of *all* states, together with the further insight that *human individuals and not states or nations must be the ultimate concern even of international organizations*, will help us to realize clearly, and to get over, the difficulties arising from the breakdown of our fundamental analogy.

(2) It seems to me that the remark that human individuals must be recognized to be the ultimate concern not only of international organizations, but of all politics, international as well as 'national' or parochial, has important applications. We must realize that *we can treat individuals fairly, even if we decide to break up the power organization of an aggressive state* or 'nation' to which these individuals belong. It is a widely held prejudice that the destruction and control of the military, political, and even of the economic power of a state or 'nation' implies misery or subjugation for its individual

citizens. But this prejudice is as unwarranted as it is dangerous.

It is unwarranted provided that an international organization protects the citizens of the so weakened state against exploitation of their political and military weakness. The only damage to the individual citizen that cannot be avoided is one to his national pride; and if we assume that he was a citizen of an aggressor country, then this is a damage which will be unavoidable in any case, provided the aggression has been warded off.

The prejudice that we cannot distinguish between the treatment of a state and of its individual citizens is also very dangerous, for when it comes to the problem of dealing with an aggressor country, it necessarily creates two factions in the victorious countries, viz. the faction of those who demand harsh treatment and those who demand leniency. As a rule, both overlook the possibility of treating a state harshly, and, at the same time, its citizens leniently.

But if this possibility is overlooked, then the following is likely to happen. Immediately after the victory the aggressor state *and* its citizens will be treated comparatively harshly. But the state, the power organization, will probably not be treated as harshly as might be reasonable because of a reluctance to treat innocent individuals harshly, that is to say, because the influence of the faction of leniency will make itself felt somehow. In spite of this reluctance, it is likely that individuals will suffer beyond what they deserve. After a short time, therefore, a reaction is likely to occur in the victorious countries. Equalitarian and humanitarian tendencies are likely to strengthen the faction of leniency until the harsh policy is reversed. But this development is not only likely to give the aggressor state a chance for a new aggression; it will also provide it with the weapon of the moral indignation of one who has been wronged, while the victorious countries are likely to become afflicted with the diffidence of those who feel that they may have done wrong.

This very undesirable development must in the end lead to a new aggression. It can be avoided if, and only if, from the start, a clear distinction is made between the aggressor state (and those responsible for its acts) on the one hand, and its citizens on the other hand. Harshness towards the aggressor state, and even the radical destruction of its power apparatus, will not produce this moral reaction of humanitarian feelings in the victorious countries if it is combined with a policy of fairness towards the individual citizens.

But is it possible to break the political power of a state without injuring its citizens indiscriminately? In order to prove that this is possible I shall construct an example of a policy which breaks the political and military power of an aggressor state without violating the interests of its individual citizens.

The fringe of the aggressor country, including its seacoast and its main (not all) sources of water power, coal, and steel, could be severed from the state, and administered as an international territory, never to be returned. Harbours as well as the raw materials could be made accessible to the citizens of the state for their legitimate economic activities, without imposing any economic disadvantages on them, on the condition that they *invite* international commissions to control the proper use of these facilities. Any use which may help to build up a new war potential is forbidden, and if there is reason for suspicion and the internationalized facilities and raw material may be so used, their use has at once to be stopped. It then rests with the suspect party to *invite* and to facilitate a thorough investigation and to offer satisfactory guarantees for a proper use.

Such a procedure would not eliminate the possibility of a new attack but it would force the aggressor state to make its attack on the internationalized territories previous to building up a new war potential. Thus such an attack would be hopeless provided the other countries have retained and developed their war potential. Faced with this situation the former aggressor state would be forced to change its attitude radically, and adopt one of co-operation. It would be forced to *invite* the international control of its industry and to facilitate the investigation of the international controlling authority (instead of obstructing them) because only such an attitude would guarantee its use of the facilities needed by its industries; and such a development would be likely to take place without any further interference with the international politics of the state.

The danger that the internationalization of these facilities might be misused for the purpose of exploiting or of humiliating the population of the defeated country can be counteracted by international legal measures that provide for courts of appeal, etc.

This example shows that it is not impossible to treat a state harshly and its citizens leniently.

[I have left parts (1) and (2) of this note exactly as they were written in 1942. Only in part (3), which is nontopical, have I made an addition, after the first two paragraphs.]

(3) But is such an engineering approach towards the problem of peace scientific? Many will contend, I am sure, that a truly scientific attitude towards the problems of war and peace must be different. They will say that *we must first study the causes of war*. We must study the forces that lead to war, and also those that may lead to peace. It has been recently claimed, for instance, that 'lasting peace' can come only if we consider fully the 'underlying dynamic forces' in society that may produce war or peace. In order to find out these forces, we must, of course, study history. In other words, we must approach the problem of peace by a historicist method, and not by a technological method. This, it is claimed, is the only scientific approach.

The historicist may, with the help of history, show that the causes of war can be found in the clash of economic interests; or in the clash of classes; or of ideologies, for instance, freedom versus tyranny; or in the clash of races, or of nations, or of imperialisms, or of militarist systems; or in hate; or in fear; or in envy; or in the wish to take revenge; or in all these things together, and in countless more. And he will thereby show that the task of removing these causes is extremely difficult. And he will show that there is no point in constructing an international organization, as long as we have not removed the causes of war, for instance the economic causes, etc.

Similarly, psychologism may argue that the causes of war are to be found in 'human nature', or more specifically, in its aggressiveness, and that the way to peace is that of preparing for other outlets for aggression. (The reading of thrillers has been suggested in all seriousness — in spite of the fact that some of our late dictators were addicted to them.)

I do not think that these methods of dealing with this important problem are very promising. And I do not believe, more especially, in the plausible argument that in order to establish peace we must ascertain the cause or causes of war.

Admittedly, there are cases where the method of searching for the causes of some evil, and of removing them, may be successful. If I feel a pain in my foot I may find that it is caused by a pebble and remove it. But we must not generalize from this. The method of removing pebbles does not even cover all cases of pains in my foot. In some such cases I may not find 'the cause'; and in others, I may be unable to remove it.

In general, the method of removing causes of some undesirable event is applicable only if we know a short list of necessary conditions (i.e. a list of conditions such that the event in question does never happen except if one at least of the conditions on the list is present) and if all of these conditions can be controlled, or more precisely prevented. (It may be remarked that necessary conditions are hardly what one describes by the vague term 'causes'; they are, rather, what is usually called 'contributing causes'; as a rule, where we speak of 'causes' we mean a set of sufficient conditions.) But I do not think that we can hope to construct such a list of the necessary conditions of war. Wars have broken out under the most varying circumstances. Wars are not simple phenomena, such as, perhaps, thunderstorms. There is no reason to believe that by calling a vast variety of phenomena 'wars', we ensure that they are all 'caused' in the same way.

All this shows that the apparently unprejudiced and convincingly scientific approach, the study of the 'causes of war' is, in fact, not only prejudiced, but also liable to bar the way to a reasonable solution; it is in fact, pseudoscientific.

How far would we get if, instead of introducing laws and a police force, we approached the problem of criminality 'scientifically', i.e. by trying to find out what precisely are the causes of crime? I do not imply that we cannot here or there discover important factors contributing to crime or to war, and that we cannot avert much harm in this way; but this can well be done after we have got crime under control, i.e. after we have introduced our police force. On the other hand, the study of economic, psychological, hereditary, moral, etc., 'causes' of crime, and the attempt to remove these causes, would hardly have led us to find out that a police force (which does not remove the cause) can bring crime under control. Quite apart from the vagueness of such phrases as 'the cause of war', the whole approach is anything but scientific. It is as if one insisted that it is unscientific to wear an overcoat when it is cold; and that we should rather study the causes of cold weather, and remove them. Or, perhaps, that lubricating is unscientific, since we should rather find out the causes of friction and remove them. This latter example shows, I believe, the absurdity of the apparently scientific criticism; for just as lubrication certainly reduces the 'causes' of friction, so an international police force (or another armed body of this kind) may reduce an important 'cause' of war, namely the hope of 'getting away with it'.

7 I have tried to show this in my *Logik der Forschung*. I believe, in accordance with the methodology outlined, that systematic piecemeal engineering will help us to build up an empirical social technology, arrived at by the method of trial and error. Only in this way, I believe, can we begin to build up an empirical social science. The fact that such a social science hardly exists so far, and that the historical method is incapable of furthering it much, is one of the strongest arguments against the possibility of large-scale or Utopian social engineering. See also my *Poverty of Historicism* (*Economica*, 1944-5).

8 For a very similar formulation, see John Carruthers' lecture *Socialism and Radicalism* (published as a pamphlet by the Hammersmith Socialist Society, London, 1894). He argues in a typical manner against piecemeal reform: 'Every palliative measure brings its own evil with it, and the evil is generally greater than that it was intended to cure. Unless we make up our minds to have a new garment altogether, we must be prepared to go in rags, for patching will not improve the old one.' (It should be noted that by 'radicalism', used by Carruthers in the title of his lecture, he means about the opposite of what is meant here. Carruthers advocates an uncompromising programme of canvas cleaning and attacks 'radicalism', i.e. the programme of 'progressive' reforms advocated by the 'radical liberals'. This use of the term 'radical' is, of course, more customary than mine; nevertheless, the term means originally 'going to the root' — of evil, for instance, or 'eradicating the evil'; and there is no proper substitute for it.)

For the quotations in the next paragraph of the text (the 'divine original' which the artist-politician must 'copy'), see *Republic*, 500e/501a.

In Plato's Theory of Forms are, I believe, elements which are of great importance for the understanding, and for the theory, of art. This aspect of Platonism is treated by J.A. Stewart in his book, *Plato's*

Doctrine of Ideas (1909), 128*ff*. I believe, however, that he stresses too much the object of pure contemplation (as opposed to that 'pattern' which the artist not only visualizes, but which he labours to reproduce, on his canvas.)

9 *Republic*, 520c. For the 'Royal Art', see especially the *Statesman*.

10 It has often been said that ethics is only a part of aesthetics, since ethical questions are ultimately a matter of taste. (Cf., for instance, G.E.G. Catlin, *The Science and Methods of Politics*, London, 1964, 315*ff*.) If by saying this, no more is meant than that ethical problems cannot be solved by the rational methods of science, I agree. But we must not overlook the vast difference between moral 'problems of taste', and problems of taste in aesthetics. If I dislike a novel, a piece of music, or perhaps a picture, I need not read it, or listen to it, or look at it. Aesthetic problems (with the possible exception of architecture) are largely of a private character, but ethical problems concern men, and their lives. To this extent, there is a fundamental difference between them.

11 For this and the preceding quotations, cf. *Republic*, 500d-501a (italics mine).

The two quotations in the next paragraph are from the *Republic*, 541a, and from the *Statesman*, 293c-e.

It is interesting (because it is, I believe, characteristic of the hysteria of romantic radicalism with its *hubris* — its ambitious arrogance of godlikeness) to see that both passages of the *Republic* — the canvas cleaning of 500d*ff*., and the purge of 541a — are preceded by reference to the godlikeness of the philosophers; cf. 500c-d, 'the philosopher becomes ... godlike himself', and 540c-d, 'And the state will erect monuments, at the expense of the public, to commemorate them; and sacrifices will be offered to them, as demigods, ... or at least as men who are blessed by grace and godlike'.

It is also interesting (for the same reasons) that the first of these passages is preceded by the passage (498d/e*f*.) in which Plato expresses his hope that philosophers may become, as rulers, acceptable even to 'the many'.

Concerning the term 'liquidate' the following modern outburst of radicalism may be quoted: 'Is it not obvious that if we are to have socialism — real and permanent socialism — all the fundamental opposition must be "liquidated" (i.e. rendered politically inactive by disfranchisement, and if necessary by imprisonment)?' This remarkable rhetorical question is printed on p. 18 of the still more remarkable pamphlet *Christians in the Class Struggle*, by Gilbert Cope, with a foreword by the Bishop of Bradford (1942). The Bishop, in his Foreword, denounces 'our present economic system' as 'immoral and unChristian', and he says that 'when something is so plainly the work of the devil, ... nothing can excuse a minister of the Church from working for its destruction'. Accordingly, he recommends 'this pamphlet as a lucid and penetrating analysis'.

A few more sentences may be quoted from the pamphlet. 'Two parties may ensure partial democracy, but a full democracy can be established only by a single party ...' (p.17). — 'In the period of transition ... the workers ... must be led and organized by a single party which tolerates the existence of no other party fundamentally opposed to it ...' (p. 19). — 'Freedom in the socialist state means that no one is allowed to attack the principle of common ownership, but everyone is encouraged to work for its more effective realization and operation.... The important matter of how the opposition is to be nullified depends upon the methods used by the opposition itself' (p.18).

Most interesting of all is perhaps the following argument (also to be found on p. 18), which deserves to be read carefully: 'Why is it possible to have a socialist party in a capitalist country if it is not possible to have a capitalist party in a socialist state? The answer is simply that the one is a movement involving all the productive forces of a great majority against a small minority, while the other is an attempt of a minority to restore their position of power and privilege by renewed exploitation of the majority.' In other words, a ruling 'small minority' can afford to be tolerant, while a 'great majority' cannot afford to tolerate a 'small minority'. This simple answer is indeed a model of 'a lucid and penetrating analysis', as the Bishop puts it.

12 It seems that romanticism, in literature as well as in philosophy, may be traced back to Plato. It is well known that Rousseau was directly influenced by him. Rousseau also knew Plato's *Statesman* (cf. the *Social Contract*, book II, ch. VII, and book III, ch. VI) with its eulogy of the early hill-shepherds. But apart from this direct influence, it is probable that Rousseau derived his pastoral romanticism and love for primitivity indirectly from Plato; for he was certainly influenced by the Italian Renaissance, which had rediscovered Plato, and especially his naturalism and his dreams of a perfect society of primitive shepherds. It is interesting that Voltaire recognized at once the dangers of Rousseau's romantic obscurantism; just as Kant was not prevented by his admiration for Rousseau from recognizing this danger when he was faced with it in Herder's 'Ideas'.

8

'Social engineering'

RUSH RHEES

'The only course open to the social sciences', says Dr Popper, 'is ...
to tackle the practical problems of our time with the help of the
theoretical methods which are fundamentally the same in *all*
sciences.... A social technology is needed which can be tested by
social engineering'[1].

On this view, then, the social sciences are concerned with
'practical problems'. And although these differ from theoretical
problems, the assumption is that the same methods may be used for
solving them.

But there are important differences. 'The social engineer believes
that man is the master of his own destiny, and that in accordance
with our aims we can influence or change the history of man just as
we have changed the face of the earth' (vol. i, p. 17). But the history
of man is fundamentally different from the face of the earth, and so
is the science of it. 'The beginning of social science ... is marked by
the distinction between two different elements in man's environment — his natural environment and his social environment'. For
there can be no social science until there is a clear grasp of the
fundamental distinction between '(*a*) *natural laws*, or laws of
nature, or positive laws, such as the law of the apparent motion of
the sun, or the law of gravity; and (*b*) *normative laws*, or standards,

Reprinted from Mind, *Vol. LVI* (1947), *by permission of* Mind. *This article has
also appeared in R. Rhees,* Without Answers (*Routledge and Kegan Paul, 1969*).

or norms, i.e. rules that forbid or demand certain modes of conduct, or certain procedures; examples are the laws of the Athenian Constitution, or the rules pertaining to the election of Members of Parliament, or the Ten Commandments' (vol. i, p. 49). These normative laws are 'decisions' and are man-made. Natural laws are independent of us. This is part of what Popper calls the 'dualism of facts and decisions'.

Granting that these are different senses of 'law', it might still seem misleading to say that natural science studies natural laws, while social science studies normative laws. No doubt the study of society takes account of norms and standards, and of how they operate — how they arise, and how they influence social developments. But then it is studying them as natural, and if it succeeds in giving any general account of their operation it is formulating natural laws.

But Popper is not thinking of the *study* of society when he speaks of social science. He is thinking of the 'scientific' *changing* of it — of the solution of 'practical problems'. That is why he thinks that if the social sciences were scientific they would be forms of social engineering.

Not all his statements about this are consistent. Towards the beginning of his book he suggests that a social engineer merely asks whether a particular institution is 'well designed and organized to serve' any aims which have been proposed. 'In his function as a citizen, who has certain ends in which he believes, he may demand that these ends, and the appropriate measures, should be adopted. But as a technologist, he would carefully distinguish between the question of the ends and their choice and questions concerning the facts, i.e. the social effects of any measure which might be taken' (vol. i, p. 19). But he generally speaks as though it were the business of social engineers to 'reform' social institutions. It is to this end that they perform 'social experiments'. Their problems are problems of how to 'improve civilization'. 'The "world"' he says (vol. ii, p. 337), 'is not rational, but it is the task of science to rationalize it. "Society" is not rational, but it is the task of the social engineer to rationalize it.' By 'rationalizing the world' I suppose he means *understanding* the world, or giving an account of it. But he does not mean that the social engineer should try only to understand society. His point is that rationalizing society is altering or improving it. That is clear from the whole of chapter 24.

So when Popper speaks of making the social sciences scientific he generally means making social *policy* scientific[2]. He is holding that there is an analogy between 'problems of social policy' and problems of science; and that they may be solved by the same methods. The science and discussion of social affairs will be a discussion of norms and of decisions; it will be a matter of justifying decisions or criticizing them. It will include the critical discussion of institutions. But progress in such discussion will be progress in working out a policy for institutions, not a theory of them.

For I take it that the dualism of facts and decisions means, for Popper, that decisions must be studied differently. That is part of what is meant by saying that they cannot be reduced to facts. I may decide that it is wrong to steal. Then my deciding is a fact, but 'It's wrong to steal' is not a fact. It is not something to be *believed*. It is something that has to be *decided* — for or against. And the utterance of it is not the expression of a belief but of a decision. If I try to influence another in respect of such utterances, I try to influence his will or his decisions, not his beliefs. I could not *disprove* his decision that it is wrong to steal, or show that it was mistaken; at least not in the way in which I might show that his beliefs about matters of fact were mistaken. I may point out to him certain consequences. But 'the decision depends on him'.

Popper's discussion of all this is confusing, and I do not know how near my paraphrase comes. But he wants to hold, I think, that *because* 'decisions or norms' cannot be reduced to facts, social science is a practical inquiry. To improve its method we must bring scientific method to decisions; at least when they are decisions of public policy.

The dualism of facts and decisions implies also that 'existing normative laws (or social institutions)' (vol. i, p. 52) depend on 'us'. It is 'we' who create or adopt them, and their existence cannot result from anything but our decision to create or adopt them. The dualism — the distinction between a mechanistic and a voluntaristic realm — is needed for the view that man is the master of his destiny and that society can be shaped and controlled by social engineering. But there are complications. We must apply engineering to social institutions. Yet it is hard to think of applying it to decisions. And we find that institutions are really a combination of normative laws and natural laws. 'There are important natural laws in social life also. For these the term "sociological laws" seems appropriate.... In institutions normative laws and sociological laws are closely interwoven[3] and it is therefore impossible to understand the functioning of two institutions without being able to distinguish between these two' (vol. i, pp. 56, 57).

There is such a dualism in institutions that Popper says different things about them. At first he uses 'normative laws' and 'social institutions' as equivalent. He says that institutions are norms or standards which we adopt and for which we are morally responsible. But he sometimes speaks of them as machines that need intelligent supervision, or as fortresses which must be manned. His main view seems to be that they are *instruments* which 'we' may use for good or evil.

When he is speaking of them as something for which we are morally responsible, he equates institutions with conventions and so with normative laws and so with norms. 'Norms and normative laws can be made and changed by man, more especially by a decision or convention to observe them or to alter them, and it is therefore man who is normally responsible for them; not perhaps for the norms which he finds to exist in society when he first begins to reflect on them, but for the norms which he is prepared to tolerate once he has found out that he can do something to alter them. Norms are man-made in the sense that we must blame nobody but ourselves for them' (vol. i, p. 51).

Here, and throughout the book, Popper is ruthless with 'man' and 'we'. 'Social institutions have been made by man' may mean only that they have arisen in the histories of human societies, or that their development is a development of human and social activities. It may mean also that they are not 'fixed' as say, human anatomy is. But this would not mean that they have arisen because anyone decided to create them, or that they persist — when they do — because anyone has decided to maintain them. Nor does it give ground for saying that 'the responsibility for them is entirely ours'. To say that 'man' is morally responsible for anything is meaningless; just as it is to say that 'man' has made a decision. But this sort of confusion helps Popper to combine an historical with a voluntarist view of society (and to hold that man makes his history, which is a history *of* his making although his making is not made).

But the passage has a further interest. It is not at first sight clear why dualism should be as important for social science as Popper says it is. There can be no social engineering unless normative laws or social institutions can be made and changed by man. But machines can also be made by man, and we have changed the face of the earth; and these are not norms. So why cannot social science hold that normative laws can be made and changed without holding to a dualism of norms and facts? Popper gives one answer when he explains that to say we make norms means that we are morally responsible for them — 'that we alone carry the responsibility for adopting them'. The earth is not responsible for the changes wrought in its face, but we are responsible for the changes in the scoiety in which we live. Theories of social engineering have been criticized on the ground that the 'engineer' must be subject to the influences he is trying to control. But this does not alter his responsibilty. He is responsible even for the ways in which those influences — existing norms — affect him. And if he tries to alter them, the way in which he does this depends entirely upon him; it is his responsibility. Social engineering is possible if you recognize this character of normative laws or institutions — this sort of 'dependence on us' which they have; and it would not be possible otherwise.

This account of what is meant by 'making' normative laws or institutions leaves the analogy with mechanical engineering rather thin. But I do not think Popper could hold to social engineering without it.

Still, when he is emphasizing the instrumental character of institutions and comparing them with machines, this feature of their dependence is left more in the background. 'Institutions are always made by establishing the observance of certain norms, designed with a certain aim in mind.... Like machines, they need intelligent supervision by someone who understands their way of functioning and, most of all, their purpose, since we cannot build them so that they work entirely automatically' (vol. i, p. 56). 'The engineer or the technologist approaches institutions rationally as means that serve certain ends ... as a technologist he judges them wholly according to their appropriateness, efficiency, simplicity, etc.' (vol. i, p. 19). Here he mentions insurance and a police force as examples. But he would clearly regard political institutions, penal systems, educational institutions, trade unions, banking institutions, scientific institutions and so on, in the same way.

I see no reason to believe that all institutions have been 'designed with a certain aim in mind'. Why should one say this of penal systems, for instance, or of many legal institutions? One might argue that they have not been designed at all, any more than language has. But anyway, as they exist now, there is apparently no *one* aim for which people support them. That is why you cannot give *the* reason why we have a public penal system, for instance. Some may advocate punishing criminals because they deserve it, others say it is needed as a deterrent, or they may give other utilitarian or sociological justifications. This is true of statesmen as well as laymen. But the penal system is there and it is carried on in that way, and it is generally supported. Similar remarks might be made of other institutions. Even when they have grown from beginnings which were designed with a certain aim in mind, the design cannot generally have included much of their present development; and it does not account for much. They have been supported and taken over and developed by influences and new developments that had no part in their beginning. And of course for the most part we simply support such institutions because they *are* there, and not because we have any aim or reason in doing so; so with property rights, contract, taxation, and so on.

So why talk of 'the purpose' of social institutions? What is the purpose of educational institutions, for instance? or, if you like, what is 'the aim of education'? Those who work in education may believe they are training people for 'life', or making them better able to fend for themselves, or that they are trying to develop personalities, or that they are training them for citizenship or merely that they are trying to give them good schooling. Such ideas may conflict, and there may be conflicts within educational institutions. But they will go on just the same.

Possibly you can talk of the purpose of a standing army; and perhaps of a police force. (Though in neither case would this be quite simple.) I do not think you can talk of the purpose of banks, though of course you would go to them for certain things and not for others. Trade unions may become 'organs of struggle' or they may become organizations for negotiating with employers and administering relief. I should not know what was meant by their 'purpose'. And what is the purpose of the theatre?

It might be answered that the purpose of the theatre is to produce drama; as it might be said that the purpose of universities is to carry on academic work. These answers would be disputed. And in a sense they are denying that there is any purpose. But such answers suggest standards of good work or of serious work in these fields. And it might be argued that unless there is concern for these standards the institutions may die out or lose any distinctive character that they have. I do not know whether this is true. But in any case it is a different proposition from Popper's view that institutions 'need intelligent supervision'.

There are conflicting tendencies in the working of any institution. But there are common ways of working there too. Otherwise the institution could not go on. And this makes it possible for those engaged in them to discuss and formulate policies for institutions (even though some opposition may remain to any declared policy). But that does not mean that the institutions are 'means' which 'serve the ends' of those engaged in them. Banking institutions are not merely instruments of those engaged in their operation. These people may make decisions in the course of their work and may contribute to the framing of policies. But these are *banking* policies, policies *of* the institutions. They are not statements of ends that banking institutions are to be used for. And similarly elsewhere.

This is obscured by Popper's statement that 'the functioning of even the best institutions will always depend, to a considerable degree, on its personnel. Institutions are like fortresses. They must be well designed *and* manned.... They cannot improve themselves. The problem of improving them is always a problem of persons rather than of institutions' (vol. i, pp. 110, 111). This idea of 'manning' institutions, as men man fortresses or man machines, is misleading. (An army may man a fortress but do the soldiers 'man' the army?) And it leads here to a false distinction between personnel problems and problems of institutions. We are told that an individual might improve an institution by working hard and setting a good example. I doubt if Popper means just this. Yet apart from this the improvement of institutions is not a matter of individual decisions and individual conscience.

And in suggesting that the institution is controlled by those who man it, and that their plans and norms and decisions are not controlled by *it* — almost as if the working of the institution itself had nothing to do with decisions and projects, as if they were no more part of that working than they are of the working of a machine — Popper is also implying that just as the effect of the machine, what it accomplishes at any time, depends on the use we put it to, so it is too with institutions. Yet the contrast between the work a machine does and the influence of a social institution is really greater than the analogy. And for reasons similar to those which interfere with the notion that institutions are manned. You can use a bulldozer for various things, or you can leave it in the garage. But with most institutions it is not like that. The sort of influence they have is largely independent of any plans we may have for them, or any use we may wish to put them to. And this is just because they *are* institutions and are not machines. They are features or forms of social existence, not instruments of it. New institutions may develop — and existing institutions may change — *with* the development of machines. So with the development of printing, telephones, means of transport, wireless, motion pictures and many others. But even so there is no control of the institutions parallel to the control of the machines.

It is sometimes said of radio that 'radio is all right; it all depends on what you do with it'. But it is not simply that 'what you do with it' is limited by the special conditions of broadcasting. Radio is *there*, and it affects the lives of people in ways that do not depend upon policies of the board of governors. The fact that broadcast material, of whatever sort, comes into the homes in this way; the fact that people want to have it always on, as a background to what they are doing; that music is 'on tap', to be turned on and off; that broadcasting makes public utterances something different from what they were — these and countless other features of it — including the fact that people cannot do without it — influence public and private living and the development of norms and 'needs' and attitudes. The fact that people have become dependent upon radio and feel lost without it means that its influence is something more than that of an instrument which 'we' may use to exert our good or evil influence.

When Popper says that institutions 'need intelligent supervision', he thinks chiefly of supervision by those with political power. (That is who 'we' are, or should be.) And in much of his discussion it is mainly political institutions he has in mind.

But political control never wholly determines the development of other institutions; though of course it influences them. And political institutions are not just instruments themselves. They influence the character of political activities and decisions. This holds, first, of the institution of state power altogether ('all power corrupts'). There is, I think, no 'purpose' of the state, no 'true end of government'. But state power not only makes it possible to enforce particular policies or insure their domination in the society. It also influences the type of policies that are enforced. It affects the life of the society altogether, though with some forms of constitution more, with others less; and affects the sort of policies that arise there. But especially it affects the policies of those who are possessed of it. However strong other influences, say economic tendencies, may be, there is no doubt that state power has a role of its own, has tendencies of its own which 'catch up' those who arrive at it. Of course these tendencies grow and change with other social developments. But the state is no more just a means or instrument than religion is.

And special political institutions (representative institutions, institutions connected with hereditary monarchy, hierarchical organization and so on) are not just instruments either. They affect the character of political activities and programmes. The publicity

of legislation influences the character of legislation and the sort
of control that governments seek to exercise. A custom of parliamen-
tary manoeuvring and intrigue may influence the way government
is carried on and help to form standards of what is permissible among
popular activities.

Popper's 'technological' view of such institutions is in line with the
Marxist view of politics which he criticizes.

Of course he cannot hold that institutions are through and
through manipulated. That is why he says that there are 'important
sociological laws connected with the functioning of social institutions'. But he holds that 'these laws play a role in our social life
corresponding to the role played in mechanical engineering by, say,
the principle of the lever' (vol. i, p. 56). And he will not admit that
the formation of policies and decisions is *part* of the working of
institutions. Decisions always depend on 'us' who 'supervise' them.

He seems to think that otherwise we should have to say that 'there
is no escape' from the tendencies of existing institutions, and that
institutions can never be 'reformed'. But that would be so only if we
overlooked the ways in which institutions interact, and the ways in
which the working of any institution may be interfered with and
altered by developments from without.

To say that men's activities are largely shaped by the institutions
they work in, is not to say that any man's activities are wholly shaped
by the working of any *one* institution (a branch of scientific research,
or trade union work, say), or that influences from elsewhere may not
operate in him as powerfully. It is partly because they do, that we
find interactions and rival tendencies within any institution. These
differences help to make the history of any institution contingent[4]
(as other social developments do also). But it is no help in
understanding them if you say that men's consciences speak differently, and leave it at that.

In any case, you do not control the development of an institution
by 'improving' or reforming it. Engineers may make a series of
improvements in the design of a machine; and then the way the
machine develops depends on the engineers. This is partly because
the machine will not show important developments without them.
But it would be a more relevant analogy here to say that the way
engineering develops depends on the engineers.

Now Popper seems to think it does. His reason for thinking that
we can control the development of institutions and progressively
improve them seems to lie mainly in his view that in science we have
an example of an institution which controls its own development

and insures its own progress. So he thinks that if you introduce the methods of science into other institutions, and especially into politics, they will be sure of progress too. We may control our destiny if only we are scientific.

If in engineering, or in any science, the methods employed do not lead to a solution of the problems, the methods themselves are criticized. And they are criticized by the methods common to scientific inquiry. This criticism is possible — as in fact the maintenance of scientific method is possible — because of the social character of science; because of the fact that scientific work is always connected with scientific institutions — laboratories, periodicals, congresses — in which many different workers are engaged. It is in these institutions that the standards of objective criticism grow up and live (vol. ii, pp. 205*ff*.).

No doubt this publicity and criticism of methods does help to maintain certain standards of scientific investigation. But these standards may be maintained while others change. Attention may come to be directed to certain features of experimental work at the expense of others. And in particular, there may be a change in the sort of problems that are regarded as important. There is nothing in the social character of scientific institutions or in their devotion to experimental techniques to prevent this. Judged by certain standards, science may degenerate, however great the 'objectivity' that is maintained in it. This seems to have happened as science has been dominated more and more by technology and by 'practical' requirements[5]. There has been a change in the dominant interest and in the character of the work in scientific institutions. And this sort of change cannot be 'corrected' by applying 'scientific method'.

The neglect or disregard of the degeneration of science is connected with the view that science is all a matter of 'the method'. This is a view that Popper explicitly shares. It is fundamental to his view that the development of science is self-controlling. But it is a naïve sort of view. It is like confusing morality with precision.

You do not control the development of technology by keeping it technological either. The same can be said of anything that Popper calls 'social engineering'. And in this case there is not really even the sort of control which the sciences do have. Popper thinks you have begun to introduce engineering into social institutions when you have public control through free criticism, as in science; and when the institutions employ 'the methods of trial and error, of inventing hypotheses which can be practically tested, and of submitting them to practical tests' (vol. ii, p. 210). If politicians began 'to look out for their own mistakes instead of trying to explain them away ... this would mean the introduction of scientific method into politics, since the whole secret of scientific method is a readiness to learn from mistakes' (vol. i, p. 144). But free criticism has not the function in social affairs that it has in science. And experimenting and learning by mistakes are not the same here either. These points are both connected with the fact that controversies in social affairs are not about the solution of problems, as they are in science. If we speak of 'social problems', that is something different.

Public criticism need not be anything like science. Consider literary criticism, for instance; or ethical criticism. Popper might say literary criticism is not criticism of public policy. But neither is scientific criticism. And he has not shown any clearer analogy in the one case than in the other. In fact, policies are criticized on *various* grounds. And the criticism may well be moral.

'Criticism', then, is not one thing. Men criticize in different ways and by different standards. And policies are defended in different ways and with different sorts of reasons. Scientific institutions function as they do because scientists agree as to the sort of evidence that justifies a conclusion or upsets it. But the sort of thing that justifies a social policy to some people may be no justification at all to others. (Compare the pacifist reaction to the justification of going to war; or the other way about. Or consider discussions as to whether strike-breaking is justified.)

Criticism may lead men to alter policies. And reasons may lead men to adopt them. But often they do not. When they do it is not like science. Arguing for a policy is not like establishing a theory, and raising objections to a policy is not like criticizing a theory. In any case, if 'public control through free criticism' means control by all citizens, this is unlike science because there are not common standards and methods of criticizing social policies.

Popper seems to think that 'potentially' there are. He thinks this follows from the social nature of argument and of reason. 'We owe our reason, like our language', he says, 'to intercourse with other men'; and so 'we must recognize everybody with whom we communicate as potentially a source of argument and of reasonable information'. This 'establishes what may be described as "the rational unity of mankind"' (vol. ii, p. 213).

But we do not owe our reason, nor our language, to intercourse with *all* other men. We do not assume the same sort of argumentation or the same standards of criticism in all connections. Nor do all men argue alike, especially about social matters. And there is

nothing in the social character of argumentation to suggest that they
ever will.

Men are led to policies, as they are to social movements or
'causes', by other factors than arguments. The influence is likely to
be the other way. The movements in which they are associated do
much to determine their standards and ways of arguing. Popper
recognizes this when he speaks of the institutional or social character
of scientific thinking. And it is not scientific reasoning that leads
men first to take up science. Men enter different movements without
reasons, and even without deciding to. And the different views they
voice on social matters do not finally rest on reasons either.

So men may well hold to their views and proceed by their
standards, no matter what arguments they meet. And if 'social
problems' are conflicts of social policies and movements, there is no
ground to think that arguments will 'solve' them. Discussion may be
important. It may clarify issues — bring out 'what is involved'. This
is sometimes needed before people can decide what attitude to take
to some proposal. In general, discussion may make reactions less
ambiguous (though it may work the other way). It may alter
decisions, too. A man may wonder whether his decision was the
right one (where to say he was 'mistaken' would mean that he would
have chosen differently if he had seen more). And you can influence
the decisions of others, in certain cases, if you make the issues
clearer to them. But this may not lead to a decision in your favour.
And it will not remove all conflicts.

Public criticism may further publicity in social affairs and help to
bring out what the various aims and movements are. For this reason
it is favoured by some movements and discouraged by others. But
this publicity will not settle any problem, in the sense either of
resolving the conflict or discovering what the outcome will be.

'The method of discussion' sometimes refers to the conference
table, and negotiations. These discussions consist largely in sound-
ing views or demands, and seeing what concessions may be made.
This sometimes leads to 'an arrangement which all parties accept';
and then a 'solution' has been reached. But this 'general accept-
ability' is not like the objectivity of science. It depends on the way
demands are pressed and what the parties are willing to concede in
order to reach an understanding. You may say they wish to avoid
conflict, and so their procedure is 'reasonable'. But this does not
play the part of public control in scientific institutions.

Popper says the 'critical rationalism' he advocates 'suggests the
idea that nobody should be his own judge, and it suggests the idea

of impartiality'. And 'this is closely related to the idea of "scientific objectivity"' (vol. ii, p. 225).

But granting that there are analogies between judicial procedures and scientific objectivity, what has this to do with political controversy? In the courts it is concerned with the effort to determine the facts of the case, and see how they stand in relation to the law. Even so it does not control or determine the *development* of law. One would not speak of scientific objectivity when a judge assesses the importance of claims and interests. In fact, on these questions judges *do* enter political controversy. And while they are not pressing personal considerations — social conflicts are not personal disputes anyway — they are voicing a particular school of thought or current of opinion on social matters. There is no 'impartiality that is closely related to scientific objectivity' on such issues. And we should not know what was meant by saying that there was.

This bears on the further point, that you cannot count on settling such differences by appealing to experience. Popper knows that what he calls 'social experiments' can never be used in social policy as physical experiments are used in engineering, if only because they are not framed so that they can be accurately repeated. But the main point is that in social matters the experiments do not decide the issue. If you speak of learning from experience here, it is a different sort of 'learning'. It means being made wiser, and you expect to see the result in conduct and in future policies. It is not like the case in which a scientist learns more about the behaviour of some material. This is the point of Popper's 'dualism of facts and decisions', or part of it. And in speaking of the 'analysis of the consequences of a moral theory' he says it 'has a certain analogy to scientific method.... But there is a fundamental difference. In the case of a scientific theory, our decision depends upon the results of the experiments.... But in the case of a moral theory we can only confront its consequences with our conscience. And while the verdict of experiments does not depend upon ourselves, the verdict of our conscience does' (vol. ii, p. 220). The same fundamental difference would hold for any adoption of a policy, I suppose. But scientific objectivity surely rests on the fact that in science the experiments *do* decide. And if there is nothing like that in social affairs, or in the settling of social problems, then what has scientific method to do with their solution?

For Popper, however, the real social problems are not conflicts; for these are not fundamental. The real problems are problems of improvement. The aim of social engineering is to 'improve matters', 'improve the lot of man' and 'improve civilization'.

'Improvement', like 'the common good', implies an all-embracing social aim or movement. It is a matter of furthering the cause of society as a whole. Popper speaks of the 'aim of civilization' (vol. i, p. 1). Social engineering is just the scientific way of furthering this aim. And 'piecemeal engineering' takes a no less 'monistic' view of society than 'total engineering' does. It plans to improve society as a whole — to make it a more 'rational' society — even though it will do this one step at a time. It is the cause of all mankind.

But we do not know what sort of enterprise this would be. As if there were some definite form of activity which was working for society; as if 'furthering society' meant anything. Yet if that means nothing, then neither does 'improving society'.

If there are conflicting ways of living, then no sort of work is working for society.

If there were not rival ways of living[6], if there were not conflicting movements, there would not be society as we know it. Any way of living is social. And accordingly it is involved in interaction and rivalry with others. This is characteristic of social existence, and we should not call anything social without it.

Humanitarianism is not a policy for society as a whole, in the sense of being a policy for all movements. It is a policy for protecting the weak; Popper calls it 'protectionism'. It pretends to universality by being a policy for all *men*, by being concerned about their 'lot'; and thus by disregarding different movements or ways of living.

With humanitarianism the dualism of decisions and facts appears in society too. And we find a distinction between those who decide and those who are protected (because they are too weak to decide).

This is not society controlling its own development. It is the domination of society by a particular group. (Whether you call it science is a matter of wisdom in advertising.) And in proportion as men do participate in running their own affairs, they will come in conflict with humanitarians and with the reasonableness of social engineers.

The idea of a 'social technology' rests on confusions about 'dependence'.

You cannot deduce principles and policies from the facts of science. And you cannot deduce the future from 'the nature of historical development'. But it does not follow that the future depends on what we decide. Nor does it follow that the principles we adopt depend only on us — unless that is just a tautology. (Popper repeats 'it is always *we* who decide', and he seems to think something

important follows from this.) Generally we do not *adopt* principles at
all. And the working of institutions does not depend upon what
principles we decide to adopt. There is some voluntary activity in
the functioning of institutions. So there is in language. But we do
not make the language we speak. Nor does its persistence depend on
our decisions. Neither do the activities for which policies are put
forward — industry, education and the rest. Policies are put forward in the day's work.

And although you cannot deduce policies from facts, this does not
point to a special realm in which special sorts of 'laws' hold. And
there is no special science — a 'practical' science — of such laws.

Notes

---

1 Karl Popper, *The Open Society and Its Enemies* (London, 1945),
vol. ii, p. 210.

2 On the common confusion between social theory and policy see J.
Anderson, 'Utilitarianism', *Australasian Journal of Psychology and
Philosophy* (September 1932), p. 167. I am indebted to other articles
by Professor Anderson and others of his school in the same journal.

3 The phrase 'closely interwoven' covers a good many difficulties, and
hardly makes the 'dualism' clearer.

4 This 'contingency' does not imply indeterminism. The point is that the
outcome depends on what happens, and there is not one outcome
which is 'necessary'. See P.H. Partridge, 'Contingency', *Australasian
Journal of Psychology and Philosophy* (April 1938).

5 Anderson remarks that in recent times '"scientific advance" has been
largely bound up with the decline of inquiry, that modern science does
not exemplify disinterested inquiry. Its spirit has been "practical", it
has been concerned with "getting things done", with facilitating transformations and translations, not just with finding out what is the case
and with the "criticism of categories" that that involves.' *Australasian
Journal of Psychology and Philosophy* (December 1945).

6 This conception of 'ways of living' I have taken mainly from Anderson.
Wittgenstein uses the phrase in a somewhat different, but I think
related, connection.

9

Between obedience and revolution[1]

CLYDE FRAZIER

Political man finds himself in many dilemmas because he is unable to create a government which will insure that only just laws are passed. Even with the best of constitutions, a government may at times commit morally outrageous acts and all the legal remedies provided by that constitution may prove ineffectual in bringing about a change. In such circumstances the conscientious citizen finds himself in a paradoxical situation. In the interests of preserving a political process that is basically just and to which he may indeed have committed himself, explicitly or otherwise, he has an obligation to perform an act at which his conscience rebels. His commitment to the system may prevent him from becoming a revolutionary, but his sense of moral outrage prevents him from being a completely loyal subject either. Because they have been continually faced with such dilemmas and have found themselves unable to eliminate them completely by framing a procedure to insure that law and justice coincide, men have tried to devise and justify a kind of political action that falls somewhere between strict obedience to the state and an attempt to overthrow it.

Reprinted from Philosophy and Public Affairs, *Vol. 1, No. 3 (1972), pp. 315-34, by permission of the author and* Philosophy and Public Affairs. © *1972 Princeton University Press.*

What follows is an effort to shed some light on the nature and variety of actions that comprise this category of extraordinary political acts. It will be my thesis, in particular, that extraordinary politics is a much broader and more inclusive category than we have generally supposed. This essay will be divided into four main parts. In the first I shall examine the literature on civil disobedience with a view to making explicit its assumptions about the nature and limits of justifiable disobedience. Next these assumptions will be traced back to their roots in traditional liberal theory and an attempt made to show that this theory actually allows a much broader range of disobedience than has generally been assumed. The third section presents a characterization and examination of the kinds of disobedience encompassed within these broader limits. The final section explores some of the considerations involved in justifying such acts.

I *Disobedience as speech*

Falling as it does between ordinary politics and revolution, extraordinary politics takes on some of the characteristics of each type of political action. It is always both inside and outside the existing legal system. It is always extralegal or illegal enough so that opponents can cry 'foul' and attempt thereby to divert attention from the substantive issues raised. It may, on the other hand, be close enough to existing legality for its proponents to claim that it should be recognized by the legal system and go unpunished[2]. The predominant tendency in the recent literature on the subject has been to emphasize only one side of this dichotomy, and to admit as morally serious disobedience only those actions which are so narrowly restricted that their obedient aspects are their main ones.

Most of this literature has focused on something called 'civil' disobedience. The underlying theme of this work is that disobedience can be justified only when it is so limited that it can be characterized as an act of political speech. Disobedience is, from this perspective, an appeal (albeit a desperate appeal) 'to the public to alter certain laws or policies that the minority takes to be incompatible with the fundamental principles of morality, principles that it believes the majority to accept'[3]. It is an attempt to address 'the sense of justice of the majority in order to urge reconsideration'[4], 'a form of persuasion'[5]. Thus conceived, the actions falling under the heading of extraordinary politics are unusual ones, but they are not totally foreign to our political traditions. They are departures from the ordinary channels of politics but they are appeals to them as well. The disobedience must, therefore, be of a limited character and designed not to overthrow or bypass the system but merely to get the system to work. The utilization of this extraordinary form of political appeal may be justified because of the shortcomings of ordinary speech. Mere speech may fail to produce change in many situations because it does not demand a response. Civil disobedience is designed to reinforce the disobedient's appeal. Direct disobedience of intrinsically objectionable laws may actually force the community to act on the issue and either enforce its laws or change them[6]. Unless the community decides to act and enforce the law in such a situation, that law may in effect be annulled by the extralegal action of the disobedient. Society becomes the tacit partner in the change through its inaction. Where a protest is indirect, involving disobedience to laws not objectionable in themselves, the rationale for disobedience is similar, if somewhat weaker. While he cannot force a response, such a disobedient, by capturing public attention or by demonstrating his own seriousness, may strengthen his appeal and make a response much more likely.

Although the recent literature on civil disobedience is divided into two major strands, both of them characterize disobedience as speech. One school of thought, following former Justice Fortas, admits as justifiable only that disobedience which presents itself as a legal appeal designed to test the constitutionality of a specific law[7]. The other school would allow a somewhat broader range of disobedience, admitting the possibility that political as well as legal appeals may be justified. One can, in this view, use disobedience in appealing to the government to change its politics even when it is clear that the policy in question is legally enacted and constitutionally permitted. In both cases disobedience is employed as a means of appeal, though the appeal is directed to different audiences: the legal system in the one case and the political system in the other.

Some differences in the types of acts disobedients may employ follow from the different characterizations of disobedience advanced by the two schools (the justifiability of indirect disobedience is a prime example); but the concern of the vast majority of writers of both schools has been to stress the limits on disobedience that flow from its characterization as speech and which they therefore hold in common. Writers of both persuasions have been almost unanimous in demanding that disobedience be open, public, limited, and respectful of the rights of other citizens. Only if all these limits are observed, they assert, can the act of disobedience be characterized as speech. Disobedients have often been advised, in addition, to accept the penalty for their disobedience willingly in order to prove their seriousness and reinforce their appeal. While most authors have agreed with John Rawls that violence is not compatible with civil disobedience as speech, since it does not invite a dialogue but demands submission[8], Marshall Cohen has defended some forms of violence, claiming that when strictly limited it can be a very effective form of expression[9]. It is revealing that although there is disagreement about the justifiability of violence, there is agreement as to the grounds on which any attempt at such justification must be made.

This very limited conception of disobedience as speech seems to have gained wide acceptance largely because it describes the kind of civil disobedience that was so successful in the civil rights campaigns of the early fifties. Later attempts to use disobedience to combat deeply rooted social segregation and to protest against the war have proven much less effective and have exposed a weakness in the rationale for the kind of disobedience that can be described as speech. The court and the public have both been unwilling to face squarely the issues raised by the disobedients and have hidden behind the banner of 'law and order' instead. Unable to resolve his moral dilemma through the use of disobedience in the narrow sense, the citizen may again find himself faced with the basic questions of obligation and obedience. If, as many contend, disobedience can only be justified as an act of speech, the only alternatives left to the unsuccessful disobedient are obedience and revolution. It is my contention that our fate is not so harsh as this and that one may, on occasion, be able to justify more radical varieties of disobedience which still fall short of revolution. It is to an examination of the possibility of such alternatives that I now turn.

II   *Radical disobedience*

A search for the reasons that it has seemed necessary to restrict disobedience so narrowly takes us back to the origins of liberal theory. Assumptions first made by Hobbes and accepted by Locke continue to inform much of contemporary thinking about disobedience. Many modern arguments against disobedience appear to be only slightly altered restatements of the original Hobbesian ones. Hobbes pointed out that we have reason to obey even a bad law because we have an interest in the preservation of a system of arbitration through which differences between citizens can be settled peacefully. Such a system is possible, he reasoned, only if each member of society is willing to forswear the use of force in disputes with his fellows and to submit them to binding arbitration by the sovereign and his laws. Hobbes felt, accordingly, that unless a member of society could be sure that others would submit to the outcome of such arbitration even when they disagreed with it, he himself would be foolish to submit when he disagreed with the outcome. The system could not be preserved unless all men agreed to submit to all laws. Hobbes's arguments have been repeated in almost identical form by many modern thinkers. When David Spitz states that 'For the sake of the greater good secured by that system through its government and its law, [citizens] accept enactments which they otherwise disapprove'[10], he is relying on the force of the Hobbesian argument.

Hobbes did not stop, however, with the proposition that the citizen is bound to obey all the laws. He claimed, using exactly the same logic, that one is obligated to obey *any* state whatsoever, irrespective of its origins or policies. The mere existence of a state, whatever its form, is sufficient reason for obedience. As long as the state provides a means for settling conflicts peacefully, one is bound to obey. A citizen might prefer that the state operate for his own benefit, or in accordance with certain principles, and Hobbes never denied that it might indeed be desirable to have it so. He insisted, however, that guarantees for citizens against the state, even though they were desirable, could never be enforced without destroying the state. Men would only forswear the use of violence and submit their disputes to adjudication, he argued, if they could be absolutely sure that their fellows would do likewise. Any attempt to set limits on the sovereign or to give the citizens guarantees against the state would open the way to irresolvable conflict, for there would be no one to render an authoritative decision should a dispute arise on these matters between the citizens and the sovereign. Any attempt to set up such an arbiter would leave unanswered the question of what guarantees the citizen would have against that arbiter. The problem of ultimate sovereignty would not be solved, it would only have been made more remote. The existence of these areas of potential conflict would, according to Hobbes, leave each citizen unsure that others would comply with the commands of the sovereign; being unsure, he would have no reason to do so himself. Men would fall back into the state of nature, which was a war of all against all.

As it stands so far, Hobbes's argument is incomplete. While he has shown that the logic of arbitration is all-encompassing, he has not shown that men must agree to arbitration in the first place. Might not a citizen choose to reject the state altogether and take his chances in the state of nature? Hobbes met this difficulty with a premise which, considering its importance to his argument, he left curiously unexamined. He simply asserted that 'the greatest [evil] that in any form of government can possibly happen to the people in general is scarce sensible in respect of the miseries and horrible calamities that accompany a civil war or that dissolute condition of masterless men, without subjection to laws and a coercive power to tie their hands from rapine and revenge ...'[11]. Men ought to obey even the harshest state, since from Hobbes's perspective even the worst state would be better than the best war. He himself recognized only a very few exceptions to this rule. When the sovereign condemned a man to die or commanded him to do something that he regarded as worse than death he had no obligation to obey[12]. Since the underlying purpose of the compact is security of life and liberty, the agreement is broken if the sovereign threatens your life or worse.

Locke denied that man had no choice but to obey any government under which he happened to find himself, and all of liberal theory has followed him in this denial[13]. Locke saw, and others have agreed, that order alone is not a sufficient condition to permit the realization of those values for which we establish government[14]. Locke's views on this matter differ from Hobbes's in at least two important respects. On the one hand, he took a more sanguine view of the condition of man in the state of nature than did Hobbes. He accused Hobbes of confusing the state of nature with the state of war, and pointed out that the former only occasionally degenerates into the latter[15]. Locke was also more keenly aware than Hobbes that the concentration of power which a state entails makes possible greater evils than the state of nature or even the state of war[16]. In their natural condition men can at least fight it out as equals, but no man would have a chance against the superior force of the state. The liberal view, following Locke, has been that when the preservation of a state compels worse evils than anarchy, the costs of that state are too high. A citizen has no reason to preserve such a state, for there is no greater good which it makes possible.

This argument was used by liberal theorists to defend the right of revolution against Hobbesian insistence on the necessity for absolute obedience, but it comprises only a part of the liberal response to Hobbes. Indeed, if taken alone, it leaves man with an even more dismal destiny than Hobbes had envisioned. While it holds that man can do worse than the state of nature, it does not establish that he can do any better. This argument alone does not challenge Hobbes's other contention, that any attempt to provide citizens with guarantees against the sovereign is bound to return them to the state of nature (if not actually to the state of war). The whole structure of liberal theory with its constitutional prescriptions and inalienable rights must depend, therefore, on the assertion of a second premise, if it is not to be mere wishful thinking. Liberal theory must depend on a premise to the effect that the logic of arbitration is not all-encompassing. This premise seemed so obvious to Locke and his followers that no one, so far as I can tell, has bothered to make it explicit; it remains, nevertheless, the implicit basis of liberal theory. Liberal theorists assume that we do not need absolute certainty that our fellow citizens will in all circumstances refrain from disobeying the sovereign in order for it to be rational for us to refrain ourselves. On the contrary, it seems more likely that only a fairly high degree of probability that they will do so is necessary. Some laws at least are clearly not essential to the maintenance of social order, for many laws are broken every day without causing the collapse of the state. Indeed, we may suspect that the non-enforcement of certain laws is in fact a condition of social stability. Nor have the much more direct threats to the legitimacy of the state represented by civil rights and antiwar disobedients (and even rioters) destroyed the fabric of law and order, though it would be foolish to contend that the fabric has not been damaged to some extent, particularly by the more violent manifestations of defiance. Some citizens probably do experience a measure of insecurity, because such occurrences make them feel that the state is no longer protecting them. But if we do not have total domestic peace, neither have we returned to the state of nature as Hobbes's theory predicts.

Though Locke never made explicit his denial of Hobbes's claims about the logic of arbitration, he clearly relied on it. He acknowledged the fact that in attempting to give citizens guarantees against the state he was leaving open the possibility of violence and revolution. There is, he admitted, no judge on earth with authority to decide the controversies that these guarantees would ignite: 'the appeal then lies nowhere but to heaven; force between either persons who have no known superior on earth or which permits no appeal to a judge on earth, being properly a state of war wherein the appeal lies only to heaven'[17]. War is a possibility and Locke never denies that it is, but this mere possibility is not enough to make men so insecure as to feel that they must return to the state of nature where each undertakes to protect himself by his own force. Liberal theory clearly assumes that man is not stuck in the state of nature, for that theory is an attempt to explore various alternatives to this undesirable state.

It is my contention that liberal theory, through its rejection of Hobbes's argument about the logic of arbitration, opens the possibility of a much wider range of disobedience than liberal theorists have generally recognized. Locke himself was not concerned with the problem of disobedience but with that of revolution. He did dispute Hobbes's contention that the citizen has no choice but to obey, but Locke felt that revolution was the only alternative open to the citizen. Hobbes's assertion that anything less than total obedience is revolutionary was supported by his argument about the logic of sovereignty. He used that same argument to deny the possibility of a limited, constitutional state. Locke had to dispute Hobbes's argument about the logic of sovereignty in order to establish the possibility of limits on the power of the government, but he failed to realize that this also undermined his (and Hobbes's) assumption that any disobedience to the state was *ipso facto* revolutionary. It seems, ironically, that the very argument by which liberal theorists established the possibility of a limited constitutional regime also established the possibility of a wide range of acts disobedient to the laws of that regime but still falling short of revolution. Locke probably failed to recognize this because he never made his own argument explicit, and because he failed to see the connection between the two different parts of Hobbes's work. He therefore continued to support Hobbes's denial of the possibility of non-revolutionary disobedience, while his own work contradicted the assumptions on which that denial was based.

Most modern theorists have made a similar mistake. They have denied the possibility of all but the most strictly limited disobedience, and the logic of their denials has been consistently Hobbesian. Louis Waldman's reasoning is typical when he states, 'Those who assert rights under the constitution and the laws thereunder must abide by that constitution and the law *if that constitution is to survive*' [18]. Notice that Waldman speaks only to those who do assert rights under the constitution. Revolution remains a possibility for anyone who is willing to forgo the benefits of constitutional guarantees, but short of that the only option is to obey. Waldman denies, as Hobbes and Locke denied, the very *possibility* that disobedience is compatible with the survival of any sort of state at all. He does not contend that all disobedience is unjustified, but holds that the justification must be a revolutionary one. The continuing prevalence of this logic is one important reason for the insistence that disobedience be limited to such an extent that it can be classified as an act of speech. Even many supporters of disobedience seem to have accepted the Hobbesian logic and to assume that if one oversteps the narrow limits which allow an act of disobedience to be characterized as a kind of speech it becomes implicitly revolutionary[19]. It almost seems as if most literature on 'civil' disobedience is attempting to show that very carefully limited disobedience is not *really* outside the system after all. Such emphasis has led to an extremely narrow notion of justifiable disobedience. There has been a failure to explore the range and character of the acts in which a non-revolutionary disobedient might engage. It is to such exploration that I turn in the next section.

III   *Varieties of resistance*

Not all students of disobedience have been blind to the existence of alternatives to traditional civil disobedience. Many have hinted that alternatives arc available[20], but they have not followed up these suggestions, and the exact nature and range of such acts remains a mystery. If the defining feature of traditional civil disobedience was that it could be characterized as a form of speech, the more radical position that I wish to explore defends the right of a citizen not only to appeal to the state but to resist it as well. In so doing the citizen is of course asserting his right to defy the state's claim to make binding decisions in a specific area. The logic of his act is coercive, and it is this movement from appeal to coercion that characterizes the radical disobedient and differentiates him from the more traditional civil disobedient. Although the great body of literature on civil disobedience has assumed that all justifiable disobedience could be characterized as speech, this more radical aspect has been present, to some degree, in almost all acts of disobedience. If we appeal to the conscience of the sovereign with an act of disobedience we certainly defy him to an extent as well, even when we are careful to do so only to a very limited degree. No matter how carefully one circumscribes a protest to make it harmonize with the spirit of the laws, there always remains an element of defiance, however small it may be. It is this element of defiance that opponents have often recognized in even the mildest forms of disobedience and used as a basis for their objection to it.

At times supporters of disobedience have recognized the presence of a coercive element in disobedience and have even included the idea of coercion as part of their definition of traditional civil disobedience[21]. The shortcoming of such analyses is that they have generally failed to differentiate acts that may vary in many respects, because they have focused on the form of an act and not on its substance or effect. It has usually been assumed in analyses of this kind that the criteria of civility are external factors: whether the act is open and public, whether the penalty is accepted willingly, and so on. It is my contention that such a focus obscures vitally important differences. A disobedient can accept the penalty for his act because he thinks it is his due or because he wants to help pack the jails and bring down the system of justice. Even some revolutionary campaigns, such as Gandhi's fight for Indian independence, have been carried on by means of acts that meet all the criteria generally set up as tests of the civility of disobedience. If an act of disobedience is to be acceptable as a form of speech it generally must have such external characteristics, but the possession of these characteristics alone is not enough to assure that it will be acceptable as speech. By focusing on external characteristics of the act, even those who have recognized the coercive element in disobedience have been prevented from seeing the full scope of possibilities open to the disobedient. They have continued to demand that disobedience remain within very narrow limits despite the implicitly radical thrust of their analysis.

Resistance to the state is, or at least can be, very radical indeed. If, as we have seen, defiance of the state does not entail revolution, there does remain a sense in which it is revolutionary. It would be neat, though much too simple, to say that the resister asserts his right to defy the state only in certain areas, while the revolutionary preaches complete defiance. It would be too simple because revolutionaries always share *some* common ground with their opponents. Rather than attempting to speak of resistance and revolution as two distinct modes of action it seems preferable to consider them as part of a continuum of actions that vary in their degree of opposition to the given order. There is, of course, a distinction between those acts that are designed to bring down the existing legal-constitutional structure and those that are not, but this distinction is not always found at the same point on the continuum. There are numerous examples both of conservative revolution and of radical resistance. I would like to devote the rest of this section to an examination of a number of variables which affect the extent to which disobedience is revolutionary and to a very general consideration of the different kinds of acts disobedience might involve.

One important aspect in which disobedient acts can vary is the degree to which they are coercive. A disobedient or group of disobedients is seldom in a position to force a society to choose a particular course of action or to prevent its choosing another. More commonly, what the disobedient is able to do is to raise the costs associated with the choice or rejection of a particular alternative, increasing the probability that the alternative chosen will be the one that he favours. For all their talk about stopping the operations of the Pentagon, it is difficult to believe that the antiwar demonstrators in 1967 actually believed that they could win an all-out fight with the troops guarding the building. What they perhaps hoped was that the government would either find it too much trouble or (more likely) would not find it morally possible to take the actions necessary to prevent an occupation of the building. The disobedient may employ minimal coercion when the public is apathetic about a policy and persists in following it not out of strong commitment but largely through inertia. In such a situation raising the costs only slightly may cause a change in public sentiment toward the policy. (Of course the disobedient also risks provoking the opposite reaction.) In general, the higher the degree of coercion an act of disobedience involves (everything else being equal), the more radical a challenge it poses to the established authority.

A second crucial variable is the scope and importance of the area in which the disobedient challenges the state's authority. Defiance of one particular law on very narrow grounds seems much less threatening to the state than defiance of a broader type which involves disobeying many different laws. The importance of the particular law in question is also a relevant factor here. Defiance of traffic laws or of laws regulating personal sexual behaviour seems hardly more than a nuisance to the state, but defiance of draft laws strikes at an area that is much more central to the state's power and authority. It is for this reason that many have seen refusal to pay taxes as being among the most radical possible actions, for if it were widespread it would render impossible the existence of any kind of government at all. One can consider the question of the scope of defiance in another sense as well. Acts of disobedience can vary greatly in the extent to which they attempt to thwart the enforcement of any particular law. The case of the moral refuser, who does not attempt to thwart the enforcement of a law but refuses for moral reasons to perform particular duties required of him by that law, is especially interesting in this respect. The draft refuser may defy the application of the law only to one of its subjects, himself. Even though his act may be highly coercive, since his refusal is absolute, his challenge to the state is less radical than many others, involving as it does such a small percentage of the citizens affected by the law.

A third major variable is the extent to which acts are purely coercive, rather than being mixed forms of coercion and appeal. The vast majority of disobedient acts, though they have involved some coercion, have relied mainly on a moral appeal. Disobedients have attempted to dramatize the injustice of government policy at the same time they tried to frustrate it by their disobedience and their willingness to suffer. While in some cases coercion and appeal are implicit in the same act, in others they may be part of the same campaign but pertain to different acts. Those who participated in the underground railroad made a moral appeal against slavery as well as trying to frustrate enforcement of the law, but they did not make this appeal by helping the slaves to escape. Any attempt to make their acts public would have undermined their effectiveness. This simultaneous appeal to both the conscience and the self-interest of the public has been one of the great strengths of traditional disobedience. Other possible forms of action may minimize the element of appeal and be almost purely coercive. Sabotage is an act of this sort, and for this reason it comes very close to the revolutionary end of the continuum. One can imagine instances, however, where a citizen might attempt to sabotage a particular government programme, the nuclear weapons development programme for example, without challenging the government in any other area. Such an action would be a difficult one to evaluate, for although it is both highly and exclusively coercive it challenges only a very limited aspect of government power.

A fourth important variable, in the democratic context at least, is the number of people involved in the protest. A democratic society bases its legitimacy on popular support, and a protest movement which had very wide support would have a kind of legitimacy in such a society. It might even go so far as to be subversive of the particular regime in power without attempting to undercut the fundamental constitutional order. It might indeed be claimed that the regime itself was subversive of the more fundamental order. It is for this reason that attempts to render the draft ineffective through mass refusal of induction have always seemed less threatening than schemes to do so by the destruction of draft files, even though the potential degree and scope of coercion is the same in both cases. An effective programme of mass refusal requires the kind of broad public support which endows it with a good measure of respectability in a democracy.

A fifth variable of importance is the proximity of the disobedience to the law or policy being protested. Direct disobedience raises the fewest challenges to the state, but it is not always possible. Disobedience to laws not directly challenged but which support the object of the protest raise a few more questions. Civil rights demonstrators continually broke trespass laws, with which they had no quarrel as such, because such laws were used to enforce segregation. Attempts to force change by disobeying laws that have no direct connection with the object of the protest seem very different indeed. Such disobedience presents a far more radical challenge to society and seems to be almost a form of social blackmail. The threatened stall-in on the freeways leading to the New York World's Fair is an example of such action, as are many (though by no means all) sit-ins. Many of the recent attempts to bomb public buildings are in this class, since the connection between the targets of the attacks and the continuation of the war is tenuous indeed.

A sixth and final consideration in evaluating the degree of threat that acts of disobedience pose to the state is the extent to which they violate the rights of other citizens. Since the guarantee of such rights is a vitally important function of any government, a disobedient who violates the rights of his fellow citizens is much more threatening than one who does not. Attempts to prevent opponents from speaking will rightly be seen as extremely subversive in a democratic order, because they violate one of the most basic political rights. Sit-ins that impede normal access to one's own property or to public property are still infringements of the rights of other citizens, but they are far less serious. Simple refusal to comply with the draft law could also be said to infringe the right of other citizens to be defended, but the connection is very indirect and the threat that it poses to the state is correspondingly weak.

I have tried in my examples to give a very rough idea of the range of actions open to the radical disobedient. It is my contention that it is in terms of the kinds of variables discussed above, and not by any external characteristics, that one must evaluate his act to determine the degree of danger it represents to the established order.

IV *Justifying resistance*

My concern so far has been only to support the claim that there exists a wide range of extraordinary political acts and to explore some of the ways in which these acts vary. I have refrained from examining the related question of their justification until now because I feel that much of the debate about the various forms of disobedience has been marred by a confusion of these two issues. Too often students of disobedience have concluded that acts of disobedience could not be justified merely because they assumed that all disobedience was revolutionary. In this final section I want to take up the question of the justification of resistance.

In one sense, at least, the notion of justifying acts of resistance to the state presents grave problems. It is clear that one cannot hope to justify such resistance in the sense of reaching commonly agreed upon criteria to distinguish justified from unjustified instances. The very recourse to disobedience in the first place seems to indicate that such common standards have broken down. There is no rule or principle one can look to as a justification for disobedience that might not itself be subject to controversy[22]. If any such standard could be agreed on, it could be incorporated into the law, and disobedience would not be necessary. There can therefore be no legal right to disobedience, although exceptions to particular laws may be made in certain cases. (The provision for conscientious objection to military service is an example of this.) This does not mean, of course, that acts of resistance are never justified. Many are (although many are not), and as actors in the political system we are constantly called on to make decisions about the justification of such acts and to behave accordingly. It does mean, however, that we cannot hope to find publicly agreed upon standards on which to base our judgments. Allowing individuals to interpret their own political obligations makes it entirely possible that irreconcilable conflicts may develop, which can be settled only by force.

To a certain extent, then, we merely pick our moral criteria and act on them, but this does not mean that we are left entirely outside the bounds of moral discourse. There is a difference between justifying an act and justifying the actor who performs it[23]. An actor can perform the wrong acts for the right kinds of reasons. Because of this we may at times face opponents who act because of deeply held beliefs which we respect but cannot share. In such cases we accept our opponent as a morally serious actor, but this does not oblige us to agree with him or to acquiesce to his wishes. In many situations we may be convinced that our opponent should act as he does (given his beliefs, etc.), even when we feel that our own duty lies in opposing his aims[24]. The realization that we are facing a morally serious actor does, however, require us to treat him as such, and to show him the kind of personal respect that precludes the use of ridicule, or degrading or inhumane treatment.

For most citizens faced with the problem of what they consider to be an immoral law, the proper course of action is far from clear. Typically, a citizen finds himself faced not with a single moral obligation but with conflicting obligations, each of which has prima facie force but neither of which is conclusive. The way he resolves such conflicts depends, of course, on the nature of his personal moral system. If the citizen's moral system is teleological (which does not necessarily imply utilitarian), he will attempt to determine his moral duty by weighing the consequences of the various courses of action open to him. Since I feel that such teleological morality is predominant in our society, I would like to turn finally to an examination of some of the problems involved in an attempt to balance these conflicting moral claims from the standpoint of a teleological moral system.

If disobedience does not imply that one is attempting to overturn the system, it does pose some danger to it, and the disobedient will have to balance this danger against the good he proposes to achieve by his act. He will have to estimate the relative weights of these factors in terms of his own system of values, but whatever system he uses it seems safe to say that the greater the good he aims at, or the greater the evil he seeks to eliminate, the easier it will be to justify an act of resistance. A disobedient must weigh not only the magnitude of the good he desires but also the chance he has of achieving it. Numerous practical considerations affecting the probability of success or failure will thus be relevant to the decision to disobey.

Against the good he proposes to achieve the potential disobedient must attempt to balance the undesirable effects of his act. One set of factors he must weigh pertains to the direct effects of the act he contemplates. Certain acts, notably acts of violence against persons, have immediate consequences which are so repulsive that most disobedients will rule them out regardless of their effectiveness. More often indirect consequences are paramount. The disobedient must weigh carefully the degree of danger that his acts pose to the state. The greater the danger entailed by his act, the more difficulty a disobedient will have in justifying it. The considerations discussed in the last section are all relevant in determining the degree of challenge to the state that any particular act poses. Some acts are very likely to be judged negatively on both counts. Acts of violence directed against persons, such as murder and kidnapping, are intrinsically repulsive as well as posing a very radical threat to the state's authority.

The extent to which a prospective disobedient approves of the system by which he is governed is also an important factor affecting the justifiability of his disobedience. To the extent that he is an enthusiastic supporter of the existing regime, his estimation of the damage his act will do will tend to dissuade him from disobedience. To the extent that he places a very low value on the existing system generally, he will be less concerned about the adverse consequences of his act for the stability of the state. He may feel that he has not much to lose by an act of disobedience even if it backfires, and thus he will not be so easily dissuaded by the fact that he may endanger social stability.

The precise manner in which a citizen's approval of the state should enter into his political decisions has not always been clearly understood. Liberal theory in particular has ignored the importance of approval and focused on the closely related factor of consent. One either consents or does not, but approval is continuous. A citizen can approve to varying degrees both of a system he does consent to obey and of those systems he does not. Without denying the relevance of consent, I would like to contend that approval is germane to the considerations of the potential disobedient as well. The failure to understand the relevance of *both* factors has, paradoxically, led liberal theorists to demand too much obedience on most occasions but too little on others.

In traditional liberal theory, if a citizen does not consent to the state he is justified in opposing or attempting to overturn it. Though an appreciation of the vital role of consent is a profound corrective to the one-sided theory of Hobbes, it is my opinion that the case for consent has often been badly overstated. David Spitz makes an exemplary error in this regard when he asserts that a political system (he is speaking of a democracy) has no moral basis for demanding obedience from those who, preferring other systems, deny its basic legitimacy[25]. Spitz is wrong here, and much of liberal theory is wrong with him, because Hobbes's argument still retains some force even if it does not have the absolute binding quality that Hobbes maintained. To the extent that a disobedient believes that the system, while imperfect, is better than anarchy, he has *some* reason not to endanger its existence. This reason will not, it is true, always lead him to reject disobedience in the face of great evil, but it does mean that he does not have *carte blanche* in the matter of disobedience. The better the system, the stronger the obligation to obey and the greater, therefore, must the improvement brought about by disobedience be if it is to justify the risks it also implies. Even weak systems, however, may have some claim to our obedience, and a strong system may be able to claim some obedience even from the partisans of another form of government.

In most cases, liberal theory has demanded too much rather than too little obedience. Focusing on consent alone, it forced the citizen to be almost totally obedient whenever he could not justify revolutionary disobedience. The case for radical disobedience is, in many ways, an attempt to dispute just this aspect of liberal theory and to point out the possibility of a wider range of non-revolutionary disobedience. I would like to add here only that even in the best state we can devise, the possibility of justifiable disobedience cannot be categorically excluded. As long as we cannot devise a procedure which guarantees that only good laws will be passed (and we cannot), the possibility of justifiable disobedience will exist.

It is commonly supposed, in our own country at least, that democracy is the best system that can be devised and that it has special claims to our obedience. In some ways the case for obedience to a democratic government suffers from the same weaknesses as the case for obedience to any other type of system. It cannot be maintained that the operation of the majority principle gives us a firmer assurance of just decisions than does the operation of any other principle of decision. There are many political questions, it is true, in which the application of the majority principle seems to yield a result that is intrinsically fair. But by no means all political decisions are of this sort. Majority decision is not, however, the only basis of democracy, nor is it necessarily the strongest. The strong claim that democracy does make is that it precludes the possibility of justifiable disobedience by providing alternative means of change. Democracy is not, of course, the only system that provides such avenues. Even the most irresponsible dictator cannot be completely deaf to appeals from his people, and in most predemocratic governments, traditionally prescribed means for appeal to the sovereign were present. Democracy, however, makes certain that these means are particularly numerous through its guarantees of political rights to citizens, and that the appeals will have a good chance of being effective once they are expressed. It seems reasonable to conclude, therefore, that the prospective disobedient in a democracy has another factor to weigh in his considerations. Not only must he weigh against the good he desires to accomplish the evil his act may bring about, but he must also weigh against it the likelihood that he can achieve the same end through normal political channels. Even in a democracy, this consideration will not absolutely preclude disobedience, for majorities can be incredibly insensitive to the claims of minorities and the processes of ordinary politics can work so slowly that conscientious citizens are driven to disobedience.

This is, of course, the dilemma of many citizens in the United States today. They are keenly aware of the value of the system under which they live, but at the same time they see that system committing what they feel are immoral acts both at home and abroad. Unable to justify revolution, many citizens have been convinced that the only remaining alternatives are obedience and ineffectual protest. Many others have become revolutionaries by default, because they feel that the evils are intolerable and have failed to recognize the existence of a wide range of possible action short of revolution. It is to be hoped that clarification of the available alternatives will make it possible for men to define their relationship to their political system more consciously and accurately.

Notes

---

1 This is a revised version of a paper originally read at the annual meeting of the American Political Science Association, 7-11 September 1971. I am indebted to more people than I can mention for helpful criticism of the earlier draft of this paper.

2 Carl Cohen, 'Law, Speech, and Disobedience', in Hugo A. Bedau (ed.), *Civil Disobedience: Theory and Practice* (New York, 1969), p. 166.

3 Marshall Cohen, 'Civil Disobedience in a Constitutional Democracy', *The Massachusetts Review*, vol. 10, no. 2 (Spring 1969), pp. 217-18.

4 John Rawls, 'The Justification of Civil Disobedience', in *Civil Disobedience*, p. 240.

5 Harris Wofford, 'Non-Violence and the Law: The Law Needs Help', in *Civil Disobedience*, p. 63.

6 Harry Prosch, 'Limits to the Moral Claim in Civil Disobedience', *Ethics*, vol. 75, no. 2 (January 1965), pp. 103-5.

7 See Fortas's book *Concerning Dissent and Civil Disobedience* (New York, 1968).

8 Rawls, 'The Justification of Civil Disobedience', p. 247.

9 Cohen, 'Civil Disobedience in a Constitutional Democracy', p. 217.

10 Spitz, 'Democracy and the Problem of Civil Disobedience', *American Political Science Review*, vol. 48, no. 2 (June 1954), p. 397.

11 Thomas Hobbes, *Leviathan* (New York, 1958), p. 152.

12 Hobbes, *The Citizen* (New York, 1949), p. 79.

13 John Locke, *The Second Treatise of Government* (New York, 1952), pp. 9-10.

14 Spitz, 'Democracy and the Problem of Civil Disobedience', p. 393.

15 Locke, *Second Treatise*, p. 12 and all of chapter 3.

16 Ibid., p. 78.

17 Ibid., p. 139.

18 Waldman, 'Civil Rights — Yes: Civil Disobedience — No', in *Civil Disobedience*, p. 107 (italics mine).

19 Cohen, 'Civil Disobedience in a Constitutional Democracy', p. 215.

20 Marshall Cohen, 'Civil Disobedience', *The Great Ideas Today, 1971* (Chicago, 1971), p. 246; and Martin Luther King, 'Letter from Birmingham City Jail', in *Civil Disobedience*, p. 78.

21 Hugo A. Bedau, 'On Civil Disobedience', *Journal of Philosophy*, vol. 58, no. 21 (1961), p. 661; and Anthony De Crespigny, 'The Nature and Methods of Non-Violent Coercion', *Political Studies*, vol. 12, no. 2 (June 1964), p. 263.

22 Bedau, 'On Civil Disobedience', p. 663.

23 Richard Lichtman, untitled remarks in Harrop Freeman (ed.), *Civil Disobedience* (Santa Barbara, Cal., 1966), p. 16.

24 H.B. Acton, 'Political Justification', in Bedau (ed.), *Civil Disobedience*, pp. 228-9.

25 Spitz, 'Democracy and the Problem of Civil Disobedience', p. 394.

PART IV

Cultural relativism

Introduction

ALAN R. DRENGSON

In their discussions of patterns of human behaviour, social scientists use a number of different terms in order to call attention to various features of human life. For example, they talk about the normal behaviour of a given people and they also talk about their values. They take note of the fact that people might, in speaking, place high value on a certain course of behaviour, but in fact the norm, that is the frequent pattern of behaviour, is not consistent with that expressed value. For example, among some North American Indians, infidelity on the part of wives was soundly condemned in the expressed attitudes of the people. When asked how infidelity was to be treated, a typical reply might have been: 'The woman will have her nose cut off and she will be banished from the tribe.' In fact, cases of infidelity rarely led to this.

Another term used to mark the different features of human culture is 'mores'. Mores are usually thought of as those patterns of behaviour and custom that are conducive to the welfare of the group. They might, in some cases, attain the status of laws or taboos. A particular set of mores might not actually be conducive to the welfare of the group, and furthermore, the mores of a given people are often not in complete harmony with their own expressed values. Inconsistencies between beliefs, conventions and ways of acting are not unusual. What all of this so far calls attention to is in some ways a commonplace. People often say one thing and do another. It is difficult, when studying human cultures, to make certain that one has understood these differences; many things should not be taken at face value.

As a result of careful studies of different cultures (other than Western), it has become clear that human behaviour, beliefs, values and customs vary widely. It is partly on the basis of this observed diversity that some social scientists and philosophers have been inclined to argue that what is important and what is of value is not an absolute matter, but is rather something that depends upon the cultural context. They say that how we perceive things, that is, how the world appears to us, is partly a function of our beliefs and our language. These we get by way of cultural conditioning. We are not born with beliefs, language and values: we learn these things. Just what we learn depends on what we are taught and this, in turn, is a function of the culture we are born into. The conclusion that is said to follow from these observations of cultural diversity is that our values, our norms and our ways of thinking and perceiving the world, are relative to the culture we are born in; and so, there is, it has been argued, no system of standards apart from those of particular cultures.

Even though the field work referred to above is a 'modern phenomena', the idea that norms, values, and even ways of perceiving the world might be, at least in part, the result of cultural conditioning, is not new. This idea was very much alive in the philosophic speculations of some early Greeks, particularly some well-educated Athenians. They recognized, as a result of their contacts with alien cultures, that the beliefs, practices, religion and world view of other people differed from their own.

People react in different ways to alien cultures. Exposure to alien ways sometimes results in the attitude that those alien ways are quaint, in some respects misguided, mistaken, or possibly sinful. People usually think that their rules, their laws and their beliefs are the right, just and true ones. Exposure to cultural diversity might not however engender such attitudes in everyone. As with some social scientists, one might conclude that cultural variation is the result of different living conditions and that there is not, nor can there be, any one set of rules, laws, etc. that are appropriate for all times and places.

One might respond, then, to perceived cultural differences by intolerance, reinforced by strong assertion of one's own practices as representing the absolute norms of all humans everywhere. This kind of intolerance has often been buttressed by assertions of religious revelation and doctrinal absolutism. Another response to perceived cultural differences has been tolerance as a result of the belief that cultural practices are not open to any sort of objective evaluation. Whether or not a given practice is proper depends, in this view, on the context. If the practice is acceptable in a given culture, then, for those in that culture, that is the right sort of thing to do in those circumstances. There is no independent right or wrong here; cross-cultural judgments are not possible. Values, rules, norms, etc. are relative to culture. In short, exposure to other cultures often results in either fervent assertion of the values of one's own culture and condemnation of alien practices, or scepticism about the values of one's own cultural practices and the belief that no lasting, independent standards of behaviour exist. The former of these responses has been stigmatized as ethnocentrism by anthropologists; the latter has been called cultural relativism and is a position that has often been taken by anthropologists and other social scientists.

What we have, then, are two dominant attitudes with respect to cultural diversity. It has been assumed throughout this discussion that there is cultural diversity. How could one deny it? People in different cultures do dress, eat, dance, marry and associate differently, do they not? This much is certainly obvious: styles, ceremonial practices, clothing, marital patterns, and the like, do differ. But the question is whether or not these differences reflect fundamental differences in what people value and think important. The fact that my neighbour drives a different kind of car, lives in a different sort of house, wears a different style of clothing from me does not, so far, establish that we have any *fundamental* differences with respect to values. One has to be certain that the obvious cultural differences are reflections of fundamental differences and not merely superficial variations. The fact that one group of people belch at the table, while another group considers this impolite behaviour, does not, so far, establish an important difference. We might find out that for the belchers, belching is an expression of enjoyment and a compliment to the host, while among the non-belchers the same compliment is expressed differently, in words, perhaps.

Moreover, even if we are able to provide a case where we have not only a difference in the way in which attitudes and values are expressed, but different values being expressed, we still have not, so far, shown that diversity establishes the soundness of the doctrine of cultural relativism. For, after all, we have differences within our own culture that reflect differences in what is thought to be of value, and also differences in beliefs about the world. Where this diversity leads some to disobey a law, neither their disagreements nor their acts establish that there is no law here. Even if we are able to clearly illustrate concrete cases of cultural diversity of the sort we have been referring to, we will not have settled the normative question, i.e., people might in fact have different values, but all of them, or some of them, might be mistaken.

Traditionally we have been confronted by two alternative doctrines with respect to relativism in morals and practices. On the one hand, the absolutist has insisted upon the universality of moral values and often too of religious truths; on the other hand, relativists have insisted that values and religious beliefs are culturally conditioned, relative to individual cultures, and that therefore cross-cultural judgments are not possible. For the relativist there are no universal moral or religious truths. These two doctrines are incompatible with one another. But is the conflict between these two views the sort of conflict one can resolve by simply getting the evidence together? Or do we have here the kind of philosophical impasse that can only be resolved by identifying the confusions common to both views and by gaining a better perspective on the issues involved? Such a perspective might lead us to reject both doctrines. As is clear from Ruth Benedict's writings the motive for arguing strenuously for cultural relativism is to combat the kind of intolerance often associated with absolutism and ethnocentrism. One problem with this is however that combating intolerance is itself an endorsement of the belief that intolerance is bad. It involves, in other words, implicit assertion of at least one standard viewed as not culturally conditioned. This kind of cultural relativism, used to combat intolerance, seems in conflict with itself, and John Cook shows that relativism itself can be seen as an ethnocentric notion.

What is important in the ethnologist's work is the realization that intolerance is often the result of failure to understand another culture, and of course intolerance itself often makes such understanding impossible. Furthermore, it is easy, when combating intolerance, to overlook and distort various features of another culture. The question is, then, can we provide sufficiently detailed examples so that we will understand why the people of culture A do things differently from the people of culture B? When we provide this detail, as Professor Cook attempts to do, usually we find that we can better understand why a people condone, for example, infanticide, and other people do not. The practice of infanticide is not isolated from other practices, but is part of a complex and inter-related system of beliefs and practices. Usually when one understands this, one sees that illustrating diversity of moral practices is not simply a matter of finding differences between two cultures as one would find the differences between two card games. Often merely illustrating cultural differences in detail answers questions we might have by showing that the apparent differences in values is the result of differences in beliefs about the world. If we believe that animals have no capacity for suffering, our attitudes towards them will probably be different from those who believe they do.

We might be inclined to think that our moral practices are governed by rules, and these rules, we might also think, either must be universal and hold for all peoples everywhere, or else they must be relative to culture. Some take examples of cultural differences, that is different practices, as evidence for relativity; others take these differences as was pointed out above — as evidence for how errant the human race is. One way of resolving such an impasse might be to show that these views are the result of a common confusion. For example, it *might* be that relativists and absolutists share the view that morality consists of rules. If the notion of 'moral rules' is shown to be confused, then both the doctrines of relativism and absolutism, *in so far as they are based* on this confused notion, will not be defensible.

So far we have been discussing some of the problems connected with cultural relativism as this has bearing primarily on morality. One might think that even where we have demonstrated differences with respect to moral values, nevertheless, there is a common public world of sense that we all share, so that in time one could resolve many of these differences, if one can just get the facts straight. But a more thorough-going form of cultural relativism than that discussed so far has sometimes been used as an argument against this possibility.

The linguist B.L. Whorf has claimed that the languages spoken by peoples of different cultures often differ radically with respect to their grammar and categories. The result of these differences is a difference in ways of understanding and perceiving the world. As a result of studying these differences we are, he says, 'introduced to a new principle of relativity, which holds that all observers are not led by the same physical evidence to the same picture of the universe, unless their linguistic backgrounds are similar, or can in some way be calibrated'[1]. The languages to which Whorf devoted most of his time studying were those spoken by the native Americans of the southwestern United States. He claims that the Hopi, for example, speak a language that is tenseless.

It recognizes psychological time, which is much like Bergson's 'duration', but this 'time' is quite unlike the mathematical time, T, used by our physicists. Among the peculiar properties of Hopi time are that it varies with each observer, does not permit of simultaneity, and has zero dimensions; i.e., it cannot be given a number greater than one ... The timeless Hopi verb does not distinguish between the present, past, and future of the event itself ...[2]

The result of this grammatical structure is that the Hopi think of the world very differently than we, who have a tensed verb, do. Whorf goes further elsewhere and claims that our perception of the world is conditioned by the language we learn, for all languages cut the world up in different ways. The language we learn controls our pattern of thought. As Whorf puts it:

[T]he forms of a person's thoughts are controlled by inexorable laws of pattern of which he is unconscious. These patterns are the unperceived intricate systematizations of his own language — shown readily enough by a candid comparison and contrast with other languages, especially those of a different linguistic family. His thinking itself is in a language — in English, in Sanskrit, in Chinese. And every language is a vast pattern-system, different from others, in which are culturally ordained the forms and categories by which the personality not only communicates, but also analyzes nature, notices or neglects types of relationships and phenomena, channels his reasoning, and builds the house of his consciousness.[3]

Whorf suggests that divergence in ways of thinking is a matter of degree: there will be less divergence among people who speak languages belonging to the same family, and in general there will be greater divergence between people whose language families differ. One supposes that if the divergence was too great there would be no hope of understanding between these people who speak radically different tongues. Thus the assumption that languages are mutually translatable, if we are only clever enough, would be false. But it is not clear that this follows, for it is not clear that this imagined divergence can be given coherent statement.

Whorf's thesis, that language profoundly affects the way in which we think and perceive the world, is not by itself original to him. His emphasis upon linguistic relativity and the way he develops it is, but the great German philosopher, Immanuel Kant, to a certain extent, held a similar view. For Kant, however, the structure of our *a priori* concepts enables us to understand the phenomenal world perceived through our senses as orderly and rule-bound. Kant held that the *a priori* categories, as rules of order, are universal; they hold for all men in all times and places. Other theorists, to a certain extent, accept the Kantian view, but reject the idea of universality. Recently, for example, Thomas S. Kuhn and others have argued that even within the history of a given culture we have examples, in the case of scientific revolution, of conceptual change and alteration that has the profound effect of altering the way in which people not only think of the world, but also the way in which they actually perceive it.

The way in which we both think and perceive the world has been said then to be conditioned by our languages, scientific theories and cultural practices. Norman's article explores some of these issues. In 'On seeing things differently' he develops a number of analogies in order to try to make sense of the idea that one person might see things differently from another. His main emphasis is on differences in world view and the effects of these differences on the way things are literally seen. He tries to bring out these differences by comparing 'seeing and seeing as'. His main illustrations involve various pictures that can be seen in different ways. His examples are the duck-rabbit picture and the picture of the old-young woman. He argues that in such cases it is not that the picture, in each case, really *is* a picture of, e.g., a rabbit or a picture of a duck. The pictures can be seen in different ways; there is not *a* right way of seeing them. He regards talk of truth and falsity, or objectivity and subjectivity, as unhelpful in this context. He argues that the same applies to the possibility of a plurality of world views and also a plurality of moral practices. He writes that where we have fundamental disagreements of, for example, a moral kind, this difference usually involves different views of the nature of man and his relation to the world, and can be understood on analogy with seeing as. If this is the case it will follow that a kind of pluralism will be true for some cultures, where, for example, there is a great diversity of beliefs, and false for others, where, for example, we have a highly cohesive tribal society. The logic of ethical discourse cannot be divorced, he argues, from concrete social and historical development.

Norman writes at times as if there were no sharp contrast between what is the case and what is believed to be the case, and this leads him to argue for a qualified sort of relativism. This is not the full-blown sort of relativism briefly referred to above. The most thorough-going relativism would supposedly deny that the notions of objectivity, truth and the idea of an objective reality, have any meaning apart from culturally conditioned modes of perceiving the world. This raises issues and problems too difficult to discuss here, but central to them is a nest of problems having to do with rationality and what it means to understand the world rationally. I refer the reader at this point to Stephen Toulmin's essay, *Human Understanding* (London, 1972), for in it he attempts to address himself to these issues. His discussion has the virtue of illustrating what some of the problems are.

Notes

1 Benjamin Lee Whorf, *Language, Thought and Reality* (Cambridge, Mass., 1956), p. 215.
2 Ibid., pp. 216-17. There is much dispute about the accuracy of these observations.
3 Ibid., p. 252.

10

Anthropology and the abnormal

RUTH BENEDICT

Modern social anthropology has become more and more a study of
the varieties and common elements of cultural environment and the
consequences of these in human behaviour. For such a study of
diverse social orders primitive peoples fortunately provide a laboratory not yet entirely vitiated by the spread of a standardized
worldwide civilization. Dyaks and Hopis, Fijians and Yakats are
significant for psychological and sociological study because only
among these simpler peoples has there been sufficient isolation to
give opportunity for the development of localized social forms. In
the higher cultures the standardization of custom and belief over a
couple of continents has given a false sense of the inevitability of the
particular forms that have gained currency, and we need to turn to
a wider survey in order to check the conclusions we hastily base upon
this near-universality of familiar customs. Most of the simpler
cultures did not gain the wide currency of the one which, out of our
experience, we identify with human nature, but this was for various
historical reasons, and certainly not for any that give us as its
carriers a monopoly of social good or of social sanity. Modern
civilization, from this point of view, becomes not a necessary
pinnacle of human achievement but one entry in a long series of
possible adjustments.

Reprinted from The Journal of General Psychology, *Vol. 10 (1934), pp. 59-82, by*
permission of The Journal Press.

These adjustments, whether they are in mannerisms like the ways of showing anger, or joy, or grief in any society, or in major human drives like those of sex, prove to be far more variable than experience in any one culture would suggest. In certain fields, such as that of religion or of formal marriage arrangements, these wide limits of variability are well known and can be fairly described. In others it is not yet possible to give a generalized account, but that does not absolve us of the task of indicating the significance of the work that has been done and of the problems that have arisen.

One of these problems relates to the customary modern normal-abnormal categories and our conclusions regarding them. In how far are such categories culturally determined, or in how far can we with assurance regard them as absolute? In how far can we regard inability to function socially as diagnostic of abnormality, or in how far is it necessary to regard this as a function of the culture?

As a matter of fact, one of the most striking facts that emerge from a study of widely varying cultures is the ease with which our abnormals function in other cultures. It does not matter what kind of 'abnormality' we choose for illustration, those which indicate extreme instability, or those which are more in the nature of character traits like sadism or delusions of grandeur or of persecution, there are well-described cultures in which these abnormals function at ease and with honour, and apparently without danger or difficulty to the society.

The most notorious of these is trance and catalepsy. Even a very mild mystic is aberrant in our culture. But most peoples have regarded even extreme psychic manifestations not only as normal and desirable, but even as characteristic of highly valued and gifted individuals. This was true even in our own cultural background in that period when Catholicism made the ecstatic experience the mark of sainthood. It is hard for us, born and brought up in a culture that makes no use of the experience, to realize how important a role it may play and how many individuals are capable of it, once it has been given an honourable place in any society....

Cataleptic and trance phenomena are, of course, only one illustration of the fact that those whom we regard as abnormals may function adequately in other cultures. Many of our culturally discarded traits are selected for elaboration in different societies. Homosexuality is an excellent example, for in this case our attention is not constantly diverted, as in the consideration of trance, to the interruption of routine activity which it implies. Homosexuality poses the problem very simply. A tendency toward this trait in our culture exposes an individual to all the conflicts to which all aberrants are always exposed, and we tend to identify the consequences of this conflict with homosexuality. But these consequences are obviously local and cultural. Homosexuals in many societies are not incompetent, but they may be such if the culture asks adjustments of them that would strain any man's vitality. Wherever homosexuality has been given an honourable place in any society, those to whom it is congenial have filled adequately the honourable roles society assigns to them. Plato's *Republic* is, of course, the most convincing statement of such a reading of homosexuality. It is presented as one of the major means to the good life, and it was generally so regarded in Greece at that time.

The cultural attitude toward homosexuals has not always been on such a high ethical plane, but it has been very varied. Among many American Indian tribes there exists the institution of the berdache, as the French called them. These men-women were men who at puberty or thereafter took the dress and the occupations of women. Sometimes they married other men and lived with them. Sometimes they were men with no inversion, persons of weak sexual endowment who chose this role to avoid the jeers of the women. The berdaches were never regarded as of first-rate supernatural power, as similar men-women were in Siberia, but rather as leaders in women's occupations, good healers in certain diseases, or, among certain tribes, as the genial organizers of social affairs. In any case, they were socially placed. They were not left exposed to the conflicts that visit the deviant who is excluded from participation in the recognized patterns of his society.

The most spectacular illustrations of the extent to which normality may be culturally defined are those cultures where an abnormality of our culture is the cornerstone of their social structure. It is not possible to do justice to these possibilities in a short discussion. A recent study of an island of northwest Melanesia by Fortune describes a society built upon traits which we regard as beyond the border of paranoia. In this tribe the exogamic groups look upon each other as prime manipulators of black magic, so that one marries always into an enemy group which remains for life one's deadly and unappeasable foes. They look upon a good garden crop as a confession of theft, for everyone is engaged in making magic to induce into his garden the productiveness of his neighbours'; therefore no secrecy in the island is so rigidly insisted upon as the secrecy of a man's harvesting of his yams. Their polite phrase at the acceptance of a gift is, 'And if you now poison me, how shall I repay you this present?' Their preoccupation with poisoning is constant; no woman ever leaves her cooking pot for a moment untended. Even the great affinal economic exchanges that are characteristic of this Melanesian culture area are quite altered in Dobu since they are incompatible with this fear and distrust that pervades the culture. They go farther and people the whole world outside their own quarters with such malignant spirits that all-night feasts and ceremonials simply do not occur here. They have even rigorous religiously enforced customs that forbid the sharing of seed even in one family group. Anyone else's food is deadly poison to you, so that communality of stores is out of the question. For some months before harvest the whole society is on the verge of starvation, but if one falls to the temptation and eats up one's seed yams, one is an outcast and a beachcomber for life. There is no coming back. It involves, as a matter of course, divorce and the breaking of all social ties.

Now in this society where no one may work with another and no one may share with another, Fortune describes the individual who was regarded by all his fellows as crazy. He was not one of those who periodically ran amok and, beside himself and frothing at the mouth, fell with a knife upon anyone he could reach. Such behaviour they did not regard as putting anyone outside the pale. They did not even put the individuals who were known to be liable to these attacks under any kind of control. They merely fled when they saw the attack coming on and kept out of the way. 'He would be all right tomorrow.' But there was one man of sunny, kindly disposition who liked work and liked to be helpful. The compulsion was too strong for him to repress it in favour of the opposite tendencies of his culture. Men and women never spoke of him without laughing; he was silly and simple and definitely crazy. Nevertheless, to the ethnologist used to a culture that has, in Christianity, made his type the model of all virtue, he seemed a pleasant fellow.

An even more extreme example, because it is of a culture that has built itself upon a more complex abnormality, is that of the North Pacific Coast of North America. The civilization of the Kwakiutl, at the time when it was first recorded in the last decades of the nineteenth century, was one of the most vigorous in North America. It was built up on an ample economic supply of goods, the fish which furnished their food staple being practically inexhaustible and obtainable with comparatively small labour, and the wood which furnished the material for their houses, their furnishings, and their arts being, with however much labour, always procurable. They lived in coastal villages that compared favourably in size with those of any other American Indians and they kept up constant communication by means of sea-going dug-out canoes.

It was one of the most vigorous and zestful of the aboriginal cultures of North America, with complex crafts and ceremonials, and elaborate and striking arts. It certainly had none of the earmarks of a sick civilization. The tribes of the Northwest Coast had wealth, and exactly in our terms. That is, they had not only a surplus of economic goods, but they made a game of the manipulation of wealth. It was by no means a mere direct transcription of economic needs and the filling of those needs. It involved the idea of capital, of interest, and of conspicuous waste. It was a game with all the binding rules of a game, and a person entered it as a child. His father distributed wealth for him, according to his ability, at a small feast or potlatch, and each gift the receiver was obliged to accept and to return after a short interval with interest that ran to about 100 per cent a year. By the time the child was grown, therefore, he was well launched, a larger potlatch had been given for him on various occasions of exploit or initiation, and he had wealth either out at usury or in his own possession. Nothing in the civilization could be enjoyed without validating it by the distribution of this wealth. Everything that was valued, names and songs as well as material objects, passed down in family lines, but they were always publicly assumed with accompanying sufficient distributions of property. It was the game of validating and exercising all the privileges one could accumulate from one's various forbears, or by gift, or by marriage, that made the chief interest of the culture. Everyone in his degree took part in it, but many, of course, mainly as spectators. In its highest form it was played out between rival chiefs representing not only themselves and their family lines but their communities, and the object of the contest was to glorify oneself and to humiliate one's opponent. On this level of greatness the property involved was no longer represented by blankets, so many thousand of them to a potlatch, but by higher units of value. These higher units were like our bank notes. They were incised copper tablets, each of them named, and having a value that depended upon their illustrious history. This was as high as ten thousand blankets, and to possess one of them, still more to enhance its value at a great potlatch, was one of the greatest glories within the compass of the chiefs of the Northwest Coast.

The details of this manipulation of wealth are in many ways a parody on our own economic arrangements, but it is with the motivations that were recognized in this contest that we are concerned in this discussion. The drives were those which in our own culture we should call megalomaniac. There was an uncensored self-glorification and ridicule of the opponent that it is hard to equal in other cultures outside the monologues of the abnormal.... All of existence was seen in terms of insult. Not only derogatory acts performed by a neighbour or an enemy, but all untoward events, like a cut when one's axe slipped, or a ducking when one's canoe overturned, were insults. All alike threatened first and foremost one's ego security, and the first thought one was allowed was how to get even, how to wipe out the insult....

In their behaviour at great bereavements this set of the culture comes out most strongly. Among the Kwakiutl it did not matter whether a relative had died in bed of disease, or by the hand of an enemy, in either case the death was an affront to be wiped out by the death of another person. The fact that one had been caused to mourn was proof that one had been put upon. A chief's sister and her daughter had gone up to Victoria, and either because they drank bad whisky or because their boat capsized they never came back. The chief called together his warriors. 'Now I ask you, tribes, who shall wail? Shall I do it or shall another?' The spokesman answered, of course, 'Not you, Chief. Let some other of the tribes.' Immediately they set up the war pole to announce their intention of wiping out the injury, and gathered a war party. They set out, and found seven men and two children asleep and killed them. 'Then they felt good when they arrived at Sebaa in the evening.'

The point which is of interest to us is that in our society those who on that occasion would feel good when they arrived at Sebaa that evening would be the definitely abnormal. There would be some, even in our society, but it is not a recognized and approved mood under the circumstances. On the Northwest Coast those are favoured and fortunate to whom that mood under those circumstances is congenial, and those to whom it is repugnant are unlucky. This latter minority can register in their own culture only by doing violence to their congenial responses and acquiring others that are difficult for them. The person, for instance, who, like a Plains Indian whose wife has been taken from him, is too proud to fight, can deal with the Northwest Coast civilization only by ignoring its strongest bents. If he cannot achieve it, he is the deviant in that culture, their instance of abnormality....

Behaviour honoured upon the Northwest Coast is one which is

recognized as abnormal in our civilization, and yet it is sufficiently close to the attitudes of our own culture to be intelligible to us and to have a definite vocabulary with which we may discuss it. The megalomaniac paranoid trend is a definite danger in our society. It is encouraged by some of our major preoccupations, and it confronts us with a choice of two possible attitudes. One is to brand it as abnormal and reprehensible, and is the attitude we have chosen in our civilization. The other is to make it an essential attribute of ideal man, and this is the solution in the culture of the Northwest Coast.

These illustrations, which it has been possible to indicate only in the briefest manner, force upon us the fact that normality is culturally defined. An adult shaped to the drives and standards of either of these cultures, if he were transported into our civilization, would fall into our categories of abnormality. He would be faced with the psychic dilemmas of the socially unavailable. In his own culture, however, he is the pillar of society, the end result of socially inculcated mores, and the problem of personal instability in his case simply does not arise.

No one civilization can possibly utilize in its mores the whole potential range of human behaviour. Just as there are great numbers of possible phonetic articulations, and the possibility of language depends on a selection and standardization of a few of these in order that speech communication may be possible at all, so the possibility of organized behaviour of every sort, from the fashions of local dress and houses to the dicta of a people's ethics and religion, depends upon a similar selection among the possible behaviour traits. In the field of recognized economic obligations or sex taboos this selection is as nonrational and subconscious a process as it is in the field of phonetics. It is a process which goes on in the group for long periods of time and is historically conditioned by innumerable accidents of isolation or of contact of peoples. In any comprehensive study of psychology, the selection that different cultures have made in the course of history within the great circumference of potential behaviour is of great significance.

Every society, beginning with some slight inclination in one direction or another, carries its preference farther and farther, integrating itself more and more completely upon its chosen basis, and discarding those types of behaviour that are uncongenial. Most of those organizations of personality that seem to us most incontrovertibly abnormal have been used by different civilizations in the very foundations of their institutional life. Conversely the most valued traits of our normal individuals have been looked on in differently organized cultures as aberrant. Normality, in short, within a very wide range, is culturally defined. It is primarily a term for the socially elaborated segment of human behaviour in any culture; and abnormality, a term for the segment that that particular civilization does not use. The very eyes with which we see the problem are conditioned by the long traditional habits of our own society.

It is a point that has been made more often in relation to ethics than in relation to psychiatry. We do not any longer make the mistake of deriving the morality of our own locality and decade directly from the inevitable constitution of human nature. We do not elevate it to the dignity of a first principle. We recognize that morality differs in every society, and is a convenient term for socially approved habits. Mankind has always preferred to say, 'It is a moral good', rather than 'It is habitual', and the fact of this preference is matter enough for a critical science of ethics. But historically the two phrases are synonymous.

The concept of the normal is properly a variant of the concept of the good. It is that which society has approved. A normal action is one which falls well within the limits of expected behaviour for a particular society. Its variability among different peoples is essentially a function of the variability of the behaviour patterns that different societies have created for themselves, and can never be wholly divorced from a consideration of culturally institutionalized types of behaviour.

Each culture is a more or less elaborate working-out of the potentialities of the segment it has chosen. In so far as a civilization is well integrated and consistent within itself, it will tend to carry farther and farther, according to its nature, its initial impulse toward a particular type of action, and from the point of view of any other culture those elaborations will include more and more extreme and aberrant traits.

Each of these traits, in proportion as it reinforces the chosen behaviour patterns of that culture, is for that culture normal. Those individuals to whom it is congenial either congenitally, or as the result of childhood sets, are accorded prestige in that culture, and are not visited with the social contempt or disapproval which their traits would call down upon them in a society that was differently organized. On the other hand, those individuals whose characteristics are not congenial to the selected type of human behaviour in the community are the deviants, no matter how valued their personality traits may be in a contrasted civilization.

The Dobuan who is not easily susceptible to fear of treachery, who enjoys work and likes to be helpful, is their neurotic and regarded as silly. On the Northwest Coast the person who finds it difficult to read life in terms of an insult contest will be the person upon whom fall all the difficulties of the culturally unprovided for. The person who does not find it easy to humiliate a neighbour, nor to see humiliation in his own experience, who is genial and loving, may, of course, find some unstandardized way of achieving satisfactions in his society, but not in the major patterned responses that his culture requires of him. If he is born to play an important role in a family with many hereditary privileges, he can succeed only by doing violence to his whole personality. If he does not succeed, he has betrayed his culture; that is, he is abnormal.

I have spoken of individuals as having sets toward certain types of behaviour, and of these sets as running sometimes counter to the types of behaviour which are institutionalized in the culture to which they belong. From all that we know of contrasting cultures it seems clear that differences of temperament occur in every society. The matter has never been made the subject of investigation, but from the available material it would appear that these temperament types are very likely of universal recurrence. That is, there is an ascertainable range of human behaviour that is found wherever a sufficiently large series of individuals is observed. But the proportion in which behaviour types stand to one another in different societies is not universal. The vast majority of the individuals in any group are shaped to the fashion of that culture. In other words, most individuals are plastic to the moulding force of the society into which they are born. In a society that values trance, as in India, they will have supernormal experience. In a society that institutionalizes homosexuality, they will be homosexual. In a society that sets the gathering of possessions as the chief human objective, they will amass property. The deviants, whatever the type of behaviour the culture has institutionalized, will remain few in number, and there seems no more difficulty in moulding the vast malleable majority to the 'normality' of what we consider an aberrant trait, such as delusions of reference, than to the normality of such accepted behaviour patterns as acquisitiveness. The small proportion of the number of the deviants in any culture is not a function of the sure instinct with which that society has built itself upon the fundamental sanities, but of the universal fact that, happily, the majority of mankind quite readily take any shape that is presented to them.

The relativity of normality is not an academic issue. In the first place, it suggests that the apparent weakness of the aberrant is most often and in great measure illusory. It springs not from the fact that he is lacking in necessary vigour, but that he is an individual upon whom that culture has put more than the usual strain. His inability to adapt himself to society is a reflection of the fact that that adaptation involves a conflict in him that it does not in the so-called normal....

The relativity of normality is important in what may some day come to be a true social engineering. Our picture of our own civilization is no longer in this generation in terms of a changeless and divinely derived set of categorical imperatives. We must face the problems our changed perspective has put upon us. In this matter of mental ailments, we must face the fact that even our normality is man-made, and is of our own seeking. Just as we have been handicapped in dealing with ethical problems so long as we held to an absolute definition of morality, so too in dealing with the problems of abnormality we are handicapped so long as we identify our local normalities with the universal sanities. I have taken illustrations from different cultures, because the conclusions are most inescapable from the contrasts as they are presented in unlike social groups. But the major problem is not a consequence of the variability of the normal from culture to culture, but its variability from era to era. This variability in time we cannot escape if we would, and it is not beyond the bounds of possibility that we may be able to face this inevitable change with full understanding and deal with it rationally. No society has yet achieved self-conscious and critical analysis of its own normalities and attempted rationally to deal with its own social process of creating new normalities within its next generation. But the fact that it is unachieved is not therefore proof of its impossibility. It is a faint indication of how momentous it could be in human society....

11

Cultural relativism as an ethnocentric notion

JOHN COOK

Those anthropologists who have advocated the doctrine of cultural (or ethical) relativism have done so with the avowed aim of combating ethnocentrism. In the pages that follow I shall argue that relativism is itself a particular form of ethnocentrism. In particular, I shall argue that this doctrine describes all cultures alike in terms that are derived from a certain aspect of our own culture.

I

When anthropologists discuss cultural relativism, whether they advocate or dispute this doctrine, they understand themselves to be concerned with morality. These discussions either presuppose or explicitly contain some account of what morality is, and it is about morality as thus conceived that they ask: is it relative or not? The following remarks by Raymond Firth provide a representative account of what morality is:

> By the moral attributes of an action is meant its qualities from the standpoint of right and wrong. Morality is a set of principles on which such judgements are based. Looked at empirically from the sociological point of view, morality is socially specific in the first instance. Every society has its own moral rules about

what kinds of conduct are right and what are wrong, and members of society conform to them or evade them, and pass judgement accordingly. For each society such rules, the relevant conduct, and the associated judgements, may be said to form a moral system. Examination of these moral systems ... is part of the work of social anthropology.[1]

Here we find morality explained as a set of 'rules' or 'principles', and we are told that moral judgments are 'based on' these rules or principles. Firth goes on to elaborate as follows on the nature of moral judgments:

From the empirical point of view, ... what are the essential elements in the exercise of moral judgements? There is the recognition that conduct is measurable by certain standards, commonly known as those of good and bad, right and wrong. These standards are regarded as not emanating from the person giving the judgement, but from outside him; they are external non-personal in their origin. Linked with this, as Durkheim has pointed out, they are invested with a special authority, they are credited with an intrinsic virtue which demands that they be obeyed. The felt necessity of obedience to this authority is termed *duty*. Yet this moral obligation is not of the order of mere yielding to superior weight. These moral standards have the character of being thought desirable in themselves — the character of *goodness*. Given this, the elements of authority and desirability, moral standards tend to be regarded as absolutes.[2]

Here we are further told that an essential element of moral judgments is that the standards on which they are based be regarded as 'not emanating from the person giving the judgement' but as being 'external in origin'. Moreover, obedience to these external standards (principles, rules) is a matter of duty.

This description of morality is so far not a relativist's account; it would be agreed to by absolutists as well. Relativism is a doctrine that arises when anthropologists offer to explain the external origin of these moral standards. Firth, once again, can serve as our guide.

What can be said about the source of these moral standards ...? The commonest answer probably in the history of Western social thought is that the source of all morality is God, that he provides both the absolute desirability of the standards and the unquestionable authority for following them. On such a view the distinction between right and wrong is absolute, universal ... On this and similar views the moral rules to be found in different types of society are various forms of approximation, according the perception or ignorance of the members of the society, to the absolute criteria springing from the central divine source. At the opposite extreme from this are the various views that morality is a thing of circumstance, ... lacking any absolute character of external necessity, any validation of universal principle. In Westermarck's conception of ethical relativity, for instance, conduct can be judged to be right or wrong only within its own social setting ... On the one view, morality ... is human by endowment and social by practice, but its origin is sought beyond man and society altogether ... On the other view, morality is essentially a social product, concomitant with the activities of man as a social being.[3]

The account that Firth gives us here of the absolutists' position is undoubtedly incomplete. There are secular versions of this view as well as the theological one he mentions. But let us pass over this point and see if we can get a fuller account of the relativist's position.

Christoph von Fürer-Haimendorf, an anthropologist who explores this subject in his book *Morals and Merit*, sets before us the sorts of considerations that have led people to embrace relativism.

Students of German drama and connoisseurs of Italian opera are familiar with the scene in which Don Carlos confesses to the horrified Marquess of Posa his love for the queen, the young wife of his father Philip II. To a Western audience the situation of a son passionately in love with his step-mother appears fraught with tragedy, and it seems inevitable that the drama should end with the hero's doom. A Tibetan audience would not understand what all the excitement is about, for Tibetans see no harm in the sharing of one wife by father and son. An arrangement which one society considers the height of immorality, is thought natural and innocuous by another. Similarly, a European peasant, beheading a woman from a neighboring village whom he happened to encounter on her way home from the fields, would be locked up as a criminal lunatic; whereas in a Naga village a youth returning with a human head captured under similar circumstances earns the insignia of a successful head-hunter. Examples of such extreme differences in the moral assessment of conduct could easily be multiplied, and there is a school of thought which considers all morality as relative and culturally conditioned.[4]

Fürer-Haimendorf goes on to remark that philosophers in constructing their moral theories 'did not pay much attention to the fact that two persons of different cultural background may react to identical circumstances in a totally different manner, even though each may be convinced of the righteousness of his conduct... Most moral philosophers had little knowledge of ethnographic data relating to the conduct and beliefs of pre-literate populations, and in their analyses of moral concepts there was hence only limited scope for any transcultural comparisons'[5]. He then gives us this account of relativism:

> The theory of the relativity of morals tentatively formulated by philosophers such as David Hume, was fully elaborated by... Westermarck, and throughout the earlier part of the twentieth century it gained the strong support of many British and American anthropologists. It was then argued that different cultures produced distinct but 'equally valid' patterns of life, and that it was impossible to pass judgement on the respective patterns in moral terms.[6]

Unfortunately he does not explain why it was thought impossible to pass judgment on the respective patterns, and in fact there is some confusion in associating Hume's name with relativism as thus explained. On Hume's view there is certainly no impossibility of passing judgment in moral terms on conduct in other cultures for it is Hume's view that 'when you pronounce any action or character to be vicious, you mean nothing but that... you have a feeling or sentiment of blame [or of "disapprobation"] from the contemplation of it'[7]. Now on such a view there is surely no impossibility of pronouncing conduct in other cultures to be vicious, for as any relativist will allow, there is no impossibility of a feeling of blame or disapprobation arising in people from the contemplation of certain of the conduct in other cultures. Thus, a view such as Hume's is no real ally of relativism, if relativism is supposed to undermine cross-cultural judgments. For a Humean there is no condition for making moral judgments which is fulfilled in the case of intra-cultural judgments but not fulfilled in the case of cross-cultural judgments. The same would hold for an egoist: if he held that the judgment 'Jones is doing wrong' should be analysed as 'I don't want Jones to do that', then on his theory there is no difference between

the case in which Jones is a member of his own culture and the case
in which Jones is a member of some other culture.

William G. Sumner gives what appears to be a properly relativistic account. He writes: '"Immoral" never means anything but
contrary to the mores of the time and place. Therefore ... there is no
permanent or universal standard by which right and truth in regard
to these matters can be established and different folkways compared
and criticized'[8]. What he means, presumably, is that to say 'Jones
is acting immorally' is to say 'Jones is acting contrary to the mores of
his group' so that if we were to say of a headhunter that in taking
heads, he is acting immorally, it could be said in reply to us: 'No,
the mores of his group allow headhunting.' The trouble with
Sumner's view is that it seems to be just plainly false. When some of
us denounced the US involvement in the Vietnam War as being not
merely wasteful but immoral, we did not mean that our involvement
there was contrary to the mores of the United States. Indeed, not a
few anti-war critics thought if someone were to say that the Naga
warriors are immoral because they engage in headhunting, he
would surely *not* mean that these Naga warriors have violated Naga
mores. Accordingly, relativism, as Sumner explains it, is just false.

The same difficulty resides in Ruth Benedict's version of relativism. She writes: 'We recognize that morality differs in every society,
and is a convenient term for socially approved habits. Mankind has
always preferred to say "It is morally good", rather than "It is
habitual" ... But historically the two phrases are synonymous'[9].
Here again we have a claim that, as stated, is plainly false. Suppose
that an old man who lives alone in an apartment building falls ill
and that a neighbour down the hall discovers this and nurses him
back to health. If the old man now says to this person, 'It was very
good of you to take care of me', he certainly does not mean that it
was *habitual* of that person to take care of him or even that it is
habitual (customary?) for people in our culture to look after sick
neighbours.

It seems altogether unlikely that either Sumner or Miss Benedict
would have folded under such criticisms and acknowledged that
relativism is false. No doubt they would have sought a less vulnerable version of relativism. Let us see, then, if we can reconstruct the
position they might have retreated to.

Perhaps the point to bear in mind here is that relativists chiefly
intend to be arguing against absolutism, which they identify with
ethnocentrism. Very likely, then, in the face of the foregoing
criticisms, a relativist would content himself with the following,

merely negative, claim. He might say: 'Moral judgments are based on moral principles. Now *if* moral principles were known to be true by means of some revelation or some moral intuition, then — and *only* then — would it be possible to *know* that all peoples everywhere ought to do certain things and not others. But the variability of moral principles is proof that there are no moral intuitions or revelation, for if there were a faculty of moral perception we would all have the same principles. So therefore it is not possible to know what all people everywhere ought and ought not to do.' This, I think, is the argument that relativists really intend to be making. It is aimed at getting people to admit that although it may *seem* to them that their moral principles are self-evidently true, and hence *seem* to be grounds for passing judgment on other peoples, in fact the self-evidence of these principles is a kind of illusion. Solomon Asch who is not himself a relativist puts this matter as well as anyone.

> Social conditions not only enforce particular practices; they also inculcate the conviction of their rightness ... Every parochial system appears to its upholders as universally valid. The varied and often contradictory beliefs about marriage or property ownership ... [are] each treated by its supporters as unquestionable. It also appears that people misconceive the ways in which they arrive at their beliefs and values. Each acts as if he has gone through a process of judging and evaluating his views independently. But an unbiased examination will show that he could not have developed them himself and that had fate cast him under other skies, he would have been a faithful member of Russian or Eskimo society. Our assumption about the rationality and self-evidence of our values is itself, it would seem, a socially bred illusion — dogmatism parading under a veneer of reason.[10]

The idea here is that Anglo-Saxons, for instance, believe that monogamy is right and that polygamy is wrong, while in other cultures there are people whose beliefs contradict these. These 'beliefs', of course, are what Firth, in the passages quoted above, called 'rules' or 'principles'. Relativism, then, is really a theory about such beliefs or rules or principles.

Here the following question might arise. If, according to relativism, our moral judgments and decisions are based on moral principles, and if these principles are not the sort of thing we could know to be true, i.e., if they are merely the effect of a process of enculturation, then does not relativism imply that these principles can have no real moral authority over even the *individual?* In other words, if an individual should ask himself 'How can the principles which have been thus inculcated in me really *oblige* me to do some things and refrain from other things?' the answer would seem to be 'They *can't!*' This, at least, is the answer that some writers have thought to be the correct one. Thus, Frank Hartung writes: 'Cultural relativity deprives us of any possible rational basis for choosing a proper life. Tolerance and equal validity also seem to imply that no moral concepts, regardless of their derivation, can possibly be given any logical or empirical authority over the conventions of any individual'[11]. Thus, cultural relativism seems to imply what might be called 'individual relativity' — an absolute relativity, as Norman Mailer once called it. In an article eulogizing the Hipster of the 1950s, Mailer wrote:

> Character ... enters then into an absolute relativity where there are no truths other than the isolated truths of what each observer feels at each instant of his existence ... What is consequent therefore is the divorce of man from his values, the liberation of the self from the Super-Ego of society. The only Hip morality ... is to do what one feels whenever and wherever it is possible, and — this is how the war of the Hip and the Square begins — to engage in one primal battle: to open the limits of the possible for oneself, for oneself alone because that is one's need.[12]

The Hipster, as Mailer says, is a 'philosophical psychopath', and it has seemed to some that relativism opens the door to such psychopathy.

At least some defenders of relativism, however, repudiate this interpretation of their doctrine. Melville Herskovits, for instance, replies to this view as follows:

> In a similar manner, we can dispose of the contention that cultural relativism negates the force of the codes that prevail at a given time in a given culture ... Each people, having standards, not only inculcate them in the young so that each generation is enculturated to the value-systems of its predecessors, but they see to it that transgressions of accepted codes are punished ...

> The point may be put in a somewhat different way. *Cultural* relativism must be sharply distinguished from concepts of the relativity of individual behaviour, which would negate all social controls over conduct ... Conformity to the code of the group is a requirement for any regularity in life.[13]

Elsewhere he reiterates the point in these words:

> Cultural relativism, which stresses the universals in human
> experience as against ethnocentric concepts of absolute values,
> in no wise gives over the restraints that every system of ethics
> exercises over those who live in accordance with it. To recognize
> that right, and justice, and beauty may have as many manifesta-
> tions as there are cultures is to express tolerance, not nihil-
> ism.[14]

Herskovits apparently thought that on this interpretation relativism
would have no nasty implications. Unfortunately he failed to realize
that his interpretation, while rejecting nihilism, has equally disastrous implications. It amounts to the view that the code of any
culture really does create moral obligations for its members, that we
really *are* obligated by the code of our culture — *whatever it may
be*. In other words, Herskovits' interpretation turns relativism into
an endorsement of tyranny. Let me illustrate. Several years ago an
Associated Press dispatch from Alcamo, Sicily, carried the following
story of a twenty-year-old girl, Franca Viola, who 'broke a thousand
years of Sicilian tradition'.

> Two years ago Franca refused to wed the rich man's son who
> kidnapped and raped her. Since the Middle Ages, kidnap and
> rape have been the sure road to the altar for a rejected Sicilian
> suitor. If the girl didn't say yes after that, she was dishonoured
> and no one else would marry her.[15]

Not only did Franca refuse to marry the man who raped her, she
took him to court, where he was convicted and sentenced to eleven
years in prison. The reaction, it seems, was violent: 'Franca and her
family were threatened with vengeance for her violation of the
ancient code.' Even so, another young man, a former acquaintance,
'became a steady caller at her home'; he proposed, she accepted,
and they were married.

Now Herskovits is surely bound by his version of cultural relativism to say that this young woman did not do the right thing, for
Herskovits' whole point was that 'conformity to a code of the group'
is a 'requirement' which relativism does not undermine. If he makes
an exception for Franca Viola, how does he avoid making an
exception for Mailer's 'philosophical psychopaths'? Notice, too, that
Sumner's position is equally clearly committed to such a consequence, for he says that 'immoral' means contrary to the mores of
the group, which commits Sumner to saying that Franca Viola acted

immorally when she brought charges against the rapist and married another man.

Thus relativism is stretched between two equally old consequences. It implicitly endorses the philosophical psychopath or it advocates tyranny. Relativism was presumably meant to tell us what morality is, but on either interpretation it fails utterly. A moral theory which can do no better than either to implicitly condemn Franca Viola or to join Norman Mailer in excusing the killing of candy store owners for kicks (see p. 314, n. 12) is a thoroughly confused theory. Where did it go wrong? Perhaps we need to scrutinize that part of the doctrine which relativism shares with absolutism, namely, the idea that morality consists of making moral judgments about actions and that these judgments are based on rules or principles. I shall argue that this is the source of confusion in relativism and is, in fact, an ethnocentric description.

II

Perhaps the essential feature of the relativist's account of morality is not merely the idea that moral judgments are based on principles, but the idea that these principles, as Firth said (p. 290 above) do not come 'from the individual giving the judgement, but from outside him; they are external, non-personal in their origin'. What this, in effect, denies is that the individual has any capacity for thinking, reflecting, about moral matters, any capacity for reaching moral decisions of his own. Now it is worth noticing that there are cultures for which this would be a fairly accurate description. Pre-war Japan would, I think, be an example. I cannot here completely justify this, but to give some substance to the example I will quote briefly from several articles by Douglas Haring. He gives at one point a brief sketch of the 'outstanding aspects of Japanese conduct and personal character' in the period before World War II, which contains the following items:

(1) Psychologically and culturally the Japanese people are unusually homogeneous. They act and think more alike than do Occidental peoples. The avowed aim of Japan's prewar Ministry of Education was to produce subjects of the Emperor so much alike as to be interchangeable for national purposes....

(2) The Japanese conform almost eagerly to numberless exact rules of conduct and exhibit bewilderment when required to act alone or in situations not anticipated in the codes ...

(3) The major sanctions of conformity to Japanese codes of conduct are ridicule and shame. Early in life every child learns that the slightest breach of proper conduct may expose his family to ridicule, and that a lapse from propriety may leave him unsupported in the face of the ridicule of the world and the wrath of his own family.

*   *   *   *   *

(8) The word *makoto* ... is charged with emotional significance in Japan ... In Japanese eyes *makoto*, utter devotion to codes of conduct, is one of the highest virtues.[16]

How does all of this come about? Haring gives a part of the explanation in this account of the education of the Japanese:

The aims of all education culminate in a single theme: the sanctity of the Emperor. Not for a moment in his school career may a Japanese forget that the purpose of life is to serve the Emperor. His history books — and above all, his 'morality' courses — insure that every Japanese thinks of himself as a loyal subject. Whatever his social class he is a subject, never a citizen ...

Shinto doctrines are impressed upon the young in their books by participation in rituals at the school, and by group worship at Government Shinto shrines. These cult activities are compulsory ...

The middle schools, junior colleges, and universities conform to similar standards. There is no relaxation of the duties of Emperor worship in the higher institutions ...

The educational system has achieved two major ends ... By the nature of the language and the system of writing with Chinese ideographs, the masses of the people cannot hope to acquire foreign ideas except as the officials permit their publication in Japanese. Even the Chinese ideographs are used in such a way that Japanese primary school graduates cannot read Chinese.

Secondly, the relatively small number of persons who achieve higher education are rendered irrevocably Japanese in the formative years of childhood. By the time they encounter foreign ideas in the colleges, they have formed emotional habits which guarantee immunity against beliefs that might threaten their patriotic devotion.[17]

Haring goes on to give a number of examples to illustrate the incapacity of these people for individual judgment. I will quote only one of these:

> The streetcar conductor also knows his place. He carries a book of rules. Therein are printed all possible questions that passengers might ask, together with correct replies. His speech is confined to these prescribed sentences, and 'whatsoever is more than these cometh of evil'. Now and then the Electric Bureau holds a contest for the best sentence for conductors to use when asked thus-and-so. The winning sentence is added to the rules book and the conductor's repertory is enlarged. But originality transcends the conductor's imagination.[18]

Now assuming that this gives us a fairly accurate picture of the pre-war Japanese, we could say that the relativist's (and the absolutist's) account of morality really does fit these people. And the important thing is that this is a quite particular case and one which differs very considerably from our own situation. The question arises, then, how the relativist, along with the absolutist, comes to adopt a very general account of 'morality' which fits only certain, rather special, cases. I suspect that the answer — or part of the answer — is that within our own culture there are elements that tend to suggest such an account of morality, not only to anthropologists but to philosophers as well. What I want to argue, then, is that relativists are deploying cross-culturally a notion of morality which is in fact a reflection of certain elements of our own culture. This is the ethnocentric feature of relativism.

III

In order to exhibit the ethnocentric character of ethical relativism, I will need to sharply define that aspect of our culture which the relativist's notion of morality reflects. To do this I will try to isolate that aspect of our culture and set it in sharp contrast with another possible culture whose members would find no plausibility in thinking of their 'morality' as a set of rules imposed from without. My strategy for doing this will be to sketch in some detail two imaginary cultures. Both will bear some similarity to our own, although the second will bear the deeper similarity and will reveal that aspect of our culture on which the plausibility of relativism depends.

I must emphasize here that the way in which these two cultures differ from our own is mostly a matter of degree. Indeed, they might even be phases of our own history. Accordingly, I will construct these imaginary cultures by simply adapting certain more or less familiar features of our own lives. Because I have not here the space to give more than a brief sketch of Islandia and Grundlegung, as I shall call them, I must restrict myself to describing dominant features and tendencies. The disadvantage of this is that my own description may create a false impression, especially in the case of the first culture to be described, Islandia[19]. The impression, unfortunately, is likely to be that of a people whose lives must be *altogether* different from our own, almost to the point of unimaginability. To counteract this impression, I can only plead with the reader to bear constantly in mind that my description is deliberately focused on only certain aspects of their culture and even then only on dominant tendencies to the exclusion of much of the leven which, if described, would show that they share with us a common humanity. With this caution, then, I turn to a brief sketch of Islandia and Grundlegung.

The best way to indicate what it is about the Islandians that chiefly interests me is to begin with some words written by Judge Learned Hand in appreciation of Benjamin Cardozo shortly after the latter's death. The relevance of this is that among the Islandians Benjamin Cardozo would not have been as rare and individual as he was among us. If we were to go among these people, we would find many whom we could describe in the language of the following quotation:

> In all of this I have not told you what qualities made it possible for him to find just that compromise between the letter and the spirit [of the law] that so constantly guided him to safety. I have not told you because I do not know. It was wisdom: and like most wisdom, has run beyond the reasons which he gave for it. And what is wisdom — that gift of God which the great prophets of his race exalted? I do not know; like you, I know it when I see it, but I cannot tell of what it is composed. One ingredient I think I do know: the wise man is the detached man. By that I mean more than detached from his grosser interests — his advancement and his gain. Many of us can be that — I dare to believe that most judges can be, and are. I am thinking of something far more subtly infused. Our convictions, our outlook, the whole make-up of our thinking, which we cannot help bringing to the decision of every question, is the creature of our past; and

into our past have been woven all sorts of frustrated ambitions with their envies, and hopes of preferment with their corruptions, which, long since forgotten, still determine our conduct. A wise man is one exempt from the handicap of such a past; he is a runner stripped for the race; he can weigh the conflicting factors of his problem without always finding himself in one scale or the other. Cardozo was such a man; his gentle nature had in it no aquisitiveness; he did not use himself as a measure of value; the secret of his humor — a precious gift that he did not wear upon his sleeve — lay in his ability to get outside of himself, and look back. Yet from this self-effacement came a power greater than the power of him who ruleth a city. He was wise because his spirit was uncontaminated, because he knew no violence, or hatred, or envy, or jealousy, or ill-will. I believe that it was this purity that chiefly made him the judge that we so much revere; more than his learning, his acuteness, and his fabulous industry. In this America of ours where the passion for publicity is a disease, and where swarms of foolish, tawdry moths dash with rapture into its consuming fire, it was a rare good fortune that brought to such eminence a man so reserved, so unassuming, so retiring, so gracious to high and low, and so serene. He is gone, and while the west is still lighted with his radiance, it is well for us to pause and take count of our own coarser selves. He has a lesson to teach us if we care to stop and learn; a lesson quite at variance with most that we practice, and much that we profess.[20]

This, of course, is a striking eulogy, and even among the Islandians such a man would not be common coin. The difference is that among us there are too many who would not even approximate to such a man, whereas among the Islandians most people share to some degree in such wisdom. This is how they differ from us. And now let us see in more detail how this is possible.

A good place to begin is with the Islandians' 'moral' literature and drama, which gives a central place to men and women who are thoughtful, wise and insightful people. (If an ethnologist went looking for their 'authority figures', these would be the only ones he would find — and, of course, the label 'authority figure' would be quite inappropriate.) Furthermore, among the Islandians there is no status to be achieved by mere prowess, by stardom in athletics, by achieving high office, or amassing great wealth. They have no Horatio Algers, no Supermen, no Jack Armstrong, the All-American

Boy. Their moral tales are concerned not so much with passing judgment on actions as with the quality of moral thinking. The 'villains' are hypocrites, self-deceivers, the insincere, the prejudiced, the opinionated, the obtuse, the smug, the callous, and so on. Their tales of virtue are, to a large extent, tales of people who manage to break out of their prejudice or callousness, who are brought into a new level of sensitivity and insight, or who triumph over their self-deception or hypocrisy. In this culture there is no body of literature that resembles our 'westerns', where characters are portrayed as the virtuous and the villainous by means merely of their deeds. Their literature is all of a far more subtle kind than this[21].

One consequence of all this is that as the children of this culture grow up, they become adept at carefully thinking about and describing situations that call for nice judgment or that require a difficult decision. They are skilful at presenting and exploring the morally relevant aspects of situations. In short, they are articulate in a way that many of us are not. Where some of us might end up saying, 'Well, all I know is that that's wrong!' they find it possible to exhibit the nature and quality of the act in dramatic and revealing ways. And they are resourceful in finding ways to do this. For instance, where appropriate they can invent parables like that which Nathan told to David to make him see the nature of his treatment of Uriah (2 Sam. 12:1). They know how to use gentle humour to expose the absurdity of someone's thoughts and rationalizations. In these and in many other ways they manage to accomplish in daily life what, among us, is accomplished only by some of our more sensitive authors (e.g. Eudora Welty's 'A Visit of Charity' and the scene in *The Brothers Karamazov* in which Zossima comes to realize what he is about to do in fighting a duel).

I do not mean that all of these people are equally competent in this respect. Some are more acute, more discerning, more intelligent than others, but even the least articulate among them never resorts to saying something like 'It's just wrong, that's all I know' or 'You just ought to, that's all!' If they find themselves in disagreement with someone and not getting anywhere, they conclude either that they have not been very successful in exhibiting the character of the action in question or that they have been stupid in not seeing what the other person was driving at in *his* account of the action. At other times, when two people begin in disagreement and fail to bridge the gap in either direction, they reach the conclusion, not that one or the other is wrong or obtuse, but that neither of them knows how to think about the matter at hand. Phrases like 'It's just a matter of opinion' and 'Everyone has his own point of view' are unheard of among them. But where there are prolonged disagreements, it is not uncommon for them to say things like 'I guess we just don't know how to think about this.'

In order that we not over-idealize this culture, I should add that what I have described here is only one aspect of their lives, a theme of their culture. I have not meant to suggest that they are constantly engaged in moral reflection, self-scrutiny and so on. And their moral literature does not loom much larger in their lives than ours does in our lives. Just as we have novels of adventure, humorous novels, and so on, so do they. Also, just as our writers and other intellectuals go through fads, so do theirs. (For instance, from time to time their lesser authors go in for grossly psychological melodrama.) Like us, they fall into temptation, get angry, frustrated, jealous, and so on. In short, they are human through and through. But even so, I would venture to suggest that a culture fitting the above description would be a great deal healthier than our own. For instance, deep prejudices would not divide them, and among their politicians there would be no demagogues. Their level of political discussion would be much higher than what we are accustomed to, and since irrational fears of foreign ideologies would not beset them, social experimentation would be far easier. I leave it to the reader to infer the differences this would make to their lives.

Let us now turn to the second culture, known as Grundlegung. These people are not altogether incapable of recognizing and talking about the quality of moral thinking. They, too, have in their vocabulary such words as 'hypocrisy', 'self-deception', 'prejudiced', 'opinionated', 'callous' and so on. But they do not have a *ready* command of these words. Neither their literature nor their conversations make much use of these notions. *Some* use, but not much. What predominates in their culture's moral literature is a concern with matters of property rights, sex, physical heroism and national honour. As a result, the villains are mostly thieves, cheats, seducers, adulterers and traitors. The moral heroes, on the other hand, are people who resist temptation to steal and seduce and who uphold their country's honour even at great cost to themselves. Self-sacrifice is a cardinal virtue, and in their children's literature there are plenty of books that eulogize the humble, forbearing poor, people who would never dream of stealing or raising a cry against an economic system that kept them in rags. I do not mean that all of their literature is of this ilk, only that such literature *can* exist in this culture and that everyone is exposed to some of it. They do have

their more thoughtful authors, and even among their non-writing
public there are some perceptive people, capable of critical judgment. But even so it is extremely rare to find among them people
who have any real facility of the kind that is developed in Islandia,
i.e., people who can carefully, yet revealingly, describe morally
complicated or novel situations. Even those whom they think of as
wise tend to be moralizers rather than sensitive thinkers; they tend
to go in for generalization rather than thoughtful attention to the
situation at hand. The vast majority of the people are given to
thinking in clichés and stereotypes. And in their inarticulateness,
they, unlike the Islandians, are given to impatiently ending disagreements by saying things like 'Well, it's just wrong, that's all I
know!' The level of their political dialogue is comparatively very
low, and in every generation there appear several highly effective
demagogues. It is not uncommon for their politicians to attack the
press and even to urge their followers not to read certain news-
papers. Naturally these people tend to be self-righteous, and especially in adolescence they cover their vulnerability in a cloak of smug-
ness and arrogance. I do not mean that they are all like this, and to
the same degree, but this is a pronounced tendency among them.

Another aspect of the moral upbringing in Grundlegung is that
there are a great many do's and don't's that have no very evident
point. Duty is a dominant moral category, so that most of these
people would recognize themselves — or a bit of themselves — in the
following lines from Rudolf Hess's autobiography, *Commandant of
Auschwitz*:

> I had been brought up by my parents to be respectful and
> obedient toward all grown-up people, and especially the elderly,
> regardless of their social status. I was taught that my highest
> duty was to help those in need. It was constantly impressed upon
> me in forceful terms that I must obey promptly the wishes and
> commands of my parents, teachers, and priests, and indeed of
> all grown-up people, including servants, and that nothing must
> distract me from this duty. Whatever they said was always right.
>
> These basic principles on which I was brought up became
> part of my flesh and blood. I can still clearly remember how my
> father, who on account of his fervent Catholicism was a deter-
> mined opponent of the Reich government and its policy, never
> ceased to remind his friends that, however strong one's opposi-
> tion might be, the laws and decrees of the state had to be obeyed
> unconditionally.

From my earliest youth I was brought up with a strong awareness of duty. In my parent's house it was insisted that every task
be exactly and conscientiously carried out. Each member of the
family had his own special duties to perform. My father took
particular care to see that I obeyed all his instructions and wishes
with the greatest meticulousness. I remember to this day how he
hauled me out of bed one night, because I had left the saddle
cloth lying in the garden instead of hanging it up in the barn to
dry, as he had told me to do.[22]

One of his more striking remarks here is his saying: 'I was taught
that my highest duty was to help those in need.' He does not say at
all that he was brought up to *care* about people in need, to care
about their problems. It is pretty clear that what we have here is a
degenerate form of Christianity: Jehovah's wrath and the so-called
legalism of the Old Testament combined with the story of the Good
Samaritan. One is reminded here of Kant's insistence, regarding the
commandment to love thy enemy, that love as a sentiment cannot
be commanded and that we must therefore interpret that commandment to mean that we are obliged to perform beneficent acts.
In any case, this is pretty much the style of the thinking of the
people of Grundlegung. They have little understanding of what they
are doing, but they feel themselves obliged to do it anyway. Again, I
don't mean that the culture is perfectly uniform in this respect. But
because this is a dominant theme of their literature and the rest of
their culture, those who deviate from this theme are rather unsure
of how to understand themselves. Some of them, especially those
who are most thoroughly disgusted with the deadening effect of all
the talk about 'duty', represent themselves as nihilists. A kind of
paradigm of the thinking of these few individuals is found in Huck
Finn's reflections on the lie he told to save Jim from being hauled
back to slavery:

They went off and I got aboard the raft, feeling bad and low,
because I knowed very well I had done wrong, and I see it
warn't no use for me to try to learn to do right; a body that
don't get started right when he's little ain't got no show — when
the pinch comes there ain't nothing to back him up and keep
him to his work, and so he gets beat. Then I thought a minute,
and says to myself, hold on; s'pose you'd 'a' done right and give
Jim up, would you feel better than what you do now. Well, then,
says I, what's the use you learning to do right when it's troublesome to do right and ain't no trouble to do wrong, and the wages

is just the same? I was struck. I couldn't answer that. So I reckoned I wouldn't bother no more about it, but after this always do whichever come handiest at the time.[23]

This nihilism, however, tends to leave these people uneasy, so like Frenchmen who have abandoned their Catholicism, they tend to seek intellectual surrogates, and as a result there grow up a variety of popular 'philosophies', existentialist and otherwise.

It goes without saying, I think, that moral philosophy will flourish in Grundlegung. And naturally one of the questions with which their philosophers become obsessed is the question 'Why should I be moral?' The reason for this is, as *we* can see, that they understand the word 'moral' to mean (as perhaps it does in most of its uses in this culture) 'adherence to duty' or something close to that. So that philosophical question poses a problem for them just because, on the one hand, much of what passes for duty in this culture is sort of sick, or at least is lacking in any *sense* for them, while on the other hand they see that to answer that there is *no* reason to be moral is to somehow open the door to murder, stealing, rape, adultery, and so on. So they go on arguing at great length over the question 'Why should I be moral?' — never recognizing the nature of their quandary. For the Islandians, of course, this question would not even make sense, for they would have no word that had quite the associations of the word 'moral' in Grundlegung. By the same token, it is inconceivable that an Islandian should become a nihilist, for there would not exist for them the sort of thing that nihilists rebel against, i.e., no Islandian could have anything like Huck's thought that he had done wrong in telling a lie to save a man from slavery.

Another aspect of their moral philosophy is that they are always talking about moral rules or moral principles, as though these were somehow the guidelines of action. Of course they never quite succeed in explaining what a moral rule or principle *is*, but also they never quite succeed in seeing what is queer about this notion, for in fact in certain respects their lives *do* look as though they were living by rules — as if, like boys at a summer camp, they needed someone to set limits and prescribe duties. (In other words, they are to some extent like the pre-war Japanese, as described by Haring. See section II above.) The kinds of things they call rules, of course, are 'It is wrong to lie', 'You ought not to steal' and 'It is one's duty to perform beneficent acts.' Naturally their philosophers wonder where these principles come from, how they know that it is one's duty to perform the beneficent acts rather than cruel acts and a whole flood of theories are developed to explain this puzzling matter. Some say that these principles come from God, and that if God had so decreed it, it would have been our duty to walk around on our hands and to kill our mothers by disembowelling them. Others say that these principles are self-evident and necessary truths which even God could not alter and that we perceive these truths with a special moral faculty. Still others insist that these are not really 'truths' at all, but expressions of our feelings. And still others, who have read some anthropology, say that these are just arbitrary rules inculcated by society — like traffic rules that tell you which side of the road to drive on. It is their notion of rules or principles, of course, that makes moral nihilism among them plausible, for naturally if the 'foundations' of morality are thought to be rules, and if these rules are found to be pretty strange things, then all of 'morality' is in danger of being called into question at once. (See the dispute over the implications of relativism in section I above.) Islandians, on the other hand, would find no plausibility in the notion that they live by rules, so there is not, for them, any way of calling all of their 'morality' into question at once. Or as I had better put it, for the Islandians there just is nothing that they can think of as 'their morality', for it is really only the notion that we have a 'set' or 'system' of moral rules that makes it appear that we have 'a morality'.

It should now be clear why I have said that cultural relativism rests on an ethnocentric notion of morality. This can be made clearer, however, if we remind ourselves of the following four features of the relativist's doctrine. The relativist maintains that:

(1) Moral judgments are concerned with *actions*.
(2) Moral judgments are based on rules or principles.
(3) The origin of these rules or principles is external to the individual; they are 'non-personal' as Firth puts it.
(4) The words of moral praise and blame are such words as 'good' and 'immoral' and these can be defined by reference to the mores of the group. Thus, 'immoral' never means anything but contrary to the mores of the group (Sumner).

Now all four of these propositions would have some plausibility as descriptions of the Grundlegung culture, but they would constitute an utter misinterpretation if offered as a description of the Islandians. Let us ask then whether they would serve as a more or less accurate description of *us*. The answer, I suppose, is yes and no. Bear in mind here that I was able to construct both Islandia and

Grundlegung from materials taken from our own culture. Thus, in so far as those four propositions reflect something of Grundlegung culture they also, although to a lesser degree, reflect something of our own culture. But also because they utterly misrepresent the Islandians, they also, although to a lesser degree, misrepresent us. This is why, in saying that the doctrine of relativism is an ethnocentric notion, I said that it reflects an *aspect* of our culture.

At this point I can imagine a relativist wanting to make several objections to my criticism. I will try to state these on his behalf.

The first objection that a relativist might want to make against me is this: 'I don't understand your Islandians at all, and hence I don't understand the distinction you have been trying to make. Do your Islandians not have a settled way of life? What about their form of marriage, for instance? Are they monogamous, polygamous, or what? You surely don't mean to say that they have no settled form of marriage and family life, for if that is what you mean to say about them, then I can assure you that this is a cultural impossibility. But on the other hand, if you are prepared to allow that they are, say, monogamous, then you must admit that this is part of their morality. If they practice monogamy, then they must believe that monogamy is *right*. Now the relativist's whole claim is that different cultures have different and contradictory beliefs about such things as marriage. And it is these beliefs that we call their "rules" or "principles" and which we claim to have an origin outside the individual. Now if you mean to say that each of your Islandians, as an individual, reflects upon the nature of marriage and that all of them have in this way "discovered" that they ought to marry monogamously, then you are surely embracing an intuitionist theory of morality — a theory which is as dubious as any theory could ever be. In short, I simply don't understand your criticism of relativism.'

How is this to be answered? First of all, nothing that I said about the Islandians was meant to suggest that they do not have a settled way of life. It is altogether consistent with what I said about them that they are a monogamous people, for example. What I would deny is that to admit that they are a monogamous people carried the further implication that they believe that monogamy is right. The above objection by the relativist claims that if a culture is monogamous, then its members believe that monogamy is right and polygamy is wrong. Now something *rather* like this *could* be true of my Islandians, but it is not what the relativist imagines. Suppose that earlier in their history the Islandians had been a polygamous people, but that at some state in their history the women began to chafe under this arrangement and succeeded in making the men see that this was a form of male chauvinism. For this reason they eventually become a monogamous culture. Now in such a case it *could* be said of them that they have moral objections to polygamy: it is a form of male chauvinism. But this *need* not be the case in every monogamous culture. Surely it is far more common for the members of monogamous cultures to have no knowledge of other forms of marriage and to have no thoughts on the subject at all. (There are exceptions, of course, as illustrated by the fate of polygamy among the Mormons in the United States. But this is a case of a religious conflict within a culture, and surely the relativist's case cannot be based on cases of this sort.) In any case, it cannot be said that just because certain practices *exist* that therefore people believe that their practices are right. It is not even clear what it could *mean* to say such a thing. In the case of my Islandians, it is clear what it would mean to say that they had moral reasons for abandoning polygamy and becoming monogamous. But the relativist's claim is supposed to apply even to an isolated, homogeneous people like the Eskimos. We are supposed to think that the Eskimos have a moral principle to the effect that monogamy is right and polygamy is wrong, and the evidence for this claim is supposed to be just that the Eskimos are a monogamous people. It is *this* claim that I do not understand, and, so far as I can see, it is the sort of thing that would be plausible only to someone who had grown up in a culture more or less like my Grundlegung.

Should the relativist now be satisfied with my criticism? I can imagine him wanting to reply as follows: 'You have underestimated the evidence we have for our account of morality. And the reason is that you have disregarded the rampant ethnocentrism that every anthropologist is familiar with. When people encounter others whose lives are very different, their underlying beliefs come to the surface. People heap scorn, ridicule and abuse on those who are different from themselves, and this shows that they believe their own ways to be the right ways. If you were not so naive, you would see that these principles are operating in the lives of all of us.'

The question now becomes: what exactly is ethnocentrism and is it really evidence for the existence of socially inculcated moral principles? The first point to bear in mind is that when relativists coined the term 'ethnocentrism', they meant to identify and condemn a certain kind of intolerance, and this means that they meant to condemn a certain kind of *unfair* or *unwarranted* judgment that we tend to make of other peoples[24]. The original thought behind the term 'ethnocentrism' was not an eagerness to get people to condone or be indifferent to mass murder or other forms of unmitigated evil. Unfortunately, relativists tended to argue for their view on a highly abstract level, so that their *reasons* for regarding certain judgments as unfair or unwarranted were lost sight of. The result was that the relativist's initial insight turned into a form of philosophical scepticism: *nothing* could be *really* right or wrong. It was this philosophical conclusion that created a difficulty for relativists in the face of the political events in Europe during the 1930s. Fürer-Haimendorf relates the oft-told story of relativists disconcerted by the undeniable existence of evil:

> This view [i.e., relativism], prevalent in the nineteen-twenties and thirties, lost some of its appeal when the rise of totalitarian regimes in Europe compelled Western intellectuals to rethink their attitude to basic moral principles. While they had argued quite happily that in the setting of the one or other primitive tribal society, headhunting or slave-raiding fulfilled useful social functions, they found it rather more difficult to adopt a similarly detached attitude towards the violation of what seemed basic human rights openly practised by the governments of powerful European States. For as long as one maintained that all morality was entirely relative and subjective, and different societies were free and justified in formulating their own rules, all of which were equally valid, it was clearly inconsistent to pass value judgments on the merits and demerits of different social and political systems. The unacceptability of such a position in regard to the practices of the totalitarian governments of various hues, showed up the flaws in the arguments against the existence of any universally valid moral principles.[25]

This perplexity along with the absurd search for 'universal principles'[26] could have been avoided if only those who had set out to combat ethnocentrism had borne in mind, or had stated more clearly for themselves, the real nature of ethnocentrism. For ethnocentrism is not plain ordinary bigotry. Bigotry is a flaw in the character of an individual, whereas ethnocentrism, properly so called, is really a misunderstanding of people whose lives are very different from one's own. Now it may be that ethnocentrism and bigotry are often found together in the same person, but they need to be distinguished and dealt with separately. This can be seen most clearly if we consider the following two kinds of cases.

A kind of example which the relativist invariably overlooks is that in which we would mistakenly over-estimate or falsely idealize a people. Irving Hallowell remarks that 'as observers of the behaviour of people in another cultural setting, it is almost inevitable that we go astray unless we have some understanding of [their motivational] orientation', and he illustrates this with a case in which we might easily make the mistake of thinking we had stumbled upon an extraordinary kind and loving people. 'Among the Ojibwa Indians', he says, 'food-sharing beyond the immediate family circle might appear to suggest unselfishness, generosity, affection, kindness, and love.' He goes on to suggest that this interpretation is 'misleading', and offers the following explanation. First of all, 'there are vicissitudes inherent in Ojibwa economy and ecology' so that 'a system of mutual sharing of food bridges lean periods for everyone'. Secondly, the Ojibwa believe in and practice sorcery. The upshot of these two facts is that someone's failure to share food with another person would suggest that he bore ill-will toward that person and thus invite a retaliation by means of sorcery. 'On the other hand, if I always share what I have, no one will have reason to sorcerize me on that score, and I will suffer much less anxiety. At the same time, by playing my expected role, any anxiety that I may have about what may happen to me in lean periods is allayed.' Thus, extensive food-sharing is not the extraordinary moral phenomenon it might at first sight appear to be[27]. Here, then, is a case in which there might easily occur a faulty moral appraisal resulting from a failure to understand another culture. And this seems to me to be as clear a case of ethnocentrism as one could find, for if among *us* someone regularly gave of his possessions as freely as the Ojibwa do, he would, in all likelihood, be an extraordinarily generous person. What this shows then is that ethnocentrism is not essentially *criticism* of another culture and is not to be thought of as a form of bigotry.

The second sort of example to be considered here is one that we have already seen one instance of (see p. 315, n. 24) but which needs to be explored in more detail. I am thinking of the case in which someone does unfairly form an unfavourable impression of another people, but where this is due, not to bigotry, i.e. not to some flaw in his character, but to a failure to understand the alien people. Consider the following example, taken from L.T. Hobhouse's discussion of the difficulty of reaching an adequate understanding of people in other cultures[28]:

We find some tribe like the Dyaks of Borneo with whom the traveller tells us it is a delight to dwell, so courteous are they, so hospitable, so full of brotherly kindliness. We begin to think there is truth in the idyllic picture of savage life so popular in the days of our great-grandfathers, until we stumble upon the fact that these same Dyaks are inveterate head-hunters, and make a practice of murdering not men only, but women and children in satisfaction of the duty of blood-vengeance, and to obtain the magical virtues inherent in an enemy's skull. At once the demon picture takes the place of the angel, and the savage world is seen as a Gehenna rather than a Paradise. We ... can hardly believe that men capable of acts so fiendish can have any trace of genuine humanity about them. The fairer view about them is that the Dyaks have a morality of their own, for many purposes as good as ours, but limited by the conditions of their life and coloured by their ideas of the supernatural. To be judged fairly, in short, both their virtues and their vices must be taken in connection with their life as a whole. What are at first sight the same ideas, the same institutions, are in reality of different value and meaning in different surroundings, and this possible source of error must always be allowed for in drawing comparisons.[29]

Hobhouse is here cautioning against the tendency to form an opinion about the actions of people in other cultures without taking into account the beliefs with which those people act. If what we know of the Dyaks is that they murder women and children, it is well-nigh inevitable that we will think of them as being like Jack the Ripper. We will think that they must be a fiendish people. But this would be unfair, as Hobhouse points out, for these 'murders' need to be understood as acts of magical cannibalism, as actions that can only be properly characterized in terms of their beliefs in the supernatural. Now the point is that if someone who did not understand their actions in this way were to regard these people as fiendish, this would not be a case of bigotry but a case of a failure in understanding. Hence, the way to correct such a judgment would *not* be to treat it as a case of bigotry and to make a plea for tolerating the murder of women and children, but rather to provide a correct understanding of these actions.

Interestingly enough, Hobhouse himself falls into the relativist's error when he says that 'the Dyaks have a morality of their own, for many purposes as good as ours'. Presumably what he means here is that the Dyaks have a different morality from ours, that they have different moral beliefs or principles, that actions which we regard as wrong, they regard as right. But to say this is to forget the very point that he himself was making here, namely, that we and they differ precisely in regard to *what* it is they are doing, i.e., we do not share their belief in the magical virtues inherent in an enemy's skull. Hobhouse himself would surely not want to say that if the Dyaks somehow gave up their supernatural beliefs and came to share our understanding of the world, they would continue their headhunting anyway because they believe it is right to murder women and children. But if that is not what Hobhouse meant to say, then what is this difference in morality he speaks of? I think we can only conclude that this relativistic talk of 'different moralities' is nothing but a confusion.

I think we have now answered the objection which we entertained above. The objection was that I had failed to undermine the relativist's account of morality for I had failed to take into account the phenomenon of ethnocentrism. Ethnocentrism, it was said, is evidence for the existence of different moral principles. My reply to this consists in pointing out, first, that what the anthropologist wants to combat and calls 'ethnocentrism' is a particular kind of unfair or unwarranted judgment and, secondly, that these judgments (opinions, attitudes) arise out of a failure (often an understandable failure) to understand the actions of people in other cultures. And finally I pointed out that once we give *this* account of ethnocentrism we shall not want to adopt the relativist's talk about 'different moralities'. Here we may point out that the relativist would not be so ready to speak of there being 'different moralities' in these cases were it not for his own ethnocentric idea of morality. His readiness to describe cultural differences in terms of different rules or principles is, I think, further evidence for my claim that the doctrine of relativism is itself a special form of ethnocentrism.

Several questions remain. First, if we abandon relativism, are we then to embrace absolutism? The answer to this should be clear: absolutism is an unqualified version of the 'rule' notion of morality. To embrace absolutism would be to choose Grundlegung over Islandia, and such a choice has nothing to recommend it. Secondly, if we abandon relativism, how are we to argue for tolerance? Well, there are perfectly good non-philosophical ways to combat intolerance, but these are not highly general, all-purpose arguments. They depend on the details of the particular case. If we find ourselves at a loss in finding and presenting such reasons, this is because we have not developed those capacities that the Islandians have. In any case, I seriously doubt that the arguments of cultural relativists have ever achieved much in combatting intolerance.

Notes

---

1 *Elements of Social Organization* (London, 1951), p. 183.
2 Ibid., p. 186.
3 Ibid.
4 *Morals and Merit* (London, 1967), p. 1.
5 Ibid., p. 2.
6 Ibid., pp. 4-5.
7 *A Treatise of Human Nature*, bk III, part I, section I.
8 William G. Sumner, *Folkways*, section 439.
9 'Anthropology and the Abnormal' in Douglas Haring (ed.), *Personal Character and Cultural Milieu*, p. 195. [Reprinted here. See p. 286.]
10 *Social Psychology* (Englewood Cliffs, NJ, 1952), chapter 13.
11 'Cultural Relativity and Moral Judgments', *Philosophy of Science*, vol. XXI (1954), p. 122.
12 'The White Negro: Superficial Reflections on the Hipster', *Dissent* (Summer 1957), pp. 289-90. Mailer's eulogy of the Hipster includes an attempt at justifying getting one's kicks by killing little old candy store owners.
13 *Man and His Works* (New York, 1960), p. 77.
14 Ibid., p. 655.
15 *Eugene Register-Guard*, 4 December 1968.
16 'Comment on Japanese Personal Character' in Douglas Haring (ed.), *Personal Character and Cultural Milieu*, pp. 425-7.
17 Ibid., pp. 405-6.
18 Ibid., p. 409.
19 The name is taken from Austin Wright's novel *Islandia* for suggestive purposes, although Wright's Islandians are not in all respects the people I mean to be describing here.
20 'Mr. Benjamin Cardozo', reprinted in Learned Hand, *Spirit of Liberty* (New York, 1952), pp. 131-3. In using this passage from Hand's eulogy, I do not intend to be endorsing that eulogy, for I know very little about Benjamin Cardozo.
21 To avoid misunderstanding, I should add here that I don't mean that evil actions don't turn up in their novels and short stories. It's rather that interest isn't focused on the action so much as on the way people

think about what has been done and about what they themselves must do — as in Humphrey Cobb's novel *Paths of Glory*.

22 *Commandant of Auschwitz* (New York, 1959), p. 32.

23 Mark Twain, *The Adventures of Huckleberry Finn*, chapter 16.

24 In Raymond Firth's *Elements of Social Organization* one finds a detailed example of the kind I have in mind here. Studying the Tikopia, Firth rather soon 'came to the conclusion that there was no such thing as friendship or kindliness for its own sake among these people' (p. 190). They seemed to be greedy, calculating people in their dealings with him. When he came to understand them better, he says, there came about a 'change in my moral attitude. I was no longer indignant at the behaviour of these calculating savages, to whom friendship seemed to be expressed only in material terms'. He came to 'accept the fact that to people of another culture, especially when they had not known one long, the most obvious foundation of friendship was material reciprocity' (p. 192). He did not, in other words, embrace the relativistic conclusion that among these people greed is right (or greediness is approved of).

25 *Morals and Merit*, p. 5.

26 An example of the absurdity I have in mind is found in Kroeber and Kluckhohn's *Culture, A Critical Review of Concepts and Definitions*, where they tell us that such things as slavery, cannibalism, and genocide are 'subject to a judgement which is alike moral and scientific. This judgement is not just a projection of values, local in time and space, that are associated with Western culture ... To say that certain aspects of Nazism were morally wrong, is not parochial arrogance. It is — or can be — an assertion based both upon cross-cultural evidence as to the universalities of human needs, potentialities, and fulfillments and upon natural scientific knowledge ... ' (Papers of the Peabody Museum, Harvard University, XLVII). Now you know what you are if you don't wait upon cross-cultural studies and developments in genetics before denouncing genocide — parochially arrogant!

27 A. Irving Hallowell, *Culture and Experience* (Philadelphia, 1955), pp. 102-3.

28 For an interesting discussion of a similar difficulty about understanding people within one's own culture, see William James' essay 'On A Certain Blindness in Human Beings'.

29 *Morals in Evolution: A Study in Comparative Ethics* (New York, 1915), p. 26.

12

On seeing things differently[1]

RICHARD NORMAN

Some moral disagreements are more fundamental than others. This is obvious. In particular, some moral disagreements are so fundamental that they are to be regarded not simply as conflicts between particular moral beliefs but as conflicts between distinct moralities. This, though less obvious, has been increasingly recognized by recent writers on ethics. Two people may disagree across a whole range of moral issues, because their specific beliefs stem from two incompatible ideologies, two distinct 'moral practices', two differing 'moral perspectives'[2]. In this paper I shall examine a particular contrast between two radically different moralities. I shall attempt to characterize the nature of the contrast, and to consider how a man might come to change his moral allegiances, to adopt one moral perspective in place of another.

The particular case I intend to look at is taken from an essay by T.E. Hulme — a somewhat neglected figure in English academic philosophy, perhaps because his academic career ended when he was sent down from Cambridge as an undergraduate, and perhaps also because he had only one important philosophical idea. This idea, however, is worth looking at. It is presented most directly in an essay entitled 'Humanism and the Religious Attitude'[3]. The distinction between the 'humanist attitude' and the 'religious attitude',

Reprinted from Radical Philosophy, *Vol. I, No. 1 (1972), pp. 6-13, by permission of the author and the Editor.*

according to Hulme, lies at the root of our more specific ethical, political and aesthetic disagreements. In using the term 'religious', he is anxious to emphasize that he is 'not concerned so much with religion, as with the attitude, the "way of thinking", the categories, from which a religion springs'. He does not discuss traditionally religious beliefs such as a belief in the existence of a god or the immortality of the soul, but rather a general conception of the nature of man and his relation to the world; he uses the word 'religious' 'because as in the past the attitude has been the source of most religions, the word remains convenient'.

The essence of the religious attitude is the recognition that the highest value does not reside in life, in either Man or Nature. Man is essentially limited and imperfect. He is endowed with *original sin*. Perfection is to be found along none of the roads by which men seek it (political, sexual, etc.). The religious attitude is thus an attitude of *renunciation*, an awareness of the tragic significance of life, the vanity of desire, the futility of human existence, as represented by the symbol of the wheel. Such an attitude lies behind all the great religions, Buddhism in particular. It enables one to make sense of moral values such as that of *chastity*. Both in ethics and in politics, it leads to an emphasis on the importance of *discipline*, for though man can never himself *be* perfect, it is through discipline that he can occasionally accomplish acts which partake of perfection. 'Order is thus not merely negative, but creative and liberating. Institutions are necessary.' The attitude also has its characteristic aesthetic manifestation, in geometrical art, which exhibits a 'digust with the trivial and accidental characteristics of living shapes' and a 'searching after an austerity ... which vital things can never have'.

Hulme takes this attitude to be the prevailing ideology of Mediaeval Europe — 'from Augustine, say, to the Renaissance'. In contrast, virtually all philosophies since the Renaissance, despite their obvious diversity, are ultimately variations of the same fundamentally humanist attitude. This picture of two contrasted periods has to be qualified somewhat. 'You may get, at any stage in the history of such a period, isolated individuals, whose whole attitude and ideology really belong to the opposed period. The greatest example of such an individual is, of course, Pascal.' But in general the antithesis between the two conceptions of man corresponds to the difference between the two historical periods.

The humanist attitude, then, emerges in the Renaissance as 'an attitude of acceptance to life', a new interest in human possibilities, in human character and personality. The same basic orientation

is to be found in virtually all subsequent ethical and political
thought. Its central feature is

> ... a refusal to believe any longer in the radical imperfection of
> either Man or Nature. This develops logically into the belief that
> life is the source and measure of all values, and that man is
> fundamentally good.... This leads to a complete change in all
> values. The problem of evil disappears, the conception of sin
> loses all meaning.... Under ideal conditions, everything of value
> will spring spontaneously from free 'personalities'. If nothing
> good seems to appear spontaneously now, that is because of
> external restrictions and obstacles. Our political ideal should be
> the removal of everything that checks the 'spontaneous growth
> of personality'. Progress is thus possible, and order is a merely
> negative conception.

Romanticism, in particular, is a further development of the humanist tradition, an exploration of the various roads along which human
fulfilment is to be found — the road of political liberation, or the
road of sex as it is treated in literature.

Hulme recognizes that this view of the changes in attitude
initiated by the Renaissance is a commonplace, but considers that
its significance has been missed. He himself is not simply interested
in presenting and contrasting the content of the two opposed
attitudes. He is concerned, as I am, with their logical status and
relationship to one another. Most frequently he refers to them as
'world-views' — *Weltanschauungen*. What are the intended implications of this term? In the first place it conveys the point which I
have already mentioned, that such an attitude is not so much a
specific belief or set of beliefs, but rather a basic orientation from
which the specific moral beliefs get their sense. It is an 'interpretation of life', an 'ideology' from which everything else springs, a
'central conception', a 'framework' within which one's moral beliefs
are situated. Hulme compares it to the 'categories' (sic) of space and
time. Like them, a *Weltanschauung* is not consciously adopted, but
it is absorbed unconsciously from one's social and cultural environment. The tradition predominant in a historical epoch moulds the
whole aparatus of one's thought; the categories in terms of which
one's thinking is done are embedded in the actual matter of one's
thought, so that one does not see them but other things through
them. Consequently, one finds in a person whose mental apparatus
is based on a different *Weltanschauung* from one's own 'a certain
obstinacy of intellect, a radical opposition, an incapacity to see

things which to us are simple'. As examples of the way in which minds dominated by a different *Weltanschauung* may have a different perception of facts Hulme refers to the influence of totemist categories on primitive man's perception of reality, or the way in which early Greek philosophy is moulded by categories inherited from primitive Greek religion[4].

However, Hulme also wants to make a distinction between the categories of a *Weltanschauung* and the 'categories' of space and time. The former are not inevitable in the way that the latter are. In this respect the categories of a *Weltanschauung* are more properly to be termed 'pseudo-categories'. We tend to regard them, like space and time, as inevitable constituents of reality, whereas in fact they simply make up one possible way of ordering our conception of reality. This brings us to a further implication of the term '*Welt-anschauung*'. Hulme attaches great importance to the distinction between a *Weltanschauung* and scientific philosophy. Genuine scientific philosophy, exemplified by Husserl and Russell, is the impersonal investigation of certain very abstract objective categories. A *Weltanschauung*, on the other hand, is 'concerned with matters like the nature and destiny of man, his place in the universe, etc.'; though masquerading as impersonal philosophy it is in fact only the expression of a personal 'standpoint'.

Here we run into difficulties. Hulme's account becomes, in fact, quite simply inconsistent. He is led to stress the plurality of possible *Weltanschauungen*: when a *Weltanschauung* is cloaked in the guise of a scientific philosophy, people are led to 'assume automatically that that all ideals must be one ideal', whereas in fact there are many possible different ideals. Burckhardt's work on the Renaissance, for example, 'describes the emergence of the new attitude towards life, of the new conception of man, as it might describe the gradual discovery of the concept of gravitation', in fact, however, 'the new attitude towards man ... was just an *attitude*, one attitude amongst other possible ones, deliberately chosen'. This pluralistic tendency on Hulme's part easily takes on the form of a traditional subjectivism. The pseudo-categories of a *Weltanschauung* are 'not objective'. When they are presented as impersonal objective science, 'you get something perfectly human and arbitrary cloaked in a scientific vocabulary'. This is what happens to 'a particular view of the relation of man to existence' when 'the people who are under its influence want to *fix* it, to make it seem not so much a particular *attitude* as a *necessary* fact ..., to give it a universal validity'. However, Hulme's own allegiances cause him to contradict these subjectivist statements. We find him declaring:

> I hold, quite coldly and intellectually, as it were, that the way
> of thinking about the world and man, the conception of sin, and
> the categories which ultimately make up the religious attitude,
> are the *true* categories and the *right* way of thinking.... The way
> in which I have explained the action of the central abstract
> attitudes and ways of thinking, and the use of the word *pseudo-*
> categories, might suggest that I hold relativist views about their
> validity. But I don't. I hold the religious conception of ultimate
> values to be right, the humanist wrong. From the nature of
> things, these categories are not inevitable, like the categories
> of time and space, but are equally objective.

I think we can understand these contradictory inclinations[5]. On
the one hand, if a *Weltanschauung* is not itself a set of beliefs but a
framework, a set of categories underlying one's beliefs, and if it is
also the case that no one Weltanschauung is inevitable but that
others are equally possible, then it is difficult to see how it could be
regarded as objectively valid, since it is difficult to see how anything
could count as supporting it. On the other hand, one who occupies
such a perspective will not see it simply as an arbitrary commitment
to one possible attitude among others, will not feel that he could just
as well have seen things differently. He will feel it supremely
important that he should adhere to this particular perspective; he
will claim that he is aware of things to which others are blind; he
will be inclined to say that, so far from nothing counting in support
of it, everything supports it.

Here, then, is what I shall try to clarify — this notion of a
Weltanschauung which is more fundamental than any of one's
particular moral beliefs, and to which the application of the
traditional objective/subjective distinction seems peculiarly prob-
lematic. At this point I want to consider one other form of words
used by Hulme, since it appears usefully suggestive. In the final
paragraph of the essay, he states that the religious attitude is

> ... perfectly possible for us today. To see this is a kind of con-
> version. It radically alters our physical perception; so that the
> world takes on an entirely different aspect.

Hulme is here echoing previous phrases of his which we have
quoted — 'We do not see the categories we employ, but see other
things through them'; 'Minds dominated by different pseudo-
categories may have a very different perception of fact'; someone

whose categories are different from ours may demonstrate 'an incapacity to see things which, to us, are simple'. This vocabulary of *vision*, implicit in the very word *'Weltanschauung'*, is worth following up. What, then, would be the nature of this 'conversion' which 'radically alters our physical perception, so that the world takes on an entirely different aspect'?

An example may enlighten us; consider therefore the following experiences which Tolstoy allots to Prince Andrew Bolkonski in *War and Peace*.

Prince Andrew is presented as a talented and successful young man who sees through and despises the superficiality of aristocratic society and is disillusioned with his recent marriage; he feels that his wife is a part of the same 'enchanted circle' of 'drawing rooms, gossip, balls, vanity, and triviality' which traps him and thwarts him. He leaves her in order to serve in the war against the French, eager for glory and for an opportunity to emulate his hero Napoleon. Preliminary successes whet his appetite, but his enthusiasm is mingled with a distaste for the echoes of court life which he finds even in the army. Before the Battle of Austerlitz, he feels that his great opportunity must surely now present itself. The Russians are routed; Andrew seizes a standard and leads a desperate and futile charge; he falls, wounded:

> 'What's this? Am I falling? My legs are giving way,' thought he, and fell on his back. He opened his eyes, hoping to see how the struggle of the Frenchman with the gunners ended, whether the red-haired gunner had been killed or not, and whether the cannon had been captured or saved. But he saw nothing. Above him there was now nothing but the sky — the lofty sky, not clear yet still immeasurably lofty, with great clouds gliding slowly across it. 'How quiet, peaceful, and solemn, not at all as I ran,' thought Prince Andrew — 'not as we ran, shouting and fighting, not at all as the gunner and the Frenchman with frightened and angry faces struggled for the mop: how differently do those clouds glide across that lofty infinite sky! How was it I did not see that lofty sky before? And how happy I am to have found it at last! Yes! All is vanity, all falsehood, except that infinite sky. There is nothing, nothing but that. But even it does not exist, there is nothing but quiet and peace. Thank God! ...'[6].

With the French victorious Andrew is left for dead. Later, having been taken to the dressing-station as a prisoner, he is addressed by Napoleon:

'Well, and you, young man,' said he. 'How do you feel, *mon brave?*' Though five minutes before Prince Andrew had been able to say a few words to the soldiers who were carrying him, now with his eyes fixed straight on Napoleon he was silent.... So insignificant at that moment seemed to him all the interests that engrossed Napoleon, so mean did his hero himself with all his paltry vanity and joy in victory appear, compared to the lofty, equitable, and kindly sky which he had seen and understood, that he could not answer him.

Everything seemed so futile and insignificant in comparison with the stern and solemn train of thought that weakness from loss of blood, suffering, and the nearness of death, aroused in him. Looking into Napoloen's eyes Prince Andrew thought of the insignificance of greatness, the unimportance of life which no one could understand, and the still greater unimportance of death, the meaning of which no one alive could understand or explain.

Prince Andrew's family receive no news of him, and fear the worst. When finally he is able to return, he arrives as his wife, against whom he had felt hostility and resentment on his departure, is dying in giving birth to a son. He sees her before she dies, but is aware only of his own powerlessness to help or communicate when faced with her look of childlike fear.

Three days later the little princess was buried, and Prince Andrew went up the steps to where the coffin stood, to give her the farewell kiss. And there in the coffin was the same face, though with closed eyes. 'Ah, what have you done to me?' it still seemed to say, and Prince Andrew felt that something gave way in his soul, and that he was guilty of a sin he could neither remedy nor forget. He could not weep.

Some months later Andrew is visited by his friend Pierre, who has become full of enthusiasm for projects of philanthropy as a result of his encounter with Freemasonry. Andrew reacts sceptically to Pierre's moral self-confidence. He declares that

'It is not given to man to know what is right and what is wrong. Men always did and always will err, and in nothing more than in what they consider right and wrong.'

To Pierre's insistence that whatever does harm to others is wrong, Andrew replies that the only real harms, the only real evils in life, are remorse and illness, and these are, by their very nature, not such as one can inflict on others. The only object of life is to avoid them in oneself. To live for others, pursuing the ideals of love for one's neighbour and self-sacrifice, is sheer pretension; it is enough that one should live in such a way as to be free of guilt or remorse. Though he may care for those who are near to him — his son, his father, his sister — this is not 'love of one's neighbour'; he lives for them simply because they are a part of his own life. Pierre cannot believe that Andrew sincerely thinks in this way —

> '...What evil and error is there in it, if people were dying of disease without help while material assistance could so easily be rendered, and I supplied them with a doctor, a hospital, and an asylum for the aged? And is it not a palpable, unquestionable good if a peasant, or a woman with a baby, has no rest day or night, and I give them rest and leisure? ... I know, and know for certain, that the enjoyment of doing this good is the only sure happiness in this life.'

Andrew retorts that though this may indeed be a genuine source of happiness for Pierre, the question of moral right and good is one which neither of them is able to pronounce upon. Similarly Andrew agrees that the liberation of the serfs would be admirable, not however because it would do them good or make them any happier but because it would rescue their proprietors from the guilt and remorse which they would otherwise bring upon themselves through being in a position to inflict punishment and cruelty. Pierre may enthuse about Masonic doctrines of brotherhood and universal harmony

> '... but it is not that which can convince me, dear friend — life and death are what convince. What convinces is when one sees a being dear to one, bound up with one's own life, before whom one was to blame and had hoped to make it right' (Prince Andrew's voice trembled and he turned away) 'and suddenly that being is seized with pain, suffers, and ceases to exist.... Why? It cannot be that there is no answer. And I believe there is.... That's what convinces, that is what has convinced me.'

Pierre takes this to be, after all, a recognition of the truths which he himself espouses —

> '...We must live, we must love, and we must believe that we live not only today on this scrap of earth but have lived and shall live

for ever, there, in the Whole,' said Pierre, and he pointed to the sky.

Prince Andrew stood leaning on the railing of the raft listening to Pierre, and he gazed with his eyes fixed on the red reflection of the sun gleaming on the blue waters. There was perfect stillness. Pierre became silent. The raft had long since stopped, and only the waves of the current beat softly against it below. Prince Andrew felt as if the sound of the waves kept up a refrain to Pierre's words, whispering:

'It is true, believe it.'

...'Yes, if only it were so' said Prince Andrew. 'However, it is time to get on,' he added, and stepping off the raft he looked up at the sky to which Pierre had pointed, and for the first time since Austerlitz saw that high everlasting sky he had seen while lying on that battlefield; and something that had long been slumbering, something that was best within him, suddenly awoke, joyful and youthful in his soul. It vanished as soon as he returned to the customary conditions of his life, but he knew that this feeling which he did not know how to develop, existed within him. His meeting with Pierre formed an epoch in Prince Andrew's life. Though outwardly he continued to live in the same old way, inwardly he began a new life.

Andrew does, in spite of himself, carry out philanthropic reforms of his estates — he frees his serfs, provides medical and educational facilities, and so on. His attitude to life nevertheless remains one of resignation. Two years later he is visiting one of his estates, and is riding through birch-forests fresh with the signs of spring; he passes an old oaktree, huge and gnarled and dead-looking, which alone 'refused to yield to the charm of spring' —

'Spring, love, happiness!' this oak seemed to say. 'Are you not weary of that stupid, meaningless, constantly repeated fraud? ... There is no spring, no sun, no happiness! Look at those cramped dead firs, and at me too, sticking out my broken and barked fingers just where they have grown, whether from my back or my sides: as they have grown so I stand, and I do not believe in your hopes and your lies.' ...

'Yes, the oak is right, a thousand times right', thought Prince Andrew.... A whole sequence of new thoughts, hopeless but mournfully pleasant, rose in his soul in connection with that tree.

During this journey he, as it were, considered his life afresh and arrived at his old conclusion, restful in its hopelessness: that it was not for him to begin anything anew — but that he must live out his life, content to do no harm, and not disturbing himself or desiring anything.

While in the district, Andrew has to visit the local Marshal, Count Rostov; he sees the Count's young daughter Natasha, and is struck by her carefree gaiety. He spends that night at the Count's, and, being unable to sleep, opens the shutters, to discover the garden and the trees brilliantly illuminated by the silvery moonlight; in the room above he hears the young Natasha rapturously enthusing over the beauty of the night. On his return journey through the forest he looks once more for the oak-tree, and scarcely recognizes it:

> The old oak, quite transfigured, spreading out a canopy of sappy dark-green foliage, stood rapt and slightly trembling in the rays of the evening sun. Neither gnarled fingers nor old scars nor old doubts and sorrows were any of them in evidence now....

> 'Yes, it is the same oak,' thought Prince Andrew, and all at once he was seized by an unreasoning spring-time feeling of joy and renewal. All the best moments of his life suddenly rose to his memory. Austerlitz with the lofty heavens, his wife's dead reproachful face, Pierre at the ferry, that girl thrilled by the beauty of the night, and that night itself and the moon, and ... all this rushed suddenly to his mind.

> 'No, life is not over at thirty-one!' Prince Andrew suddenly decided finally and decisively. 'It is not enough for me to know what I have in me — every one must know it: Pierre, and that young girl who wanted to fly away into the sky, every one must know me, so that my life may not be lived for myself alone while others live so apart from it, but so that it may be reflected in them all, and they and I may live in harmony.'

One might at first be inclined to regard this sequence of experiences primarily as a series of changes of mood. Certainly there is this aspect to it — the process of depression and emotional renewal. One might then suppose that the appearance of rational argument and decision on Andrew's part simply hides the reality of emotional responses. Tolstoy himself sometimes encourages this extreme emotivist interpretation; after the last-quoted incident he comments ironically:

On reaching home Prince Andrew decided to go to Petersburg that autumn and found all sorts of reasons for this decision. A whole series of sensible and logical considerations kept springing up to his mind. He could not now understand how he could ever even have doubted the necessity of taking an active share in life. … It now seemed clear to him that all his experience of life must be senselessly wasted unless he applied it to some kind of work and again played an active part in life. He did not even remember how formerly, on the strength of similar wretched logical arguments, it had seemed obvious that he would be degrading himself if he now, after the lessons he had had in life, allowed himself to believe in the possibility of being useful and in the possibility of happiness or love.

Nevertheless, Andrew's own sense that on each occasion he had made a *discovery*, had acquired a new *awareness* of something in the world, cannot be seen as a mere illusion. Through his vision of the sky on the battlefield he discovers the futility of martial glory and the insignificance of human greatness; confronted with the pained and bewildered expression on his dead wife's face, he discovers the reality of human guilt and remorse; with Pierre at the ferry, he becomes aware of 'that which is best within him'; through his visit to Count Rostov he becomes aware of the bonds which tie him to other human beings. This sense of acquiring new knowledge is emphasized by Tolstoy when Andrew first recovers consciousness after being wounded at Austerlitz:

'Where is it, that lofty sky that I did not know till now, but saw today?' was his first thought. 'And I did not know this suffering either,' he thought. 'Yes, I did not know anything, anything at all till now.'

Here we can begin to make connections with Hulme's talk of 'world-views'; for Andrew's 'discovery' is in each case the acquisition of an enlarged and clearer view of human nature and of a man's relation to the world. Tolstoy speaks of Andrew's 'new outlook'. None of the views which Andrew comes to adopt coincides precisely with either of Hulme's two world-views. Nevertheless it is clear that the same kinds of question are being raised — questions of the vanity of human desires, the possibilities of human fulfilment, the meaning of 'sin' and 'remorse', the necessity or futility of positive human relationships.

We must be aware of distorting and oversimplifying the situation which Tolstoy describes. He of all novelists deals least in abstract general types; and he effectively reminds us of the danger of doing so[7]. We have mentioned that the change of outlook ascribed to Prince Andrew is not exactly a change from one to the other of Hulme's two basic world-views. We have also mentioned that it is not simply a change of outlook. Tolstoy's hints of self-deception, of the way in which appeals to logical argument can mask underlying irrationalities, of the ease with which moral conceptions are exaggerated or misunderstood, are a constant reminder that he is portraying the particular struggles and doubts of a single individual rather than presenting a consistent and easily classifiable ideal type. For all that, Prince Andrew's experiences can, I think, be seen as examples of a 'conversion' experience, and can throw some light on Hulme's use of that term.

What, then, entitles us to speak of a 'conversion' here? First, and most obviously, there is the fact that Andrew's way of life is radically changed. But men may change their behaviour without having undergone any 'conversion'. More important, then, is the nature of the experience which leads to the change. In Andrew's case we might suppose that the 'conversion' is constituted by the suddenness of the change, the momentary flash of insight — encapsulated in the vision of the sky, the sight of the oak. But this is not what is essential. The development of insight may equally be a gradual one, and even if it is instantaneous, it may reflect back on previous thoughts and experiences which have prepared the ground for it. Thus, on the night before the battle of Austerlitz, Andrew imagines to himself the glory which may await him, but these reveries have to struggle against the half-suppressed awareness that what may equally await him is his own death, and that this possibility mocks at all human aspirations after glory and renown. His subsequent vision of the sky is then the moment at which he admits to himself the truth of this recognition. Similarly, his discovery of the need for any human life to find an answering response in others is forced upon him by Natasha's exuberance and by the new life of the oak-tree, but the seeds have already been sown by Pierre's insistent argument. Thus, even if the experience is a sudden one, the suddenness is symptomatic of something more important. What is crucial, I think, is the experience of seeing a whole range of things with which one is familiar, but seeing them in a new light, as though for the first time. This we have already remarked upon — Andrew, we saw, speaks of having 'known nothing till now'. 'How was it I did not see that lofty sky before?' he asks. But in what sense hadn't he? He had never seen it *as* something infinite in comparison with human concerns, *as* something which dwarfs human aspirations and reduces them to insignificance in the light of its own vast serenity. Thus it is the vocabulary of 'seeing as' that we are driven to use here. The 'conversion' experience is one of seeing things in a new light, seeing the same things and yet seeing them differently — like the well-known examples used by Gestalt psychologists such as the switch from seeing a picture of a young woman to seeing the same picture as that of an old woman, or seeing the same lines now as a duck and now as a hare[8]. This analogy does seem to fit at least certain aspects of Andrew's experience. It also returns to us, and enables us

to find an application for, Hulme's talk of a 'conversion' which 'radically alters our physical perception, so that the world takes on an entirely different aspect. In the remainder of this paper I want to consider how far this analogy will take us, and how appropriate it is in moral philosophy.

Let us first attempt to establish the relation between 'ways of seeing the world' and specifically *moral* considerations. We found in Hulme the suggestion that the religious attitude enables one to make sense of notions such as 'chastity' and 'original sin'. Why, it may be asked, should there be any difficulty about 'making sense of them'? Are they not simply certain ultimate evaluations which some people just happen to have made? Think, however, of the way in which writers in the humanist tradition have talked about the 'virtues' of abstinence, self-denial, asceticism. Think of David Hume on the 'monkish virtues':

> And as every quality which is useful or agreeable to ourselves or others is, in common life, allowed to be a part of personal merit, so no other will ever be received where men judge of things by their natural, unprejudiced reason, without the delusive glosses of superstition and false religion. Celibacy, fasting, penance, mortification, self-denial, humility, silence, solitude, and the

whole train of monkish virtues — for what reason are they everywhere rejected by men of sense but because they serve to no
manner of purpose.... We justly, therefore, transfer them to the
opposite column and place them in the catalogue of vices; nor
has any superstitution force sufficient among men of the world
to pervert entirely these natural sentiments. A gloomy, hair-
brained enthusiast, after his death, may have a place in the
calendar, but will scarcely ever be admitted when alive into
intimacy and society, except by those who are as delirious and
dismal as himself.[9]

Hume does not simply present celibacy, fasting and the rest as odd
things to value; he presents them as absurd and irrational. (One
might compare Bentham's dismissal of asceticism, and J.S. Mill's
rejection of 'wasted' self-renunciation.)

How is it that Hume makes such values appear nonsensical? What
he has done is to detach them from any context that would render
them meaningful. Conversely, by considering them from the perspective of what Hulme calls the religious *Weltanschauung*, or in
the light of something like Prince Andrew's experience at Austerlitz
and after the death of his wife, that one could begin to do so. If one
sees man's relation to the world as making human activity essentially
futile, if one is struck by the vanity of all specifically human
satisfactions, one may then come to see human desires as existing
not to be satisfied but to be denied, as fetters on the soul which tie it
to the delusions of the physical world, imprisoning it and tyranni-
zing over it. The concept of 'original sin' may then start to become
intelligible; one may be led to consider worldly desires as *by their
very nature* corrupt, and the gratification of them as a matter of
'yielding' to them. If a contrast is then made between the futility
and despair of human existence and the purity of something infinite
and eternal which surpasses the human world, virtue may come to
be positively identified with resistance to the desires. Such virtues as
chastity then become genuinely intelligible. Moreover, they are
understood in their true sense, whereas humanist moralists who
have wanted to retain the concept of chastity have never succeeded
in talking anything but nonsense. (Hume, for example, thinks that
chastity is useful as a guarantee that a man's children are his
own[10].)

I am not concerned here with the presentation of, still less with
the advocacy of, the aforementioned perspective, which may seem a
commonplace or, less disparagingly, a perennial moral tradition in

which such thinkers as Plato, Augustine, Pascal, Schopenhauer, Kierkegaard could be variously situated. I am concerned with its philosophical significance. What is important here is the notion of a 'background'[11]. The 'way of seeing the world' does not *necessitate* or *entail* such moral values as chastity or self-denial (it might equally lead to an attitude of sheer pessimism and despair). But it does, as I have said, make them intelligible, give them a sense. And if the 'ways of seeing' which constitute the background of different moral values are indeed comparable to a visual Gestalt — if we can speak, in the moral as in the perceptual case, of two people confronted with what is in a sense the same object of experience yet seeing it differently — then this may explain how someone thinking within a particular perspective may simply fail to see the sense of some other morality. It will explain how the monkish virtues can be made to appear irrational, and how, conversely, when one is thinking within the 'religious' tradition one can give no point to any talk of, for example, 'repression' or 'liberation' in relation to human desires.

But why should the analogy of 'seeing as' be necessary? Why should the so-called 'way of seeing' or *'Weltanschauung'* not be regarded just as a set of very general value-judgments from which are deduced all the more specific moral judgments going to make up a particular morality? The high-level judgments, it might be suggested, are in effect judgments of approval and disapproval such as 'Human desires are bad', 'Freedom from the power of desires is good', and these, together with minor premises specifying particular instantiations of 'desire', entail various more concrete moral judgments.

The simple answer is that the judgments in question are not of this kind. They are judgments about the *futility* of human activity, the *vanity* of human desires, the *transitoriness* of human existence, the *tyrannical power* of worldly satisfactions — and about other conceptions which are the converse of these. In other words, they are judgments as to the correct characterization of certain states of affairs.

At this point, however, we can expect the Humean[12] guillotine to be put into operation: 'If a *Weltanschauung* is not a set of value-judgments, it must be a set of ordinary statements of fact which can in principle be empirically verified or falsified.' Our suggestion that a morality is somehow grounded in, even if not entailed by, a *Weltanschauung* might then be interpreted as an argument for some kind of ethical naturalism. It might be supposed, for example, that a claim about the futility of all attempts to satisfy human desires is just such an empirically verifiable or falsifiable statement. As such, of course, it would be plainly false. It would amount to a claim that no one ever gets what he wants; and yet, in a purely psychological sense, it must surely be the case that some people are sometimes satisfied. Consider now, however, a riposte of the following kind:

> The vanity of existence is revealed in the whole form existence assumes: in the infiniteness of-time and space contrasted with the finiteness of the individual in both; in the fleeting present as the sole form in which actuality exists; in the contingency and relativity of all things; in continual becoming without being; in continual desire without satisfaction, in the continual frustration of striving of which life consists.... Time is that by virtue of which everything becomes nothingness in our hands and loses all real value.... In ... a world where no stability of any kind, no enduring state is possible, where everything is involved in restless change and confusion and keeps itself on its tightrope only by continually striding forward — in such a world, happiness is not so much as to be thought of.... It is all one whether [a man] has been happy or not in a life which has consisted merely in a succession of transient present moments and is now at an end.[13]

Schopenhauer is not here denying (although he is often rather inclined to do so) that what we ordinarily call 'satisfaction' or 'happiness' sometimes occurs. Rather he is suggesting that what looks like the satisfaction of desires from one point of view comes to be seen as sheer futility when set against the inexorability of time. Within this perspective the concepts of 'futility' and 'satisfaction' are transformed. They are brought into association with concepts such as 'vanity', 'transitoriness', 'infiniteness', all of which, in the sense in which they are here understood, would simply not be employed by someone who did not share this perspective. When they are employed, they give rise to certain 'descriptions' of the 'facts'; but these descriptions cannot be regarded as straightforwardly open to empirical verification or falsification, since the question of their truth or falsity would simply not arise for someone employing a different perspective. Here the metaphor of vision is quite natural. In challenging Schopenhauer's assertions, I should not claim that they are straightforwardly false; my own response would be 'I don't see the matter that way, I don't see it in those terms.' Such a form of words comes naturally in this context.

The fact/value dichotomy, then, appears singularly inappropriate when applied to cases of this kind. We are dealing with questions of 'fact', but the facts appear as they do only because they are already viewed from a particular moral perspective. This way of putting it, however, may suggest one further means of trying to preserve the fact/value dichotomy. Should the 'factual descriptions' within a *Weltanschauung* perhaps more properly be regarded as evaluatively-loaded interpretations of the facts? The argument might proceed as follows: 'There must be some neutral characterization of the facts which are variously interpreted in one or another *Weltanschauung* and this residual neutral substratum is alone "factual" in the strict sense; the evaluation interpretations must accordingly be seen as conforming to the logic of evaluation in general, the logic of approval and disapproval.'

The question of value-neutrality is a difficult one, and would properly take us beyond the limits of this paper. Forgoing a full discussion, let us provisionally admit that there are innumerable particular facts which are 'neutral' in the sense that they do not in themselves possess any specific practical significance or demand any specific human response. But the crucial question is this: is there some general way of representing man's relationship to the world and to other human beings which is 'neutral' and is prior to any ethical interpretation? Is there any neutral substratum of which Hulme's 'religious attitude' and 'humanist attitude' are alternative interpretations? A certain kind of neutrality is indeed possible. Consider the mode of consciousness exemplified by Meursault in Camus's *L'Etranger* — a consciousness of the world as totally indifferent, totally detached and foreign, lacking all human significance. Because Meursault is confined within this kind of consciousness, he is incapable of any attachments or allegiances, either to persons or to values. It is all one whether he loves his mistress or does not love her[14]; whether he kills a man or does not kill him, it comes to the same thing[15]. He commits a murder, but is aware of his doing so more as an arbitrary event in the world, something which just happens to him, than as an action which he has performed and for which he has any motive or any responsibility. His typical way of experiencing the world is as a series of unrelated sense-impressions[16]. To see the world in this way is, in a sense, to see it in neutral terms. But it does not follow that this kind of consciousness has any epistemological priority. It is not the underlying basis of normal human consciousness; rather it is itself simply one particular, and in fact highly unusual, mode of consciousness. It is not more fundamental than any 'evaluative interpretation'; it is itself one interpretation among others — which is perhaps to say that the very term 'interpretation' may be misleading here, since there is nothing further for it to be an interpretation of.

This point is effectively demonstrated by the novel itself, and by Camus's essay *The Myth of Sisyphus*. So far from possessing a neutral awareness of the facts on which he can subsequently build an ethical interpretation, Meursault comes to recognize that his way of experiencing the world is one which assigns to it its true ethical significance. He 'lays open his heart to the benign indifference of the universe'[17]. He has been brought face to face with what Camus himself calls the 'inhuman', the 'denseness and strangeness of the world' — the 'absurd'. To assign to it any different significance would be, in his view, sheer dishonesty and self-deception.

Does our suggested analogy between an ethical world-view and a visual Gestalt hold good at this point? Certainly, philosophers have claimed that perception is necessarily theory-laden, and that the notion of basic perceptual data prior to any interpretation is an inadmissible one[18]. Of course, it is not the possibility of *value*-neutrality that is in question there. Nevertheless the parallel is important.

If the traditional fact/value dichotomy obstructs a proper understanding of moral world-views, we shall not be surprised to find that the objective/subjective dichotomy becomes equally questionable. This, it will be remembered, was the point on which Hulme appeared confused. We saw that Hulme wanted to claim objective validity for his own allegiances, but was at the same time led into a form of subjectivism by his emphasis on the plurality of possible world-views, no one of which is either demonstrably more correct or inevitable. The 'seeing-as' analogy can, I suggest, help us to remove this confusion. It reveals the possibility of pluralism without subjectivism. A figure can be seen equally as a picture of an old woman and as a picture of a young woman; neither is *the correct* way of seeing it. But this does not mean that the two ways of seeing it have the status of subjective responses. Are they then 'objective'? The following can at any rate be said:

(1) The figure cannot be seen in just *any* way. We can see it as an old woman, and we can see it as a young woman, but we cannot

see it as anything we like. There are strict limits to the possibilities.
The possibilities are made available by the concepts in our language; what it is possible for us to see depends upon how it is possible
for us to conceptualize our experience. And any concept obviously
carries with it a distinction between correct and incorrect applications of it. Thus the figure can correctly be seen both as an old
woman and as a young woman, but it cannot correctly be seen as a
man. Similarly the possible ways of seeing man's nature and his
place in the universe are made available by the moral and intellectual traditions within one's culture. Thus there are limits to what
can be said. And what is said can be more or less appropriate. The
available traditions do not confine us once and for all; new ways of
seeing can be developed and extended — but not arbitrarily.

(2) Someone who is unable to see the figure as a picture of an
old (or young) woman is missing something which is there to be
seen. There is something about the picture which he has failed to
see. Similarly, someone who simply cannot see the force of a
particular world-view is missing something which is there to be seen.
(However, there are complications here to which we shall return.)

(3) I cannot 'choose' or 'decide' to see the figure in a certain
way. If I am able to see it as a picture of an old woman, this is
because that way of seeing it *forces* itself upon me. We can speak of
the *dawning* of an aspect, of the way in which the picture *strikes*
me[19]. Similarly, I do not 'choose' or 'decide' to adopt a particular
world-view. In the Tolstoy examples, Prince Andrew does not opt
for a new way of seeing things, as though he should say 'I'll try this
one for a change'. The appropriate vocabulary is precisely that of

the 'dawning' of an aspect which 'strikes' him and 'forces itself upon him'. We can speak of his gaining a new 'insight'.

(4) If someone is unable to see the figure as a picture of an old woman, can we give him *reasons* or *grounds* for seeing it as such? Well, at any rate, we can point to all the elements which go to make up that way of seeing it. We can tell him that whereas the young woman is turning away and looking over her shoulder, the old woman is in profile and looking down towards the bottom left of the picture. We can point out that the young woman's chin becomes the old woman's nose, and so on. What is interesting is that he will be able to understand these points only once he has already come to see the figure as a picture of an old woman. He can accept the correctness of these assertions only when he has accepted that for which they are supposed to be reasons. Nevertheless, it certainly *is* by saying 'This is the nose', 'This is the chin', and so on, that we could get him to see it as a picture of an old woman. And I think it can legitimately be said that we are thereby supplying 'grounds' for seeing it in that way. Similarly, one who wished to combat the view which sees human aspirations as essentially corrupt and futile might point to particular human achievements — artistic creations, the growth of human knowledge, the development of technological skills which make it increasingly possible to eliminate disease and suffering etc.; and one who wished to support the view in question might point to the impassioned and ceaseless strivings of men's hearts, the vastness of their ambitions, and contrast them with the brevity of human life, and the inexorability of the eternal round of birth, procreation and death. Now of course precisely what is in question is whether the things they point to are to be seen as fulfilment or futility. The 'evidence' each gives will be understood in the relevant way only by one who is already convinced. Nevertheless it is important that each of them *can* back up his world-view by referring to these particular facts which bear it out and give substance to it. And if one wished to convince someone of the appropriateness of one's world-view, one would quite legitimately invoke such facts.

With regard both to visual 'seeing-as' and its moral analogue, the objective/subjective dichotomy is perhaps best discarded. But if it is retained, the considerations we have just reviewed entitle us to assert the possibility of a plurality of world-views which are nevertheless all objective and equally valid.

It may be thought that, in saying this, we are contravening in a quite facile way the Law of Non-Contradiction. To do so explicitly, we should have to be making some claim to the effect that alternative world-views can be equally *true*. So far I have avoided any such claim, and I am inclined to think that to talk of 'truth' and 'falsity' in this context is out of place. Indeed, I have in effect been arguing that any idea of 'the *true* morality' ought to be rejected. But if we are to abandon all claims on 'truth' on the part of different world-views, it is important to insist that a world-view may nevertheless be perfectly *objective*; nor do I see any reason to baulk at the conceptual separation of 'objectivity' and 'truth' which is implied.

Perhaps, however, this is where the analogy with visual 'seeing-as' begins to break down. In the latter case there appears to be no comparable problem about truth or falsity. The simplest way of obviating the problem would be to say for example: 'It's neither an old woman nor a young woman, it's a picture — a picture which can be seen either as a picture of an old woman's head or as a picture of a young woman's head.' In other words, there is no problem about the incompatibility of the two statements 'It's an old woman' and 'It's a young woman', since neither is asserted[20]. The examples which I have quoted, and which are most often quoted, have indeed been examples of *pictures* which can be seen in different ways. But I do not think that this is essential. Consider, for example, the possibility of seeing the sun two-dimensionally as a small flat disc and seeing it as a huge and very distant ball of fire, or of seeing a mountain as a kaleidoscope of colours and as a solid towering mass. What is more to the point is that where something can be seen as *a* and as *b*, nothing further need be said than that it is *both*. Once we have become aware of the possibility of seeing the figure both as a picture of an old woman and as a picture of a young woman, there is no further problem, nothing more to be said. This is just where the case of conflicting moral perspectives is different. One can see a thing in two different ways without feeling this as a tension, but one cannot live on the basis of two incompatible moral perspectives — or rather, if one finds oneself doing so, this presents itself as a moral conflict which demands to be resolved. This is what constitutes the real importance of the notion of 'commitment' and 'choice' in ethics. And we saw that Hulme's own theoretical difficulties were created by his own commitment to a particular moral perspective.

What is it, then, that ultimately determines a man to see the world one way rather than another, to act from within one world-view rather than another? If we think back to Tolstoy examples, the answer there must clearly be: 'Experience'. Prince

Andrew is led to a new moral perspective by his experience of the realities of a military campaign, his confrontation with the possibility of his own death, his reactions at his wife's death-bed, and so on. One whose experience was different would be likely to see things differently. The question is: can we speak of anything more than a *causal* relation between Prince Andrew's experience and his commitment to a particular moral perspective? Is the relation merely comparable to that between, say, a man's moroseness and his having slept badly? Or is there some sense in which Andrew's experience constitutes a *verification* or *confirmation* of this view of the world?

I think that there is. But we shall not see it if we look for 'verification by experience' in the traditional empiricist sense. The differences are worth examining.

(1) The experience in question is not the passive recording of perceptual data, but essentially a matter of *activity* — the work one does, the things one has achieved or failed to achieve, the relationships one has entered into, and so on. In Prince Andrew's case, as we saw, the relevant experience includes his participation in war, his hopes of glory, his coming close to death, the development of his relationship with his wife, etc.

(2) Since this kind of experience is not the passive awareness of an object but is primarily activity, that which provides the 'verification' of a world-view is not an object of experience, but the nature of the experience itself, the relation which it involves between the self and its world.

(3) The fact that this experience is not an awareness of a public objective world helps to explain why the kind of verification it provides is something specific to the individual. This is why we refer to individuals' experience to account for the *differences* in their ways of seeing the world. Of course two persons may equally differ in their perceptual awareness of a public object; but their account of the content of this perceptual experience will be presented as claims about the nature of an impersonal, public object of experience. Thus, perceptual experience, by the manner of its formulation, presents itself as a way of *resolving* individual differences rather than of *accounting for* them.

(4) The way in which experience in this active sense serves to 'confirm' a world-view is not a matter of matching a hypothesis against the corresponding observation(s). Rather, one finds that a certain perspective enables one to *make sense of* and to *render intelligible* the experiences which one has lived through. Thus Prince Andrew's vision of the sky enables him to look back at his

previous experiences and see them for what they were — the empty
gestures of military heroism, the feverish and impassioned activity
for the sake of trivial rewards, his own deliberate refusal to face
certain aspects of his life. I can only add that whether or not this
kind of 'verification by experience' appears philosophically acceptable, it is what does happen. This just *is* the form that people's
moral development characteristically takes. One encounters a certain view of the world, and realizes that one's past actions,
experiences, emotions and relationships, hopes and fears all fit into
place when seen in this light.

(5) We have spoken of a 'world-view' as a view of men's relations
to the world and to one another. Now, in so far as experience is
regarded primarily as activity, it is not merely a means of *discovering* these relations, but itself serves to *define* them. Men *create* their
own relationships to one another and to the non-human world. The
formulation of a world-view is then an attempt to grasp these
relations as human activity has defined them. For example, whether
the world presents itself to men as something which surpasses and
transcends them and before which they can only bow in submission,
or as the material from which human achievements can be built,
depends upon what men do. But this activity is also the means by
which they are enabled to *recognize* the nature of the relationship.

(6) Since a world-view is an *overall* view of these relations, it is
confirmed not by particular experiences but by the totality of one's
experience. Hence the differences from visual 'seeing-as'. There,
one's *different* experiences of something enable one to describe it in
different ways. Seeing the figure as a picture of an old woman and
as a picture of a young woman are themselves two separate
experiences, and neither can override the other. But a world-view
has to make sense of one's experience taken as a whole, and thus a
commitment to one or another view is demanded.

Perhaps what we have been saying about the relation between
men's activity and their world-view is part of what Marx means in
passages such as the following[21]:

> The ideas which ... individuals form are ideas either about their
> relation to nature or about their mutual relations or about their
> own nature. It is evident that in all these cases their ideas are the
> conscious expression — real or illusory — of their real relation-
> ships and activities, of their production and intercourse and of
> their social and political organization.... The production of
> ideas, of conceptions, of consciousness is directly interwoven

with the material activity and the material relationships of men, the language of actual life.... The same applies to intellectual production as expressed in the language of politics, laws, morality, religion, metaphysics, etc. of a people.... Consciousness can never be anything else than conscious existence, and the existence of men is their actual life-process.

My relationship to my surroundings is my consciousness.... Consciousness is at first ... consciousness of nature, which first appears to man as a completely alien, all powerful and unassailable force.... Hence it is a purely animal consciousness of nature (natural religion) — for the very reason that nature is not yet modified historically.[22]

Passages such as these add a further dimension to our discussion. Marx emphasizes the aspect of historical and social development. If active human experience both defines men's relationshp to the world and to one another and confirms their view of these relationships, it will follow that, as human activity and experience varies from one age to another and from one social group to another, so the world-view current in a society or epoch will vary accordingly. We are reminded of Hulme's association of the 'religious' and 'humanist' attitudes with the pre-Renaissance and post-Renaissance periods respectively. Marx's position is forcefully stated in another well-known passage:

Is the view of nature and of social relations which shaped Greek imagination and Greek art possible in the age of automatic machinery and railways and locomotives and electric telegraphs? Where does Vulcan come in as against Roberts and Co.? Jupiter as against the lightning conductor? and Hermes, as against the *Credit Mobilier*? All mythology masters and dominates and shapes the forces of nature in and through the imagination; hence it disappears as soon as man gains mastery over the forces of nature.[23]

In quoting this passage I do not intend to equate Greek mythology with Hulme's 'religious attitude', but I do consider that the point which is made here is a relevant one. We thus seem driven towards some kind of relativism, such as Hulme wanted to avoid; but if this is so, it needs to be properly formulated.

A reference back to the 'seeing-as' analogy may be helpful. Although differences in the situation of the observers may account for how they see the figure, this does not entitle us to say it *is* one thing for anyone in situation *a* and another thing for anyone in situation *b*. Similarly we cannot say that a certain world-view is 'valid' for one historical epoch but not for another, for one individual or society but not for another. This would be to formulate a second-order philosophical point in the first-order language appropriate to the expression of one's own commitments. To assert the validity of a particular world-view is to express one's own commitment, and to do so on the basis of one's own experience. Since people's experience differs, they will be committed to different world-views. There is no impersonal experience to arbitrate between these differences. One can say that as the characteristic experience of one epoch or society varies from that of another, so a different world-view will tend to be predominant in each. But this is not itself a statement about the 'validity' of the one or the other world-view. Thus, when Hulme says that the religious attitude is 'a perfectly possible one for us today', in one sense I would agree. Nothing about contemporary society, as compared with other human societies, entails the falsity of the religious world-view. It may nevertheless be the case that the kinds of experience which have been taken as confirming the religious world-view are no longer characteristic of contemporary human society.

I conclude with some second-order remarks about what I have been doing in this paper.

I must first emphasize that the two world-views I have been discussing are essentially ideal types, and that the contrast between them will rarely be found in such a simplified form in actual moral experience. Complexities arise in a number of ways.

(1) The moral beliefs of an individual or of a social group will typically involve a variety of moral conceptions drawn from different world-views. It is characteristic of moral experience that one's moral standpoint reveals internal tensions. One finds oneself torn between conflicting moral tendencies, pulled in different directions by the different moral traditions within which one's ideas are located. This is what lies behind the experience of deep-rooted moral conflicts *within* oneself.

(2) The relation of different world-views to one another is not simply one of opposition. As we came to see in the previous section, they are also related to one another historically. Thus in order to understand properly the relation of the humanist world-view to the religious world-view, we should have to consider how the one *grew out of* the other. And in view of this process of historical development,

we shall not be able to draw a clear line between the one world-view and the other, nor can particular thinkers be located easily and automatically within one or the other. If we consider such thinkers as Spinoza, or Kant, or Blake, we can see how in varied ways, religious conceptions and a religious vocabulary have gone into the making of important elements in humanist morality. We can see, too, how the religious tradition has itself developed from a morality of life-denial to a morality of life-affirmation.

(3) The conflict between world-views which I have been discussing is only one particular moral disagreement. I have not been trying to characterize 'moral disagreement' in general. There are certainly other kinds of moral disagreement: cross-cultural differences, where different cultures employ a totally different moral vocabulary, and where we can perhaps hardly speak of 'disagreement' at all, but only of non-communication; disagreements about consequences, straightforwardly empirical disagreements about what will happen and how certain things can be achieved; disagreements where the disputants are working within the same moral tradition and are disagreeing about its application when extended to new situations; and so on. Moreover, any particular case of moral conflict may involve any or all of these elements. Think, for example, of the present conflict between those who wish to re-affirm traditional standards of sexual or other morality and those who challenge them in the name of liberation. One element in this may well be the clash between the two world-views I have been discussing; but certainly many other kinds of disagreement are involved — disagreements about empirical matters such as the incidence of VD, or the effects of pornography and of censorship, or, less straightforwardly, about the role of the family in bourgeois society, or the psychological effects of exclusiveness in personal relations. Accordingly I would not characterize this particular conflict simply as one between different ways of seeing man and the world; on the contrary, I would maintain strongly that the campaigners against 'moral pollution' exhibit a mass of sheer confusion and ignorance.

What, then, in positive terms, have I been saying? I am committed to the defence of two claims:

(a) that the particular disagreement which I have been considering is a *fundamental* one; i.e. that the difference between the virtues of self-denial, chastity, etc., and the values of human fulfilment and achievement does lie behind a great many particular moral conflicts;

(b) that this difference does involve different views of the nature of man and his relation to the world, and is properly understood on the model of 'seeing-as', i.e. that it cannot be assimilated to one of the other kinds of disagreement mentioned above. (Thus, for example, it might be argued instead that the disagreement is really one about the most effective means of achieving human satisfaction and wellbeing. Or again, taking up the point I have previously made about the historical relationship between religious and humanist morality, it might be suggested that these are really different manifestations of the same moral tradition.)

Clearly both kinds of question can be settled only by looking at the *content* of moral disagreements. In other words, we have to find out what people disagree *about*. For it might turn out to be the case that, although the kind of disagreement I have outlined is a perfectly possible one, men do not as a matter of fact disagree in this way. The truth or falsity of ethical pluralism cannot be decided *a priori*.

It should also be apparent that the answers we give may be true of some societies and not of others. If it is the case that there are fundamental differences of ethical perspective within contemporary society, then this ethical pluralism is surely a reflection of the pluralistic nature of our society — the high degree of stratification, the radical extent of the division of labour, the existence of social classes and subcultures, a radical dichotomy between public life and private conviction, etc. Conversely in a highly cohesive tribal society ethical pluralism is likely to be false. Thus the logic of ethical discourse cannot be considered in abstraction from the concrete nature of human social life and historical development. The consideration of these issues will take us up to, and beyond, the limits of analytical philosophy.*

*I should like to thank Tony Skillen, Peter Winch and James Cameron for valuable comments on this paper; I am also grateful for conversations with students and friends on the issues presented here.

Notes

1 This article originally appeared in *Radical Philosophy*, vol. I, no. 1, together with an article by Tony Skillen, 'Seeing Things Indifferently?', which contained some important criticisms of it. I am not persuaded by Mr Skillen's criticisms, but I would suggest that they should be carefully considered by any reader who is inclined to be convinced by my own arguments.

2 I take these terms respectively from Alan Montefiore, 'Fact, Value and Ideology', in B. Williams and A. Montefiore (eds.), *British Analytical Philosophy* (London, 1966); D.Z. Phillips and H.O. Mounce, *Moral Practices* (London, 1970); and Peter Winch, *Moral Integrity* (Oxford, 1969).

3 In T.E. Hulme, *Speculations*, edited by Herbert Read (London, 1936), pp. 3-71, 3, 8*f*., 10*f*., 14*f*., 18, 20, 22, 24*f*., 25, 33*f*., 46*f*., 47*f*., 49, 56, 58*f*., 61, 64, 66, 66-9, 67-70, 70.

4 Op. cit., p. 67*f*. Hulme's references here are to Levy-Bruhl and, I presume, to F.M. Cornford, *From Religion to Philosophy* (New York, 1958).

5 My own contradictory inclinations would lead me to assert a) that both are equally possible attitudes; b) that the *humanist* attitude is the right one, the *religious* attitude the wrong one. I wish to emphasize this, since I shall have to present the religious attitude in a way which may tend to give the impression that I adhere to it. This is not so.

6 *War and Peace*. All references are to the translation by Louise and Alymer Maude (London, 1967), pp. 300, 310, 312*f*., 351, 413, 414, 419, 420, 455, 458*f*., 459.

7 A danger which I shall mention later — see the final section of this paper.

8 And numerous other examples. For philosophical discussions of these, see *inter alia* L. Wittgenstein, *Philosophical Investigations* (London, 1968), pp. 193*ff*.; N.R. Hanson, *Patterns of Discovery* (Cambridge, 1958), chapter 1; T.S. Kuhn, *The Structure of Scientific Revolutions* (Chicago, 1970), chapter 10 *et passim*, all with a view to philosophical problems different from those I am concerned with here, but all, I think, relevant.

9 *An Inquiry Concerning the Principles of Morals*, Section IX, *Conclusion* (p. 91 in 'Library of Liberal Arts' edition).

10 *A Treatise of Human Nature* (Oxford, 1941), book III, part II, section XII.

11 Cf. Phillipa Foot, 'When is a Principle a Moral Principle?', in Aristotelian Society Supplementary Volume XXVIII (1954).

12 Or neo-Humean. The attribution of the fact/value dichotomy to Hume has rightly been questioned.

13 Arthur Schopenhauer, *Essays and Aphorisms*, translated by R.J. Hollingdale (Harmondsworth, 1970), pp. 51-2.

14 p. 48. All references are to the Penguin edition of the English translation by Stuart Gilbert.

15 p. 62 — but I have been informed by Miss Susan Quick that the English translation puts this more forcibly than does the French text.

16 p. 27, *et passim*.

17 p. 120.

18 Cf. Hanson, op. cit., chapter 1.

19 But if I am already able to see it in more than one way then I can subsequently 'choose' to see it in one of those ways, in the sense that I can concentrate my attention on those features which go to make up that aspect.

20 This is a point made to me by Tony Skillen.

21 It is certainly not the *whole* of what he means.

22 Marx and Engels, *The German Ideology*, translated by Roy Pascal and Clemens Dutt (Moscow, 1964), pp. 37 and 42. I have also drawn on the translation in L.D. Easton and K.H. Guddat, *Writings of the young Marx on Philosophy and Society*, pp. 414 and 421.

23 David McLellan, *Marx's Grundrisse* (London, 1971), p. 44*f*.

PART V

Community

Introduction

ALAN R. DRENGSON

In *Crito* Socrates asks, does the individual have an obligation to obey the laws of the state? In modern states the answer to this question has usually been 'yes'. Not only is it said that we, as citizens, have an obligation to support the laws of our state, it is also widely held that we even have an obligation to give our lives, if necessary, in its defence. In some states national defence has been thought to require organized violence practised far from the shores of the native land. This has led some people to ask, how can there be any conceivable relationship between a nation's security and insurgency in a far distant land? This, in turn, has led to the more general question, by what right does a state command its citizens to bear arms, by what right does it conscript its youth into military service?

That states have the *legal* right to do a number of these things is not questioned here. The issue is whether a state has a *moral* right to require obedience of its citizens. This issue is explored by A.E. Murphy. He focuses upon the concept of community as this concept has bearing on the concepts of rights, moral ends, etc. Murphy argues it is only in so far as a state is in some respects a community that it can morally obligate us in any way, for morality has to do with the relationships between persons and entails a mutuality of interest and respect that can rationally commend itself to us. Thus, the very concept of a community is, according to Murphy, a moral concept, and so it is, he says, an important analytic truth that to the community we have certain obligations.

Murphy's account of 'community' can perhaps help us with our original question. Our question was whether or not the state has a moral right to make certain claims upon its citizens. According to Murphy, we can say that the state, in so far as it is a community, has the right to ask certain things of its citizens; they are obligated to it in so far as it has the features of a community. This leaves unanswered of course the difficult problem of how community is to be realized in large modern states. What we have said so far about the state is, on Murphy's analysis, logically entailed by the very concepts that we have. Murphy goes on to argue that we not only have a duty to serve our community, but also a duty to 'create the community'. But what is it we are obligated to do in order to create the community? And are we able, through deliberate action, to 'create community'? Or, is the shape of human society beyond our grasp?

If we compare different societies, and what they give to their members, we will see that some are not worthy of our support. If one has moral obligations to a state and its government only in so far as the state is a community, does one have an obligation to not support, or even attempt to overthrow, a corrupt state? Many eighteenth-century political thinkers thought that citizens had an obligation to overthrow oppressive and tyrannical governments. In any event, governments and forms of government do change. Can these changes ever be construed as a result of a clear choice made knowingly by the people? To what extent, in other words, can we control our societies? This is a question to which Simone Weil addresses herself. She claims that certain features of the natural world, and the kind of organizations we must develop to cope with them, seem inevitably to result in oppression. If these conditions are unavoidable, how can we give sense to the assertion that we ought to create community? If we are unable to do so, then it would seem pointless to say that we ought to do so. For certainly, as Kant observed, one cannot be obligated to do something that one cannot do: the moral 'ought' *implies* an unconditional 'can'.

According to Weil, the problems that modern people face cannot be solved by the egalitarian organization characteristic of many primitive food-gathering societies. Modern states require, in her view, two kinds of people: those who command, and those who obey. This is so because modern industrial states have complex economies and technologies that require enormous organization. This kind of co-ordination can only be accomplished if some individuals are in positions of power and are able to determine what others shall do, and this usually results in oppression. It looks then as if we are faced with a dilemma. If we could create simple food-gathering societies such as those of the past, we would be very much at the mercy of natural forces; if, on the other hand, we strive for dominion over nature so that we will no longer be at the mercy of flood, famine and pestilence, then we seem forced to develop vast organizations in which some will command. In either case it appears, in Weil's view, that we must be enslaved 'to the twin domination of nature and society'. Or, are there other alternatives as yet unrealized? Weil says that in order to answer these questions we must attempt to find out why we have usually had to pay for our power over nature with oppression. Also, we must determine what position would allow for the least enslavement by nature and society. Finally, we must find out how, given our current situation, we can realize a state of little or no oppression. These are difficult and tangled issues, and they raise a number of questions, some philosophical and some empirical, and we cannot explore all of them here.

Weil claims that our first task must be to form a clear idea of what social arrangement would be the least unhappy one for us in the sense of least oppressive. The answer we can give, so far, is conceptual. In so far as we succeed in realizing community, we will have done away with oppression and regimented control. In a community humans do not do things because some super bureaucrat manipulates them, but because they freely chose to do what it is they do. Their associations are not based upon inequality and power, but upon mutual respect and co-operation.

Could such an association exist in the modern world? This is in part an empirical question for it points towards actual possibilities open to us given our situation and the material conditions of the world. We must remind ourselves that many things which appear necessary are not necessary at all. For example, we do not *need* to use large quantities of fossil fuels in order to live satisfying lives. What we want to see is that there are possibilities open to us, that many things that appear necessary are not. Let us, for purposes of illustration focus then upon farming.

The production of food in the West has, on the whole, become an energy-intensive industry, dependent upon a vast system of refinement and transport. This, in turn, has resulted in pollution, environmental degradation and decreased land fertility, all as a consequence of systematic application of various chemicals. These chemicals require large amounts of energy to produce, and so farming, as it has developed in the West, particularly since the last World War, has come to ultimately depend upon consumption of large quantities of energy whether on the farm or in the factory. The real costs of this energy consumption have not been borne by the farming industry alone, although to be sure fuel shortages in recent years have hurt farmers. Many of these costs have been simply deferred, particularly the environmental ones. When energy supplies become more limited our farm industries are going to suffer more, and the price of farm commodities is going to rise sharply. The only kind of farm industry that is going to survive, in significant percentages, is going to be the industrial type of managed farm. All of these processes lead to further urbanization and have other side effects.

Now we might think that there is nothing we can do about these trends. We might think there is no other way to practise farming and at the same time support our large urban populations. There are two things to be said about this. First, why think that our current population levels are ideal? We could aim at a lower population by lowering our birth rates. Second, there are alternative methods of farming, that are not energy-intensive, which will support large urban populations. Let us look at the second of these points in more detail.

A number of groups and individuals have experimented with other methods of farming, i.e., alternative to those that use energy-intensive methods which rely upon pesticides, chemical fertilizers, etc. These alternatives do not necessarily involve more hand labour as tractors and other farm machines are still used[1]. In place of pesticides, biological and botanical controls are used, and there is less reliance on large-scale monoculture. Instead of chemical fertilizers, crop rotation, surface tilling, animal and green manures, composting and mulches are used to enhance soil fertility. With these methods it is possible to increase per-acre yields, and at the same time reduce run-off of chemicals that pollute surface and subsurface waters. Composting and mulching used together reduce irrigation requirements and increase soil warmth. A farm which practises these methods, often referred to as 'organic farming', consumes far less energy from fossil fuels, and, over the years, the soil actually, in contrast to the petro-chemical approach, becomes more productive rather than less.

If we were to adopt these organic methods of farming, we would obviously have to alter current practices. The former require more careful thought and planning, and must be more carefully adjusted to the natural rhythms and cycles of the earth. They are not, in other words, as mechanical as current practices. None the less, even though these 'organic methods' are alternatives to current practices, we might still be inclined to think that we cannot change those practices. There seems so much inertia involved in our current ways of doing things, that we are almost overwhelmed when we think about altering them. But these practices, we must remind ourselves, are not our jailers. They are the result of custom and habit. They did not develop because we aimed at them, for we aimed at no particular end. If we are to change them however we will have to aim at specific ends. If we accept them as unchangeable, any change that comes about will not be change we have chosen.

Let us cite one further example in connection with this discussion. We sometimes think that in countries such as the United States and Canada, private motor cars are necessary forms of transportation. The great distances between places within the two countries would seem to make such transport a necessity. But of course when we think this way we overlook the fact that it really is not necessary for most people to travel as much as they do. They could stay at home, and their homes could be planned so that they could easily walk or cycle to work; further, public transport could be more efficiently developed. We find it necessary to travel as we do, because in part we think that it is necessary and have not conceived of, still less planned for, alternatives. What we think is necessary will, regardless of whether it is or not, become a necessity for us; it will be one of our limits. Now all of this is related to the problem of creating community, for that depends in part on how we conceive of ourselves and our aims; altering our society and creating community are to a large extent connected with altering ourselves and our behaviour.

It is usually at this point that social engineers and others of their ilk can be heard to say 'all social problems are the result of human behaviour. If there are social problems, they can be dealt with by modifying human behaviour.' In order to create the community that is desirable we have only to condition people in the appropriate ways. What is then proposed is the sort of thing outlined in *Walden II*. Walden II is a planned society where human behaviour is manipulated, where people are conditioned to behave in the 'right' ways. Positive reinforcement, behaviour modification, operant conditioning, etc., these are the tools available to students of the twentieth-century sciences of human behaviour. But, as Murphy makes clear, no society conceived and created in this way could bring community into existence. Its moral foundations will be unacceptable ones.

We then have to think carefully about what sorts of things are important in human life. Whether, for example, gadgets and even such things as air conditioning are more important than the things we seem forced to sacrifice for them. Some philosophic traditions have emphasized that it is only by changing our desires and interests that we can achieve fulfilment[2]. The thought is that the world is in many respects beyond our reach, whereas our own desires and interests are not. If we think that wealth and possession of things is important, then that is what we will pursue. But such pursuits have a way of becoming all-consuming and incapable of satisfaction, for the possession of some wealth seems to lead to the desire for more. These desires seem unlimited. Our consumption of energy is like this. The curve of increasing demand is tangential, and the time during which the doubling of consumption occurs grows shorter with the passage of time. It is clear that this kind of growth is malignant and insatiable. The solution to the energy crisis is not to be found by mining the last reserves of fossil fuels, for unless we reflect upon our basic practices our 'needs' will soon be doubling every five to ten years. At this rate we would soon consume the entire planet.

I began this discussion with an attempt to explore what things stand between us and the creation of community. A number of problems have been touched upon, and we are now face to face with major difficulties. We have failed to realize community in our modern industrial states in part as a result of the very practices that these states seem to rest upon. In the modern economy, efficiency in economic terms is the by-word, productivity is the goal. But these goals have seemed to require that we sacrifice many important things that are necessary for community. And the irony is that many of these practices turn out to be inefficient in terms of human needs. We seem locked into an industrial, technological machine that controls us and we sacrifice our own interests to it. Modern farming with its petro-chemical investment seems necessary to keep up food production, but this causes decreased soil fertility, increased problems with pests, and pollution of valuable streams and lakes. The recreational and scenic values of the land and the waters decrease; congestion from private motorcars frustrates our efforts to find relief from the confusion and noise of the large city; computers invade our privacy and bureaucracy reduces us to impersonal cyphers. But with respect to two of these areas we have given examples that illustrate that there are alternatives. While it is no doubt true that our interests and wants are conditioned by the societies we live in, none the less we affect those societies and make them what they are. Community seems to require a certain kind of person, but community seems required in order for persons to be a certain way. We have, if we are to create community, to begin somewhere, and certainly we each have the capacity to change our own behaviour; we can, for example, learn to walk and cycle once more. If Murphy's dictum is to be taken seriously, the duty to create community seems to require that we change ourselves, for we must start somewhere. A change in our thinking, in consciousness (as the current saying goes), is the first place we might start. The lack of community that characterizes the modern industrial state contributes to and is one of the causes of some forms of alienation and anomie. However, there are other sources of alienation and anomie. The paper by Steven Lukes discusses some of these issues.

Most discussions of alienation and anomie are bound up with assumptions about human nature and the interaction between it and society. There is a wide divergence of views about these matters. If two thinkers have different views about human nature, they will not be very apt to have the same views about alienation and society. Given our current knowledge, or lack of it, it might not be possible when we theorize about human nature to clearly separate those issues that are empirical from those that are not. There have been endless disputes among social scientists about the nature of human nature. In the course of these disputes scientists sometimes accuse one another of unwittingly making value judgments in place of scientific hypotheses. Once we get involved in these disputes we get the feeling that we no longer know our way about: definitions become entangled with factual claims, factual claims become entangled with judgments. In an attempt to remain objective about these issues, social scientists have attempted to refrain from making value judgments, but, as we have seen in earlier chapters, this is not always easy.

Some theorists have claimed that humans are so plastic that they are essentially without nature. Others have claimed that humans are basically aggressive and selfish, and that we must be disciplined by a rigid social order, otherwise we will have chaos. Some have thought that humans are basically good, and all we need do is create free societies that allow this 'good' nature to develop and show itself. Now as long as we are confused about these issues we will not be able to clearly see what possibilities are open to us in community design. How we are to resolve these issues is not itself clear. What we will accept as evidence for one view over the other is not independent of beliefs we already hold, beliefs that are often neither the result nor the subject of scientific inquiry.

When we talk of human nature then it is far from clear what we are talking about. Yet we cannot expect to get very far in our attempts to form a clear idea of our possibilities, with respect to community, without having some clear idea of what we are. We must, at the very least, try to identify what about us is not subject to change and whether we have basic social, as well as physical, needs.

This introduction has focused on questions related to the creation of community. Although the essays in this section do not always directly discuss community, they none the less relate to it. We can see this if we consider the following. Murphy, for example, addresses the issue of whether a rule account of morality is sound. His article focuses on this in more detail than it does on community *per se*. None the less, this discussion is closely related to community, since community is a moral concept which is tied to our understanding of moral agency. As Murphy shows, moral agency cannot be understood in terms of rule-bound action, nor can it be independent of the community. Moral agents develop, they do not simply change, within the context of community. Understanding and judgment mature from reflection on our *shared* experiences, and not from following rules. Moral agency has its home in human community, and the lack of community gives rise to the patterns of alienation and anomie described by Lukes. Finally, as Weil suggests, the use we make of the natural world can determine whether or not our communities become exploitative cultures, for exploitation of the earth usually results in oppression. Weil asks whether there can be a balanced community that exploits neither person nor nature, for the dilemma she sketches implies that either we subdue nature to escape its domination and end dominated by our own oppressive societies, or else we remain forever at the mercy of natural cycles and are dominated by nature. In either case oppression appears to be our lot, unless we succeed in creating community as Murphy describes it.

Notes

---

1 For more details see *Organic Gardening and Farming* published monthly by Rodale Press. Also see E.H. Faulkner, *Plowman's Folly* (Norman, Okla., 1963).
2 '[H]e who knows that enough is enough will always have enough' and 'Without desire there is tranquility.' Lao Tzu, *Tao Te Ching*.

13

Reason, rules and the 'community'

A. E. MURPHY

There is a persistent misunderstanding to which a theory of practical reason is open and which, if not explicitly corrected, will lead to a distorted picture of the nature and the work of practical reason. Right actions, we have said, are warrantable by reasons. It is only as thus warrantable that the characterization of an action as right has a normative force or cogency that makes practically justifying sense. And in answer to the questions: where do we get such reasons? and how can we understand and use them in this way? we have replied that we learn their use and cogency as we become responsibly participating members in the communities in which, in practice, the distinction between right and wrong ways of acting functions as a guide to justifiable conduct. Here training must precede questioning and argument. The man who in such training has learned the difference between right and wrong understands, in some instances at least, what it is to act justifiably or for good reasons, and the man who does not know this cannot significantly ask for the reason for an action for which a practically justifying 'because' would provide a relevant answer. He would not have the understanding — the mastery of the conceptual structure of the practice — required to make practical sense of such a reason if he saw one.

Reprinted from A.E. Murphy, The Theory of Practical Reason (*Open Court Publishers, 1965*), *pp. 186-220, by permission of the publishers.*

So much, I have maintained, is true and of fundamental importance for our subject. But it is at just this point that the misunderstanding referred to above may arise, and too often does. For when we look for the content of the reasons that in this way and initially we learn, we find it in the accepted rules and approvals of the social groups in which such training actually is given. And if to act justifiably is simply to conform our actions to such rules, then the work of practical reason seems to be 'in the end' just that of following learned instructions. In its beginning is its end, so far as being reasonable is concerned.

C.S. Peirce expressed and embraced this implication, for moral reasoning at least, with characteristic explicitness.

> We all know what morality is: it is behaving as you were brought up to behave; that is, to think you ought to be punished for not behaving. But to believe in thinking as you were brought up to think defines *conservatism*. It needs no reasoning to perceive that morality is conservatism. But conservatism again means, as you will surely agree, not trusting to one's reasoning powers. To be a moral man is to obey the traditional maxims of your community without hesitation or discussion. Hence, ethics, which is reasoning out an explanation of morality, is — I will not say immoral [for] that would be going too far — composed of the very substance of immorality.[1]

Not many philosophers are as forthright as Peirce or as ready to carry a wrong-headed argument to its logical conclusion. But, as we shall see, there are some contemporary accounts of moral reasons that appear, though more equivocally, to lead us in the same direction. And these accounts have, in some respects, a disturbing similarity to our own. They, too, stress practices and learning and community. And some of them have learned from Wittgenstein to describe practically justifiable behaviour as the mastery of a technique in which games are played and rules followed according to learned instructions. It may even be suspected that this is what we also ought to say. For, if we bring the learning of moral reasons back to training *of this sort*, what more can be learned from it than to behave as you were brought up to behave? If this is all there is to learning moral reasons in the beginning, what more than this can there be to a 'rational' use of them in the end? And if there were a 'more', of what nature could it be?

The answer is, of course, that this is not all there is to moral training (or to any other in which it is *reasons* that are to be understood and used) in the beginning. An account that so represents the matter is wrong not merely incidentally or on minor issues but fundamentally. It does not have the root of the matter in it. But since there are strong temptations, both analytical and practical, not to understand it, we shall perhaps be well-advised to say it again, as explicitly as possible and in specific contrast to those theories that sound, in some respects, like our own but whose sense is by no means the same. Such a statement will enable us to bring together and get clearly into focus considerations so far discussed piecemeal, and in this way to sum up what we have to say about the reasonableness of practical, and especially of moral, reasons in their proper and distinctive use.

'Morality is behaving as you were brought up to behave; that is, to think you ought to be punished for not behaving.' The 'that is' in this sentence suggests that the clause that follows it says nothing more than was asserted in the one by which it is preceded. It takes but little reasoning, however, to show that this is not the case. To behave as you were brought up to behave is, so far, not to 'behave' morally at all. Dogs and other dumb creatures are trained to behave in this way as well as men and whether or not such behaviour is moral is not the question as to whether or not the training has been successful. The expectation of punishment may play a part in such training, but it does not always do so. 'Position re-enforcement' is more basic than negative and may do the job by itself. But to think one ought to be punished for not behaving is thinking of a different kind than this. The action that ought to be punished is one that deserves or merits punishment. And to think of one's own actions in this way is to view them in a certain light, *as* right or wrong, and of oneself as rightly held responsible for them, as justified or unjustified in their performance.

The categories in whose terms such thinking is done and the language in which they have a practically significant use are not those of behavioural conditioning but of moral understanding, of practical action, agent and justifying or normatively cogent reasons. Until we have learned to view our own conduct and that of others in this light nothing moral has been learned and the training given is not moral training. A man whose behaviour was appropriately conditioned might behave all his life as he had been brought up to behave and still be a moral moron. How far this is the case with what Peirce calls 'conservatism' the reader, from his own political experience, may judge.

What, then, is *moral* training? The account in Plato's *Protagoras* will be useful here. The formula for such instruction, it will be recalled, is not just 'do this' under specified conditions, but 'this is right: do this'. If this is 'right' were understood merely as a reiterated command, from those we are afraid of, or as verbal bait for the performance ordered, like fish for trained seals, such instruction would reduce without remainder to the 'conditioning' we have just considered. We have seen that such reductions have been attempted and that, and why, they make no moral sense. No doubt what passes for 'moral' training is often given and understood in just this way. But this is not the way in which a man learns to become, and to conduct himself as, a moral agent. Those who learned no more than this would rightly be regarded not as men we could respect as persons but, morally, as cases of arrested development. Peirce is quite right in saying that in such 'morality' there is no place for reasoning. Indeed, he understates the case. For men thus trained what would be the sense or use of justifying reasons? They would need only to remember their instructions and in fear and trembling or with a glow of conformist satisfaction or just as a matter of course, of social habit and routine, to do as they had long ago been told. They would 'obey the traditional maxims of their community without hesitation or discussion'. What, with respect to the morality of the action, would there be to discuss? But he is wrong in describing this as 'thinking as you were brought up to think'. It is rather a way of behaving as you were brought up to behave in situations in which you were brought up *not* to think. To suppose that it is in such 'bringing up' as this that we learn the meaning and the use of moral reasons would be patently absurd.

But what other use than this *could* there be for the 'right' that is a distinctive factor in moral instruction? There is one at least. Here 'right' functions as an admonition to the learner to look at his action in a distinctive way, to consider it not merely as something he is told to do or not to do but as something that he, of his own will, ought or ought not to do 'because' — where the ground for so doing is specified in the reasons that show the action to be in this way right or wrong. 'Wrong', *thus understood*, is not the name of a class of not-to-be-done acts any more than 'poisonous' is the name of a class of not-to-be-eaten foods. A poison is a not-to-be-eaten thing not just because our instructors tell us to avoid it but because it is lethal and should as such be shunned by a man concerned to preserve his life even when no one in authority has ordered him to shun it. A man who has not learned that has not learned how to deal rationally with poisons. No matter how docile he might be in following instructions, he would be quite helpless in a situation that they did not cover or where they had been wrongly given. His not to reason why; his but to eat and die. For he would so far have nothing to reason with, or about. His training would not have taught him to think and act as a practical agent.

So for 'right'. 'This is right', where it makes rational sense at all, is a 'move' in a different game from that of the conditioning of behaviour by peremptory and/or persuasive speech. The action is something to be done or not done for a reason, and 'right' in its moral use is an indicator of the kind of reason that would here be relevant to warrant action. 'Look at it this way.' To characterize an action as honourable or as dishonourable, or in any other moral terms, is to place it in this practical context, to give a reason why it should or should not be done. Unless the 'done thing' is *in this way* understood as the ought-to-be-done thing it has no moral warrant and in the teaching of it nothing moral has been taught.

Such admonitions are addressed to men *as* moral agents, and it is in this capacity that they can practically respond to them as such. Moral training is the training of actual human beings to become and act as such agents — men who, in their own persons can distinguish between right and wrong and will sometimes, of their own will, act accordingly. For the right is, as we have seen, a necessity by which men are bound only in so far as they are free. This must be a training of a different sort than that used for trained dogs or seals. For it is training in the development and right exercise of *this* capacity. Here the appeal to justifying reasons has a distinctive and essential place. A 'right' thus understood has a 'because' in it and until this 'because' has been given, the 'normative force' of right has not been established for a responsible moral agent. To learn what moral reasons are is to learn what considerations are in this way grounds for right action, to learn their justifying use and cogency in *this* 'game'. A training that does not teach this is not moral training and the use in it of terms that claim a moral cogency is analytically a categorial confusion and practically a fraud.

Our first and primary answer, then, to those who in this way 'analyse' morality and moral training is that they have here confused their 'games'. They are trying to get a language of justifying reasons out of procedures of social conditioning in which this kind of justification, with the reasons that support it, has no place. It is not surprising to discover that in such 'training' nothing normatively cogent can be learned, and that moral reasons, thus understood, can have no practically rational use. It is, on the contrary, exactly what, by this time, we should expect.

What, then, *is* moral training? Before the use of justifying reasons can be taught, there must *be* such a use. The 'game' in which they have a normative cogency must be played. A society that offers effective training in such use must practise what it preaches, for it is in this practice that the preaching makes practical sense. And if the training is to be moral, this practice must be that of a community in which a going concern for right action is an effective factor in the way of life in which the learner is called upon responsibly to share. It is in such sharing that a child can learn what it is to have good reasons for what he does, and to do an action for such reasons. Admonitory speech has a useful part in such training, and reward and punishments may support it, but unless the practice itself supports it in a different way, by example and not by punishment and precept merely, only the timid or the gullible will in the long run be imposed on by it. Here as elsewhere we learn to do by doing, under the practical guidance of those who do well the thing that we are learning how to do. And what, in this case we are learning how to do is to act as moral agents. At what point in a child's development he can be reached by considerations of this sort is a question 'child psychologists' must answer, where that term refers to their subject-matter and not to the conceptual discernment of their treatment of it. Obviously the child's behaviour must be 'conditioned' in other ways before he is able so to act. But this, when and as it becomes possible, is what moral training is, and without it no amount of conditioning will be the training of a moral agent.

Of course, the content of such training, as formulated in familiar maxims, will be the accepted moral precepts of the group in which the training is given. It is only on the basis of an agreed or understood consensus that there can be common grounds for action, and a ground that is not in its intention 'common' is not a practical reason. If everything in a moral situation were arguable or questionable at once there could be no significant questioning or argument. And until the learner has acquired this working basis of understanding, until he knows in some cases what good reasons are, he will have nothing to reason with or about when he is called on in his own person to distinguish between actions that are right and wrong. *Of course* his having promised is a reason why he ought to do a promised act; a man who could not understand this, or other reasons of a similarly rudimentary nature, would be one with whom we could never hope to reach a moral understanding on the issues of our common life. But while this is the beginning of moral wisdom it cannot in principle, or in hard cases, be the end. For such reasons are not reasons for themselves, self-evident bits of final moral truth, to be cognitively cherished on their own account. They are grounds *for* actions to be done, and whether in specific cases they are sufficient grounds is a question that cannot be answered by an appeal to their initial unquestioning acceptance as reasons. And this question is inherent in their right use *as reasons* from the start, though, fortunately, in many instances, it need not be raised. In moral training, as in any other, we must begin with the rudiments. There cannot be exceptions to rules unless there are rules and the rule, as a moral maxim, is the norm for normal cases. But the rudiments must have the root of the matter in them, else the seed thus planted could not grow up to bear the fruit which is moral agency and moral judgment. And this root is precisely the understanding and use of the reasons taught *as reasons* as grounds for action to be done not because that is the way we learned it, or because it is the done thing but because, for good and sufficient reasons, it is right. The learner thus equipped is launched on a voyage of discovery that can carry him a long way from his starting point. For the process of the use of reasons is a self-correcting process. The customary acceptance with which it begins are the grounds for action each of us has learned to respect in the local communities in which he was brought up to play his part well as a son, a team mate or a citizen. In many situations they are good enough. If they were not the group that taught him what it is to be a responsible agent would not be itself a moral community. But in changing conditions and in the larger situations with which he and his group, since it is never morally isolated, have to deal, they are sometimes not good enough. There are issues that cannot on their local and parochial terms be adequately met and other people's reasons to be weighed that are not those he learned in childhood to respect. And if he has not merely been 'brought up' but has grown up he must come to understand and use the better reasons here required — better in the same way in which these are good, as requirements for a moral *modus vivendi* — but adequate, as those that he initially learned are not, to serve here as foundations for a good society. Moral learning is not for children merely; we must go on learning all our lives if the requirements of our moral situation are rightly to be met. The point of moral training is to supply a starting point and to develop the concern and capacity with which we can thus go on. It is a teaching that prepares us to go beyond our instructions and to solve a problem for ourselves. And it is in just this way that it is a training in the practical use of reason.

Do we ever get this kind of training? Indeed we do — not in admonitory verbal slaps and sweetmeats, though for the very young and for those who never do grow up such admonitions have a social use, but in living and working with those who in their own persons embody this kind of excellence and, by precept and example, can bring out the best in us. It is in this way and in the light of their achievement that we come to understand what makes good reasons 'good' and how, in their terms, to distinguish between right and wrong as we share with them in the concerns and responsibilities of a way of life in which such goodness has a practical sense and use. And if we have learned to understand their reasons, not just to mimic their behaviour, we can go on to do for ourselves what in our own situation, which may not be theirs, it is our business to do. This capacity to go on is the authentic mark of the mastery of the technique of this practice and it is in the right use of it that all that is moral in 'moral training' is fulfilled. That much of what is offered as moral falls far short of this we must not merely admit but emphasize. There are those who believe that men are made morally good by the kind of conditioning that would train a monkey or a seal, and that compulsory indoctrination in 'our ideology' will somehow 'make man free'. But moral persons are not made; they grow. And it is in the exercise of freedom that we become free men. The training that can fruitfully foster this growth is indeed a special kind of training. For to become such a person is a special kind of achievement. That achievement and nothing less is the point of moral training.

A subtler form of the same misconception is embedded in what is currently known as the 'rules' or 'practice' conception of obligation and of duty. Here the language of justifying reasons is employed and it is recognized that the 'why' required to make sense of it is that of moral justification. It turns out, however, on this analysis, that there are really two different 'whys' here — each the answer to a quite distinct problem and applicable in a special area of conduct. The area of duty and obligation is that of actions covered by the rules of a practice in which the individual has a definitely assignable role, the area, roughly, of 'my station and its duties'. Here, it is alleged, to justify an action is just to show that there is a rule that governs it and is thus binding on the individual in his role or 'office' within the practice. That the rule exists is a social fact, the fact that it is accepted as a justifying norm for action. Within the practice, references to the rule, as thus accepted, are reasons that justify doing, or refusing to do, a particular action, and they owe their 'moral force' to this reference. As H.L.A. Hart puts it, 'The morality of duty and obligation is that of principles which would lose their moral force unless they were wisely accepted in a particular group'[2]. For they are the principles or rules of this specific practice, and it is as they are thus accepted that there *is* this practice. This game is played.

The 'why' of obligation is answered by reference to the rules as thus existing. It's three strikes and you're out in the old ball game, for that is the way this game is played. If there is any doubt on this point, we need only refer to the official rule book to confirm it. And it is the duty of the umpire to enforce this rule, not because he wants to, or thinks on other grounds that it is a good idea, but because as an umpire it is his office to do so. This is the 'why' inside the game, and, in its own domain, it is quite final.

For the rules themselves, however, there is no 'why' of this sort at all. They simply are the structure of the way this game is played and unless we act in accordance with them it is not this game that we are playing. Their correct observance is a conceptual *must* of the practice that, as a social fact, exists. In this way promising is one of the practices of our society. As Toulmin puts it, '"It is wrong to keep this book because it is wrong to break a promise" is accepted in our society because making and keeping promises is one of the things we do; "the promise" is one of our institutions'[3]. Given this acceptance the 'obligation' is clear. Rawls states it succinctly: 'The promisor is bound because he promised. Weighing the merits of the case is not open to him'[4].

The analysts of this persuasion are emphatic in affirming that this 'why' of rule-bound behaviour does not cover the whole area of moral action. On the contrary, they insist, there is another sphere of morality, beyond obligation and duty, in which we are not thus bound at all. The wrong of inflicting gratuitous suffering, Hart tells us, does not depend on its actual acceptance by the social group but is something by which we may judge the morality of social groups. Here what we ask for is the 'why' of the rules themselves and it is obviously not by reference to the rules as socially existing that we can get an answer to this question. How, then, are we to get it? By reference to the good or interests of the society to whose welfare the observance of the rules, and of the practice they define, contributes. The question that we cannot raise within the practice can and should be asked about it and about the good of it. Of the nature of this good the analysts have so far not had much to say. Their remarks concerning it are utilitarian in a large, loose way; it is to be estimated somehow in terms of consequences and of welfare for 'society'. But they are careful to leave the door open for it and to point out that the rule-bound morality of duty and obligation, or of 'practices' with which they chiefly deal, is morally incomplete without it.

This is a plausible and ingenious theory. But it seems to me, as it stands, to be seriously misleading. For it cuts the 'why' of moral justification up into two quite different 'whys', neither of which makes moral sense by itself nor, as thus analysed, in combination with the other. The 'why' of obligation, as thus elucidated, is something less than moral and the 'why' of the good unbound by obligation is morally equivocal. From their juxtaposition we get an analytically distorted picture of the authentic cogency of moral reasons. And since the language of the analysis is, in some respects, much like our own, it is important that we see how and why this is the case.

Consider first the why of action for which a reference to the socially accepted rules of a practice is supposed to supply not only a sufficient but the only logically possible justification. Why did you — or why should I — pay this man this sum of money? Because I or you promised to do so, and that one keeps a promise is a rule of a practice which is one of our institutions. This rule defines the status of the promisor within the practice and specifies what, in a particular case, it is his office, or his obligation, to do. A man who did not understand this would not know what it was to make a promise, just as one who thought that he could steal a base in baseball by picking up the bag and walking away with it would not know what it was, in that game or practice, to steal a base. If he asked *why* he could not steal it that way, an elucidation of the rules would provide a logically conclusive answer. For it is only on the terms set by the rules that stealing a base counts as a move in this game at all, and the rules do not permit this move. This does not mean, of course, that a man might not in fact pick up the bag and make off with it but that if he did he would not be playing baseball. His action would count as 'stealing' not in the official boxscore of the game but rather, perhaps, in a police court. So equally for promising, and, on this account, for all behaviour that is in this way 'covered by rules'.

Now there is evidently a stage — normally an early one — in learning to play baseball at which this kind of misunderstanding might arise, and it is by this sort of instruction that it would properly be corrected. Here, as Rawls well says, one does not so much justify a particular action as explain it. 'When a particular action is specified by a practice there is no justification possible of the particular action of a particular person save by reference to the practice'[5]. And if it is this kind of 'justification' that is wanted, this surely is the way to give it.

But is it what is wanted when a man asks for — or offers — moral grounds for action? The question here is not, save incidentally or in special cases, as to what the rules are but rather as to the account he ought to take of them in his conduct. So this is the way baseball or 'the institution of the promise' is played. So what? If the explanation given is understood merely *as* an explanation or elucidation it leaves the man who accepts it as practically uncommitted as before. 'If the game is not thus played it will not be baseball as the rules define it.' 'Of course not. Should it be? Why so?' 'Baseball is one of our institutions. This game is played.' 'I accept this as sociological information but I do not see how I am morally bound by it. Why should I do the done thing?' 'It has been empirically established that the playing of baseball by these rules contributes to the interests of society.' 'Perhaps so. If I had a clearer notion what you took to be the interest of society I might be able to agree or disagree with that assertion. But, in any case, why should I so act as to contribute in this way to the interests of society? So far you have given me a logical elucidation, some sociological information, and a very loose generalization about the interests of society. But you have given me no moral grounds for doing anything at all. And it was for such grounds that I asked.'

Obviously the man who plays his part well and fairly in the game of baseball or any other does not in this way understand the rules, or his own role or office with respect to them. He is 'bound' by them not logically or sociologically but morally. To respect and follow them is a requirement for the right playing of this game in which he is involved as a responsible participant, and as such an obligation which he ought to meet. Only as thus understood can a reference to the rules, however analytically precise, provide a moral ground for action. The 'practice' analysts have not reduced the justifying sense of obligation to the explanatory sense of a conceptual elucidation of socially accepted rules. On the contrary, it is only when what is thus elucidated is understood *as* a ground of obligation that it has any relevance to moral problems, or can be *in this way*, a justifying reason. We often have an obligation to follow socially accepted rules — though we sometimes also have an obligation to break them.

But the moral sense of the rule is in the obligation and it is only by bringing back into the picture what their analysis cuts out of it that we can make such sense of what the analysts tell us about rules.

At this point we shall be told, perhaps, that we have misunderstood the theory. Its aim is not at all to eliminate the 'why' of obligation, in its use as a moral reason, but rather to show more clearly in what this consists and how, for analytic or 'linguistic' purposes, it is to be understood. Its purpose is to clarify *this* use — not to substitute another for it. Perhaps, but in that case our objection must be that this is precisely what it fails to do. For what it tells us is that where obligation is in question the only justifying 'why' for action is an explanation or elucidation of the rules themselves. And when we ask how this elucidation provides a ground for action it tells us that, within the practice itself, there is no more to be said than that as socially accepted the rules thus elucidated have 'moral force', i.e., that their acceptance as thus cogent is a social fact. And neither of these considerations, nor both together, are the reasons that, for the moral grounding of our actions, we need. If they were so understood, they would be the wrong kind of reasons. It is true, of course, that if the rules were not socially accepted in this way they would have no 'moral force', for then *this* game would not be played and it is within this game, and as responsible participants, that we have an obligation to respect them. If baseball were not played, no one would have an obligation, as a baseball player, to abide by its rules. But the moral force — i.e., the normative cogency — of the obligation does not consist in its social acceptance. That the rules are so accepted is not a sufficient answer to the 'why' of duty. If it were, social conformity, or doing the done thing, would be the final *ground* of moral obligation. When the analysts so far forget themselves as to import a moral significance into their elucidations, the words are those of the (informal) logician, but the voice is that of the games master, or football coach exhorting us to 'play up and play the game' or 'pull, pull together'. It is not surprising that those who have thus understood them have interpreted what they have to say as an expression of the ideology of socially respectable conservatism.

We are assured that this is a misunderstanding — that in fact what is offered is *only* an analysis and elucidation which has as such no moral import. What we do — or ought to do — with the rules thus elucidated and moored to their appropriate social context is another question altogether. But if this is so, then what was offered was not an account of moral reasons in their morally justifying or normatively cogent use — i.e., it was not an account of the 'why' of obligation and of duty. It was *this* 'why', in the whole area of obligation and of duty, that the analyst was supposed to elucidate, and if this in his terms is all that justification comes to, then so far we have not got a moral reason. The irony of the situation is that we *must* 'misunderstand' what is thus offered *as* a moral reason if we are to understand it in a moral sense at all. For this is the sense of 'justification' as a ground for morally right action.

Here, however, we shall be reminded that we have so far left out half the theory. The game has not only rules but a point, and the question of why the rules should be followed, which cannot be raised within the game itself, since here a reference to the rules as socially accepted is all the justification that there logically can be, can be raised about it. Is such rule-bound behaviour conducive to the general welfare or to the interests of society? Should this game be played? Here we do not accept the rules as the final norm of justification but demand that they be justified in their turn. This is the other side of moral reasoning, not bound by rules or obligations at all but free to examine all our social practices from an obligation-free standpoint and hold fast only those that are good. If the rule-bound side of moral justification seemed to imply conservatism, this one is 'liberal' indeed.

For what is this 'good' and why should the rightness of our practices be measured in its terms? 'Good' in general, as we have seen, is tautologously what we ought to seek and a 'larger' good in preference to a lesser one. But whose good, how achieved, and on what terms shared by those for whom an *obligation* to seek it has a moral sense? The answers given here are vaguely utilitarian in tone. It is the good of all concerned, or most of them at least, and if it is not pleasure — the modern Utilitarian is usually too cautious to say that — it is welfare, or the satisfaction of interests or the like. How it is to be achieved is a problem for the social planners — the Sidney and Beatrice Webbs of the future, perhaps. With such questions the linguistic analyst of moral language is not professionally concerned. His job is simply to point out what kind of questions they are and what, in principle, would be an answer to them.

Our objection must be that he has done this job badly and that, given his account of obligation and duty, he was bound to do so. For just as there is no obligation that makes moral sense without good, so there is no normatively cogent good that does not have its roots in obligation, understood not as rule-bound conformity to the formal requirements of a game, but as obligation-bound acceptance of the requirements of a way of life. Utilitarianism is by no means a no-obligation theory. Rather it is a doctrine that sets up one obligation — to maximize 'happiness' no matter whose, or of what sort, or how attained if only in the total felicific balance it be 'more' — as unconditionally binding, and treats all others as empirical maxims concerning ways in which this 'more' is normally to be achieved. That an action is in this way happiness-producing is the final, and finally the only reason why, on moral grounds, we ought to do it. Other rules have exceptions, but it allows none and is as inflexible as the strictest Puritan could ask. In invoking this philosophy, there-fore, we have not reached an obligation-free standpoint. For in our estimate of the good that ought to be produced we are still bound by an obligation and a very rigid one. And we cannot appraise the moral cogency of this rule from the outside, for it is only on the terms it sets that 'good' has normative significance for action. If 'rule-bound' means obligation-bound action then in Utilitarianism there is no moral action that is not 'rule-bound'.

This, however, is not what the analysts have in mind when they talk of rules and obligations. They would limit the application of such terms to principles socially accepted in *particular* groups which would lose their moral force without such acceptance. Where right and wrong are not thus localized but would hold (as socially accepted?) in any society, they are not in this way grounds of obligation. Thus Hart tells us, 'It is absurd to speak of a moral *duty* not to kill another human being, or an *obligation* not to torture a child'[6]. The 'right' of happiness-maximizing actions is presumably of this practice-transcending character and can therefore be used as a standard by which the morality of accepted practices can be judged. It was in this way, certainly, that Bentham tried to use it.

Is this narrowing of the sense of duty and of obligation helpful here? I should have thought that it at least made sense in our society to say that the observance of the Sixth Commandment was a moral duty. At Oxford it may not be so. But linguistic proprieties of this sort are not the major issue here. The question rather is about the meaning of a right and wrong from which the content of particular obligations, within a morally structured community, has been eliminated as mere rule-bound conformity to the requirements of a socially accepted practice. 'Torture' or the infliction of gratuitous suffering is universally disapproved. But that is because 'torture', in this use, is itself a condemnatory term and any action to which it is properly applied is so far condemned. If moral language is to have a coherent use at all, this much must be true. But when is it properly

applied? What infliction of suffering on children is 'gratuitous'? Is
corporal punishment 'torture'? Or allowing a child to be hurt by the
consequences of his own wilful act? Or requiring him to be quiet
when he wants to make a noise? Here a Spartan parent may judge
the rightness of an action differently than would a devotee of
progressive education. These differences are not extrinsic to the
moral significance of the action. They are bound up with conceptions of what it is to be a child and to become a man — of what is
essential and what is admirable in the preservation of a moral order.
And the same, of course, is true of 'welfare' and of 'happiness'.
Whatever merits these eulogistic designations is thereby established
as a worthy end of action. It is the function of such words of praise
to present it in this status. But what kind of living can rightly be thus
characterized, and on what terms can such a life be rightly lived? Is
welfare to be identified with a multiplication of creature comforts
on equalitarian terms? Or happiness with a sum of pleasures
distinguished from all lesser 'goods' only by the fact that somehow it
is more? And what does the achievement of such a good require of
men who would *justly* share it? These are questions that a reference
to universal moral platitudes does not answer. Yet an answer to
them is presupposed in any appeal to happiness or welfare as a
worthy end of action that makes practical sense and can thus serve
as a normative guide to action. The 'felicity' for whose attainment
Bentham laid down legislative rules was not that of the whole
sentient creation, calculated from the point of view of the Universe,
but that of respectable, sensibly self-interested, law-abiding
Englishmen, calculated from the point of view of a reformer who for
the most part shared the business-like values of the community to
which his 'moral arithmetic' was addressed and was concerned to
bring its penal procedures, for example, into line with such a
reasonably calculable good. In this context his appeal to utility
makes good moral sense. Divorced from it, and set up as a
'principle' about good in general, it becomes morally indeterminate
and hence equivocal in its practical implications. Whose pleasure,
how secured and how enjoyed? To say that 'in the end' these
considerations matter only instrumentally as means to the attainment of more pleasure 'on the whole' is morally preposterous. Yet if
happiness, now identified as pleasure, is *the* good, and right action
that which maximizes it, what else is there to say? In the making of
responsible moral judgments we must have grounds more relative
than this. And these grounds are just the obligations of a morally
structured community whose practices have a justifying 'why' in

them and whose good is the fulfilment of their own intent. There is no morally acceptable good without obligations and there are no obligations whose 'why' is not a requirement for the attainment of such a good.

When we try to combine the 'why' of rule-bound action with the obligation-free good of generalized welfare or social interest what, more specifically, do we get? *Within* the practice, as we have seen, the question of good cannot be raised. As Rawls says: 'The promisor is bound because he promised. Weighing the case on its general merits is not open to him'[7]. Outside the practice, however, the question of general merits is the only one that counts. Thus we may ask whether the practice of keeping promises is in general beneficial to society. If it is, then this game should be played, and if it is played it must be played in this way; the promisor must abide by the rule and is 'bound' accordingly. What such general merits would be and how they could be ascertained in abstraction from the requirements of a way of life in which 'merit' already had a moral meaning it is difficult to see. But let us suppose that these questions could be cogently answered and that, in terms of such an answer, it could be established that the playing of the promise-keeping game was in general, in its consequences, beneficial to such social interests. This would still not take us far toward the solution of any moral questions about the right of keeping a specific promise. Almost nobody would deny that *in general* promises should be kept. The serious question is that of whether *this* action, which would be the keeping of a promise, should be done when it would also be, e.g., giving aid and comfort to enemies of my country and this, in general, is something that I ought *not* to do. Here the 'practice' that we are morally involved in is not just that of promise keeping. There are no *merely* moral practices. It involves the whole network of relations in which a man is involved as a promisor, of course, but also as a citizen and much more besides, and the merits of the case as specified by *all* these obligations are profoundly relevant to what in this case and in his 'office' as a moral agent, he ought or ought not to do. It is not only open to him here to take account of such merits; it is his duty as a responsible moral agent to do so. To say 'It is good in general or on the whole that the game of promise-keeping should be played and therefore, as a promisor, I am bound to keep my promise without regard for any other obligation than that which the rule for promise-keeping defines' would be, in practice, a highly *un*-reasonable procedure. That is not the way in which *this* game — the game of rational justification — is played by those who understand the meaning and the use of moral reasons.

Almost no one who is not infatuated by a theory would suppose it was. The rules of such a practice must be in some way 'defeasible' — exception must be made for cases in which it would be morally unreasonable to follow a 'rule' thus simple-mindedly understood and 'defences' allowed for those who, in the interests of good sense and fairness, refuse, in such instances, to conform to it. The question is as to how this defeasibility and these exceptions are to be understood. One way is that of legalism. We must somehow get the 'defences' into the rule itself. If the rule has all allowable exceptions in it, it can, as thus qualified, be followed without exception, and a reference to it will be sufficient in particular cases to tell us what it is our 'obligation' to do. It is, as Hart as observed[8], where obligations are 'legally coloured' that this version of the matter is most plausible. We may, indeed, suspect that it is just to the legal colouring that it plausibly applies. In the administration of the law this kind of legalism has its plain and proper place, though even here considerations of 'general merit' sometimes rightly guide the decisions of judges. But where the issue is moral there is little to be said for it. For here we are not just giving previously promulgated laws to ourselves but judging a particular moral issue on its merits. To suppose that all that is relevant to such an estimate is embalmed in 'exceptions' designed to deal with past cases and duly canonized in our rule book is moral superstition. It is not merely that old rules will not adequately 'cover' new cases. The question, as we have seen, is that of how, and on what grounds, the exceptions got into the rule in the first place. Those who put them there did not have antecedent rules for so doing. *They* must have made a judgment on the merits of the case. And to suppose that we, in the complex, novel and demanding world that now confronts us, are called on to do less is dangerously simple-minded.

The other way is that of moral judgment and the reasons that support it. Here moral rules are understood as maxims that rightly claim our allegiance and respect. But to respect them *as reasons* is not to set them up as the logical requirements of games that, in the general interest, it is good to play. Their defeasibility is not that of laws with built-in loopholes (exceptions) in them. It is rather that of grounds for action which, though good as *so far* cogent, may be insufficient for the resolution of concrete problems on their specific merits. Here an obligation, as a ground for action, is in one way less, and in another more, than the 'rules' conception would make of it. It is less in the sense that it is never, simply as it stands, a final justification for moral action. In normal circumstances, it is a sufficient reason for an action to be done. And if circumstances were not usually normal, the 'rule' as a maxim would have no moral standing. But in some circumstances it may not be, and where *on moral grounds* the question of its adequacy can be fairly raised, a reference to the rule as final will not meet the issue, for it is precisely its *moral* finality in this instance, not its justification in general that is here in question. But, in another sense, it is more. For, as it stands, it is a moral reason and as such a ground for action, as no elucidation of *de facto* rules could ever be. It is a good reason, the right *kind* of reason, and if in specific cases it is not good enough, the better reasons that can justify a different action than the one which, by itself, it warrants, will themselves be obligations, understood as requirements for the achievement of a moral order which it genuinely, but so far incompletely, serves to specify. The right that can carry us beyond our customarily accepted maxims is an ought that is *in* them, as grounds for justifiable action, and it is the right playing of this game that their intent in this use is adequately fulfilled. Unless the new commandments were the fulfilment of the old, we could not morally understand them. But when we do thus understand them we are launched on a voyage of discovery that no rule book yet devised can adequately chart.

Why is it that a theory with so much truth in it should with such ingenuity in this way go wrong? The answer is, I think, two-fold. There is a deeply ingrained notion in 'linguistic analysis' that an account of moral justification in moral terms has not really done its job. We *begin* with 'obligation' and 'duty', understood in a specifically moral sense, but if we are *really* to clarify them, we must end with something else — with a logical elucidation of rules, or a social fact or something like a legal system. And perhaps even these are not really basic. It may be that on metaphysical analysis assertions of these kinds 'unfold into facts' of a still more basic and rudimentory sort. If this should prove to be the case, how simple (ultimately) everything would be. This kind of analysis does, indeed, have its attractions.

There is a practical persuasiveness about it, too. If we could just bring moral reasons (at least those of obligation) back to logical truths and sociological, legal and/or linguistic facts, we could 'finally' reach a point at which we were relieved of the responsibility of making moral judgments. The question of meaning could be handed over to the (informal) logician and that of fact to the scientists or near-scientists of the areas in question. As analysts we should not be required to accept the moral implications of the considerations we identified as justifying reasons for as thus processed, they would have no moral implications. And if any area of moral justification — that of 'good', for example — remained uncovered by such an analysis, we could safely leave it in that realm of edifying generalities in which traditional 'liberal' ethical theorizing — Utilitarianism for example — has enshrined it. All this seems modest, circumspect and in harmony with approved academic procedure.

The one major difficulty with it, as we have seen, is that under such analysis 'moral reasons' lost their moral sense and use. This loss is a high price to pay for an observance of academic proprieties — too high if our purpose is so to understand the 'language' of morality that we can use it reasonably for practical ends. Hence, while we may respect the good intentions and admire the skill of the analysts of this persuasion we cannot follow their example nor expect to find in their description of morality the substance of the thing we seek. They have, for their own purposes, changed the subject.

Just as the moral use of 'reasons' and 'rules' may, in our current climate of opinion, be analytically misunderstood, so, too, may that of 'community', and with comparable results. We have held that the requirements of morality are those for the maintenance of a moral order, or *modus vivendi* in the communities to which men belong as moral agents, and that it is to such agents that moral claims on conduct are significantly addressed. Experience has shown that there are those who will suppose at once that they understand us here, and will agree with what they take to be our main conclusion, though they will be unhappy about the unduly moralistic terms in which it is presented. For 'community' they will substitute 'society', for the moral agent the socialized 'self' or 'me' of the will-conditioned organism, and for 'obligations' the pressures of 'the group' as these are 'internalized' and generalized in individual behaviour as goals and guides for socially normalized behaviour. Such a substitution appears to put the discussion on a sound factual basis and to bring it into fruitful connection with the advancing sciences of sociology and social psychology. Nothing is lost save a scientifically outmoded terminology and, on the level of the engineering of human attitudes, there is a world to win. If only philosophers would say plainly that this is what they mean, what profitable interdisciplinary and crossfertilizing research projects might be organized with at least one philosopher on every team.

This, of course, is not what we mean. And, if taken as an account of the moral meaning of 'community' it is not only theoretically incorrect but morally indefensible. The reader who has followed our account so far will hardly need to be told that and why this is the case. But since the urge to such misunderstanding is strong and the terminology for its articulation academically well established, it will perhaps be wise to sum the matter up as explicitly as possible.

What such a theory — sometimes called 'social behaviourism' — tells us is that what we call moral obligations are the pressures of society upon its members, generalized as rules of good behaviour and internalized through social training as the 'self' or 'me' of the behaving organism. Moral principles are the directives of such generally sanctioned behaviour as these are accepted and acted on voluntarily by the socially adjusted individual. The voice of the generalized other is the voice of conscience and to be a self is to respond in this way — taking the role of the other — to one's own organic responses and 'behaving oneself' accordingly. Since such theories claim to be factually descriptive in the best scientific manner, there can be no question here of whether conduct thus controlled is 'really' right. Within the group in which such conditioning effectively functions it will be what is called right and as such a norm for the normalized individual. And those who conform to it will be acting rightly in the only sense of that term which here makes sociological sense.

The 'facts' stressed by such theories, so far as they are factually confirmed, are instructive. And since the moral process is at least a social process, they are clearly relevant to our subject. But as an account of moral action they are theoretically incongruous and practically misleading. An obligation, as a ground for action, is not a social pressure. A moral self is not a mechanism of social control built into the individual by the appropriate conditioning of his responses. And a community that can rightly claim the loyalty of its members is not a pressure group thus organized. Something has been left out here that makes all the difference between a social tool, however well processed, and a moral person. And it is not really difficult to see what this something is. For it is just morality itself.

Why should I conform to the pressures of society? For the 'social self' this could not be a moral question, for these pressures themselves, as generalized and internalized in 'conscience', are the only moral 'should' he knows. But there is often urgent need for us to ask them, if we are to live as free men in the socially engineered world that now confronts us. And what kind of answer can 'society' give to such a question? Because it is the done thing? But sometimes it is not done. That is why pressures are required to bring 'deviant' conduct into conformity with it. It is not as the done thing merely but as the ought-to-be-done thing that it is supposed to influence my conduct. What gives it this status? Is it because this is what society requires of me and I am a social being? But the voice of 'society' may here be anything from the shouts of a lynching mob to the dictates of Mrs Emily Post. Gangsters, pickpockets and prostitutes are no less social in their fashion than are men and women of distinction. Is it what the best people do, or at least approve of others doing? Who, then, are the best? Those whose social status establishes them as the elite of the society in question? If the wife of the President of General Motors approves of Gladiola Cake Mix or contributes to the United Fund is there not a clear social mandate for Mrs Jones and Mrs Robinson to 'do so as well'? Or is it simply those who by one sort of 'conditioning' or another have the power to exert this kind of influence on my thought and conduct? Here 'might' (if we include all forms of social power and not mere physical force) does indeed, and tautologically, make 'right'. For 'right' in this use is just 'internalized' conformity to this sort of might. Other societies with a different sort of power structure will, of course, have different 'rights' and, where these practically conflict only might (including that of propaganda) can decide which 'right' is to prevail. If it really does prevail a future generation, if not ours, will be trained as 'social selves' to accept its dictates as their 'moral' principles. Their 'consciences' will have been conditioned to this end.

Just as the 'right' thus established is not moral right, so the self that thus responds to it is not a moral agent. He is the adjustable man and one of the ways in which he can be thus adjusted is by the use of generalized directives whose dictates he is trained, by moral engineering, to impose upon 'himself'. The voice of the generalized other speaks in him; it is, for moral purposes, the only voice he has. The language of traditional morality is often effectively employed in the processing of such dictates for generalized consumption. In such a use they lose nothing but their rationally justifying sense. For beings thus conditioned, however, this loss would not appear as a defect. For they would not know what to make of such a justification if they had it. Their 'responses' to 'moral' issues are conditioned in a different way and, if they have been well conditioned, 'society' will do their thinking for them. 'Oh brave new world, that has such people in it.'

A society thus organized would have great power at its command. But there is one sort of 'force' that cannot be thus commanded. That is the moral force or cogency of a valid claim on the loyalty of men as moral agents. The words in which such claims have traditionally been made are still available to it — 'community', 'right', 'freedom' and the like — but their use will be a different one and their sense will alter with that use. They may excite or intimidate or soothe those trained in this way to respond to them, but they can justify nothing, for the grounds of obligation that would warrant their cogency in such a use will no longer have a rationally examinable meaning, nor would those to whom they were addressed be morally or rationally in a position to examine them. To such individuals anything could be 'justified' — i.e., made socially acceptable — by those who had the power to control the instruments of conscience-making. But nothing could be justified by being shown to be right. For a social pressure, thus imposed, is not a moral reason. And whether any given 'pressurizing' was itself justifiable could be answered only by more justification (pressurizing) which would establish 'right' to the degree that it was socially effective. To say that this is not what we meant when we spoke of moral reasons as addressed to men as members of communities is not an overstatement.

To see precisely where the difference lies between the two accounts, we need only take a closer look at 'community'. This is a word of many uses and I do not claim that the one here followed is its only proper use. It is, however, a common and distinctive one, and I have tried to adhere consistently to it throughout. In this use, a 'community' is not just any group that influences the behaviour of its members. It is a group whose members are related in a quite distinctive way, the way of moral understanding, and the group is a community only in so far as they are thus related. The categories that make sense of this relationship are those of practical reason: of action, agent, public right and common good. And they make this kind of sense only in their normatively cogent or justifying use. That an action will further the 'interests' of the community is a reason why I ought to do it. How so? What is the community to me, or I to it, that I should work for it? Why should its interests have precedence over mine, when these are prima facie different? If the interests of the community define a good that is somehow my good, too — a common good to whose achievement I am morally committed and in which I can rightly share, these questions can have a reasonable answer. But the 'I' that can *thus* share in a good that can in truth be common to all who will rightly meet the requirements of its shared achievement is a free moral agent, not the manipulable end product of whatever processes of social conditioning have successfully been brought to bear on him. Such an 'I' needs reasons for his action that the persuasive reiteration of the word 'community' cannot supply. Is the pressure group that makes demands on me in fact such a community? Is the 'good' in whose name it speaks in truth a common good or rather a false front for interests whose pretensions and claims will not bear rational inspection? It is not in internalized conformity to generalized directives that such questions can be significantly asked or rightly answered. For the answers may well lead to a rejection of demands thus made and to a counter-demand that the social directives of 'the group' be altered for the better achievement of the common good whose interests it claims to represent. Considered in their normative cogency its pretensions are examinable by those who have the concern and capacity to act on them as reasons, i.e., by moral agents, and it is only for such agents that they can have a rationally justifying sense.

What 'social behaviourism' does in practice is to strip the concept of community of this justifying use and sense and at the same time to trade on its persuasive or 'engineering' potency as propaganda. We are still urged to serve 'the community', for 'community' is a 'good' word for manipulative purposes. And 'togetherness' has recently been a very good word indeed, in this use, though it appears now to be losing something of its glamour. That there are ways in which men can be 'together' where, for the good of their soul, they had much better be apart, and that well-fed gregariousness is not as such the moral equivalent of virtue are here considerations 'of no interest' — who in such a 'community' would be concerned or competent to make such a judgment? There is in this use a kind of sentimental cynicism, a combination of tongue in the cheek and tear in the eye that sometimes leaves even the engineer of our attitudes deeply moved. For he, too, is the product of his social environment and is playing out his 'role' as senselessly as are the rest of us. That this is not the role of a moral agent is not surprising. In the world of social behaviourism there is no place for such a role.

It is not, then, by inadvertence, or as a concession to philosophically customary ways of speaking, that we have described the community that makes sense of moral action in morally loaded rather than in sociologically neutral terms. For it is precisely this moral loading which is its normatively relevant and cogent import and it is as considered in this light that the interests of 'the community' make sense as grounds for moral action. The attempt to 'clarify' this sense, or to evade its normatively rational commitments by reducing moral obligation to social pressures is based on a categorial confusion — the confusion it has been our aim throughout to eliminate. We must respectfully refuse to play on the social scientist's team, for it is not his game that we are playing. But ours though moralistic and, by current research standards, old fashioned is a game that all of us are obliged to play, not as professional researchers merely, but as men. It is of some importance therefore that its normative requirements be adequately understood.

There is one further source of misunderstanding that should be noted here. Even if we are careful to distinguish the normative claims of community as moral from the *de facto* pressures of existing social groups, does not a theory that holds that it is only for men as responsible participants in such communities that moral reasons have a moral use require us to conclude that a right action simply *is* one that serves the community of which one is a member? Does not this mean that our duty 'in the end' is just to 'serve and preserve the community'? And what is this but the identification of moral right with the 'service' of existing institutions on the terms that their existing structure sets? In his very enlightening discussion in *Rights and Right Conduct* Melden tells us that 'It is self-evident — analytic — that it is right that one maintain the moral community of which one is a member. There is no further feature over and above this one that is the rightness and that needs to be connected with it'[9]. I do not think that, in its context, this assertion need or should be interpreted as a kind of analytic Hegelianism, a reduction of moral rightness to the maintenance of 'my station and its duties'. But since it has been so interpreted we had best point out, even at the cost of some repetition, that no such implication follows from a theory of the sort here presented. On the contrary, such a theory provides the grounds on which it can, and should, be decisively rejected.

The first thing to be noted is that it is the *moral* community of which Melden speaks, and no existing social institution is *as such*, or as 'socially existing' a community in this sense. It is entitled to this status and can, accordingly, make valid claims of right upon our conduct, only in so far as it can show itself to be, in rationally warrantable terms, a moral order. *Of course*, in so far as the families, or 'teams' or nations or churches of which we are *de facto* members are in this way moral communities it is right that we serve and preserve them, for in so doing we are serving and preserving moral right. No *further* feature needs to be connected with this to establish rightness, for this connection is already made when 'the community' is characterized as in this way moral. But so to characterize existing institutions is to make a claim that sometimes needs very careful scrutiny indeed. That right actions are those that serve a *moral* community is indeed analytic, for in this context, it is a tautology. It tells us that it is right to preserve existing institutions in so far as they are genuinely the embodiment of a moral right which it is our duty to maintain, i.e., that it is right to do right actions. It is illuminating in so far as it refers us to the context in which right can have a moral use and meaning. But as it stands it justifies the *de facto* demands of no existing social institution. It only indicates the light — which is that of moral reason itself — in which we must consider such demands if we are to judge their moral cogency.

Putting the issue in this light enables us to see quite clearly what is wrong with the morality of 'my station and its duties'. For moral relations are essentially and inescapably relations between persons. My duty is not to 'the family' or 'the state' or 'the community' as such. It is to other men united with me in activities whose normatively practical requirements, as mutually acknowledged, can give our common life a moral meaning. My *moral* station in any community is that of such a person, and its duties are not the grooved conformities of the 'organization man' but the responsibilities of one who acts in his own person for a right that makes a valid claim upon his conduct. It is only *in* a social context that he has such duties. But it is only *as* a moral agent that he has them, and what they are is something he, and not the institution, must judge. For institutions have no minds of their own, and only men with minds and wills of their own can constitute a free society. What constitutes a state, in the sense in which the state is a community that rightly claims the loyalty of its citizens? In the words of a poem quoted by Thomas Jefferson, it is not battlements and towers — nor guided missiles, we might add, though these have their uses — but men: 'High-minded men — men who their duties know but know their rights and, knowing, dare maintain. These constitute a State'[10]. This, too, when the state is thought of as a moral community, is an analytic truth. But, for our times particularly, it is an enlightening one.

Moreover, when we understand the concept of community in this sense — and it is in this sense only that we have used it as a moral notion — we can see that our duty is not merely to serve and preserve but to create 'the community'. *What* community? The groups in which we have our moral roots are to some degree communities in this sense. If they were not, we could not have learned in them, as we have, how obligations can be moral reasons. But they are incomplete, one-sided and in many ways parochial in the range and level of their moral understanding. The good reasons we have learned in them are sometimes not good enough for the achievement of an effective moral order in our actual social relations. The communities in which their moral intent could be adequately fulfilled has still in large measure, and under great difficulties, to be built. To treat the limits of existing social acceptances or institutional organization as the ultimate boundaries of such understanding whose 'preservation' is our final duty would be a betrayal of the continuing work to which, in the use of moral reasons, we are rationally and morally committed. Those who have not seen this still do not adequately understand the sense and use of moral reasons.

The main conceptual outlines of our theory of practical reasons have now been drawn. We have said, and tried to show, that in their appropriate use its categories make rational sense and that this sense is practically relevant to our conduct. So far this relevance has been indicated only in a rather general way. But it is not the business of moral philosophy to end in generalities. The cogency of such a theory is to be found not in its own inner luminosity but in what, in its light, we can understand about the right solutions of our moral problems....

Notes

---

1 Charles Hartshorne and Paul Weiss (eds), *Collected Papers of Charles Sanders Peirce* (Cambridge, Mass., 1931), chapter I, paragraph 666.
2 In 'Legal and Moral Obligation', in A.I. Melden (ed.), *Essays in Moral Philosophy* (Seattle, 1958), p. 101.
3 *The Place of Reason in Ethics* (Cambridge, 1950), p. 170.
4 'Two Concepts of Rules', *The Philosophical Review* (January 1955), p. 16.
5 Ibid., p. 32.
6 Op. cit., p. 82.
7 Op. cit.
8 Op. cit.
9 A.I. Melden, *Rights and Right Conduct* (Oxford, 1959), p. 71.
10 In a letter to John Taylor, dated 28 May 1816. The letter is printed in *The Life and Selected Writings of Thomas Jefferson* (New York, 1944), pp. 668-73.

14

Oppression

SIMONE WEIL

Among all the forms of social organization which history has to show, there are very few which appear to be really free from oppression; and these few are not very well known. All of them correspond to an extremely low level of production, so low that the division of labour is pretty well unknown, except between the sexes, and each family produces little more than its own requirements. It is sufficiently obvious, moreover, that such material conditions necessarily rule out oppression, since each man, compelled to sustain himself personally, is continually at grips with outside nature; war itself, at this stage, is war of pillage and extermination, not of conquest, because the means of consolidating a conquest and especially of turning it to account are lacking. What is surprising is not that oppression should make its appearance only after higher forms of economy have been reached, but that it should always accompany them. This means, therefore, that as between a completely primitive economy and more highly developed forms of economy there is a difference not only of degree, but also of kind. And, in fact, although from the point of view of consumption there is but a change-over to slightly better conditions, production, which is the decisive factor, is itself transformed in its very essence. This transformation consists at first sight in a progressive emancipation

Reprinted from Simone Weil, Oppression and Liberty (*Routledge and Kegan Paul, 1965, newly issued 1973*), pp. 500-10, *by the permission of the publisher.*

with respect to nature. In completely primitive forms of production — hunting, fishing, gathering — human effort appears as a simple reaction to the inexorable pressure continually exercised on man by nature, and that in two ways. To start with, it takes place, to all intents and purposes, under immediate compulsion, under the ever-present spur of natural needs; and, by an indirect consequence, the action seems to receive its form from nature herself, owing to the important part played therein by an intuition comparable to animal instinct and a patient observation of the most frequent natural phenomena, also owing to the indefinite repetition of methods that have often succeeded without men's knowing why, and which are doubtless regarded as being welcomed by nature with special favour. At this stage, each man is necessarily free with respect to other men, because he is in direct contact with the conditions of his own existence, and because nothing human interposes itself between them and him; but, on the other hand, and to the same extent, he is narrowly subjected to nature's dominion, and he shows this clearly enough by deifying her. At higher stages of production, nature's compulsion continues certainly to be exercised, and still pitilessly, but in an apparently less immediate fashion; it seems to become more and more liberalized and to leave an increasing margin to man's freedom of choice, to his faculty of initiative and decision. Action is no longer tied moment by moment to nature's exigencies; men learn how to store up reserves on a long-term basis for meeting needs not yet actually felt; efforts which can be only of indirect usefulness become more and more numerous; at the same time a systematic co-ordination in time and in space becomes possible and necessary, and its importance increases continually. In short, man seems to pass by stages, with respect to nature, from servitude to dominion. At the same time nature gradually loses her divine character, and divinity more and more takes on human shape. Unfortunately, this emancipation is only a flattering semblance. In reality, at these higher stages, human action continues, as a whole, to be nothing but pure obedience to the brutal spur of an immediate necessity; only, instead of being harried by nature, man is henceforth harried by man. However, it is still the same pressure exerted by nature that continues to make itself felt, although indirectly; for oppression is exercised by force, and in the long run all force originates in nature.

The notion of force is far from simple, and yet it is the first that has to be elucidated in order to formulate the problems of society. Force and oppression — that makes two; but what needs to be understood above all is that it is not the manner in which use is made of some particular force, but its very nature, which determines whether it is oppressive or not. Marx clearly perceived this in connection with the State; he understood that this machine for grinding men down, cannot stop grinding as long as it goes on functioning, no matter in whose hands it may be. But this insight has a far more general application. Oppression proceeds exclusively from objective conditions. The first of these is the existence of privileges; and it is not men's laws or decrees which determine privileges, nor yet titles to property; it is the very nature of things. Certain circumstances, which correspond to stages, no doubt inevitable, in human development, give rise to forces which come between the ordinary man and his own conditions of existence, between the effort and the fruit of the effort, and which are, inherently, the monopoly of a few, owing to the fact that they cannot be shared among all; thenceforward these privileged beings, although they depend, in order to live, on the work of others, hold in their hands the fate of the very people on whom they depend, and equality is destroyed. This is what happens to begin with when the religion rites by which man thinks to win nature over to his side, having become too numerous and complicated to be known by all, finally become the secret and consequently the monopoly of a few priests; the priest then disposes, albeit only through a fiction, of all of nature's powers, and it is in their name that he exercises authority. Nothing essential is changed when this monopoly is no longer made up of rites but of scientific processes, and when those in possession of it are called scientists and technicians instead of priests.

Arms, too, give rise to a privilege from the day when, on the one hand, they are sufficiently powerful to render any defence by unarmed against armed men impossible, and, on the other, the handling of them has become sufficiently advanced, and consequently difficult, to require a long apprenticeship and continuous practice. For henceforth the workers are powerless to defend themselves, whereas the warriors, albeit incapable of production, can always take forcible possession of the fruits of other people's labour; the workers are thus at the mercy of the warriors, and not the other way about. The same thing applies to gold, and more generally to money, as soon as the division of labour is so far developed that no worker can live off his own products without having exchanged at any rate some of them for those of others; the organization of exchange then becomes necessarily the monopoly of a few specialists who, having money under their control, can both obtain for themselves, in order to live, the products of others' labour, and at the same time deprive the producers of the indispensably necessary.

In short, wherever, in the struggle against men or against nature, efforts need to be multiplied and co-ordinated to be effective, co-ordination becomes the monopoly of a few leaders as soon as it reaches a certain degree of complexity, and execution's primary law is then obedience; this is true both for the management of public affairs and for that of private undertakings. There may be other sources of privilege, but these are the chief ones; furthermore, except in the case of money, which appears at a given moment of history, all these factors enter into play under all systems of oppression; what changes is the way in which they are distributed and combined, the degree of concentration of power, and also the more or less closed and consequently more or less mysterious character of each monopoly. Nevertheless, privileges, of themselves, are not sufficient to cause oppression. Inequality could be easily mitigated by the resistance of the weak and the feeling for justice of the strong; it would not lead to a still harsher form of necessity than that of natural needs themselves, were it not for the intervention of a further factor, namely, the struggle for power.

As Marx clearly understood in the case of capitalism, and as a few moralists have perceived in a more general way, power contains a sort of fatality which weighs as pitilessly on those who command as on those who obey; nay more, it is in so far as it enslaves the former that, through their agency, it presses down upon the latter. The struggle against nature entails certain escapable necessities which nothing can turn aside, but these necessities contain within themselves their own limits; nature resists, but she does not defend herself, and where she alone is involved, each situation presents certain well-defined obstacles which arouse the best in human effort. It is altogether different as soon as relations between man and man take the place of direct contact between man and nature. The preservation of power is a vital necessity for the powerful, since it is their power which provides their sustenance; but they have to preserve it both against their rivals and against their inferiors, and these latter cannot do otherwise than try to rid themselves of dangerous masters; for, through a vicious circle, the master produces fear in the slave by the very fact that he is afraid of him, and vice versa; and the same is true as between rival powers.

What is more, the two struggles that every man of power has to wage — first against those over whom he rules, secondly against his rivals — are inextricably bound up together and each is all the time rekindling the other. A power, whatever it may be, must always tend towards strengthening itself at home by means of successes gained abroad, for such successes provide it with more powerful means of coercion; besides, the struggle against its rivals rallies behind it its own slaves, who are under the illusion they have a personal interest in the result of the battle. But, in order to obtain from the slaves the obedience and sacrifices indispensable to victory, that power has to make itself more oppressive; to be in a position to exercise this oppression, it is still more imperatively compelled to turn outwards; and so on. We can follow out the same chain of events by starting from another link; show how a given social group, in order to be in a position to defend itself against the outside powers threatening to lay hands on it, must itself submit to an oppressive form of authority; how the power thus set up, in order to maintain its position, must stir up conflicts with rival powers; and so on, once again. Thus it is that the most fatal of vicious circles drags the whole society in the wake of its masters in a mad merry-go-round.

There are only two ways of breaking the circle, either by abolishing inequality, or else by setting up a stable power, a power such that there exists a balance between those who command and those who obey. It is this second solution that has been sought by all whom we call upholders of order, or at any rate all those among them who have been moved neither by servility nor by ambition; it was doubtless so with the Latin writers who praised 'the immense majesty of the Roman peace', with Dante, with the reactionary school at the beginning of the nineteenth century, with Balzac, and is so today with sincere and thoughtful men of the Right. But this stability of power — objective of those who call themselves realists — shows itself to be a chimera, if one examines it closely, on the same grounds as the anarchists' Utopia.

Between man and matter, each action, whether successful or not, establishes a balance that can only be upset from outside; for matter is inert. A displaced stone accepts its new position; the wind consents to guide to her destination the same ship which it would have sent off her course if sails and rudder had not been properly adjusted. But men are essentially active beings and have a faculty of self-determination which they can never renounce, even should they so desire, except on the day when, through death, they drop back into the state of inert matter; so that every victory won over men contains within itself the germ of a possible defeat, unless it goes as far as extermination. But extermination abolishes power by abolishing its object. Thus there is, in the very essence of power, a fundamental contradiction that prevents it from ever existing in the true sense of the word; those who are called the masters, ceaselessly compelled to reinforce their power for fear of seeing it snatched away from them, are for ever seeking a dominion essentially impossible to attain; beautiful illustrations of this search are offered by the infernal torments in Greek mythology. It would be otherwise if one man could possess in himself a force superior to that of many other men put together; but such is never the case; the instruments of power — arms, gold, machines, magical or technical secrets — always exist independently of him who disposes of them, and can be taken up by others. Consequently all power is unstable.

Generally speaking, among human beings, since the relationships between rulers and ruled are never fully acceptable, they always constitute an irremediable disequilibrium which is continually aggravating itself; the same is true even in the sphere of private life, where love, for example, destroys all balance in the soul as soon as it seeks to dominate or to be dominated by its object. But here at any rate there is nothing external to prevent reason from returning and putting everything to rights by establishing liberty and equality; whereas social relationships, in so far as the very methods of labour and of warfare rule out equality, seem to cause madness to weigh down on mankind in the manner of an external fatality. For, owing to the fact that there is never power, but only a race for power, and that there is no term, no limit, no proportion set to this race, neither is there any limit or proportion set to the efforts that it exacts; those who give themselves up to it, compelled to do always better than their rivals, who in their turn strive to do better than they, must sacrifice not only the existence of the slaves, but their own also and that of their nearest and dearest; so it is that Agamemnon sacrificing his daughter lives again in the capitalists who, to maintain their privileges, acquiesce lightheartedly in wars that may rob them of their sons.

Thus the race for power enslaves everybody, strong and weak alike. Marx saw this clearly with reference to the capitalist system. Rosa Luxemburg used to inveigh against the aspect of 'aimless merry-go-round' presented by the Marxist picture of capitalist accumulation, that picture in which consumption appears as a 'necessary evil' to be reduced to the minimum, a mere means for keeping alive those who devote themselves, whether as leaders or as workers, to the supreme object, which is none other than the manufacture of capital equipment, that is to say of the means of production. And yet it is the profound absurdity of this picture which gives it its profound truth; a truth which extends singularly beyond the framework of the capitalist system. The only characteristic peculiar to this system is that the instruments of industrial production are at the same time the chief weapons in the race for power; but always the methods pursued in the race for power, whatever they may be, bring men under their subjection through the same frenzy and impose themselves on them as absolute ends. It is the reflection of this frenzy that lends an epic grandeur to works such as the *Comédie Humaine*, Shakespeare's *Histories*, the *chansons de geste*, or the *Iliad*. The real subject of the *Iliad* is the sway exercised by war over the warriors, and, through them, over humanity in general; none of them knows why each sacrifices himself and all his family to a bloody and aimless war, and that is why, all through the poem, it is the gods who are credited with the mysterious influence which nullifies peace negotiations, continually revives hostilities, and brings together again the contending forces urged by a flash of good sense to abandon the struggle.

Thus in this ancient and wonderful poem there already appears the essential evil besetting humanity, the substitution of means for ends. At times war occupies the forefront, at other times the search for wealth, at other times production; but the evil remains the same. The common run of moralists complain that man is moved by his private interest: would to heaven it were so! Private interest is a self-centred principle of action, but at the same time, restricted, reasonable and incapable of giving rise to unlimited evils. Whereas, on the other hand, the law of all activities governing social life, except in the case of primitive communities, is that here each one sacrifices human life — in himself and in others — to things which are only means to a better way of living. This sacrifice takes on various forms, but it all comes back to the question of power. Power, by definition, is only a means; or to put it better, to possess a power is simply to possess means of action which exceed the very limited force that a single individual has at his disposal. But power-seeking, owing to its essential incapacity to seize hold of its object, rules out all consideration of an end, and finally comes, through an inevitable reversal, to take the place of all ends. It is this reversal of the relationship between means and end, it is this fundamental folly that accounts for all that is senseless and bloody right through history. Human history is simply the history of the servitude which makes men — oppressors and oppressed alike — the plaything of the instruments of domination they themselves have manufactured, and thus reduces living humanity to being the chattel of inanimate chattels.

Thus it is things, not men, that prescribe the limits and laws governing this giddy race for power. Men's desires are powerless to control it. The masters may well dream of moderation, but they are prohibited from practising this virtue, on pain of defeat, except to a very slight extent; so that, apart from a few almost miraculous exceptions, such as Marcus Aurelius, they quickly become incapable even of conceiving it. As for the oppressed, their permanent revolt, which is always simmering, though it only breaks out now and then, can operate in such a way as to aggravate the evil as well as to restrict it; and on the whole it rather constitutes an aggravating factor in that it forces the masters to make their power weigh ever more heavily for fear of losing it.

From time to time the oppressed manage to drive out one team of oppressors and to replace it by another, and sometimes even to change the form of oppression; but as for abolishing oppression itself, that would first mean abolishing the sources of it, abolishing all the monopolies, the magical and technical secrets that give a hold over nature, armaments, money, co-ordination of labour. Even if the oppressed were sufficiently conscious to make up their minds to do so, they could not succeed. It would be condemning themselves to immediate enslavement by the social groupings that had not carried the same change; and even were this danger to be miraculously averted, it would be condemning themselves to death, for, once men have forgotten the methods of primitive production and have transformed the natural environment into which these fitted, they cannot recover immediate contact with nature.

It follows that, in spite of so many vague desires to put an end to madness and oppression, the concentration of power and the aggravation of its tyrannical character would know no bounds were these not by good fortune found in the nature of things. It behoves us to determine roughly what these bounds can be; and for this purpose we must keep in mind the fact that, if oppression is a necessity of social life, this necessity has nothing providential about it. It is not because it becomes detrimental to production that oppression can come to an end; the 'revolt of the productive forces', so naïvely invoked by Trotsky as a factor in history, is a pure fiction. We should be mistaken likewise in assuming that oppression ceases to be ineluctable as soon as the productive forces have been sufficiently developed to ensure welfare and leisure for all. Aristotle admitted that there would no longer be anything to stand in the way of the abolition of slavery if it were possible to have the indispensable jobs done by 'mechanical slaves', and when Marx attempted to forecast the future of the human species, all he did was to take up this idea and develop it. It would be true if men were guided by considerations of welfare; but from the days of the *Iliad* to our own times, the senseless demands made by the struggle for power have taken away even the leisure for thinking about welfare. The raising of the output of human effort will remains powerless to lighten the load of this effort as long as the social structure implies the reversal of the relationship between means and ends, in other words, as long as the methods of labour and of warfare give to a few men a discretionary power over the masses; for the fatigues and privations that have become unnecessary in the struggle against nature will be absorbed by the war carried on between men for the defence or acquisition of privileges. Once society is divided up into men who command and men who execute, the whole of social life is governed by the struggle for power, and the struggle for subsistence only enters in as one factor, indispensable to be sure, of the former.

The Marxist view, according to which social existence is determined by the relations between man and nature established by production, certainly remains the only sound basis for any historical investigation; only these relations must be considered first of all in terms of the problem of power, the means of subsistence forming simply one of the data of this problem. This order seems absurd, but it merely reflects the essential absurdity lying at the very heart of social life. A scientific study of history would thus be a study of the actions and reactions which are perpetually arising between the organization of power and the methods of production; for although power depends on the material conditions of life, it never ceases to transform these conditions themselves. Such a study goes very far beyond our possibilities at the moment; but before grappling with the infinite complexity of the facts, it is useful to make an abstract diagram of this interplay of actions and reactions, rather in the same way as astronomers have had to invent an imaginary celestial sphere so as to find their way about among the movements and positions of the stars.

We must try first of all to draw up a list of the inevitable necessities which limit all species of power. In the first place, any sort of power relies upon instruments which have in each situation a given scope. Thus you do not command in the same way, by means of soldiers armed with bows and arrows, spears and swords, as you do by means of aeroplanes and incendiary bombs; the power of gold depends on the role played by exchanges in economic life; that of technical secrets is measured by the difference between what you can accomplish without them; and so on. As a matter of fact, one must always include in this balance-sheet the subterfuges by which the powerful obtain through persuasion what they are totally unable to obtain by force, either by placing the oppressed in a situation such that they have or think they have an immediate interest in doing what is asked of them, or by inspiring them with a fanaticism calculated to make them accept any and every sacrifice. Secondly, since the power that a human being really exercises extends only to what is effectively under his control, power is always running up against the actual limits of the controlling faculty, and these are extremely narrow. For no single mind can encompass a whole mass of ideas at once; no man can be in several places at once; and for master and slave alike there are never more than twenty-four hours in a day. Collaboration apparently constitutes a remedy for this drawback; but as it is never absolutely free from rivalry, it gives rise to infinite complications. The faculties of examining, comparing, weighing, deciding, combining are essentially individual, and consequently the same thing applies also to power, whose exercise is inseparable from these faculties; collective power is a fiction, at any rate in final analysis. As for the number of interests that can come under the control of one single man, that depends to a very large extent on individual factors such as breadth and quickness of intelligence, capacity for work, firmness of character; but it also depends on the objective conditions of the control exercised, more or less rapid methods of transport and communication, simplicity or otherwise of the machinery of power. Lastly, the exercise of any form of power is subject to the existence of a surplus in the production of commodities, and a sufficiently large surplus so that all those engaged, whether as masters or as slaves, in the struggle for power, may be able to live. Obviously, the extent of such surplus depends on the methods of production, and consequently also on the social organization. Here, therefore, are three factors that enable one to conceive political and social power as constituting at each moment something analogous to a measurable force. However, in order to complete the picture one must bear in mind that the men who find themselves in relationship, whether as masters or as slaves, with the phenomenon of power are unconscious of this analogy. The powerful, be they priests, military leaders, kings or capitalists, always believe that they command by divine right; and those who are under them feel themselves crushed by a power which seems to them either divine or diabolical, but in any case supernatural. Every oppressive society is cemented by this religion of power, which falsifies all social relations by enabling the powerful to command over and above what they are able to impose; it is only otherwise in times of popular agitation, times when, on the contrary, all — rebellious slaves and threatened masters alike — forget how heavy and how solid the chains of oppression are.

Thus a scientific study of history ought to begin by analysing the reactions brought to bear at each moment by power on the conditions which assign to it objectively its limits; and a hypothetical sketch of the play of these reactions is indispensable in order to conduct such an analysis, far too difficult, incidentally, considering our present possibilities. Some of these reactions are conscious and willed. Every power consciously strives, in proportion to the means at its disposal — a proportion determined by the social organization — to improve production and official control within its own sphere; history offers many an example of this, from the Pharaohs down to the present day, and it is on this that the notion of enlightened despotism is founded. On the other hand, every power strives also, and again consciously, to destroy among its competitors the means whereby to produce and govern, and is the object on their part of a similar attempt. Thus the struggle for power is at the same time constructive and destructive, and brings about economic progress or decadence, depending on whichever aspect wins the day; and it is clear that in a given civilization destruction will take place to an extent all the greater the more difficult it is for a power to expand without coming up against rival powers approximately as strong as itself. But the indirect consequences of the exercise of power are far more important than the conscious efforts of the wielders of power.

Every power, from the mere fact that it is exercised, extends to the farthest possible limit the social relations on which it is based; thus military power multiplies wars, commercial capital multiplies exchanges. Now it sometimes happens, through a sort of providential accident, that this extension gives rise, by some mechanism or other, to new resources that make a new extension possible, and so on, more or less in the same way as food strengthens living beings in full process of growth and enables them thus to win still more food so as to acquire still greater strength. All régimes provide examples of such providential accidents; for without them no form of power could endure, and consequently those powers that benefit from them are the only ones to subsist. Thus war enabled the Romans to carry off slaves, that is to say workers in the prime of life, whom others had had to provide for during childhood; the profit derived from slave labour made it possible to reinforce the army, and the stronger army undertook more important wars which brought in new and bigger consignments of slaves as booty. Similarly, the roads which the Romans built for military purposes later facilitated the government and exploitation of the conquered provinces, and thus contributed towards storing up resources for future wars.

If we turn now to modern times, we see, for example, that the extension of exchanges has brought about a greater division of labour, which in its turn has made a wider circulation of commodities indispensable; furthermore, the increased productivity which has resulted from this has furnished new resources that have been able to transform themselves into commercial and industrial capital. As far as big industry is concerned, it is clear that each important advance in mechanization has created at the same time resources, instruments and a stimulus towards a further advance. Similarly, it was the technique of big industry which came to provide the means of control and information indispensable to the centralized economy that is the inevitable outcome of big industry, such as the telegraph, the telephone, the daily press. The same may be said with regard to the means of transport. One could find all through history an immense number of similar examples, bearing on the widest and the narrowest aspects of social life. One may define the growth of a system by the fact that all it needs to do is to function in order to create new resources enabling it to function on a larger scale.

This phenomenon of automatic development is so striking that one would be tempted to imagine that a happily constituted system, if one may so express it, would go on enduring the progressing endlessly. That is exactly what the nineteenth century, socialists included, imagined with regard to the system of big industry. But if it is easy to imagine in a vague way an oppressive system that would never fall into decadence, it is no longer the same if one wants to conceive clearly and concretely the indefinite extension of a specific power. If it could extend endlessly its means of control, it would tend indefinitely towards a limit which would be something like ubiquity; if it could extend its resources endlessly, everything would be as though surrounding nature were evolving gradually towards that unqualified abundance from which Adam and Eve benefited in the earthly paradise; and, finally, if it could extend indefinitely the range of its own instruments — whether it be a question of arms, gold, technical secrets, machines or anything else — it would tend towards abolishing that correlation which, by indissolubly linking together the notions of master and of slave, establishes between master and slave a relationship of mutual dependence.

One cannot prove that all this is impossible; but one must assume that it is impossible, or else decide to think of human history as a fairy-tale. In general, one can only regard the world in which we live as subject to laws if one admits that every phenomenon in it is limited; and it is the same for the phenomenon of power, as Plato had understood. If we want to consider power as a conceivable phenomenon, we must think that it can extend the foundations on which it rests up to a certain point only, after which it comes up, as it were, against an impassable wall. But even so it is not in a position to stop; the spur of competition forces it to go ever farther and farther, that is to say to go beyond the limits within which it can be effectively exercised. It extends beyond what it is able to control; it commands over and above what it can impose; it spends in excess of its own resources. Such is the internal contradiction which every oppressive system carries within itself like a seed of death; it is made up of the opposition between the necessarily limited character of the material bases of power and the necessarily unlimited character of the race for power considered as relationship between men.

For as soon as a power goes beyond the limits assigned to it by the nature of things, it narrows down the bases on which it rests, renders these limits themselves narrower and narrower. By spreading beyond what it is able to control, it breeds a parasitism, a waste, a confusion which, once they have appeared, increase automatically. By attempting to command where actually it is not in a position to compel obedience, it provokes reactions which it can neither foresee nor deal with. Finally, by wishing to spread the exploitation of the oppressed beyond what the objective resources make possible, it exhausts these resources themselves; this is doubtless what is meant by the ancient and popular tale of the goose with the golden eggs. Whatever may be the sources from whence the exploiters draw the material goods which they appropriate, a day arrives when such and such a method of development, which was at first, as it went on spreading, more and more productive, finally becomes, on the other hand, increasingly costly. That is how the Roman army, which had first of all brought wealth to Rome, ended by ruining it; that is how the knights of the Middle Ages, whose battles had first of all brought a relative security to the peasants, who found themselves to a certain extent protected against acts of brigandage, ended in the course of their interminable wars by laying waste the countryside which fed them; and it certainly seems as though capitalism is passing through a phase of this kind. Once more, it cannot be proved that it must always be so; but it has to be assumed, unless the possibility of inexhaustible resources is also assumed. Thus it is the nature itself of things which constitutes that justice-dealing divinity the Greeks worshipped under the name of Nemesis, and which punishes excess.

When a specific form of domination finds itself thus arrested in its development and faced with decadence, it does not follow that it begins to disappear progressively; sometimes it is then, on the contrary, that it becomes most harshly oppressive, that it crushes human beings under its weight, that it grinds down body, heart and spirit without mercy. However, since everyone begins little by little to feel the lack of the resources required by some to maintain their supremacy, by others to live, a time comes when, on every hand, there is a feverish search for expedients. There is no reason why such a search should not remain fruitless; and in that case the régime can only end by collapsing for want of the means of subsistence and being replaced, not by another and better organized régime, but by a disorder, a poverty, a primitive condition of existence which continue until some new factor or other gives rise to new relationships of force. If it happens otherwise, if the search for new material resources is successful, new patterns of social life arise and a change of régime begins to form slowly and, as it were, subterraneously. Subterraneously, because these new forms can only develop in so far as they are compatible with the established order and do not represent, in appearance at any rate, any danger for the powers that be; otherwise nothing could prevent these powers from destroying them, so long as they remain the stronger. For the new social patterns to triumph over the old, this continued development must already have brought them to play effectively a more important role in the functioning of the social organism; in other words, they must have given rise to more powerful forces than those at the disposal of the official authorities. Thus there is never really any break in continuity, not even when the change of régime seems to be the result of a bloody struggle; for all that victory then does is to sanction forces that, even before the struggle, were the decisive factor in the life of the community, social patterns that had long since begun gradually to replace those on which the declining régime rested. So it was that, under the Roman Empire, the barbarians had begun to occupy the most important posts, the army was disintegrating little by little into armed bands led by adventurers, and the system of military colonies gradually replaced slavery by serfdom — all this long before the great invasions. Similarly, the French bourgeoisie did not by any means wait until 1789 to get the better of the nobility. The Russian Revolution, thanks to a singular conjunction of circumstances, certainly seemed to give rise to something entirely new; but the truth is that the privileges it abolished had not for a long time rested on any social foundation other than tradition; that the institutions arising out of the insurrection did not perhaps effectively function for as long as a single morning; and that the real forces, namely big industry, the police, the army, the bureaucracy, far from being smashed by the Revolution, attained, thanks to it, a power unknown in other countries.

Generally speaking, the sudden reversal of the relationship between forces which is what we usually understand by the term 'revolution' is not only a phenomenon unknown in history, but furthermore, if we examine it closely, something literally inconceivable, for it would be a victory of weakness over force, the equivalent of a balance whose lighter scale were to go down. What history offers us is slow transformations of régimes, in which the bloody events to which we give the name 'revolutions' play a very secondary role, and from which they may even be absent; such is the case when the social class which ruled in the name of the old relationships of force manages to keep a part of the power under cover of the new relationships, and the history of England supplies an example. But whatever may be the patterns taken by social transformations, all one finds, if one tries to lay bare the mechanism, is a dreary play of blind forces that unite together or clash, that progress or decline, that replace each other, without ever ceasing to grind beneath them the unfortunate race of human beings. At first sight there seems to be no weak spot in this sinister mesh of circumstances through which an attempt at deliverance might find its way. But it is not from such a vague, abstract and miserably hasty sketch as this that one can claim to draw any conclusion.

We must pose once again the fundamental problem, namely, what constitutes the bond which seems hitherto to have united social oppression and progress in the relations between man and nature? If one considers human development as a whole up to our own time, if, above all, one contrasts primitive tribes, organized practically without inequality, with our present-day civilization, it seems as if man cannot manage to lighten the yoke imposed by natural necessities without an equal increase in the weight of that imposed by social oppression, as though by the play of a mysterious equilibrium.

And even, what is stranger still, it would seem that if, in fact, the human collectivity has to a large extent freed itself from the crushing burden which the gigantic forces of nature place on frail humanity, it has, on the other hand, taken in some sort nature's place to the point of crushing the individual in a similar manner.

What makes primitive man a slave? The fact that he hardly orders his own activity at all; he is the plaything of need, which dictates each of his movements or very nearly, and harries him with its relentless spur; and his actions are regulated not by his own intelligence, but by the customs and caprices — both equally incomprehensible — of a nature that he can but worship with blind submission. If we consider simply the collectivity, men seem nowadays to have raised themselves to a condition that is diametrically the opposite of that servile state. Hardly a single one of their tasks constitutes a mere response to the imperative impulsion of need; work is accomplished in such a way as to take charge of nature and to organize her so that needs can be satisfied. Humanity no longer believes itself to be in the presence of capricious divinities whose good graces must be won over; it knows that it has merely to handle inert matter, and acquits itself of this task by methodically following out clearly conceived laws. At last we seem to have reached that epoch predicted by Descartes when men would use 'the force and actions of fire, water, air, the stars and all the other bodies' in the same way as they do the artisans' tools, and would thus make themselves masters of nature. But, by a strange inversion, this collective dominion transforms itself into servitude as soon as one descends to the scale of the individual, and into a servitude fairly closely resembling that associated with primitive conditions of existence.

The efforts of the modern worker are imposed on him by a constraint as brutal, as pitiless and which holds him in as tight a grip as hunger does the primitive hunter. From the time of that primitive hunter up to that of the worker in our large factories, passing by way of the Egyptian workers driven by the lash, the slaves of antiquity, the serfs of the Middle Ages constantly threatened by the seigniorial sword, men have never ceased to be goaded to work by some outside force and on pain of almost immediate death. And as for the sequence of movements in work, that, too, is often imposed from outside on our workers, exactly as in the case of primitive men, and is as mysterious for the ones as it was for the others; what is more, in this respect, the constraint is in certain cases incomparably more brutal today than it has ever been. However tied and bound a primitive man was to routine and blind gropings, he could at least try to think things out, to combine and innovate at his own risk, a liberty which is absolutely denied to a worker engaged in a production line. Lastly, if humanity appears to have reached the stage of controlling those forces of nature which, however, in Spinoza's words, 'infinitely surpass those of mankind' — and that in almost as sovereign a fashion as a rider controls his horse — that victory does not belong to men taken individually; only the largest collectivities are in a position to handle 'the force and actions of fire, water, air... and all other bodies that surround us'; as for the members of these collectivities, both oppressors and oppressed are alike subjected to the implacable demands of the struggle for power.

Thus, in spite of progress, man has not emerged from the servile condition in which he found himself when he was handed over weak and naked to all the blind forces that make up the universe; it is merely that the power which keeps him on his knees has been as it were transferred from inert matter to the human society of which he is a member. That is why it is this society which is imposed on his worship through all the various forms that religious feeling takes in turn. Hence the social question poses itself in a fairly clear manner; the mechanism of this transfer must be examined; we must try to find out why man has had to pay this price for his power over nature; form an idea of what would constitute the least unhappy position for him to be in, that is to say the one in which he would be the least enslaved to the twin domination of nature and society; and lastly, discern what roads can lead towards such a position, and what instruments present-day civilization could place in men's hands if they aspired to transform their lives in this way.

We accept material progress too easily as a gift of the gods, as something which goes without saying; we must look fairly and squarely at the conditions at the cost of which it takes place. Primitive life is something easy to understand; man is spurred on by hunger, or at any rate by the anguished thought that he will soon go hungry, and he sets off in search of food; he shivers in the cold, or at any rate at the thought that he will soon feel cold, and he goes in search of heat-creating or heat-preserving materials; and so on. As for the way in which to set about the matter, this is given him in the first place by the habit acquired in childhood of imitating his seniors, and also as a result of the habits which he has given himself in the course of innumerable tentative efforts, by repeating those methods which have succeeded; when caught off his guard, he continues to proceed by trial and error, spurred on as he is to act by a sharp urge which never leaves him a moment's peace. In all this process, man has only to yield to his own nature, not master it.

On the other hand, as soon as we pass to a more advanced stage of civilization, everything becomes miraculous. Men are then found laying by things that are good to consume, desirable things, which they nevertheless go without. They are found giving up to a large extent the search for food, warmth, etc., and spending the best part of their energy on apparently unprofitable labours. As a matter of fact, most of these labours, far from being unprofitable, are infinitely more profitable than the efforts of primitive man, for they result in an organization of outside nature in a manner favourable to human existence; but this efficacy is indirect and often separated from the actual effort by so many intermediaries that the mind has difficulty in covering them; it is a long-term efficacy, often so long-term that it is only future generations which will benefit from it; while, on the other hand, the utter fatigue, physical pains and dangers connected with these labours are felt immediately, and all the time. Now, everybody knows from his own experience how unusual it is for an abstract idea having a long-term utility to triumph over present pains, needs and desires. It must, however, do so in the matter of social existence, on pain of a regression to a primitive form of life.

But what is more miraculous still is the co-ordination of labour. Any reasonably high level of production presupposes a more or less extensive co-operation; and co-operation shows itself in the fact that the efforts of each one have meaning and efficacy only through their relationship to and exact correspondence with the efforts of all the rest, in such a way that all the efforts together form one single collective piece of work. In other words, the movements of several men must be combined according to the manner in which the movements of a single man are combined. But how can this be done? A combination can only take place if it is intellectually conceived; while a relationship is never formed except within one mind. The number 2 thought of by one man cannot be added to the number 2 thought of by another man so as to make up the number 4; similarly, the idea that one of the co-operators has of the partial work he is carrying out cannot be combined with the idea that each of the others has of his respective task so as to form a coherent piece of work. Several human minds cannot become united in one collective mind, and the expressions 'collective soul', 'collective thought', so commonly employed nowadays, are altogether devoid of meaning. Consequently, for the efforts of several to be combined, they all need to be directed by one and the same mind, as the famous line in *Faust* expresses it: 'One mind is enough for a thousand hands.'

In the egalitarian organization of primitive tribes, it is not possible to solve a single one of these problems, neither that of privation, nor that of incentive to effort, nor that of co-ordination of labour; on the other hand, social oppression provides an immediate solution, by creating, to put it broadly, two categories of men — those who command and those who obey. The leader co-ordinates without difficulty the efforts of those who are under his orders; he has no temptation to overcome in order to reduce them to what is strictly necessary; and as for the stimulus to effort, an oppressive organization is admirably equipped for driving men beyond the limit of their strength, some being whipped by ambition, others, in Homer's words, 'under the goad of a harsh necessity'.

The results are often extraordinary when the division between social categories is deep enough for those who decide what work shall be done never to be exposed to feeling or even knowing about the exhausting fatigue, the pains and the dangers of it, while those who do it and suffer have no choice, being continually under the sway of a more or less disguised menace of death. Thus it is that man escapes to a certain extent from the caprices of blind nature only by handing himself over to the no less blind caprices of the struggle for power. This is never truer than when man reaches — as in our case — a technical development sufficiently advanced to give him the mastery over the forces of nature; for, in order that this may be so, co-operation has to take place on such a vast scale that the leaders find they have to deal with a mass of affairs which lie utterly beyond their capacity to control. As a result, humanity finds itself as much the plaything of the forces of nature, in the new form that technical progress has given them, as it ever was in primitive times; we have had, are having, and will continue to have bitter experience of this. As for attempts to preserve technique while shaking off oppression, they at once provoke such laziness and such confusion that those who have engaged in them are more often than not obliged to place themselves again almost immediately under the yoke; the experiment was tried out on a small scale in the producers' co-operatives, on a vast scale at the time of the Russian Revolution. It would seem that man is born a slave, and that servitude is his natural condition.

15
Alienation and anomie[1]

STEVEN LUKES

Both Marx and Durkheim were profound critics of industrial society
in nineteenth-century Europe. What is striking is the markedly
different bases of their criticisms of the ills of their societies, which
can best be brought out by a careful consideration of the different
assumptions and implications that belong to the two concepts of
alienation and anomie, which they respectively employed[2]. These
concepts were elaborated by the two thinkers in their earliest
writings and remain implicit as basic and integral elements in their
developed social theories. Thus a study of the differing perspectives
which they manifest should be fruitful. I shall argue: first, that they
are both socio-psychological concepts, embodying hypotheses about
specific relationships between social conditions and individual
psychological states; second, that they differ precisely in the sorts of
hypotheses they embody; and third that this difference derives in
part from a fundamental divergence in the views of human nature
they presuppose. Fourth, I shall examine the nature of that
divergence, and in particular the extent to which the dispute is an
empirical one. I shall conclude by asking to what extent such
approaches to the analysis of society remain relevant and important
today.

First, however, I need to make the negative point that contemporary

Reprinted from P. Laslett and W.G. Runciman (eds), Philosophy, Politics and
Society, Third Series (Blackwell, 1967), pp. 134-56, by permission of A.D. Peters
and Company.

uses of the notions of alienation and anomie, while claiming to derive from Marx and Durkheim, are not for our purposes a useful starting-point. 'Alienation' in particular has achieved considerable and widespread contemporary currency, but it has become debased in consequence. Its evident resonance for 'neo-Marxist' thinkers, in both the West and the East, for existentialist philosophers and theologians, for psychiatrists and industrial sociologists, for *déraciné* artists and intellectuals and student rebels, has meant that it has been widely extended and altered in the interests of a number of contemporary preoccupations; as a result the core of Marx's concept has been lost[3]. 'Anomie' has been less widely used, but it too has achieved a new life, within American social science. In particular, Robert Merton's paper 'Social Structure and Anomie'[4] (published 1938) has led to an extensive literature of conceptual refinement and empirical research, chiefly concerned with 'deviance' in all its forms[5]. But here too, much of the original meaning of the concept has been lost: in particular, most writers have followed Merton in discarding Durkheim's theory of human nature.

Furthermore, modern versions of these concepts vary widely in the range of their empirical reference. In the work of sociologists they are often taken as synonymous or else one is taken to be a sub-type of the other. Thus Nettler, Seeman and Scott in recent attempts to develop typologies of alienation count anomie as a variant, while Srole[6] counts alienation as a variant of anomie. Worse, there has been endless dispute in the case of both concepts about whether they are to be taken as sociological or psychological, or as socio-psychological and, if the last, in what sense. Thus Merton defines 'the sociological concept of anomie' as 'a breakdown in the cultural structure, occurring particularly when there is an acute disjunction between the cultural norms and goals and the socially structured capacities of members of the group to act in accord with them'[7], and Robin Williams observes that 'Anomie as a social condition has to be defined independently of the psychological states thought to accompany normlessness and normative conflict'; while, for example, Riesman, MacIver, Lasswell and Srole[8] take it to refer to a state of mind. Similarly, 'alienation' is sometimes taken to refer to an objective social condition, which is to be identified independently of people's feelings and beliefs, as in the work of Lukacs and those who follow him: men live within 'reified' and 'fetishist' social forms and the task is precisely to make them *conscious* of their history, which is 'in part the product, evidently unconscious until now, of the activity of men themselves, and in part the succession of the processes in which the forms of this activity, the relations of man with himself (with nature and with other men) are transformed'[9]; on the other hand, very many writers take alienation to be a state of mind (e.g. existentialist writers, theologians, psychiatrists, American sociologists). One writer even takes alienation to be synonymous with frustration of any kind, arguing that it 'lies in every direction of human experience where basic emotional desire is frustrated'[10].

Concepts can embody hypotheses and, in the case of these two concepts, when the focus is sociological there is frequently assumed to be a psychological correlate, and vice versa. Thus, e.g., Merton classifies the psychological states resulting from sociological anomie, while others make assumptions about the social causes of psychological anomie; similarly, Marxist sociologists make assumptions about the psychological effects of alienated social forms, while, e.g., Eric Fromm sees the psychological state of alienation as a function of market society.

A basic unclarity thus exists about the range of reference of each of these concepts and, even where the concepts are clearly used to embody hypotheses about relationships between social conditions and mental states, the very diversity of such hypotheses makes an analytical comparison of the concepts in their modern forms unmanageable in a short space. Where 'alienation' can mean anything from 'bureaucratic rules which stifle initiative and deprive individuals of all communication among themselves and of all information about the institutions in which they are situated'[11] to 'a mode of experience in which the person experiences himself as an alien'[12], and where 'anomie' can extend from the malintegration of the cultural and social structure to 'the state of mind of one who has been pulled up by his moral roots'[13], then the time has come either to abandon the concepts or return to their origins for guidance.

I

(a) Marx distinguishes four aspects of alienated labour: (1) 'the relationship of the worker to the *product of labour* as an alien object which dominates him'. Thus, 'the more the worker expends himself in work the more powerful becomes the world of objects which he creates in face of himself, the poorer he becomes in his inner life, and the less he belongs to himself'; (2) 'the relationship of labour to the *act of production*', with the result that 'the work is *external* to the worker, that it is not part of his nature; and that, consequently, he does not fulfil himself in his work but denies himself, has a feeling of misery rather than wellbeing, does not develop freely his mental and physical energies but is physically exhausted and mentally debased. The worker, therefore, feels himself at home only during his leisure time, whereas at work he feels homeless. His work is not voluntary but imposed, *forced labour*. It is not the satisfaction of a need, but only a *means* for satisfying other needs'; (3) the alienation of man from himself as a 'species-being', from 'his own active function, his life-activity', which is 'free, conscious activity'. Man is thus alienated from 'his own body, external nature, his mental life and his *human* life'; (4) the alienation of man 'from other *men*. When man confronts himself he also confronts other men ... in the relationship of alienated labour every man regards other men according to the standards and relationships in which he finds himself placed as a worker.' Social relations 'are not relations between individual and individual, but between worker and capitalist, between farmer and landlord, etc.' Further, men's lives are divided up into different spheres of activity, where conflicting standards apply: 'The nature of alienation implies that each sphere applies a different and contradictory norm, that morality does not apply the same norm as political economy, etc., because each of them is a particular alienation of man; each is concentrated upon a specific area of alienated activity and is itself alienated from the other.'

'Alienation' thus refers to the relationship of the individual to elements of his social and natural environment and to his state of mind, or relationship with himself. Marx contends that 'the division of labour ... impoverishes the worker and makes him into a machine', that 'the division of labour offers us the first example of how... man's own deed becomes an alien power opposed to him, which enslaves him instead of being controlled by him. For as soon as labour is distributed, each man has a particular exclusive sphere of activity, which is forced upon him and from which he cannot escape.' In conditions where men must work for the increase of wealth, labour is 'harmful and deleterious'; the division of labour, which develops in such conditions, causes the worker to become 'even more completely dependent ... upon a particular, extremely one-sided mechanical kind of labour'. All the aspects of alienation are seen to derive from the worker's role in production: his view of his work, his products, the institutions of his society, other men and himself. In general, the capitalist economic system 'perfects the worker and degrades the man'. Thus Marx's socio-psychological hypothesis concerning alienation is that it increases in proportion to the growing division of labour under capitalism, where men are forced to confine themselves to performing specialized functions within a system they neither understand nor control.

(b) Durkheim uses 'anomie' in *The Division of Labour* to characterize the pathological state of the economy, 'this sphere of collective life (which) is, in large part, freed from the moderating action of regulation', where 'latent or active, the state of war is necessarily chronic' and 'each individual finds himself in a state of war with every other'. In *Suicide* it is used to characterize the pathological mental state of the individual who is insufficiently regulated by society and suffers from 'the malady of infinite aspiration': 'unregulated emotions are adjusted neither to one another nor to the conditions they are supposed to meet: they must therefore conflict with one another most painfully'. It is accompanied by 'weariness', 'disillusionment', 'disturbance, agitation and discontent', 'anger' and 'irritated disgust with life'. In extreme cases this condition leads a man to commit suicide, or homicide. It is aggravated by sudden crises, both economic disasters and 'the abrupt growth of power and wealth': with increased prosperity, for instance, anomie '... is heightened by passions being less disciplined, precisely when they need more discipline'. Anomie is the peculiar disease of modern industrial man, 'sanctified' both by orthodox economists and by extreme socialists. Industry, 'instead of being still regarded as a means to an end transcending itself, has become the supreme end of individuals and societies alike'. Anomie is accepted as normal, indeed 'a mark of moral distinction', and 'it is everlastingly repeated that it is man's nature to be eternally dissatisfied, constantly to advance, without relief or rest, toward an indefinite goal'. Religion, governmental power over the economy and occupation groups have lost their moral force. Thus 'appetites have become freed of any limiting authority' and 'from top to bottom of the ladder, greed is aroused without knowing where to find ultimate foothold. Nothing can calm it, since its goal is far beyond all it can attain'. The lives of 'a host of individuals are passed in the industrial and commercial sphere', where 'the greater part of their existence is passed divorced from any moral influence ... the manufacturer, the merchant, the workman, the employee, in carrying on his own occupation, is aware of no influence set about him to check his egoism'[14].

'Anomie', like 'alienation', thus also refers first to the relationship of the individual to elements of his social environment and second to his state of mind. Durkheim initially thought that the division of labour itself has a 'natural' tendency to provide the necessary regulative force, that it produces solidarity because 'it creates among men an entire system of rights and duties which link them together in a durable way', for 'functions, when they are sufficiently in contact with one another, tend to stabilize and regulate themselves'. Anomie is prevalent because of the rapid growth of the market and big industry, for since 'these changes have been accomplished with extreme rapidity, the interests in conflict have not yet had time to be equilibrated'; also there is the harmful existence of 'the still very great inequality in the external conditions of the struggle'. Later he came to believe that it was primarily due to the lack of occupational groups which would regulate economic life by establishing 'occupational ethics and law in the different economic occupations': anomie 'springs from the lack of collective forces at certain points in society; that is, of groups established for the regulation of social life'. Both explanations are consistent with Durkheim's socio-psychological hypothesis concerning anomie, which is that it is a function of the rapid growth of the economy in industrial society which has occurred without a corresponding growth in the forces which could regulate it.

II

Alienation and anomie have in common the formal characteristic that they each have a multiple reference to: (1) social phenomena (states of society, its institutions, rules and norms); (2) individual states of mind (beliefs, desires, attitudes, etc.); (3) a hypothesized empirical relationship between (1) and (2); and (4) a presupposed picture of the 'natural' relationship between (1) and (2). Thus, whereas Marx sees capitalism as a compulsive social system, which narrows men's thoughts, places obstacles in the way of their desires and denies the realization of 'a world of productive impulses and faculties', Durkheim sees it as a state of moral anarchy in the economic sphere, where men's thoughts and desires are insufficiently controlled and where the individual is not 'in harmony with his condition'. We will later notice the extent to which (3) is related to (4) in the two cases. Let us here concentrate on (3), and in particular on the difference between the hypotheses in question.

Compare what the two thinkers have to say about the division of labour. For Marx it is *in itself* the major contributing factor in alienation, in all its forms, and not just for the worker but for all men. All men are alienated under the division of labour (for, as he says, 'capital and labour are two sides of one and the same relation' and 'all human servitude is involved in the relation of the worker to production, and all the types of servitude are only modifications or consequences of this relation'). Men have to enter into 'definite relations that are indispensable and independent of their wills', they are forced to play determined roles within the economic system, and, in society as a whole, they are dehumanized by social relations which take on 'an independent existence' and which determine not only what they do, but the very structure of their thought, their images of themselves, their products, their activities and other men. Alienated man is dehumanized by being conditioned and constrained to see himself, his products, his activities and other men in economic, political, religious and other categories — in terms which deny his and their human possibilities.

Durkheim sees the division of labour as being (when properly regulated) the source of solidarity in modern industrial society: the prevalence of anomie is due to a lag in the growth of the relevant rules and institutions. Interdependence of functions (plus occupational groups) should lead to growing solidarity and a sense of community, although the division of labour in advanced society is also (ideally) accompanied by the growth of the importance of the individual personality and the development of values such as justice and equality. For Durkheim the economic functions of the division of labour are 'trivial in comparison with the moral effect it produces'. By means of it 'the individual becomes aware of his dependence upon society; from it come the forces which keep him in check and restrain him'. When educating a child, it is 'necessary to get him to like the idea of circumscribed tasks and limited horizons', for in modern society 'man is destined to fulfil a special function in the social organism, and, consequently, he must learn in advance how to play this role'. The division of labour does not normally degrade the individual 'by making him into a machine': it merely requires that in performing his special function 'he feels he is serving something'. Moreover, 'if a person has grown accustomed to vast horizons, total views, broad generalities, he cannot be confined, without impatience, within the strict limits of a special task'.

By now it should be apparent that alienation, in Marx's thinking, is, *in part*, what characterizes precisely those states of the individual and conditions of society which Durkheim sees as the solution to anomie: namely, where men are socially determined and constrained, when they must conform to social rules which are independent of their wills and are conditioned to think and act within the confines of spcialized roles. Whereas anomic man is, for Durkheim, the unregulated man who needs rules to live by, limits to his desires, 'circumscribed tasks' to perform and 'limited horizons' for his thoughts, alienated man is, for Marx, a man in the grip of a system, who 'cannot escape' from a 'particular, exclusive sphere of activity which is forced upon him'[15].

Whence does this difference derive? In part, obviously, from the fact that Marx and Durkheim wrote at different periods about different stages of industrial society. Also it is clear that Marx was concerned chiefly to describe the alienated worker, while Durkheim saw economic anomie as primarily characterizing employers. But there is also a theoretical difference that is striking and important: these concepts offer opposite and incompatible analyses of the relation of the individual to society.

Compare Marx's statements that 'it is above all necessary to avoid postulating "society" once again as an abstraction confronting the individual' and that communism creates the basis for 'rendering it impossible that anything should exist independently of individuals' with Durkheim's that society is 'a reality from which everything that matters to us flows', that it 'transcends the individual's consciousness' and that it 'has all the characteristics of a moral authority that imposes respect'. Marx begins from the position that the independent or 'reified' and determining character of social relationships and norms is precisely what characterizes human 'pre-history' and will be abolished by the revolutionary transition to a 'truly-human' society, whereas Durkheim assumes the 'normality' of social regulation, the lack of which leads to the morbid, self-destructive state of 'non-social' or Hobbesian anarchy evident in unregulated capitalism. Social constraint is for Marx a denial and for Durkheim a condition of human freedom and self-realization.

III

It is my contention that one can only make sense of the empirical relationships postulated between social conditions and individual mental states which are held to constitute alienation and anomie by taking into account what Marx and Durkheim see as the 'natural' (or 'human' or 'normal' or 'healthy') condition of the individual in society. Alienation and anomie do not identify themselves, as it were, independently of the theories from which they derive: witness the diversity of contemporary uses of the terms, discussed above.

They are, in fact, only identifiable if one knows what it would be *not* to be alienated or anomic, that is, if one applies a standard specifying 'natural' states of institutions, rules and norms and individual mental states. Moreover, this standard must be external. That is, neither the individual mental states nor the social conditions studied can provide that standard, for they themselves are to be evaluated for their degree of alienation and anomie.

Thus despite recent attempts to divest these concepts of their non-empirical presuppositions[16], they are in their original form an inextricable fusion of fact and value, so that one cannot eliminate the latter while remaining faithful to the original concepts.

The standard specifying the 'natural' condition of the individual in society involves, in each case, a theory of human nature. Marx's view of man is of a being with a wide range of creative potentialities, or 'species powers' whose 'self-realization exists as an inner necessity, a need'. In the truly human society there will be 'a new manifestation of *human* powers and a new enrichment of the human being', when 'man appropriates his manifold being in an all-inclusive way, and thus is a whole man'. Man needs to develop all his faculties in a context where neither the natural nor the social environment are constraining: 'objects then confirm his individuality ... the wealth of subjective human sensibility ... is cultivated or created' and 'the practical relations of everyday life offer to man none but perfectly intelligible and reasonable relations with regard to his fellow men and to nature'. With the end of the division of labour, there will be an end to 'the exclusive concentration of artistic talent in particular individuals and its suppression in the broad mass'. The 'detail worker of today', with 'nothing more to perform than a partial social function', will be superseded by 'an individual with an all-round development, one for whom various social functions are alternative modes of activity'[17]. Furthermore, with the end of the social determination of 'abstract' individual roles, man's relationship with man and with woman will become fully human, that is, fully reciprocal and imbued with respect for the uniqueness of the individual. As Marx says, 'the relation of man to woman is the most *natural* relation of human being to human being.... It also shows how far man's needs have become human needs, and consequently how far the other person, as a person, has become one of his needs, and to what extent he is in his individual existence at the same time a social being.' Thus Marx assumes that the full realization of human powers and 'the return of man himself as a *social*, i.e. really human, being' can only take place in a world in which man is free to apply himself to whatever activity he chooses and where his activities and his way of seeing himself and other men are not dictated by a system within which he and they play specified roles.

Durkheim saw human nature as essentially in need of limits and discipline. His view of man is of a being with potentially limitless and insatiable desires, who needs to be controlled by society. He writes:

> To limit man, to place obstacles in the path of his free develop-
> ment, is this not to prevent him from fulfilling himself? But ...
> this limitation is a condition of our happiness and moral health.
> Man, in fact, is made for life in a determinate, limited environ-
> ment....

'Health' for man in society is a state where 'a regulative force' plays 'the same role for moral needs which the organism plays for physical needs', which makes men 'contented with their lot, while stimulat- ing them moderately to improve it' and results in that 'calm, active happiness ... which characterizes health for societies as well as for individuals'. Durkheim's picture of a healthy society in modern Europe is of a society that is organized and meritocratic, with equality of opportunity and personal liberty, where men are attached to intermediary groups by stable loyalties rather than being atomized units caught in an endemic conflict, and where they fulfil determinate functions in an organized system of work, where they conform in their mental horizons, their desires and ambitions to what their role in society demands and where there are clear-cut rules defining limits to desire and ambition in all spheres of life. There should be 'rules telling each of the workers his rights and duties, not vaguely in general terms but in precise detail' and 'each in his sphere vaguely realizes the extreme limit set to his ambitions and aspires to nothing beyond ... he respects regulations and is docile to collective authority, that is, has a wholesome moral constitution'. Man must be governed by 'a conscience superior to his own, the superiority of which he feels': men cannot assign them- selves the 'law of justice' but 'must receive it from an authority which they respect and to which they yield spontaneously'. Society alone 'as a whole or through the agency of one of its organs, can play this moderating role'. It alone can 'stipulate law' and 'set the point beyond which the passions must not go'; and it alone 'can estimate the reward to be prospectively offered to every class of human functionary, in the name of the common interest'.

IV

The doctrines of Marx and Durkheim about human nature are representative of a long and distinguished tradition of such doctrines in the history of political and social theory. The difference between them is also representative of that tradition (and parallel differences can be traced back to the Middle Ages). Doctrines of this general type can be seen to underlie, for example, the work of Hobbes, Rousseau, the Utopian Socialists and Freud; and it is evident that, in large measure, Durkheim sides with Hobbes and Freud where Marx sides with Rousseau and the Utopians. For the former, man is a bundle of desires, which need to be regulated, tamed, repressed, manipulated and given direction for the sake of social order, whereas, for the latter, man is still an angel, rational and good, who requires a rational and good society in which to develop his essential nature — a 'form of association in which each, while uniting himself with all, may still obey himself alone ...'[18]. For the former, coercion, external authority, and restraint are necessary and desirable for social order and individual happiness; for the latter, they are an offence against reason and an attack upon freedom.

I want here to ask two difficult questions. First, how is one to understand Marx's and Durkheim's theories of human nature, and, in particular, what is their logical and epistemological status? And, second, how is one to account for their divergence?

(a) Statements about human nature can be construed in many different ways. They commonly include such terms as 'need', 'real self', 'real will', 'basic desires', 'human potentialities', 'human powers', 'normal', 'healthy', and so on. Statements of this sort might be taken to refer to: (1) man as existing before or apart from society,(2) man considered analytically, with those factors due to the influence of society abstracted, (3) man considered in an *a priori* manner, i.e. according to some *a priori* definition, (4) man considered from the point of view of features which seem to be common to men in all known societies, (5) man considered from the point of view of features which are held to characterize him in certain specifiable social conditions as opposed to others[19].

My suggestion is that very often, and in particular in cases I am discussing, the last is the most accurate way to read statements about human nature. It is, in general, not absurd to take statements about human needs, 'real' wants, potentialities and so on as asserting that individuals in situation S are unable to experience satisfactions that situation S_1 is held to make possible for them and which they would experience and value highly. Now, it is, in my view, not necessary that such statements refer to actual *discontents* of individuals in situation S: both Marx and Durkheim, for example, were clear that individuals could acquiesce in and even value highly their alienated or anomic condition. What is required is that, once they are in S_1, they experience satisfactions unavailable in S.

Thus far it is evidently an empirical matter. It is an empirical and testable question (1) whether the satisfactions in question are precluded in S; (2) whether they would be available in S_1, and (3) whether they would be actually experienced by individuals in S_1 and would be important and valuable to them. (1) can in principle be investigated directly. To take easy examples, it is not difficult to show that work on the assembly line precludes work-satisfaction or that the life of the highly ambitious businessman precludes a mental condition of harmonious contentment. (2) and (3) can be investigated indirectly or directly. To do so indirectly would involve looking at evidence available in S and, indeed, in other societies, which provides a strong presumption in their favour. Thus Marx can write of what happens when "communist artisans form associations'. When 'French socialist workers meet together', he writes, 'society, association, entertainment which also has society as its aim, is sufficient for them: the brotherhood of man is no empty phrase but a reality, and the nobility of man shines forth upon us from their toil-worn bodies'. And he writes in *The Holy Family* that one 'must be acquainted with the studiousness, the craving for knowledge, the moral energy and the unceasing urge for development of the French and English workers to be able to form an idea of the *human* nobleness of that movement'. Durkheim can appeal to countless examples of cohesive social groups — primitive tribes, medieval guilds, rural Catholic communities, the Jews, and to the evidence of, e.g., differential suicide rates. He compares, for instance, the poor with the rich and argues that 'everything that enforces subordination attenuates the effects of (anomie). At least the horizon of the lower classes is limited by those above them, and for this same reason their desires are more modest. Those who have only empty space above them are almost inevitably lost in it....' *Direct* investigation of (2) and (3) can be pursued only by social experiment. Thus the final test for Marx's theory of human nature is the communist revolution; and that for Durkheim's is the institution of a kind of centralized guild-socialism.

We have analysed statements about human nature as empirical

statements (in this case, hypothetical predictions) about the condition of man in S_1. But our analysis is as yet incomplete, for they also involve the affirmation that this condition is privileged — that it is evaluated as preferable to all other conditions. How is one to analyse this evaluation: is it also empirical, that is, a ranking in accordance with what men actually want, or is it non-empirical — a mere exhortation to look at the world in one way rather than another?

If it is empirical, the question arises: by *whom* is the condition of man in S_1 said to be preferred — which men's wants are relevant here? If one believes, as Marx and Durkheim did, that man is largely conditioned by social circumstances, that new needs are generated by the historical process, that his very picture of himself and others is a function of his situation, then the problem becomes even more acute, for no one is in a position genuinely to compare and evaluate alternatives, like Mill's wise man deciding between higher and lower pleasures. An appeal to men in S_1 is self-defeating, for it carries the presumption that their evaluations are privileged, which is what is at issue. An appeal to men in S will not do either, for they would not ordinarily have the necessary evidence, and, again, why should their judgments be privileged? Worse still, what criteria are appropriate? If men in S_1 are satisfied, fulfilled, contented in certain ways, what is privileged about judgments which value these states rather than others?

Both Marx and Durkheim *thought* that they had found solid empirical ground upon which to base statements about human nature. They both had a picture of history as a process of the progressive emergence of the individual and both thought that man's potentiality for individual autonomy and for genuine community with others (both of which they evisaged differently) was frustrated by existing social forms. They thought that they had found conclusive evidence for their respective views of human nature in present and past societies: they assumed that, despite the continual generation of new needs throughout history, men's fundamental aspirations, more or less hidden, and the conditions of their ultimate happiness had always been and would continue to be the same. They were both impressed by the growth of industrialism and by the possibilities it had opened up for human fulfilment[20] and they believed that men were, despite the present, and temporary, obstacles, increasingly becoming (and would continue to become) what they had it in them to be; one could identify *this* by looking at their miseries and sufferings, as well as at their strivings and aspirations towards 'human' or 'healthy' forms of life, and at historical examples of societies or institutions in which alienation or anomie were less severe or even absent. Yet this evidence about men's wants is itself selected and interpreted, and that requires a prior perspective, providing criteria of selection and interpretation.

It would seem, therefore, that statements about human nature, such as those examined here, are partly empirical and partly not. One can often get a long way with support of the empirical part, for evidence of all kinds is relevant to the question of what men's lives would be like in alternative circumstances. The hypothetical prediction about S_1 may be verifiable; at least one would know how to verify it, and one could in principle point to evidence which strongly supports it. The claim, however, that life in S_1^- is to be judged superior, though it may rest on an appeal to evidence about men's wants, is ultimately non-empirical, for that evidence has been selected and interpreted in the light of the claim. Which men's wants and which of their wants has already been decided. Moreover, the claim of superiority does not follow logically from the evidence: one must add the premise that certain wants and satisfactions are more 'human' or 'healthy' than others. In the end what is required is a perspective and an initial set of evaluations.

(b) It is precisely here that Marx and Durkheim differed radically. Marx wrote that the 'socialist perspective' attributed importance to 'the wealth of human needs, and consequently also to a *new mode of production* and to a new *object* of production' as well as to a 'new manifestation of human powers and a new enrichment of the human being'. He began from an image of man in society, where a morality of duty would be unnecessary because irrelevant, an image in which *aesthetic* criteria were of predominant importance in assessing the quality of man's relationship with the natural and social world[21].

Yet where Marx wrote in the *Theses on Feuerbach* from 'the standpoint of ... human society', Durkheim argued in the *Rules of Sociological Method* that it was 'no longer a matter of pursuing desperately an objective that retreats as one advances but of working with steady perseverance to maintain the normal state, of re-establishing it if it is threatened, and of rediscovering its conditions if they have changed'. He was haunted by the idea of man and society in disintegration. Here he appealed to the remedy of moral rules, defining and prescribing duties in all spheres of life, especially where men's anarchic and unstable desires had the greatest scope. This is a moral vision, for, as he said, 'the need for order, harmony and social solidarity is generally considered moral'[22].

Where Marx valued a life in which in community with others 'the individual' has the means of 'cultivating his gifts in all directions', and where the relations between men are no longer defined by externally imposed categories and roles — by class and occupation — and men freely come together in freely-chosen activities and participate in controlling the conditions of their social life, Durkheim held that 'we must contract our horizon, choose a definite task and immerse ourselves in it completely, instead of trying to make ourselves a sort of creative masterpiece', and hoped to see men performing useful functions in a rationally organized society, in accordance with clearly defined roles, firmly attached to relevant groups and under the protective discipline of rules of conduct at home, at work and in politics. They both sought liberty, equality, democracy and community, but the content which they gave these notions was utterly different.

V

What is the relevance of these concepts today? This question needs to be subdivided into three more specific questions, which follow the lines of the preceding argument. First, how valid is the empirical hypothesis which each embodies? To what extent do they succeed in identifying and adequately explaining phenomena in modern industrial societies? Second, how plausible is the theory of human nature which each presupposes? What does the evidence from past and present societies, from sociology and psychology, suggest about the plausibility of their respective hypothetical predictions, and about the nature of the changes which men and institutions would have to undergo to attain the conditions they predict and advocate? And third, how desirable is the ideal, how attractive is the vision to which each ultimately appeals? How today is one to evaluate these ideals: what degree of approximation to either, or both (or neither), are we to think desirable?

These questions are challenging and far-reaching. Here I shall raise them and offer tentative suggestions as to how one might begin to answer them.

(1) One problem in answering the first question is to know at what level of generality it is being posed. How *specifically* is one to read Marx's account of alienation and Durkheim's of anomie? Marx and Durkheim identified certain features of their own societies and offered explanations of them. But they may also be seen to have identified features characteristic of a number of societies including

their own; indeed, one may even see them, to some extent, as having identified features which may be said to characterize any conceivable society. Is it a specific type of technology, or form of organization, or structure of the economy, or is it the existence of classes or of private property, or the accumulation of capital, or the division of labour, or industrial society, or the human condition which is the crucial determinant of alienation? Is it the lack of a specific type of industrial organization (technical or administrative?), or the absence of appropriate occupational groups, or an economy geared to the pursuit of profit, or the cultural imperatives of a 'success ethic', or the fact of social mobility, or the erosion of a traditionally stable framework of authority, or social change, or industrial society, or the human condition, that is the major factor leading to anomie? Alienation and anomie are phenomena which have particular aspects, unique to particular forms of society or institution, other aspects which are more general and still others which are universal. We may attempt to identify new forms of these phenomena, using these concepts and the hypotheses they embody in the attempt to describe and explain them. They are in this sense concepts of 'the middle range'. They allow for specific new hypotheses to account for particular new forms, or they may account for them by means of the existing, more general hypotheses. In general, the contemporary forms of alienation and anomie are best approached on the understanding that their causes are multiple and to be sought at different levels of abstraction. A systematic investigation of alienation and anomie would range from the most particular to the most universal in the search for causes.

Marx and Durkheim attributed, as we have seen, certain types of mental condition (specified positively, in terms of what occurs, and negatively, in terms of what is precluded) to certain types of social condition. Marx pointed to meaninglessness of work and a sense of powerlessness to affect the conditions of one's life, dissociation from the products of one's labour, the sense of playing a role in an impersonal system which one does not understand or control, the seeing of oneself and others within socially-imposed and artificial categories, the denial of human possibilities for a fully creative, spontaneous, egalitarian and reciprocal communal life. He attributed these, in particular, to the form taken by the division of labour under capitalism and, more generally, to the fact of class society. Durkheim pointed to greed, competitiveness, status-seeking, the sense of having rights without duties, the concentration on consumption and pleasure, the lack of a sense of community with others, of a feeling of limits to one's desires and aspirations, and of the experience of fulfilling a useful function and serving a purpose higher than one's own self-interest, and the denial of human possibilities for an ordered and balanced life, where everyone knows his station and its duties. He attributed these, in particular, to the industrial revolution and the failure of society to provide appropriate groups to adjust to it, and, more generally, to social disorganization.

We are familiar with countless examples of these phenomena, though in many cases not all the features isolated by the concepts are necessarily present. Let me give just two examples.

Alienation is found today in perhaps its most acute form among workers in assembly-line industries, such as the motor-car industry, where, as Blauner writes in his sensitive study of workers' alienation, 'the combination of technological, organizational and economic factors has resulted in the simultaneous intensification of all the dimensions of alienation'. Here, in the extreme situation, 'a depersonalized worker, estranged from himself and larger collectives, goes through the motions of work in the regimented milieu of the conveyor-belt for the sole purpose of earning his bread', 'his work has become almost completely compartmentalized from other areas of his life, so that there is little meaning left in it beyond the instrumental purpose', and it is 'unfree and unfulfilling and exemplifies the bureaucratic combination of the highly rational organization and the restricted specialist. In relation to the two giant bureaucracies which dominate his life, he is relatively powerless, atomized, depersonalized, and anonymous'[23].

Likewise, anomie is noticeably evident and acute among 'the Unattached', well described by Mary Morse, especially those in 'Seagate' — the drifting, purposeless and unstable teenagers, who felt no connection with or obligation to family, work, school or youth organization, the children of *nouveau riche* parents, suffering from 'a sense of boredom, failure and restlessness' and refusing 'to accept limitations, whether their own or external'. Often there was 'a failure to achieve unrealistic or unattainable goals they had set for themselves or had had set for them'; also there was 'a general inability to postpone immediate pleasure for the sake of future gain', there was 'a craving for adventure', and 'leisure-time interests were short-spanned, constantly changing and interspersed liberally with periods of boredom and apathy'. Finally, they showed 'pronounced hostility towards adults', adult discipline was quite ineffective and, in general, 'all adults in authority were classed as "them" — those who were opposed to and against "us" '[24].

These are merely two instances, but they illustrate the general point made above. The causes of alienation and anomie must be sought at different levels of abstraction. At the most specific level, all sorts of special factors may be of primary importance. In a case of alienation, it may be the technical or organizational character of an industry or the structure of a bureaucracy; in a case of anomie, it may be a combination of personal affluence and a breakdown, rejection or conflict of norms of authority at home, at school and at work. But clearly, too, the nature of the wider society is of crucial importance. The extent and nature of social stratification, the structure of the economy, the character of the political system, the pace of industrialization, the degree of pluralism, the nature of the predominant social values — all these will affect the nature and distribution of alienation and anomie. Again, one can plausibly argue that *some* degree of alienation and of anomie is inseparable from life in an industrial society, characterized as it is, on the one hand, by the ramifying growth of organization and bureaucracy in all spheres of life, by economic centralization and by the increasing remoteness and technical character of politics; and, on the other, by built-in and permanent social changes, by the impermanence of existing status hierarchies and the increasing role given to personal ambition and career mobility. And at the most general level, they may each be seen to relate to the most universal features of social structure and social change. In this sense, some alienation must exist wherever there are reified social relations, socially-given roles and norms; while some anomie must exist wherever hierarchies disintegrate and social control is weakened.

(2) What about the plausibility of Marx's and Durkheim's theories of human nature? They each had definite views about men's needs, which they believed to be historically generated and empirically ascertainable. How plausible today is the picture of mutually co-operative individuals, each realizing a wide range of creative potentialities, in the absence of specific role-expectations, lasting distinctions between whole categories of men and externally imposed discipline, in conditions of inner and social harmony, where all participate in planning and controlling their environment? What, on the other hand, is the plausibility of the view of human happiness, in which men are socialized into specific roles, regulated, and to some extent repressed, by systems of rules and group norms (albeit based on justice, equality of opportunity and respect for the individual), serving the purposes of society by

fulfilling organized functions — all of which they accept and respect as constituting a stable framework for their lives?

These questions confront all those who hold versions of these ideals today. One cannot begin to appraise either, or compare them with one another, until one has come to some view about the likelihood of either being realized. What evidence is there that if the social conditions are constituted in the way Marx and Durkheim wanted, men would experience and would value highly the satisfactions of which they speak? Here one would, for example, need to examine all the accumulated evidence throughout history of experiments in community-living and in workers' control, of communes, collective farms and kibbutzim, on the one hand; and of experience in 'human relations' and personnel management, of professionalism and of life in organizations, on the other. There is a vast amount of such evidence available, but it has never been systematically reviewed in this light.

Let us look at two examples in this connection. In the opinion of Friedmann the Israeli kibbutz represents 'an original and successful application, on a limited scale, of communist principles', nearer to 'the ethical ideal defined by the philosophy of Marx and Engels (for instance, with regard to the role of money, the distinction between manual and intellectual labour, family life)' than life in Moscow or on a kolkhoz. 'The kibbutz movement,' he writes, 'despite its limitations and its difficulties, constitutes the fullest and most successful "utopian" revolutionary experiment, the one which approximates most closely to the forms of life which communism has assigned itself as an aim. It is in the kibbutzim that I have met men of ample culture, and even creators, artists, writers, technicians, among whom the contradiction between intellectual and manual work, denounced by Marx, is truly eliminated in their daily life.' Friedmann goes on, of course, to qualify and elaborate this: in particular, he outlines the perpetual confrontation between the kibbutzim and the wider society, devoted to economic growth and 'imbued with models of abundance, where, with the development of the private sector, there is proclaimed a sort of material and moral New Economic Plan'[25]. He examines the attempts of the kibbutzim to reduce to a minimum the tensions and frustrations of community life and asks the crucial questions: whether the kibbutz will be able to adapt to the economic and technical demands of an industrial society, while retaining its essential values; and whether the wider society will evolve in a direction that is compatible or incompatible with these values.

Let us take a second example, which relates to the plausibility of

Durkheim's ideal, the overcoming of anomie. Perhaps the best instance is the evidence accumulated and interpreted by the theorists of modern managerialism, concerned to remedy 'the acquisitiveness of a sick society'[26] and treating the factory, the corporation and the large organization as 'a social system'. Particularly relevant are the writings of the 'organicists', whose aim is to promote 'the values of social stability, cohesion and integration'[27] and to achieve, within the 'formal organization' (the 'explicitly stated system of control introduced by the company') the 'creation and distribution of satisfactions' among the members of the system[28]. Selznick, who typifies the attempt to explore communal values within large corporations and administrative organizations, argues that the organization requires 'stability' in its lines of authority, subtle patterns of informal relationships, 'continuity' in its policies and 'homogeneity' in its outlook[29]. Another writer describes its reification and normative significance for those who participate in it in the following terms — terms of which Durkheim might well have approved: 'One might almost say that the organization has a character, an individuality, which makes the name real. The scientist will not accept any such reification or personalizing of an organization. But participants in these organizations are subject to no such scientific scruples and generations of men have felt and thought about the organizations they belonged to as something real in themselves'[30]. For Selznick, social order and individual satisfaction are reconciled when 'the aspirations of individuals are so stimulated and controlled, and so ordered in their mutual relations, as to produce the desired balance of forces'[31].

I have merely suggested two areas in which one might look for evidence that is relevant to the plausibility of the hypothetical predictions which partially constitute Marx's and Durkheim's theories of human nature. Clearly there is much else that is relevant in, for instance, the work of industrial sociologists, social psychologists, in community studies and the writings of organization theorists. It is also important to look at what evidence there is about the prevalence of existing tendencies in modern societies which favour or hinder the sorts of changes which would be necessary in order to approach these ideals. Here it would be necessary to look, for example, at the changes in the nature of occupations brought about by automation — the replacement of the detail worker by the more educated and responsible technician; at the effects of economic planning on small-scale decision-making; at the effects of the growth of organizations on status aspirations; at contemporary trends in consumption patterns. All this, and much else, is relevant to an assessment of the costs of approaching either ideal in our societies. Without these detailed inquiries, it is hardly possible to state firm conclusions, but it would appear that Durkheim's ideal is much nearer to and easier of realization in the industrial societies of both West and East than is that of Marx.

(3) Finally, how is one to evaluate these ideals? To do so involves a commitment to values and an assessment of costs. Either may be seen to conflict with other values or may not be considered to be worth the cost of its realization. Both sociological evidence and conceptual inquiry are relevant in the attempt to decide these matters, but in the end what is required is an ultimate and personal commitment (for which good, or bad, reasons may, none the less, be advanced). One may, of course, hold, as both Marx and Durkheim in different ways did, that one's values are, as it were, embedded in the facts, but this is itself a committed position (for which, again, good, or bad, reasons may be advanced).

This is no place to argue about these matters at the length they require. Let it be sufficient to say that these two quite opposite and incompatible ideals represent in a clear-cut form two major currents of critical and normative thinking about society, to be found throughout the whole tradition of political and social theory in the West and still very much in evidence.

It is becoming increasingly common for that tradition to be attacked, by the advocates of a 'scientific' social and political theory, as being rudimentary and speculative, and lacking in scientific detachment. It is all rather like Sir James Frazer's view of primitive religion as 'bastard science'. What is required, it is argued, is the abandonment of concepts which are internally related to theories of the good life and the good society. Evaluation of this sort should be kept strictly apart from the process of scientific inquiry.

Yet the desire for scientific rigour is not in itself incompatible with the sort of inquiry which is concerned precisely to put to the task of empirical analysis concepts which have the type of relation I have outlined to theories of human nature and thereby to prior evaluative perspectives. This type of inquiry is exactly what has primarily characterized social and political theory in the past (under which heading I include the writings of the classical and many modern sociologists). The case for eliminating it necessarily involves advocating the abandonment of the application of models of alternative and preferred forms of life to the critical analysis of actual forms. That case has yet to be made convincing.

Notes

1 My thanks are especially due to Dr S. Avineri, Professor Sir I. Berlin and Mr J.P. Plamenatz for their kind and helpful comments on an earlier draft of this article.

2 For other discussions of these concepts, treating them together but in ways rather different both from one another and from that adopted here, see J. Horton, 'The Dehumanisation of Anomie and Alienation', *British Journal of Sociology*, vol. XV, no. 4 (December 1964), and E.H. Mizruchi, 'Alienation and Anomie', in I.L. Horowitz (ed.), *The New Sociology: Essays in Social Science and Social Theory* (New York, 1964).

3 Robert Nisbet writes: 'The hypothesis of alienation has reached an extraordinary degree of importance. It has become nearly as prevalent as the doctrine of enlightened self-interest was two generations ago', *The Quest for Community* (New York, 1953), p. 15. There is even an 'alienation reader' (E. and M. Josephson, *Man Alone*, New York, 1962).

4 R.K. Merton, *Social Theory and Social Structure* (Glencoe, revised edition, 1957), chapter IV.

5 According to a recent article on the subject (H. McClosky and J.H. Schaar, 'Psychological Dimensions of Anomy', *American Sociological Review*, vol. 30, 1965) there have been since Merton's paper first appeared about 35 papers on 'anomy'. 'In addition, the concept has been used in a large number of books and essays and applied to discussions of an astonishing variety of topics, ranging from delinquency among the young to apathy among the old, and including along the way such matters as political participation, status aspirations, the behavior of men in prisons, narcotics addiction, urbanization, race relations, social change, and suicide'. Op. cit., p. 14.

6 G. Nettler, 'A Measure of Alienation', *American Sociological Review*, vol. 22 (1957). M. Seeman, 'On the Meaning of Alienation', *American Sociological Review*, vol. 24 (1959). M.B. Scott, 'The Social Sources of Alienation', *Inquiry*, vol. 6 (1963). L. Srole, 'Social Integration and Certain Corollaries', *American Sociological Review*, vol. 21 (1956).

7 Op. cit., chapter V, p. 162.

8 R. Williams, *American Society* (New York, 1951), p. 537. D. Riesman, *The Lonely Crowd* (New Haven, Conn., 1950), p. 287. R. MacIver, *The Ramparts We Guard* (New York, 1950), pp. 84-5. H. Lasswell, 'The Threat to Privacy' in R. MacIver (ed.), *Conflict of Loyalties* (New York, 1952), and Srole, op. cit., p. 712.

9 G. Lukacs, *Histoire de Classe et Conscience de Classe* (Paris, 1960), p. 230.

10 L. Feuer, 'What is Alienation? The Career of a Concept', *New Politics* (1962), p. 132.

11 C. Lefort in 'Marxisme et Sociologie', *Les Cahiers du Centre d'Etudes Socialistes*, vols 34-5 (1963), p. 24.

12 E. Fromm, *The Sane Society* (New York, 1955), p. 120.

13 MacIver, *The Ramparts We Guard*, p. 84.

14 Durkheim, *Professional Ethics and Civic Morals*, tr. C. Brookfield (London, 1957), p. 12. This quotation, incidentally, confirms that, despite Durkheim's attempt to distinguish 'anomie' from 'egoism' in *Suicide*, they are not in the end conceptually distinct. See B.D. Johnson, 'Durkheim's One Cause of Suicide', *American Sociological Review*, vol. 30, no. 6 (1965), pp. 882-6.

15 But Durkheim obviously did not want to see men treated as commodities or as appendages to machines (see *Division of Labour*, pp. 371-3), and Marx had much to say, especially in vol. III of *Capital*, about avarice and unregulated desires prevalent under capitalism (see also his account of 'raw communism' in the 1844 manuscripts).

16 See e.g. B.F. Dohrenwend, 'Egoism, Altruism, Anomie and Fatalism: A Conceptual Analysis of Durkheim's Types', *American Sociological Review*, vol. 24 (1959), p. 467, where anomie is described as 'ambiguous … indistinct … and infused with value judgments about what is "good" and "bad" ', and, e.g., Seeman, op. cit.

17 Cf. the famous passage from the *German Ideology* in which Marx writes of 'communist society, where no one has one exclusive sphere of activity but each can become accomplished in any branch he wishes' and where it is 'possible for me to hunt in the morning, fish in the afternoon, rear cattle in the evening, criticize after dinner, just as I have a mind, without ever becoming hunter, fisherman, shepherd or critic'. See also *Capital* (Moscow, 1959), vol. I, pp. 483-4, and Engels, *Anti-Dühring* (Moscow, 1959), pp. 403 and 409. On the other hand, Marx seems to have changed his attitude at the end of his life to a concern with leisure in the 'realm of freedom'.

18 J.-J. Rousseau, *The Social Contract*, tr. G.D.H. Cole (London, 1913), p. 12.

19 These possibilities are distinguished for analytical purposes. Clearly, in most actual cases they are combined. Rousseau, for instance, combines (1) and (2) while Pareto combines (2) and (4). I shall in the end argue that Marx and Durkheim combine (4) and (5).

20 As Marx says, 'The history of *industry* and industry as it *objectively* exists is an *open* book of the *human faculties*' (*Early Writings*, ed. T.B. Bottomore, London, 1963, p. 162); and, as Durkheim says, 'society is, or tends to be, essentially industrial' (*Division of Labour*, ed. G. Simpson, Glencoe, 1933, p. 3) and what characterizes its morality is 'that there is something more human, and therefore more rational' about modern, organized societies (ibid., p. 407).

21 This image is, I would argue, ultimately Romantic in origin. Compare the following from Schiller's *Briefe ueber die aesthetische Erziehung des Menschen:* ' ... enjoyment is separated from labour, the means from the end, exertion from recompense. Eternally *fettered* only to a single little fragment of the whole, man fashions himself only as a fragment; ever hearing only the monotonous whirl of the wheel which he turns, he never displays the full harmony of his being ... ' (*Sixth Letter*). For Schiller, and, I believe, for Marx it is 'the aesthetic formative impulse' which 'establishes ... a joyous empire ... wherein it releases man from all the fetters of circumstance, and frees him, both physically and morally, from all that can be called constraint' (ibid., *Twenty-Seventh Letter*).

22 *Division of Labour*, p. 63. Whereas Marx's model of disalienated work is artistic creation, Durkheim writes that 'art is a game. Morality, on the contrary, is life in earnest' and 'the distance separating art and morality' is 'the very distance that separates play from work' (*Moral Education*, New York, 1961, p. 273). This is the protestant ethic transposed into Kantian terms: 'the categorical imperative is assuming the following form: Make yourself usefully fulfil a determinate function' (*Division of Labour*, p. 43). As to self-realization, Durkheim writes, 'As for a simultaneous growth of all the faculties, it is only possible for a given being to a very limited degree' (*Division of Labour*, p. 237, amended translation, S.L.).

23 R. Blauner, *Alienation and Freedom: The Factory Worker and his Industry* (Chicago and London, 1964), pp. 182 and 122.

24 M. Morse, *The Unattached* (Harmondsworth, 1965), pp. 75-6 and 28-9.

25 G. Friedmann, *Fin du Peuple Fuif?* (Paris, 1965), pp. 95, 99, 96.

26 E. Mayo, *The Human Problems of an Industrial Civilisation* (New York, 1933), pp. 152-3.

27 I am particularly indebted in the discussion of this example to the pages on this subject in S.S. Wolin, *Politics and Vision* (London, 1961), pp. 407-14.

28 F.J. Roethlisberger and W.J. Dickson, *Management and the Worker* (Cambridge, Mass., 1939), p. 551.

29 Wolin, op. cit., p. 412.

30 E.W. Bakke, *Bonds of Organization*, quoted in Wolin, op. cit., p. 506.

31 P. Selznick, *Leadership in Administration*, quoted in Wolin, p. 413.

Select bibliography

Part I Forms of social life

The controversies concerning the place of convention in social life, and the possibility of an inquiry yielding objective understanding and appraisal of one's own or alien societies, are inter-related, and range over many books and journals. Among the most helpful and interesting contributions are: Peter Winch, *The Idea of A Social Science* (Routledge and Kegan Paul, 1958), a short book which has provoked a forest of pages in reply; Peter Winch, *Ethics and Action* (Routledge and Kegan Paul, 1972), especially the papers 'Understanding a Primitive Society' and 'Human Nature'; Alasdair MacIntyre, *Against the Self-Images of The Age* (Duckworth, 1971); Bryan Wilson (ed.), *Rationality* (Blackwell, 1970), a collection of papers by anthropologists and philosophers; C. Borger and F. Cioffi, *Explanation in the Behavioural Sciences* (Cambridge University Press, 1970), a larger collection which includes an illuminating reply by Winch to one of his critics; and Stephen Lukes, *Durkheim: His Life and Work* (Allen Lane, 1973). See also the entries under part II below.

Concerning morality itself the literature, ancient and modern, is almost inexhaustible. Three interesting and reasonably brief essays are D.Z. Phillips and H.O. Mounce, *Moral Practices* (Routledge and Kegan Paul, 1970); D.H. Monro, *Empiricism and Ethics* (Cambridge University Press, 1967); and Bernard Williams,

Morality: An Introduction to Ethics (Harper and Row, 1972). See also John Cook's essay in part IV of this volume; and (especially) the collection of papers by Peter Winch, *Ethics and Action* noted above, and Iris Murdoch, *The Sovereignty of Good* (Routledge and Kegan Paul, 1970).

For the Platonic and Hegelian traditions in moral philosophy see Michael Foster, *The Political Philosophies of Plato and Hegel* (Oxford University Press, 1968); R.C. Cross and A.D. Woozley, *The Republic of Plato* (Macmillan, 1964); J.C.B. Gosling, *Plato* (Routledge and Kegan Paul, 1973); Charles Taylor, *Hegel* (Cambridge University Press, 1975). And see the note at the end of this section.

There exists no comprehensive work in English on ethics in the Marxist tradition. For an introductory essay see Eugene Kamenka, *Marxism and Ethics* (Macmillan, 1969). The most thorough works at present on Marx's philosophy of action are John Plamenatz, *Karl Marx's Philosophy of Man* (Oxford University Press, 1975), and Bertell Ollman, *Alienation: Marx's Conception of Man in Capitalist Society* (Cambridge University Press, 1971). (But see the critical notice of this book by Christian Lienhardt in *Canadian Journal of Philosophy*, vol. III, no. 3, 1974.)

For recent contractarian work in ethics see John Rawls, *A Theory of Justice* (Harvard, The Belknap Press, 1971). For work opposed to this tradition see, in addition to the works already noted, Michael Oakeshott's *Rationalism in Politics and Other Essays* (Methuen, 1961); A.I. Melden, *Rights and Right Conduct* (Blackwell, 1959); and the excellent discussion of Rawls's work by Brian Barry, *The Liberal Theory of Justice* (Oxford University Press, 1973) and Robert Paul Wolff, *Understanding Rawls* (Princeton University Press, 1977).

The themes pursued in H.O. Mounce's paper can be very helpfully followed up in the volumes by Winch, Wilson and MacIntyre referred to above.

[*Note*: A beginning may be made in the study of the moral and social philosophies of Plato, Augustine, Hobbes, Locke, Rousseau, Kant, Hegel, Nietzsche, Sartre, and others, by consulting in each case the relevant volume in the *Modern Studies in Philosophy* series, edited by various people under the general editorship of Amelie Rorty, for Anchor Books. In addition to the papers collected in each volume, there is a helpful bibliography of books and articles appended at the end.]

Part II   Social inquiry and social reality

In the case of John Cook's paper the immediate work to be consulted is that which Cook addresses his discussion to. See the references provided in his paper. In addition to these, see the works by Peter Winch, Michael Oakeshott and others noted above under part I. See also the essay by John Anderson, 'Freudianism in Society', in the volume of his collected papers, *Studies in Empirical Philosophy* (Angus and Robertson, 1962).

Two elementary studies in the philosophy of social science, the second more introductory than the first, are Frank Cunningham, *Objectivity in the Social Sciences* (University of Toronto Press, 1973), and Alan Ryan, *The Philosophy of The Social Sciences* (Macmillan, 1970). A third, introductory work is Richard Rudner, *The Philosophy of Social Science* (Prentice-Hall, 1966). Alan Ryan has collected a number of very relevant papers in the paperback volume *The Philosophy of Social Explanation* (Oxford University Press, 1973).

Two more ambitious and difficult works are Charles Taylor, *The Explanation of Behaviour* (Routledge and Kegan Paul, 1964), and S. Toulmin, *Human Understanding* (Princeton University Press, 1972).

Reading complementary to Noam Chomsky's essay might include, in addition to the papers by John Cook and Charles Taylor in this section: Frank Ebersole, 'Where the Action Is', in his book *Things We Know* (University of Oregon Press, 1967); Charles Taylor, 'Neutrality in Political Science', in P. Laslett and W.G. Runciman (eds), *Philosophy, Politics and Society*, Third Series (Blackwell, 1967); and Noam Chomsky, 'Objectivity and Liberal Scholarship', in his collection *American Power and the New Mandarins* (Vintage Books, 1969).

On the concept of ideology see Georg Lichtheim, *The Concept of Ideology and Other Essays* (Random House, 1967), and John Plamenatz, *Ideology* (Macmillan, 1971).

Perhaps the clearest and most helpful introductory essay on freedom is the long historical introduction by John Plamenatz to his volume *Readings from Liberal Writers* (Allen and Unwin, 1965). In addition to the introduction, a representative selection of utterances by Locke, Montesquieu, Rousseau, Burke, and others, concerning freedom and the institutions upon which it depends make the entire volume worth study. For an illuminating contrast to this selection see Marx's essays on 'The Jewish Question', together with what have become known as the Economic and Philosophical Manuscripts — collected for example in David McLellan (ed.), *Karl Marx: The Early Texts* (Blackwell, 1971). See also 'Oppression' by Simone Weil and 'Alienation and Anomie' by Steven Lukes in part V of this volume, and the book from which Simone Weil's discussion is taken, *Oppression and Liberty* (Routledge and Kegan Paul, 1958 and 1973).

The classic libertarian tract is John Stuart Mill's *On Liberty*. A contemporary essay by Isaiah Berlin has also been deservedly widely studied. Berlin's essay is now collected with three others under the title *Four Essays on Liberty* (Oxford University Press, 1969). In the introduction to this printing Berlin replies to many of the people who were provoked by his essay to write about freedom. The details of these critical writings are given by Berlin in his notes to this discussion. See also H.J. McCloskey, 'A Critique of the Ideals of Liberty', *Mind* (1965); Alan Ryan, 'Freedom', *Philosophy* (1965); Maurice Cranston, *Freedom: A New Analysis* (Longmans, 1953); Felix Oppenheim, *Dimensions of Freedom* (St Martin's Press, 1961); F.A. von Hayek, *The Constitution of Liberty* (Chicago University Press, 1960); R. Nozick, *Anarchy, State and Utopia* (Basic Books, 1974).

Concerning equality, the most imaginative and seminal beginning is still Rousseau's essay 'Discourse on the Origins and Foundations of Inequality'. Two recent papers worth study are Ralf Dahrendorf, 'On the Origin of Social Inequality', in P. Laslett and W.G. Runciman (eds), *Philosophy, Politics and Society*, Second Series (Blackwell, 1964); and John Plamenatz, 'Equality of Opportunity', in J. Rachels and F. Tillman (eds), *Philosophical Issues* (Harper and Row, 1972). See also David Braybrooke, *Three Tests for Democracy: Personal Rights, Human Welfare, Collective Preference* (Random House, 1968); and N. Rescher, *Welfare* (University of Pittsburgh Press, 1972).

For competing accounts of the extent to which *political* equality exists, or is possible, in advanced capitalist societies see Ralph Milliband, *The State in Capitalist Society* (Weidenfeld and Nicolson, 1969) and John Plamenatz, *Democracy and Illusion* (Longmans, 1973). See also the issues of the recent radical journal published in England, *Radical Philosophy*, for a continuing discussion of the state, ideology, and political domination.

Charles Taylor's book, *The Explanation of Behaviour* obviously connects up with his essay printed here. See also his paper 'Neutrality in Political Science' cited above. For a critical reaction to Taylor's 'Interpretation and the Sciences of Man' see Kai Nielsen, 'Social Science and Hard Data', *Cultural Hermeneutics*, 1 (1973).

Part III   Social institutions and social change

Some of the most patient and illuminating writing on social institutions and social change is to be found in the work of John Plamenatz, in his discussions of major social theories. See especially his books *The English Utilitarians* (Blackwell, 1958), the second edition, particularly the last chapter; and the two-volume work, *Man and Society* (Longmans, 1963), especially the chapters on Montesquieu, Rousseau, Burke, Hegel and Marx; and his last book, *Karl Marx's Philosophy of Man* (Oxford University Press, 1975).

See also Simone Weil, *The Need for Roots* (Routledge and Kegan Paul, 1952); Steven Lukes, *Durkheim: His Life and Work* (Allen Lane, 1973); H.L.A. Hart, *The Concept of Law* (Oxford University Press, 1962); H.B. Acton, *The Illusion of the Epoch* (Cohen and West, 1955); M. Bober, *Karl Marx's Interpretation of History* (Morton Library, 1965); Bertell Ollman, *Alienation: Marx's Conception of Man in Capitalist Society* (Cambridge University Press, 1971).

Concerning revolution see Karl Marx and Frederick Engels, *The Communist Manifesto*, and Marx's writings on France and Germany (for the titles to these refer to the chapter on revolution in D. McLellan, *The Thought of Karl Marx*, Macmillan, 1971); John Plamenatz, *The Revolutionary Movement in France* (Longmans, 1952 and 1965); H. Marcuse, 'Ethics and Revolution', in R.T. De George, *Ethics and Society* (Doubleday, 1966); R. Tucker, *The Marxian Revolutionary Idea* (Norton, 1970); Kai Nielsen, 'On The Choice Between Reform and Revolution', and Peter Caws, 'Reform and Revolution', both in V. Held, K. Nielsen and C. Parsons (eds), *Philosophy and Political Action* (Oxford University Press, 1972).

Part IV   Cultural relativism

There is a discussion of moral relativism in D.Z. Phillips and H.O. Mounce, *Moral Practices* (Routledge and Kegan Paul, 1970), and in Kai Nielsen, *Reason and Practice* (Harper and Row, 1971). See also V.A. Howard, 'Do Anthropologists become Moral Relativists by Mistake?', *Inquiry*, vol. XI (1968); and M. Ginsberg, *On The Diversity of Morals* (Routledge and Kegan Paul, 1956). See also Gilbert Harman, 'Moral Relativism Defended', *Philosophical Review* (January 1975).

Part V Community

The following may be found to be helpful: Peter Laslett, 'The Face to Face Society', in P. Laslett, *Philosophy, Politics and Society*, First Series (Blackwell, 1956); Simone Weil, *The Need for Roots* (Routledge and Kegan Paul, 1952); S. Wolin, *Politics and Vision* (Allen and Unwin, 1960). See also A.E. Murphy, *A Theory of Practical Reasoning* (Open Court, 1965), and Robert Paul Wolff, chapter 5 in his *The Poverty of Liberalism* (Harper and Row, 1970).

In addition to the last two items, A.R.D. suggests the following writings on community. For an analysis of the various uses of the term 'community' see John Ladd, 'The Idea of Community', *New England Journal*, vol. 1, no. 1 (August 1972). For the connections between community and ecosystems see the following: Thomas B. Colwell, Jr, 'The Ecological Basis of Human Community', *Educational Theory*, vol. 21, no. 4 (Fall 1971), pp. 418-53; Baker Brownell, *The Human Community* (Harper Brothers, 1950); Marvin W. Harris, *Cows, Pigs, Wars and Witches* (Vintage Books, 1974), especially the chapter on the Maring; Rene Dubos, *A God Within* (Scribners, 1972), especially chapter 6. For older sociological theories of community see: Ferdinand Toennies, *Community and Association* (Routledge and Kegan Paul, 1955); R.M. MacIver, *Community: A Sociological Study* (Frank Cass, 1970); and for more recent studies of communes and intentional communities in the US and Britain see: Rosabeth Kanter, *Commitment and Community* (Harvard University Press, 1974); D. Abrams and A. McCulloch, *Communes, Sociology and Society* (Cambridge University Press, 1976). Finally, for a collection of papers some of which are on the philosophy of community, see Carl J. Friedrich (ed.), *Community* (New York: Liberal Arts Press, 1959).

R.B.

Index

absolutism, 272, 274
aesthetic criteria and quality of life, 413
aesthetics, 233n.
Agamemnon, 386
alienation
    and capitalism, 187-93, 403, 406
    and labour, 402, 406
    Marx's analysis of, 402
alienation and anomie
    assumptions about human nature
        and, 353
    and capitalism, 405
    common features of, 405
    and community, 354
    contemporary uses of these terms,
        400 ff.
    as defined by social scientists, 401 ff.
    examples of, 416
    Marx and Durkheim on, 400-20
        comparison of Marx to Durkheim
            on, 407 ff.
        evaluation of their views on, 414
    as the natural conditions of mankind
        in society, 407 ff.
    as socio-psychological concepts,
        400 ff.
    theories of as involving a fusion of
        fact and value, 408
    see also separate entries under
        anomie *and* alienation

Almond, G. (and Powell, G.B.), 102-4,
    189
anarchy, 255, 265
Anglo-Saxons, 188, 294
anomie
    and capitalism, 405
    as a disease peculiar to modern
        industrial man, 404
    and division of labour, 406
    Durkheim's analysis, 404
Anscombe, G.E.M., 199
Archimedes, 222
Aristotle, 12-13, 46, 51, 184, 199,
    388 ff.
asceticism, discussed in connection with
    Utopian engineering and Plato,
    219-22
Asch, S., 294
Augustine, 330
Aurelius, Marcus, 388
Azande, 59-76

Balzac, H., 385
Bay, C., 102-7
behaviour modification and condition-
    ing, 351, 357
behaviouralism (behaviourism), 83-5,
    91-199
beliefs, 271-3
Benedict, R., 274, 293

Bentham, J., 32-3, 53-4, 81, 329,
 368 ff.
Bergson, H., 276
bigotry, 310
Blake, 341
Blanshard, B., 93-4
Brecht, A., 94-100
Britain, 207
Brookings Institution, 206
Buddhism, 317
Burckhardt, J., on the Renaissance, 319
Burke, E., 36

Camus, A., 332 ff.
Canada, 192, 351
capitalism, 226n., 227n., 234n., 384,
 386 ff.
capitalist ideology, 102-7, 139, 140-9,
 187-93
Cardoza, B., 300, 314n.
catalepsy and trance, 280, 287
Catholicism, 280, 306, 411
Chesterton, G.K., 69-70, 72
child-sacrifice, 15-16
Christianity, 34, 305
civil disobedience and social change,
 251-67
civil rights, 253, 256, 262
Cohen, M., 253
Collingwood, R.G., 69, 75
colour-discrimination, 16
communication, 21 ff.
community
 analysed, 376
 categorial confusion in the analysis
  of, 377 ff.
 comparison between Russian and
  Israelis, 418
 duty to create, 348 ff., 353, 379 ff.
 as frustrated by social forms, 416
 general discussion of, 135-49, 184-
  93, 373-80
 intersubjective meanings necessary
  for, 108 ff.
 involving respect and co-operation,
  349 ff.
 and Marx, 414 ff.
 moral, 19
 as a moral concept, 347 ff.
 moral order and requirements for
  community, 373 ff.

Community, *cont.*,
 moral reasons, 376 ff.
 moral structure, 369
 possibility of creating and social
  change, 349
 problems in creating, 352 ff.
 scientific, 19
 and society, 373 ff.
comparative politics, 183-4
Comte, A., 94-5
Condorcet, Marquis de, 94
conservatism defined, 356
convention, 12-31, 56-7
conversion and change of life
  compared, 327 ff.
 as seeing things in a new light, 327 ff.
Crito, 347
cultural diversity, examples of, 279-88
cultural relativism
 Benedict on, 280-8
 Cook on, 289 ff.
 general introduction to, 273-8
cultural relativism as absolute relativity, 295
customs, 272, 278

Dahl, R., 185
Dante, 385
Darwin, C., 204
democracy, 101-7, 187-93, 261, 266,
 267
Descartes, R., 396
desires and interests
 as subject to change, 352
 as unlimited, 352
development explained and contrasted
  with change, 203-4
Dobu, 282, 287
drug abuse, 206-9
Durkheim, E., 290, 400-20
Dyaks, 279, 312 ff.

Eastman, M., 223n.
Easton, D., 101-2
education, 105
Eliot, G., 51
energy consumption, 352
England, 395
ethical pluralism, 342
ethics, 233n., 286

ethnocentrism
  and belief, 313
  compared to bigotry, 310 ff.
  defined, 310 ff.
  general discussion of, 273 ff.
  origin of, 313
  original intent behind term, 310
Europe, 203-5
experience and world view, 337 ff.
  as activity, 338
  as defining and creating relations,
    338 ff.

facts and values, alleged dualism of,
    13 ff., 83-4, 91 ff., 185 ff., 235-42,
    247, 332 ff.
Fanon, F., 103-4
Faust, 399
Fijians, 279
Finn, Huck, 305 ff.
Firth, R., 289-91, 294, 297, 307, 315n.
food production
  alternative attitudes towards, 349 ff.
  as energy intensive, 349 ff.
force and oppression, 382
Fortus, Justice Abe, 252
Frazer, J., 69, 420
freedom, 86, 112-13, 125-6, 131-5,
    149-51, 184-5, 362
French bourgeoisie, 395
French and English workers, 411
Freud, S., 410
Fromm, E., 402
Fürer-Harmendorf, C. von., 291, 310

Gandhi, M., 259
Gay, P., 119
Glaucon, 221
God, 290, 307
good in utilitarianism, 367 ff.
Greaves, H.R.G., 102
Greek mythology, 339, 386
Greeks, 272, 281, 394

Hallowell, I., on the Ojibwa, 311
Hand, Learned, 300, 314n.
happiness as the good, 369
Haring, D., on Japan, 297-9, 306
Hart, H.L.A., 363, 368, 371
Hayek, F.A. von., 224n., 225n.
Hegel, G.W.F., 81, 216, 378

Herder, G., 234n.
Herrnstein, R., 136-49
Herskovits, M., 295, 296
Hess, R., 304 n.
historical laws, 203-4, 219
historicism, 219, 225n., 230n., 231n.
history
  general remarks on, 228n., 387 ff.
  as progressive, 412
  scientific study of, 389, 391
Hitler, A., 93, 128
Hobbes, T., 20-1, 81, 185, 253, 254-8,
    265, 407, 410
Hobhouse, Q.T., 311 ff., 312 ff.
Homer, 399
homosexuality, 280-1, 287
Hopis, 275 ff., 278
Houyhnhnms, 247
Hulme, T.E., 316-39
human life, primitive and civilized
    compared, 397 ff.
human nature, 110, 194-9
  alternative descriptions of, 353 ff.
  and self-realization, 408
  theories of
    empirical elements of, 411 ff.
    historical antecedents, 410 ff.
    Marx and Durkheim on, 408
      differences between, 413 ff.
      evaluation of, 417 ff.
humanist attitude, 317 ff.
  and religious attitude contrasted,
    317 ff.
humanitarianism, 248
Hume, D., 97-8 ff., 292, 328 ff.
Husserl, E., 319

ideology, 140 ff., 193 ff.
  see also capitalist ideology
Iliad, 387, 389
India, 287
indoctrination, 105
infanticide, 274
institutions, 241-9
  and moral agents, 379
integrity, connection of social institu-
    tions to, 28 ff.
intelligibility, 16 ff., 194-9
interests, 102 ff., 189-90
intolerance, 222
Islandia and Grundegung, 300 ff.

James, W., 315n.
Japan, 297-9
Jefferson, 379
Jews, 411
justice, 12-13

Kant, I., 43, 223n., 234n., 276 ff.,
    305, 341, 348, 354, 423n.
Kierkegaard, S.A., 330
Kirk, R., 92-4, 97-9
Koestler, A., 119-20
Kuhn, T.S., 277
Kwakiutl, 282-5, 287

labour, 135-46, 187-93, 398 ff.
language, 10-11, 20 ff.
Lasswell, H., 401
League of Nations, 227n.
legalism in ethics, 371
legitimacy, 184-9
Lenin, V.I., 221
Lewes, G.H., 51
liberal theory
    general discussion of, 255
    and revolution, 255-8, 265-7
liberty, 86, 112-13, 125-6, 131-5, 149-
    51, 184-5
linguistic relativism, 275-7
Lipset, S.M., 185-6
Locke, J., 81, 253, 255-7
logic, 16-17 ff., 54, 62
Lukacs, G., 401
Luxemburg, R., 386

Machiavelli, 36
MacIntyre, A., 184, 200
MacIver, R., 401
magic, 7-10, 59, 281
Mailer, N., 295
managerialism, 419
Marx, K., 81, 204-5, 219, 338 ff., 383,
    384, 386, 389, 400-20
Marxists, 243, 276n., 389, 402
master and slave, 392 ff.
means for ends, as the essential evil, 387
mechanical engineering, as contrasted
    with social engineering, 218 ff.
mediaeval Europe, 317, 393, 396, 410
Melden, A.I., 19, 378
Merton, R., 401, 402
Mill, J.S., 32, 47, 392, 412

Moore, G.E., 33
moral agency, 358
    and moral relations, 379 ff.
    and the self, 375
moral beliefs, 340 ff.
moral criticism, 263
moral disagreement and world view,
    341 ff.
moral laws
    in connection with social change,
    235-49
    moral and legal obligations dis-
    tinguished, 342 ff.
moral obligation, 264
moral order, as necessary for com-
    munity, 373 ff.
moral reasons
    account of, 356
    appeal to rules and the possibility
    of misunderstanding, 372 ff.
moral rules
    as absolute or relative, 290
    criticism of rule conception, 364
    Durkheim on, 413
    exceptions to, 371
    general discussion of, 275, 290
    and justification of actions, 362
moral theory, 247
moral training, 356
    and the achievement of personhood,
    362
    as contrasted with conditioning, 357
morality
    alternative, as a function of ways of
    seeing the world, 320
    as consisting of rules and judgments,
    297, 306
    general remarks on, 5-7, 12-31, 32-58
    idea of distinct moralities, 316
mores, 271, 293, 307
Murphy, A.E., 93-4, 351 ff., 353 ff.

Napoleon, 321 ff.
nations, 228n.-230n.
natural laws, 235-49
nature, 12-31, 51, 56-7
Nazis, 7, 55-7
nemesis, 394
nihilism, 305 ff.
normal-abnormal, as a function of
    culture and cultural norms, 280-8

Norman, R., 277-8
norms, 13 ff., 235-42, 247
North American Indians, 271, 281

Old-young woman, 277, 333 ff.
oppression
    and developed economies, 381 ff.
    as exercised by force, 382
    and monopoly, 383 ff.
    and natural boundaries, 388
    by nature, 396 ff.
    and nature's power, 382
    and objective conditions, 383
    and power, 384
    and progress, 395 ff.
    and religious rites, 383
    as residing in human society, 397 ff.
    and slavery, 391 ff.

Pascal, B., 317, 330
Peirce, C.S., 356 ff.
Pentagon, The, 260
persons and community, 353
persuasion, 123-6
Pharaohs, 391
physics
    changes in, 15 ff.
    understanding, 15 ff.
piece-meal social engineering
    defined, 212 ff.
    general discussions of, 212-22, 235-49
    introduction to Popper and Rhees
        on, 209-10
    utilitarianism and, 223n. ff.
    values of, 217 ff.
    von Hayek and, 224n.-225n.
    see also 232n.
Plamenatz, J., 208-9
Plato, 213, 216, 219-22, 232n., 233n.,
    234n., 281, 330, 357 ff., 393
Polanyi, M., 24
police state, 131-3, 149-50
political obedience, 248
Popper, K., 13, 209-10, 235-49
possibilities, as related to conceptual
    abilities and language, 334
Pound, R., 223n., 225n.
Powell, G.B. (and Almond, G.), 102-4,
    189

power
    as containing an internal contradic-
        tion, 386 ff., 393 ff.
    defined, 387
    its enslaving aspects, 384 ff.
    limitations of, 390 ff.
    race for, 386 ff.
    social organization and, 390
    social relations and, 391
practical reason, account of, 355
Protagoras, 357 ff.

racism, 110, 145-9
radicalism, discussed in connection
        with Utopian engineering and
        Plato, 219-22
    see also 232n., 233n.
rationality, 8-9, 61 ff., 66 ff., 278
Rawls, J., 253, 363, 365, 370
relativism
    criticisms of, 308 ff.
    as ethnocentrism, 299, 304 ff.
    and evil, 310 ff.
    as philosophical psychopathy, 295,
        297
    and 'seeing as', 339 ff.
    as a theory about rules, beliefs and
        principles, 294, 306
    as tyranny, 296, 297
religious attitude, the, 317 ff., 339 ff.
Renaissance, 317 ff.
revolution
    general discussion of, 250-67
    justifications for, 263
    justifications of in liberal thought,
        255
    problems in defining, 255
    social change and, 250 ff.
    social change as independent of, 395
    varieties of, 258
Riesman, D., 401
right action
    and community, 354
    and reasons, 358 ff.
rights, 257, 263
Roman army, 393
Roman Empire, 394
Romans, 391
Romanticism, 29, 222, 234n., 318,
        423n.

Rome, 393

Rousseau, J.-J., 81, 234n., 410

rule — games model, as failing to account for rational justification of moral action, 371

rules
of justice, 12-13
legal, 12
moral (*see under* moral rules)

Russia, 214, 221

Russian Revolution, 395

Schopenhauer, A., 330, 331

science, 13, 83-5, 94-9, 111-20, 147-51
difference from morality, 19 ff., 94 ff.

scientific method, 244 ff., 247

scientific objectivity, 247

scientism, 224n.-225n.

Searle, J., 199

'seeing and seeing as', 277
and world views, 333, 338 ff., 342 ff.

Selznik, P., 419

sensation, connection to action and concepts, 18

Shakespeare, W., 387

Sidgwick, H., 32

Skinner, B.F., 110-35, 149-51

social behaviourism as a theory, 374 ff.

social blackmail, 262

social criticism and other forms of criticism, 245

social engineering, 235-49, 288

social engineers, 351

social experiment, 317

social improvement, 247-9

social organizations free from oppression, 381 ff.

social sciences, 81-9, 89-199

socialism, 233n., 234n.

Socrates, 220-1, 347

Socratic, 226n.

Sophists, 13

Spencer, H., 95

Spinoza, B., 51-2, 341

Spitz, D., 254, 265

Stalin, J., 93

state of nature, 254-8

state of war, 254-8

Strauss, L., 91, 97, 107

subjectivism and objectivism contrasted, 319 ff., 333

Sumner, W.G., 293, 296, 307

teleological moral system, 264

Tolstoy, L.N., example from *War and Peace*, 321, 334 ff., 336 ff.

totalitarian control, 131-3, 149-50

Toulmin, S., 278, 363

Trotsky, L., 388

truthfulness, 22-8

USA, 187-93, 205-9, 267, 293, 351

utilitarianism, 32 ff., 46 ff., 223n., 368 ff., 373

Utopian engineering
aestheticism and radicalism in, 220 ff.
compared to mechanical engineering, 218 ff.
criticized, 214
defined, 212 ff.
general discussions of, 212-22, 235-49
introduction to Popper and Rhees on, 207-10
Marx on, 219 ff.
Plato on, 216
see also 223n.-225n., 232n.

Utopian socialists, 410

value-neutrality, 91-109, 110-55, 156-99, 332 ff.

values, 271

Vico, G., 11, 21, 29, 81

Vietnam, 103 ff., 293

Viola, F., 296 ff.

violence, 196, 253, 256, 264, 265

visual gestalt, 330, 333

Voltaire, 234n.

Walden II, 351

war and peace, 228n.-232n.

Webb, B. and S., 367

Weil, S., 348 ff., 354

Weltanschauung
and categories, 319 ff.
as contrasted with scientific philosophy, 319
differences in, 318 ff.
effects on perception, 320 ff.

Weltanschauung, cont.,
  and facts and values, 332 ff.
  as related to 'seeing as' and ways of
    seeing the world, 329 ff.
  verification and confirmation, 337 ff.
  as world-views (a basic orientation),
    318 ff.
Westermarck, B., 291, 292
western civilization, crisis of, 189-99
Whorf, B.L., 275 ff.

wisdom, 300 ff.
Wisdom, J., 25-6
witchcraft, 59-76
Wittgenstein, L., 21-2, 27-8, 59, 62 ff.,
    73, 356
working class, 187 ff.
world view, *see Weltanschauung*

Yakats, 279